CHICANA FEMINIST THOUGHT

THE BASIC HISTORICAL WRITINGS

CHICANA FEMINIST THOUGHT

THE BASIC HISTORICAL WRITINGS

EDITED BY

ALMA M. GARCÍA

Sociology/Ethnic Studies
Santa Clara University

Routledge
New York   London

Published in 1997 by

Routledge
29 West 35 Street
New York, NY 10001

Published in Great Britain by

Routledge
11 New Fetter Lane
London EC4P 4EE

Library of Congress Cataloging-in-Publication Data

Chicana feminist thought : the basic historical writings / edited by
   Alma M. García.
      p.   cm.
    ISBN 0-415-91800-6 (hb). — ISBN (invalid) 0-415-91800-4 (pb)
     1. Feminism—United States.   2. Feminist theory—United States.
   3. Mexican American women—Political activity.   4. Mexican American
women—Social conditions.   I. García, Alma M.
   HQ1421.C52   1997
   305.48′868′72073—dc21   96-49916
                                            CIP

British Library Cataloging-in-Publication Data also available.

For my mother, Alma Araiza García,
whose life exemplifies feminist struggle and
perserverance in the midst of adversity.

Contents

CONTENTS

Acknowledgments

First and foremost, I would like to pay tribute to all the Chicana feminists whose writings document lives of activism during this historical period in Chicana/Chicano history. I thank them for chronicling their struggles for social justice.

The idea for this volume belongs to Professor Mario T. García, who, under contract to Routledge Press, co-edited the entire manuscript with me from beginning to end. He graciously allowed my name to appear as the sole editor, even though, in fact, we are both co-editors.

Many colleagues provided me with the opportunity to engage in numerous discussions on questions related to the interplay of gender, ethnicity, and feminism. Their moral and intellectual support was constant, critical, and always insightful. I would like to offer a very special thanks to: Richard A. García, my brother and fellow scholar and Francisco Jiménez, my colleague and dear friend, for carefully reading many of the collected essays and introductions; and Janet Flammang, for sharing with me her expertise in the politics and development of feminist movements and for generously allowing me access to her personal archives on Chicana feminist activities. I would also like to acknowledge and thank the following individuals for their assistance: Cecelia Cancellaro for her support and enthusiasm during the early stages of the publication process; Lillian Castillo-Speed, Chicano Studies Library at the University of California at Berkeley, for her outstanding assistance in helping me locate many of the documents on Chicana feminist thought; and Raul Ruíz, former publisher and editor of *La Raza,* for generously providing me with the photographs included in this anthology. I would like to commend Abigail Baxter for her outstanding work in securing the necessary permissions for the articles included in this anthology.

Several research assistants—our future colleagues in Ethnic and Chicano Studies—provided me with their valuable skills at different stages of this project. At Santa Clara University, Anna Sampaio organized the documents during the early stages; Perlita Dicochea and Tomás Jiménez provided me with their computer skills in preparing this manuscript. Their hard work and commitment was invaluable in allowing me to meet our publication deadline and, in addition, I profited from our numerous intellectual conversations on feminism. At the University of California, Santa Barbara, I am particularly grateful to Magdalena Torres.

I would like to give our sincere thanks to the following departmental administrative assistants at Santa Clara University. Rosa Dueñas, Women's Studies Program, managed every technical aspect in producing this work and, most importantly, her patience and understanding gave me critical moral support. Leslie Bethard, Political Science Department, assisted me with new computers, printers, and many other technical tasks. Lastly, a very special thanks to Sandra Chiaramonte, Anthropology/Sociology Department, for her willingness to assist me with what I considered to be perplexing computer problems. Sandee always solved all these problems with ease, efficiency, and remarkable patience.

Various sources provided me with funding for the completion and publication of *Chicana Feminist Thought: The Basic Historical Writings*. Santa Clara University supported my research through its Irvine Foundation Grant Term Professorship directed by Francisco Jiménez. I was also supported by a Thomas Terry Research Grant, the Ethnic Studies Program, the Women's Studies Program; and the Anthropology/Sociology Department.

Lastly, I offer my most sincere thanks and appreciation to Heidi Freund, Routledge, for her unwavering commitment and dedication to this project.

Copyright Information

Introduction

Alma M. García

"Sisterhood is powerful"
—Robin Morgan

"There is a pretense to a homogeneity of experience covered
by the word sisterhood that does not in fact exist"
—Audre Lorde

"Chicanas identify
Chicanas communicate chicanas
Let your spirits not die"
—Anna Nieto-Gómez

"Look at our women. They are strong you can feel it. They
are the rocks on which we really build"
—Dolores Huerta

During the turbulent years of the 1960s and throughout the 1970s, a generation of Chicana feminists raised their voices in opposition to the gender tensions and conflicts that they were experiencing as women within the Chicano social protest movement. Although the Chicano movement—an insurgent uprising among a new political generation of Mexican-Americans—challenged persistent patterns of societal inequality in the United States, it ignited a political debate between Chicanas and Chicanos based on the internal gender contradictions prevalent within El Movimiento. Chicana feminists produced an ideological critique of the Chicano cultural nationalist movement that struggled against social injustice yet maintained patriarchal structures of domination. Chicana feminist thought reflected a historical struggle by women to overcome sexist oppression but still affirm a militant ethnic consciousness. As they forged a feminist consciousness, Chicana feminists searched for the elusive "room of their own" within the socio-historical and political context of the Chicano movement.

El Movimiento: The Paradox of Civil Rights and Ethnic Nationalism

Influenced by the Black nationalist movement and the Mexican-American community's historical legacy of discrimination and structural inequality in American society,

1

a generation of Mexican-Americans channeled their collective energies into a militant civil rights and ethnic nationalist movement in the late 1960s and 1970s. Surrounded by a radical climate of national political protests and insurgency such as the Black power movement, the anti-Vietnam War movement and the second wave of the women's movement, the movimiento focused on social, political, and economic self-determination and autonomy for Mexican-American communities throughout the United States.[1] This focus at the same time manifested a paradoxical agenda of civil rights and equal opportunity demands, on the one hand, and a more separatist ethnic nationalist rebellion, on the other.

This paradox revealed not a monolithic political base, but a Chicano movement that evolved from various struggles with specific leaders, agendas, and organizational strategies and tactics. The New Mexico land grant movement, for example, headed by Reies López Tijerina fought for the rights of dispossessed Hispanos, as those from New Mexico called themselves, whose lands had been lost as a result of the war between the United States and Mexico (1846–1848).[2] In California, César Chávez and Dolores Huerta organized migrant farm workers into the United Farm Workers union whose strikes, boycotts, and victories against the state's agribusiness would become the soul and inspiration of the Chicano movement as well as a national and international symbol of a struggle for social justice and equal rights.[3] The urban-based Colorado Crusade for Justice, spearheaded by Rodolfo "Corky" Gonzales, mobilized Mexican-American communities around the issues of political self-determination and community autonomy.[4] In Texas, José Angel Gutiérrez founded a third political party—the Raza Unida Party—and challenged the state's political system for its systematic exclusion of the Mexican-American community. Gutiérrez and the Raza Unida Party's electoral revolt and victory in Crystal City, Texas, in 1970, became a political metaphor for the strength and tenacity of El Movimiento.[5] In high schools and universities throughout the Southwest, Mexican-American students organized their collective efforts into a radical confrontation with an educational system that they indicted for its patterns of discrimination.[6] Generations of Mexican-American parents had identified the educational system as a barrier to their children's achievement of the American dream: upward social mobility. After decades of educational neglect, young Chicanos and Chicanas organized school boycotts, known as blowouts, as a sign of militant protest.[7]

Drafted in large numbers into the military and out of proportion to their population in the country, Chicanos organized their own significant anti-war movement. This protest reached its zenith when over 20,000 demonstrators, mostly Chicano, protested the war in the National Chicano Anti-War Moratorium in East Los Angeles on August 29, 1970.

Culturally, the movement released a new energy of artistic and literary expression in what constituted a "Chicano Renaissance." Poets, writers, playwrights, and artists mobilized art as a political weapon for "La Causa"—the Chicano movement. The movement was not the first time that Mexican-Americans had protested their second-class status. Indeed, a strong historical legacy of protest existed, but the movement was the largest and most widespread expression of Mexican-American discontent.[8]

Cultural Nationalism: Ideology of a Movement

In 1967, Corky Gonzales's epic poem, "*I Am Joaquín*" reverberated "a triumphant vision, a tearful lamentation, and affirmation of . . . Chicano people. [W]ritten in fire,

shouted in song and whispered in pain."⁹ Sharing ideological roots with Black cultural nationalism, Chicano cultural nationalism—*Chicanismo*—advocated an ideology
and spirit of active resistance within Mexican-American communities throughout the
United States. Gonzales's poem, representative of a resurgent Chicano cultural renaissance, echoed a collective social and political lament throughout the movement:

> I am Joaquín
> Lost in a world of confusion,
> Caught up in a whirl of gringo society . . .¹⁰

Chicanismo emphasized cultural pride as a source of political unity and strength
capable of mobilizing Chicanos and Chicanas into an oppositional political group
within the dominant political landscape in the United States. As an ideology, *Chicanismo* crystallized the essence of a nationalist ideology: a collective ethnic conscious-
ness.¹¹ Chicano cultural nationalism placed the socio-historical experiences of Mexican-Americans within a theoretical model of internal colonialism. Chicano communities represented ethnic "nations" or "internal colonies" under the domination and
exploitation of the United States.¹²

As a result, Mexican-Americans in the 1960s still faced fundamental inequities
in comparison to many other ethnic groups especially Euro-Americans. More than
one-third of all Mexican-Americans lived in poverty and the average educational attainment for Mexican-Americans was less than eighth grade, the lowest in the country. Job and wage discrimination added to poor housing opportunities only compounded the Mexican-Americans position in the United States.

Chicanismo served as a dynamically effective tool capable of mobilizing divergent
struggles within the Chicano movement. By the late 1960s, cultural nationalism
served a dual political purpose. *Chicanismo* provided a unifying worldview for El
Movimiento while, at the same time, it provided the ideological link which cut across
such groups as the Raza Unida Party, the United Farm Workers, the Crusade for Justice, and the student movement.

In time, *Chicanismo* gave rise to a parallel movement of ideological opposition
that began to gain momentum. Many Chicanas, active within every sector of the
movement, raised their voices in a collective feminist challenge to the sexism and
male domination that they were experiencing within the movimiento. Developing
first as cultural nationalists, these Chicanas began to see and experience some of the
contradictions of *Chicanismo*, specifically as it applied to women. From their nationalist base, these Chicana activists began to evolve also as feminists.

The Struggles of Chicana Feminists

Chicanas participated actively during this entire period of social protest and community mobilization. Their work within each of the strands of the movement undermined long-standing stereotypes of Mexican-American women. Chicanas struggled
for social equality during this period as had past generations of Mexican women in
the United States.¹³

Chicana feminists inherited a historical tradition of political activism dating
back to the immigrant generation of Mexican women, who together with their families, crossed the border into the United States at the turn of the century. Mexican immigrant women and their families fled the upheaval produced by the Mexican Revolution of 1910 as well as from economic displacement and poverty. Communities of
Mexican immigrant families settled throughout the Southwest joining pre-existing

communities created after the U.S.-Mexico war of 1848. El Paso, San Antonio, San Diego, Los Angeles, and Santa Barbara—all experienced dramatic societal transformations that would shape future generations of Mexican-Americans.[14] Throughout contemporary Mexican-American history, women played active roles in their communities in a struggle against persistent patterns of societal inequality. Their political activism shaped the course of major reform movements within communities of Mexicans in the United States. Recent scholarship is recovering this historical legacy by documenting the participation of women at all political levels.[15]

The political struggles of Chicana feminists during the late 1960s and late 1970s reflected a continuation of women's activism that paralleled the experiences of other women of color in the United States. A Chicana feminist movement, like that of African-American women, originated within the context of a nationalist movement. As Chicanas assessed their role within the Chicano movement, their ideological debates shifted from a focus on racial oppression to one that would form the basis for an emergent Chicana feminism discourse: gender oppression.

Chicana feminists shared the task of defining their feminist ideology and movement with other feminists, specifically other women of color. Like African-American, Asian-American, and Native-American feminists, Chicana feminists struggled to gain gender equality and racial/ethnic equality. Like other feminist women of color, Chicanas recognized that their feminist movement involved a confrontation with both sexism and racism.[16] As a result, feminism, as articulated by women of color, represented an ideological and political movement to end patriarchal oppression within the structure of a cultural nationalist movement. Chicana feminists shared a common experience with other women of color whose life histories were shaped by the multiple sources of oppression generated by race, gender, and social class.[17] Thus, a Chicana feminist movement represented a struggle that was both nationalist and feminist. Ultimately, the inherent constraints and cross-pressures facing Chicana feminists within the Chicano movement led to the broader development of Chicana feminist thought.

The Social Construction of Chicana Feminist Thought

Historically, women's participation in revolutionary struggles or mass socio-political movements has been linked with the development of a feminist consciousness. Studies of women involved in revolutionary movements such as the Chinese, the Cuban, Mexican, and Nicaragua revolutions document the origins of feminist movements within the context of a male-dominated national struggle.[18] Similarly, case studies of the white feminist movement in the United States during the 1960s document the tensions experienced by women both in the New Left Movement and in the Civil Rights Movement.[19] Male domination within each of these socio-political movements precipitated the rise of a feminist movement among white women during the 1960s. African-American feminists have also traced the origins of their feminist movement to their experiences with sexism in the Black nationalist movement.[20] Although cultural, political, and economic constraints limited the full development of a feminist consciousness and movement among Asian-American women during this period, the cross- pressures resulting from the demands of a nationalist and feminist struggle led Asian-American women in time to organize feminist organizations.[21] Native-American women activists also voiced a feminist agenda as they clashed with sexism among their male counterparts.[22]

Similarly, Chicana activists traced the emergence of their feminist "awakening" to the internal struggles within the cultural nationalist Chicano movement. In the course of their political activism, directed at reforming the structures of social in-equality embedded in American society and of proposing alternative structuring, Chi-cana activists turned part of their attention inward, embarking on a feminist journey that would change dramatically the course of El Movimiento.

In a special issue on Chicanas published by *Regeneracíon*, Chicana feminist ac-tivist Anna NietoGomez argued that sexism within El Movimiento represented a key issue facing Chicana feminists. NietoGomez called for a mobilization of Chicana feminists in order to unite against the issue of male-domination prevalent within the movement.[23] Similarly, Francisca Flores, another leading Chicana feminist and editor of the Chicana feminist publication, *Regeneracíon*, captured the early momentum that galvanized Chicana feminists:

> [Chicanas] can no longer remain in a subservient role or as auxiliary forces in the [Chicano] movement. They must be included in the front line of communication, leadership and organizational responsibility. . . . The issue of equality, freedom and self-determination of the Chicana—like the right of self-determination, equality, and liberation of the Mexican [Chicano] community—is not negotiable. Anyone opposing the right of women to organize into their own form of organization has no place in the leadership of the movement.[24]

Supporting this position, Bernice Rincón argued that Chicana feminists, through their efforts to gain full equality for women, would strengthen El Movimien-to by eradicating internal sources of oppression. The dynamic process through which a feminist agenda was forcefully introduced into the Chicano movement by other Chicana feminists, such as Marta Cotera and Enriqueta Longeaux Vasquez who raised their voices in collective protest, proved to be a contentious political struggle. Like other feminist women of color, Chicana feminists experienced male resistance as their nascent feminism challenged traditional gender roles. Their efforts to redefine them-selves as equal participants transformed them into an oppositional group in relation to their male counterparts and female counterparts who supported the view that femi-nism was a divisive force within the Chicano movement. Nevertheless, Chicana femi-nists continued their struggle to gain equality by challenging sexism. NietoGomez summarized the impact of Chicana feminism:

> Chicana feminism is in various stages of development. . . . It is recognition that women are oppressed as a group and are exploited as part of la Raza people. It is a direction to be responsible to identify and act upon the issues and needs of Chi-cana women. Chicana feminists are involved in understanding the nature of women's oppression.[25]

Throughout the 1970s, this initial generation of self-proclaimed Chicana femi-nists viewed the struggle against sexism within the Chicano movement and the strug-gle against racism in the larger society as central ideological components of their fem-inist thought.

Although many issues contributed to the development of Chicana feminist thought, the ideological critique of sexism or *machismo*, the term most frequently used within a Chicano context, contributed significantly to the formation of Chicana fem-inism. Chicana feminists, as active participants in the Chicano movement, experi-enced the immediate constraints of male domination in their daily lives. Their writ-ings express their concern with traditional gender roles within Chicano families that relegated women into secondary roles. Chicana feminist challenged the portrait of the so-called "Ideal Chicana" drawn by Chicano cultural nationalists. This portrayal was inspired by a cultural nationalism that indiscriminately equated Chicano cultural survival with the glorification of traditional gender roles for Chicanas. Thus, Chicano cultural nationalist praised the "Ideal Woman" of El Movimiento for representing strong, long-suffering women who endured social injustice, maintained the family as a safe "haven in a heartless world" for their families, and, as a result, assured the survival of Chicano culture.[26] As in the Black nationalist movement, the culturally accepted role of women, as defined by a cultural nationalist ideology, relegated women to subordinate positions within the Chicano movement. Chicana feminists responded with scathing rebuttals that ultimately shaped the social construction of Chicana feminist thought. As one Chicana feminist argued:

> Some Chicanas are praised as they emulate the sanctified example set by [the Virgin Mary]. The woman par excellence is mother and wife. She is to love and support her husband and to nurture and teach her children. Thus, may she gain fulfillment as a woman. For a Chicana bent upon fulfillment of her personhood, this restricted perspective of her role as a woman is not only inadequate but crippling.[27]

A common trope found in many of the basic writings by Chicana feminists is the recognition that the existence and perpetuation of patriarchy represents an essential source of women's oppression. Their writings vary in terms of analyzing the source of this oppression. Many view the origins of patriarchy and sexism within Chicano communities as a result of individual choices and actions. For others, "machismo" was a myth created by the larger Anglo society to maintain a system of racial/ethnic oppression. Most importantly, these historical writings document the evolvement of an analysis of patriarchy and sexism as rooted in social structures permeating all levels of society. For most Chicana feminists, the origins of a Chicana feminist consciousness were directly linked to sexism within El Movimiento and the larger society. Gender oppression constituted "a serious obstacle to women anxious to play a role in the struggle for Chicano liberation."[28] Many Chicanas feminists eventually analyzed gender oppression as a collective problem and answered with a collective solution: a Chicana feminist ideology and feminist activities within Chicano communities and Chicano organizations. Nevertheless, Chicanas fought for gender equality always cognizant of the interplay between race/ethnicity and gender. Marta Cotera—a leading Chicana feminist and prolific writer—captured the emergent roles of Chicana feminists:

> There has always been feminism in our ranks and there will continue to be as long as Chicanas live and breathe in the movement . . . Chicanas will direct their own destiny.[29]

Chicana feminists came under attack for their explicit critique of Chicano cultural nationalism. Some were criticized as followers of white feminists or as lesbians. Their feminist concern with patriarchal oppression was labeled by their opponents as secondary in importance to the more salient issue of racial or even class oppression. Chicana feminist discourse responded directly to such feminist-baiting attacks by stressing the universal aspect of sexism. Their writings reflected their views that Chicano cultural values could not be extolled from a cultural nationalist perspective without a critical analysis of sexism.

Chicana feminist lesbians contributed to the further development of Chicana feminist discourse and, as such, precipitated more virulent feminist-baiting. As a result of the oppressive climate, Chicana feminist lesbians voices were generally silenced. They participated in Chicana feminist activities, but it was not until the later years of the 1970s that they made their protests significantly vocal. By the end of this decade, conference proceedings and resolutions began to include references to the specific oppression experienced by lesbians within the Chicano movement and the Chicana feminist movement. Chicana feminist lesbians brought to the Chicana feminist movement an additional voice from the margins. Their writings revealed the societal contradictions experienced by Chicana feminists whose sexual orientation and lifestyle was not only misunderstood by many within the Chicano movement but vehemently criticized by many Chicanos and Chicanas, revealing basic homophobic sentiments. In a political climate that viewed a Chicana feminist ideology with suspicion and, often, disdain, Chicana feminist lesbians confronted even more strident political attacks. Cherríe Moraga eloquently summarized the multiple sources of oppression that Chicana feminist lesbians encountered in their daily lives. Ultimately by the 1980s and now throughout the 1990s, Chicana feminist lesbians have contributed to the further development of Chicana feminist thought. As Moraga states in her essay in the path-breaking anthology *This Bridge Called My Back: Writings by Radical Women of Color:*

> My lesbianism is the avenue through which I have learned the most about silence and oppression. . . . In this country, lesbianism is a poverty—as is being brown, as is being a woman, as is being just plain poor. The danger lies in ranking the oppressions. The danger lies in failing to acknowledge the specificity of the oppression.[30]

Documenting Chicana Feminist Thought

Chicana feminist discourse developed as Chicanas struggled in opposition to the unresolved gender tensions and contradictions that they experienced both within the Chicano movement and their communities. As a result of their collective efforts to overcome racial and gender oppression, Chicana feminists constructed a feminist ideology based on their specific experiences as women of color. Ideological discussions over Chicana feminism took place at multiple levels. Ideological debates emerged within the ranks of Chicana feminists; between Chicana feminists and the "Loyalists"- Chicanas who eschewed feminism or were ambivalent about organizing as feminists; between Chicana feminists and Chicano males whose cultural nationalist ideology continued to view Chicana feminism as a threat to El Movimiento; and between Chicana feminists and Chicano males who sympathized and supported a Chicana feminist agenda. Similarly, Chicana feminists engaged in contentious debates with white feminists whose feminism was often blinded by strands of racism directed at women of color feminists.

The writings of Chicana feminists represent a significant contribution to the history of feminist movements. Beginning in the late 1960s, Chicana feminist writings began to document the ideological debates that intensified throughout this period of social protest. The historical evolution of Chicana feminist discourse unfolds within the essays, speeches, newsletters, editorials, and conference proceedings, collected in this anthology.[31] Although many Chicano publications, particularly newspapers, originated as an outgrowth of the Chicano movement and the Chicano cultural renaissance, Chicana feminists believed that these early publications did not provide adequate coverage of feminist issues, and did not have a representative number of women on their editorial boards. Chicana feminists believed that these publication units did not provide Chicanas with an adequate or appropriate outlet to voice their concerns.

Chicana feminists devised specific strategies in their efforts to overcome these constraints in order to reach a larger audience of Chicanas. First, Chicanas adopted a strategy of submitting their works to Chicano publications which they then followed with a strategy of exerting pressure on editorial boards to publish their feminist writings. A few Chicano publications published Chicana feminist writings; some even printed special issues on Chicanas. The Berkeley-based Chicano journal, *El Grito*, issued a special volume on Chicanas in 1973. Chicana feminist writings also appeared in periodicals such as *Aztlán, El Magazín de Tejas, La Raza, Consafos, De Colores*, and *La Luz*.

A second strategy adopted by Chicana feminists, and one perhaps more important for the development of Chicana feminist discourse, was the development of their own small but influential feminist publications. One journal, *Regeneración*, edited by long-time activist Francisca Flores, appeared in 1970. In addition to its regular features on Chicanas, it printed a special issue on Chicanas in 1971 and 1973. Chicana feminists at California's Long Beach State also published a newspaper, *Hijas de Cuauhtémoc*, that served as a major outlet for the discussion of feminist issues. In the spring of 1973, this newspaper was reorganized into the first feminist Chicana journal, *Encuentro Femenil*. Anna NietoGomez and Adelaida Del Castillo served as the journals first editors. The first issue focused on the social and economic status of Chicanas; the second examined the historical and contemporary stereotypes of Chicanas.

Two Chicana feminists from New Mexico, Enriqueta Longeaux Vasquez and Elizabeth Martínez, edited the newspaper *El Grito Del Norte* from 1968 to 1973. Community organization newsletters such as the *Comisión Femenil Mexicana Newsletter* and the *Chicana Service Action Center Newsletter*, both published in Los Angeles, provided Chicana feminists with an additional important publishing outlet. Similarly, many colleges and universities witnessed the development of Chicana newsletters. *El Popo Femenil* came out of the Chicano student organization at California State—Northridge. The San Francisco Chicana feminist organization, Concilio Mujeres, began publication of its newspaper *La Razón Mestiza* in 1974 under the leadership of Dorinda Moreno: writer, poet and Chicana feminist activist. Moreno also published a 1973 anthology of Chicana feminist writings, *La Mujer—En Pie de Lucha*.[32]

In 1976, Marta Cotera, a Chicana feminist from Texas, published two major monographs of Chicana feminist writings. Cotera wrote one of the earliest histories of Chicanas. Her book, *Diosa y Hembra: The History and Heritage of Chicanas in the United States*, was used widely in courses on "La Chicana" at several universities.[33] Cotera's *Profile on the Mexican-American Woman* contained additional historical writings by Cotera in addition to primary documents on Chicana feminism.[34] Cotera also compiled a series of her own essays and speeches on Chicanas in the historical anthology, *The Chicana Feminist*, published in 1977.[35]

Chicana feminist publications served as a mobilizing tool for Chicanas. Their writings reflected a growing community of Chicana feminists and the widespread emergence of feminist activities within their communities. Chicana feminists organized conferences and workshops during the 1970s that served as critical forums for the development of Chicana feminist discourse. One of the earliest Chicana workshops was held in 1969 at the first National Youth Liberation Conference held in Denver and sponsored by the Crusade for Justice. The Chicana workshop's resolution that "Chicanas did want to be liberated" would become one of the conference's most controversial statements, and the one most open to conflicting interpretations. Marta Cotera was one among many Chicana feminists that later interpreted this resolution as indicating that Chicana feminists, finding themselves at a conference that was politically charged with intense cultural nationalism, decided not to take a stand on Anglo feminism within such a context. Resolutions passed by Chicana feminists at subsequent conferences and symposiums document the emergence of Chicana feminist discourse. Conferences included the Chicana Regional Conference held in Los Angeles in 1971, the National Chicana Conference held in Houston in 1971, the Chicana Caucus of the Texas Women's Political Caucus State Convention held in Texas in 1972, the Chicana Curriculum Workshop held in 1973 at UCLA, and the Chicana Identity Conference held in 1975 in Houston, Texas. The speeches, essays, conference proceedings and resolutions produced by Chicana feminists provide key historical documentation for tracing the social construction of a Chicana feminist ideology. As early as 1971, Chicana feminists assessed their hopes for the future contribution of a Chicana feminist movement:

> We expect that this great force of women power will give the [Chicano] move-
> ment one great *empuje* [push] to raise it one giant step higher in the drive for lib-
> eration. . . .For peace and economic improvement for those who today are living
> in poverty and squalor, victims of a social and political system which is based on
> discrimination.[36]

Documents from these conferences and workshops trace the development of ideological debates and differences that surfaced during this historical period. Chicana feminist thought evolved with several divergent, often competing, views. Chicana feminists confronted divisions based on social class, particularly the division between academic women and grass roots community women, sexual orientation, political strategies, political goals and objectives, the relationship between autonomous Chicana feminist organizations and white women's feminist organizations, and their relationships with Chicano organizations and Chicano men in general. Chicana feminists were aware of the diversity of views among Chicano men regarding their evolving feminist movement and organizations. Nevertheless, Chicana feminists generally agreed that the dominant attitude towards feminism among Chicanos, particularly among the most unyielding of Chicano cultural nationalists, was one of intolerance, if not disdain.

Chicana Feminist Thought: The Basic Historical Writings

This anthology records the historical evolution of Chicana feminist writings beginning in the late 1960s and through the mid-1970s—the heyday of the Chicano movement. These feminist documents stand as a historical tribute to Chicana feminists whose activism represented lives of struggle and triumph. They are testimony that some Chicanas during the movement years did not simply decry their victimization, but more importantly displayed their agency in combating injustice. During this historical juncture, the gender contradictions that shaped their daily lives produced a feminist awakening that was ultimately channeled into a proliferation of feminist documents. *Chicana Feminist Thought: The Basic Historical Writings* brings together key historical feminist texts. This volume traces the development of a Chicana feminist discourse that, like other feminist discourses by women of color, is in the process of being recovered into the historical record.

Chicana Feminist Thought: The Basic Historical Writings follows in the tradition of Gerda Lerner's *Black Women in White America*, originally published in 1972 and reprinted twenty years later in 1992[37]. Lerner's objective was "to define major themes in the history of black women as suggested by source material available; to bring to light important unknown or little-known documents; and to focus on those women leaders whose influence was recognized and significant in their own time."[38] Similar to the work of other feminist historians such as Joan W. Scott, Lerner's anthology attempted to rewrite women into history and reformulate historical investigations using gender as a "useful category of historical analysis." [39] Lerner's anthology answered the critical question raised by Scott: "Why (and since when) have women been invisible as historical subjects, when we know they participated in the great and small events of human history?"[40]

Lerner's *Black Women in White America* traces the historical participation of African-American women: a moving testimony of courage under the most severe adversities. Maya Angelou commended Lerner for collecting "the thoughts and writings of this doubly jeopardized segment of America, and [holding] them up for all to see."[41] Lerner concluded that:

> American women have also been denied their history, but this denial has not yet been widely recognized. History, in the past largely written by white male historians, has simply failed to ask those questions which would elicit information about the female contribution, the female point of view. Women as a group have been denied knowledge of their legitimate past and have been profoundly affected individually by having to see the world through male eyes.[42]

Since the 1972 publication of Lerner's *Black Women in White America*, African-American women have made significant contributions to the field of feminist thought. Anthologies and monographs by Angela Davis, Paula Giddings, bell hooks, Gloria "Akasha" Hull, Audre Lorde, Barbara Smith, Alice Walker, and others have succeeded in reconceptualizing feminist thought by placing the experiences of women of color at the center of feminist discourse.[43] More recently, Patricia Hill Collins' *Black Feminist Thought* traces the development of a feminist framework that combines an analysis of race, gender, and class.[44] Collins' theoretical and interpretive framework has been a valuable model in compiling this anthology on Chicana feminism.

This edited volume of the historical writings by Chicana feminists will allow the reader to see the world through the eyes of women who confronted the walls of racism and sexism with a nascent collective feminism. They struggled to achieve equality in the broadest sense. At the time of their publication, these writings represented the efforts of Chicana feminists to resolve the many problematic issues constraining their full participation in the Chicano movement. For many of these authors, their articles represented their "coming to voice" for the first time.[45] These writers included young college women, community activists, graduate students, academic women, professional women, and working class women. Some women were veteran activists in Chicano communities while others were experiencing their first politicalization. Some essays reveal all the problems and challenges that confront emerging writers. Many of the women whose works are collected in this anthology had never published and did not see themselves as writers. Their essays, primary documents in Chicana feminist thought, developed during a politically charged period of tumultuous protests, demonstrations, and conferences. Often times, their works represented first drafts written under urgent conditions of political struggle and short publication deadlines. Many publishing outlets, either at the university or community level, operated with limited editorial staffs. In some cases, the publishing unit consisted of little more than a mimeograph machine in the office of a student or community organization. Proofreading and other editorial assistance were often not available. In addition, several essays, written by Chicana feminists with limited writing experience, reveal distinct language patterns such as grammatical style; sentence construction; English and Spanish slang; specific Spanish syntax, grammar, and style often found among U.S. born Mexicans; and regional idiomatic expressions from California, Texas, and New Mexico. Other essays represent more experienced writers whose works had already appeared in various newspapers and journals. This anthology includes both in order to most accurately recreate the political climate within this era of Chicana feminism. Only minor editorial changes have been made, such as correcting typographical errors and errors in spelling and punctuation. Where necessary, Spanish words and phrases were translated for the reader and appear in brackets. If the translation appeared in the original text, italics are only used if the writer used them. Some documents were shortened, but only to the extent that the original intent of the writer was maintained.

Furthermore, the writings by this generation of Chicana feminists document divergent strands of feminism. Many writings adamantly identified all Chicano males as inherent oppressors of Chicanas. Similarly, another often recurring generalization inferred that white women were inherently racist and classist. Another common ideological trope of Chicana feminism thought consisted of a revised ethnic nationalism that incorporated gender equality as a basic foundation. Some Chicanas adopted a Marxist theoretical approach and reduced their conditions of oppression to a ruthless capitalist economic system. This particular approach often included support for the struggles of post-colonial, Third World women. By the late 1970s, Chicana feminist lesbians began to articulate their growing demands. Not surprisingly, Chicana feminist writings of this period often reveal strands of all these approaches within a single essay. Such ideological diversity became a significant issue at various conferences where Chicana feminists either viewed such differences as divisive or as a basis for the formation of a united coalition.

The voices of Chicana feminists emerged, strong and forceful, during a historical period of social protest within the United States. Any historical analysis of the Chicano movement and the women's movement and, indeed, of the social movements of the 1960s is seriously compromised without a systematic integration of the Chicana feminist movement and its ideological foundations.

Chicano Studies, as a particular field of scholarly inquiry which emerged out of the Chicano movement, is only now beginning to re-examine the movement itself. With increased distance in time, Chicano Studies historians as well as other scholars are attempting to better understand the character and impact of the Chicano movement. To date, however, little attention or focus has been given to the role of women and in particular Chicana feminists in the Movement. Ignacio García's fine study of La Raza Unida Party, *United We Win*, for example, fails to integrate the role of women in the party.[46] Carlos Muñoz, Jr.'s overview of the Chicano movement, *Youth Identity and Power*, likewise gives little attention to gender issues.[47] Armando Navarro's in-depth examination of MAYO (the Mexican-American Youth Organization) in Texas recognizes the participation of Chicanas in MAYO and the role of sexism in the organization but does not make these topics central to his otherwise excellent study.[48] As the Chicano movement becomes more of a major field of study, it is critical that the role of women and especially feminists not be once again marginalized. Our volume of the writings and documents of Chicana feminists is our attempt to prevent such marginalization and to encourage the centralization of gender issues in the developing scholarship on the Chicano movement.

Similarly, these historical writings by Chicanas will contribute to the process through which the historical development of contemporary feminism is recontextualized. Feminist women of color have been critical of historical studies of twentieth century feminist movements in the United States for generally neglecting to include the participation of women of color in feminist movements within their communities.[49] In their attempt to fill this historical gap, women of color have directed their at-

tention to rewriting the scholarship on feminist theory and history whose "exclusionary practices" have resulted in only limited attention, if any, to the differences among
women regarding, race, ethnicity, class, and sexual orientation.[50]

   Although several anthologies in feminist studies have made concerted efforts to
include writing by women of color, a strong tendency to contextualize "the women's
movement" and "feminist thought" in terms that exclude women of color persists.
Most recently, for example, Miriam Schnier's *Feminism in Our Time: The Essential Writings, World War II to the Present (1994)*, claims to bring together "the major literature
and documents that inspired and shaped modern feminism."[51] Schnier's collection of
essays includes six contributions by African-American women. All other women of
color—Asian-Americans, Native-Americans, Chicanas and other Latinas—are invisible. Schneir's comment on this exclusion is based on her view that women of color
are only now beginning to engage in feminist discourse:

> as the [women's] contemporary movement enlarges its agenda to encompass a
> wider range of issues, it is certain to attract a broader constituency; we can antici-
> pate valuable *new* feminist insights from Asian-American women and Latinas *in the
> coming years* [bold and italics ours].[52]

   Women of color feminists, critical of the persistent omission of feminist writings
and anthologies, such as Schnier's, have been advocating that feminist scholarship redefine the discipline's views on gender by calling for feminist scholarship that inte-
grates additional sources of women's oppression such as race and ethnicity. Women of
color have a rich, historical legacy of feminist activism and written records of feminist
discourse. These historical documents are not invisible despite Schnier's contention.
They exist and are available for those with a desire to use them.

   Thus, *Chicana Feminist Thought: The Basic Historical Writings* documents a feminist
discourse that emerged from the struggles of Chicana feminists beginning in the late
1960s. The selections in this anthology are arranged thematically and chronologically.
Part One, for example, concerns the initial expression by Chicana feminists about the
role of patriarchy and sexism in Mexican-American culture. Part Two focuses on five
core themes in Chicana feminist thought. These include: (1) Chicana feminism and
the politics of the Chicano movement; (2) analyzing the dynamics of Chicana oppression; (3) mapping a Chicana feminist agenda; (4) the relationship between Chicana
feminists and white feminists; and (5) Chicana feminists as an evolving future. Finally,
Part Three reveals the influence that Chicana feminists in the movement had on post-
movement Chicana feminists in the 1980s and 1990s.

   The origins of this study lie, at one level, in the recognition that the roots of
contemporary Chicana feminism are to be found in the crucial years of the Chicano
movement and, at another level, in the evidence of these roots readily available in the
existant newspapers and other documents generated by the movement. Our task was
to bring together the historical record of Chicana feminist thought during the period
of the Chicano movement. We did not have to strain to find sufficient documentation. Our dilemma was to select from a bounty of writings. Our selections were based
on the following criteria: (1) the substance of the document; (2) the historical importance of a particular document; and (3) the historical importance of a particular
writer. We want to stress that by no means is this collection of writings comprehensive. Such a volume would have resulted in one twice the size if not more that the
present one. It is a selective volume of what we believe to be the basic and key documents to an understanding and appreciation of the roots and evolution of Chicana
feminist thought. It should likewise be clear that the focus of this volume is historical.

It is not a collection of contemporary Chicana feminist writings which would obviously have included many more writers. Part Three of our volume contains a selection of more contemporary writings but only with the intent of suggesting the connection between Chicana feminists of the Chicano movement and Chicana feminists of the post-movement years. As a historical document our volume concentrates on the initial expression of Chicana feminist discourse during the late 1960s and the first part of the 1970s—the major years of the Chicano movement. Today, the writings of this generation of Chicana feminists stand as a legacy to their determination, bravery, and strength in struggling, often against all odds, to build a world free of racial, class, and gender oppression. Their vibrant voices resound in each of these essays and will echo for future generations of women and men who will experience their own feminist awakenings as they confront their own gender struggles.

NOTES

1. On the rise of the Chicano Movement, see Mario Barrera, "The Study of Politics and the Chicano," *Aztlán* 5 (1974): 9-26; Carlos Muñoz, Jr., *Youth, Identity, Power: The Chicano Movement* (New York: Verso, 1989); Armando Navarro, "The Evolution of Chicano Politics," *Aztlán* 5 (1974): pp. 57-84; Rodolfo Acuña, *Occupied American: A History of Chicanos*, 3rd ed. (New York: Harper-Collins, 1988); Ignacio M. García, *United We Win: The Rise of La Raza Unida Party* (Tucson: University of Arizona Mexican-American Studies & Research Center, 1989); Juan Gómez-Quiñones, *Chicano Politics: Reality and Promise, 1940–1990* (Albuquerque: University of New Mexico Press, 1990). Also see the four-part television documentary, *Chicano!* produced by the National Latino Communication Center in association with KCET-TV in Los Angeles and first aired in 1996. Also see the accompanying text of this documentary by F. Arturo Rosales, *Chicano: The History of the Mexican-American Civil Rights Movement* (Houston: Arte Publico Press, 1996).

2. See Peter Nabokov, *Tijerina and the Courthouse Raid* (Albuquerque, NM: University of New Mexico Press, 1969).

3. See Eugene Nelson, *Huelga: The First Hundred Days of the Great Delano Grape Strike* (Delano, CA: Farmworkers Press, 1966); John Dunne, *Delano: Story of the California Grapestrike* (New York: Farrar, Straus & Giroux, 1967); Peter Matthiesen, *Sal Si Puedes: César Chávez and the New American Revolution* (New York: Random House, 1969); Sam Kushner, *Long Road to Delano* (New York: International Publishers, 1975); Richard Griswold Del Castillo and Richard A. García, *César Chávez: A Triumph of Spirit* (Norman: University of Oklahoma Press, 1995).

4. See Christine Marín, *A Spokesman for the Mexican-American Movement: Rodolfo "Corky" Gonzales and the Fight for Chicano Liberation, 1966–1972* (San Francisco: R & E Research Associates, 1977); Richard A. García, *Political Ideology: A Comparative Study of Three Chicano Youth Organizations* (San Francisco: R & E Research Associates, 1977); Richard A. García, "The Chicano Movement and the Mexican-American Community, 1972–1978: An Interpretive Essay," *Socialist Review* 8 (July, 1978): 117–136. Matt S. Meier and Feliciano Ribera, *Mexican-Americans/American Mexicans: From Conquistadors to Chicanos* (New York: Hill and Wang, 1993).

5. See John Shockley, *Chicano Revolt in a Texas Town* (South Bend, IN: University of Notre Dame Press, 1974); García, *United We Win*.

6. Guadalupe San Miguel, *Let All of Them Take Heed: Mexican-Americans and the Campaign for Educational Equality in Texas, 1910–1981* (Austin: University of Texas Press, 1987).

7. Muñoz, Jr., *Youth, Identity, Power*.

8. For historical studies of an earlier generation of Mexican-American protest see Mario T. García, *Mexican-Americans: Leadership, Ideology, & Identity, 1930–1960* (New Haven: Yale University, 1989; Richard A. García, *Rise of the Mexican-American Middle Class: San Antonio, 1929–1941* (College Station: Texas A & M University Press, 1990); Mario T. García, *Mem-

ories of Chicano History: The Life and Narrative of Bert Corona (Berkeley: University of California Press, 1994).

9. Rodolfo Gonzales, *I Am Joaquín: An Epic Poem*, 1967.

10. Gonzales, *I Am Joaquín*, p. 3.

11. Muñoz Jr., *Youth, Identity, Politics*, p. 77.

12. For analyses of Chicano communities as an internal colony see Tómas Almaguer, "Historical Notes on Chicano Oppression," *Aztlán* 5 (1974): 27–56 and Mario Barrera, *Race and Class in the Southwest: A Theory of Racial Inequality* (Notre Dame, Ind.: University of Notre Dame Press, 1979).

13. For one of first anthologies on Chicanas see Magdalena Mora and Adelaida R. Del Castillo, eds., *Mexican Women in the United States: Struggles Past and Present* (Los Angeles: UCLA Chicano Studies Research Center Publication, 1980). See also Alfredo Mirandé and Evangelina Enríquez, *La Chicana: The Mexican-American Woman* (Chicago: University of Chicago Press, 1979); Adelaida R. Del Castillo, ed., *Between Borders: Essays on Mexicana/Chicana History* (Encino, CA: Floricanto Press, 1990); Vicki L. Ruiz, *Cannery Women/Cannery Lives: Mexican Women, Unionization, and the California Food Processing Industry, 1930-1950* (Albuquerque, NM: University of New Mexico Press, 1987). See also Mario T. García, "The Chicana in American History: The Mexican Women of El Paso, 1880–1920, A Case Study," *Pacific Historical Review*, Vol. 49, no. 2 (May, 1980): pp. 315–337.

14. For historical studies of some these communities see Mario T. García, *Desert Immigrants: The Mexicans of El Paso, 1880–1920* (New Haven: Yale University Press, 1981); Richard A. García, *Rise of the Mexican-American Middle Class: San Antonio, 1929–1941* (College Station: Texas A & M University Press, 1990); Richard Griswold del Castillo, *La Familia: Chicano Families in the Urban Southwest, 1848 to the Present* (Notre Dame, Ind.: University of Notre Dame Press, 1984); Albert Camarillo, *Chicanos in a Changing Society: From Mexican Pueblos to American Barrios in Santa Barbara and Southern California, 1848–930* (Cambridge, MA: Harvard University Press, 1979); George Sánchez, *Becoming Mexican-American: Ethnicity, Culture, and Identity in Chicano Los Angeles, 1900–1945* (New York: Oxford University Press, 1993).

15. For a collection of Chicana Studies scholarship see Adela De La Torre and Beatrice M. Pesquera eds., *Building With Our Hands: New Directions in Chicana Studies* (Berkeley: University of California Press, 1993); Norma Alarcón, et.al., *Chicana Critical Issues* (Berkeley: Third Woman Press, 1993).

16. For analyses of feminism among women of color see bell hooks, *Ain't I a Woman: Black Women and Feminism* (Boston: South End Press, 1981); bell hooks, *Feminist Theory: From Margin to Center* (Boston: South End Press); Lucie Cheng, "Asian-American Women and Feminism," *Sojourner* 10 (1984): pp. 11–12; Esther Ngan-Ling Chow, "The Development of Feminist Consciousness Among Asian-American Women," *Gender & Society* 1 (1987): pp. 284–299; Alma M. García, "The Development of Chicana Feminist Discourse, 1970–1980," *Gender & Society* 3 (June 1989): pp. 217–238.

17. See Angela Davis, *Women, Race and Class* (New York: Random House, 1983); Bonnie Thornton Dill, "Race, Class, and Gender: Prospects for an All-Inclusive Sisterhood," *Feminist Studies* 9 (1983): pp. 131–150; Frances White, "Listening to the Voices of Black Feminism," *Radical America* 18 (1984): pp. 7–25; Paula Gunn Allen, *The Sacred Hoop: Recovering the Feminine in American Indian Tradition* (Boston: Beacon Press, 1986); Maxine Baca Zinn and Bonnie Thornton Dill, "Difference and Domination," in *Women of Color in U.S. Society*, ed. Maxine Baca Zinn and Bonnie Thornton Dill (Philadelphia: Temple University Press, 1994), pp. 3–12.

18. See Shiela Rowbotham, *Women, Resistance and Revolution: A History of Women and Revolution in the Modern World* (New York: Vintage, 1974); Anna Macias, *Against All Odds: The Feminist Movement in Mexico to 1940* (Westport, CT: Greenwood, 1982).

19. Jo Freeman, "On the Origins of Social Movements," in *Social Movements of the Sixties and Seventies*, ed. Jo Freeman (New York: Longman, 1983), pp. 8–30; Jo Freeman, "The Women's Liberation Movement: Its Origins, Structure, Activities, and Ideas," in *Women: A Feminist Perspective*, ed. Jo Freeman (Palo Alto, CA: Mayfield, 1984): pp. 543–556; Flora Davis, *Moving the Mountain: The Women's Movement in America Since 1960* (New York: Simon & Schuster,

1991); Alice Echols, *Daring To Be Bad: Radical Feminism in America 1967–1975* (Minneapolis: University of Minnesota, 1989); Sara Evans, *Personal Politics, The Roots of Women's Liberation in the Civil Rights Movement and the New Left* (New YorK: Knopf, 1979).

20. Frances Beale, "Slave of a Slave No More: Black Women in Struggle," *Black Scholar* 6 (1975): pp. 6–10; Patricia Hill Collins, *Black Feminist Thought: Knowledge, Consciousness and the Politics of Empowerment* (New York: Routledge, 1990).

21. See Katheryn M. Fong, "Feminism is Fine, But What's It Done For Asian America?" *Bridge* 6 (1978): pp. 21–22; Germaine Q. Wong, "Impediments to Asian-Pacific-American Women Organizing," in *The Conference on the Educational and Occupational Needs of Asian Pacific Women* (Washington, DC: National Institute of Education, 1980), pp. 89–103.

22. See Rayna Green, "Native-American Women," *Signs: Journal of Women in Society and Culture*, 7 (1980): pp. 248–267.

23. Anna NietoGomez, "Chicanas Identify," *Regeneración* 1 (1971): p. 9.

24. Francisca Flores, "Comisión Femenil Mexicana," *Regeneración* 2 (1971), p. 6.

25. Anna NietoGomez, "Sexism in the Movement," *La Gente* 6 (Vol. 4, 1976): p. 10.

26. The phrase "haven in a heartless world" comes from Christopher Lasch, *Haven in a Heartless World: The Family Besieged* (New York: Basic Books, 1977).

27. Consuelo Nieto, "The Chicana and the Women's Rights Movement," *Civil Rights Digest* 6 (Spring 1974), p. 39.

28. Mirta Vidal, "New Voice of La Raza: Chicanas Speak Out," *International Socialist Review* 32 (October 1971), p. 8.

29. Marta Cotera, *The Chicana Feminist* (Austin: Information Systems Development, 1977), p. 12.

30. Cherríe Moraga, "La Güera," in *This Bridge Called My Back: Writings by Radical Women of Color*, (eds.) Cherríe Moraga and Gloria Anzaldúa (Watertown, MA: Persephone, 1981), p. 28–29.

31. See Alma García, "The Development of Chicana Feminist Discourse."

32. Dorinda Moreno, *La Mujer—En Pie de Lucha* (Mexico: Espina del Norte Publications, 1973). For an early anthology of documents from the Chicano Movement that includes several essays by Chicana feminists see, Richard A. García, *The Chicanos in America: 1540–1974: A Chronology and Fact Book* (New York: Oceana Publications, 1977).

33. See Marta P. Cotera, *Diosa y Hembra: History and Heritage of Chicanas in the United States* (Austin, TX: Information Systems Development, 1976.

34. See Marta P. Cotera, *Profile on the Mexican-American Woman* (Austin, TX: National Educational Laboratory Publishers, Inc.).

35. See Marta P. Cotera, *The Chicana Feminist* (Austin, TX: Information Systems Development, 1977).

36. Moreno, *La Mujer*, p. 29.

37. See Gerda Lerner, ed., *Black Women in White American: A Documentary History* (New York: Vintage Books, 1972). Lerner's book was reprinted in 1992 by Vintage Books.

38. Lerner, *Black Women*, p. xx.

39. Joan Wallach Scott, *Gender and the Politics of History* (New York: Columbia University Press, 1988), p. 28.

40. Scott, *Gender and the Politics*, p. 50.

41. This quote by Maya Angelou is taken from the first page of the 1992 edition of *Lerner's Black Women In White America*.

42. Lerner, *Black Women*, (1992) p. xvii.

43. For basic writings by African-American women on feminism see: Angela Davis, *Women, Race and Class* (New York: Random House, 1981); Angela Davis, *Women, Culture and Politics* (New York: Random House, 1989); Paula Giddings, *When and Where I Enter: The Impact of Black Women on Race and Sex in America* (New York: William Morrow, 1984); bell hooks, *A'int I a Woman: Black Women and Feminism* (Boston: South End Press, 1981); bell hooks, *Feminist Theory: From Margin to Center* (Boston: South End Press, 1984); bell hooks, *Talking Back: Thinking Feminist* (Boston: South End Press, 1989); Gloria T. Hull, Patricia Bell Scott and Barbara

Smith, ed., *But Some of Us Are Brave* (Old Westbury, NY: Feminist Press, 1982); Audre Lorde, *Sister Outsider* (Trumansberg, NY: The Crossing Press, 1984); Alice Walker, *In Search of Our Mothers' Gardens* (New York: Harcourt Brace Jovanovich, 1983).

44.   Hill Collins, *Black Feminist Thought.*

45.   bell hooks, *Talking Back.*

46.   García, *United We Win.*

47.   Muñoz, Jr., *Youth, Identity, Power.*

48.   Armando Navarro, *Mexican-American Youth Organization.*

49.   Davis, *Moving the Mountain*, addresses the tendency to overlook the participation of women of color in historical and contemporary analyses of the "women's movement." She includes a chapter, "Diversity: From the Melting Pot to the Salad Bowl," that examines feminism and women of color. Similarly, Elizabeth Spelman, *Unessential Woman: Problems of Exclusion in Feminist Thought* (Boston: South End Press, 1988) criticizes white feminists for using white middle class heterosexual women as the norm, relegating women of color feminists to the margins of feminist discourse.

50.   Barbara A. Smith, ed. *Home Girls: A Black Feminist Anthology* (New York: Kitchen Table Press, 1983); Maxine Baca Zinn et. al., "The Cost of Exclusionary Practices in Women's Studies," *Signs: Journal of Women in Society and Culture,* 11 (1986): pp. 290–303; Alma M. García, "Studying Chicanas: Bringing Women into the Frame of Chicano Studies," in Teresa Córdova, et. al, ed., *Chicana Voices: Intersections of Class, Race, and Gender* (Austin: Center for Mexican American Studies, 1986):pp. 19–29; Baca Zinn and Thornton Dill, *Women of Color,* 1994.

51.   Miriam Schnier, ed., *Feminism in Our Time: The Essential Writings World War II to the Present* (New York: Vintage Books, 1994), p. ix.

52.   Schnier, *Feminism in Our Time,* p. xiii.

I

VOICES OF
CHICANA FEMINISTS:
AN EMERGING
CONSCIOUSNESS

Introduction

First surfacing as Chicana nationalists and perhaps influenced by strong female role models within their own families, some Chicanas by the early 1970s began to seriously question the very cultural nationalism—Chicanismo—that had first engaged them in the movement. Their critique was based on their experiences and observations within the movement which suggested to them certain contradictions in Chicano nationalism as it related to gender issues. The glorification and romanticization, for example, of the Chicano family and the traditional role of women within the family by the movement appeared to these Chicanas to maintain women as second-class citizens of El Movimiento.

As a result, emerging Chicana feminists initiated a critique of the very concept of the Chicano family and of the traditional role of women within Mexican-based culture. The following essays in this section illustrate this dialogue among Chicana feminists concerning the need to question particular family and cultural traditions including the role of the Catholic Church steeped in patriarchy and sexism. Such traditions, Chicana feminists asserted, contradicted the movement's stress on freedom and liberation. Who was to be freed and liberated? Only men?

Yet while Chicana feminists challenged some of the very cultural traditions that the Chicano movement was extolling, they did not in a blanket fashion condemn all

17

traditions nor did they place all of the burden of their oppression on male domination. Chicana feminists, for example, observed that within the very culture that they were critiquing was to be found the inspiration for their own cause. As Anna Nieto-Gómez noted in her essay in this section, contrary to the stereotype of the passive Mexican woman, history revealed strong female role models who represented the origins of Chicana feminism. Expanding Chicano nationalism to include the role of assertive and strong Chicanas, Chicana feminists recognized that their questioning of their own culture represented only one aspect of their struggle. They stressed that besides the internal gender wars that they had to engage in, that they at the same time had to join Chicano males in their common struggle against race and class oppression.

The following essays document the difficult and sensitive efforts by Chicana feminists to challenge the essentialism of the movement and at the same time mobilize their opposition by staying within their own cultural boundaries.

La Nueva Chicana (1971)

The old woman going to pray
does her part,
The young mother hers,
The old man sitting on the porch,
The young husband going to work,
But let's not forget the young
Chicana,
Bareheaded girl fighting for
equality,
Unshawled girl living for a better world,
Let's not forget her,
Because,
She is LA NUEVA CHICANA
Wherever you turn,
Wherever you look,
You'll see her,
She's still the soft brown-eyed
beauty you knew,
There's just one difference,
A big difference,
She's on the go spreading the word.
VIVA LA RAZA
Is her main goal too,
She is no longer the silent one,
Because she has cast off the
shawl of the past to show her face,
She is LA NUEVA CHICANA

Ana Montes

Protest march in Los Angeles, California, early 1970s. Courtesy of Raul Ruiz, *La Raza* magazine, Los Angeles, California.

1

New Voice of La Raza:
Chicanas Speak Out*

Mirta Vidal

At the end of May [1971], more than 600 Chicanas met in Houston, Texas, to hold the first national conference of Raza women. For those of us who were there it was clear that this conference was not just another national gathering of the Chicano movement.

Chicanas came from all parts of the country inspired by the prospect of discussing the issues that have long been on their minds and which we now see not as individual problems but as an important and integral part of a movement for liberation.

The resolutions coming out of the two largest workshops—"sex and the Chicana" and "marriage—Chicana style"—called for "free, legal abortions and birth control for the Chicano community; controlled by *Chicanas*." As Chicanas, the resolution stated, "we have a right to control our own bodies." The resolutions also called for "24-hour childcare centers in Chicano communities" and explained that there is a critical need for these since "Chicana motherhood should not preclude educational, political, social and economic advancement."

While these resolutions articulated the most pressing needs of Chicanas today, the conference as a whole reflected a rising consciousness of the Chicana about her special oppression in this society.

With their growing involvement in the struggle for Chicano liberation and the emergence of the feminist movement, Chicanas are beginning to challenge every social institution which contributes to and is responsible for their oppression, from inequality on the job to their role in the home. They are questioning "machismo," discrimination in education, the double standard, the role of the Catholic Church, and all the backward ideology designed to keep women subjugated.

This growing awareness was illustrated by a survey taken at the Houston conference. Reporting on this survey, an article in the Los Angeles magazine *Regeneración* states: "84% felt that they were not encouraged to seek professional careers and that higher education is not considered important for Mexican women. . . . 84% agreed that women do not receive equal pay for equal work." The article continues: "On one question they were unanimous. When asked: Are married women and mothers who attend school expected to also do the housework, be responsible for childcare, cook and do the laundry while going to school, 100% said yes. 88% agreed that a social double

*From *International Socialist Review*, October, 1971: pp. 7–9, 31–33.

standard exists." The women were also asked if they felt that there was discrimination toward them within La Raza: 72% said yes, *none* said no and 28% voiced no opinion.

While polls are a good indicator of the thoughts and feelings of any given group of people, an even more significant measure is what they are actually doing. The impressive accomplishments of Chicanas in the last few months alone are a clear sign that Chicanas will not only play a leading role in fighting for the liberation of La Raza, but will also be consistent fighters against their own oppression as Chicanas around their own specific demands and through their own Chicana organizations.

Last year, the women in MAPA (Mexican-American Political Association) formed a caucus at their annual convention. A workshop on women was also held at a Latino Conference in Wisconsin last year. All three Chicano Youth Liberation Conferences—held in 1969, 1970, and 1971 in Denver, Colorado—have had women's workshops.

In May of this year, women participating at a Statewide Boycott Conference called by the United Farm Workers Organizing Committee in Castroville, Texas, formed a caucus and addressed the conference, warning men that sexist attitudes and opposition to women's rights can divide the farmworker's struggle. Also in May, Chicanas in Los Angeles organized a regional conference attended by some 250 Chicanas, in preparation for the Houston conference and to raise funds to send representatives from the Los Angeles area.

Another gathering held last year by the Mexican-American National Issues Conference in Sacramento, California, included a women's workshop which voted at that time to become the Comisión Femenil Mexicana (Mexican Feminine Commission) and function as an independent organization affiliated to the Mexican-American National Issues Conference. They adopted a resolution which read in part. "The effort of Chicana/Mexican women in the Chicano movement is generally obscured because women are not accepted as community leaders either by the Chicano movement or by the Anglo establishment."[1]

In Pharr, Texas, women have organized pickets and demonstrations to protest police brutality and to demand the ousting of the city's mayor. And even in Crystal City, Texas, where La Raza Unida Party has won major victories women have had to organize on their own for the right to be heard. While the men constituted the decision-making body of Ciudadanos Unidos (United Citizens)—the organization of the Chicano community of Crystal City—the women were organized into a women's auxiliary-Ciudadanas Unidas. Not satisfied with this role, the women got together, stormed into one of the meetings and demanded to be recognized as members on an equal basis. Although the vote was close, the women won.

The numerous articles and publications that have appeared recently on la Chicana are another important sign of the rising consciousness of Chicanas. Among the most outstanding of these are a special section in *El Grito del Norte*, an entire issue dedicated to and written by Chicanas published by *Regeneración* and a regular Chicana feminist newspaper put out by Las Hijas de Cuauhtémoc in Long Beach, California. This last group and their newspaper are named after the feminist organization of Mexican women who fought for emancipation during the suffragist period in the early part of this century.

These facts, which are by no means exhaustive of what Chicanas have done in this last period, are plainly contradictory to the statement made by women participating in the 1969 Denver Youth Conference. At that time a workshop held to discuss the role of women in the movement came back to report to the conference: "It was the consensus of the group that the Chicana woman does not want to be liberated."

Although there are still those who maintain that Chicanas not only do not want to be liberated, but do not need to be liberated, Chicanas themselves have decisively rejected that attitude through their actions.

"Machismo"

In part, this awakening of Chicana consciousness has been prompted by the "machismo" she encounters in the movement. It is adequately described by one Chicana, in an article entitled "Macho Attitudes," in which she says:

> When a freshman male comes to MEChA [Movimiento Estudiantil Chicano de Aztlán—a Chicano student organization in California] he is approached and welcomed. He is taught by observation that the Chicanas are only useful in areas of clerical and sexual activities. When something must be done there is always a Chicana there to do the work. "It is her place and duty to stand behind and back up her Macho!". . . . Another aspect of the MACHO attitude is their lack of respect for Chicanas. They play their games, plotting girl against girl for their own benefit. . . . They use the movement and Chicanismo to take her to bed. And when she refuses, she is a *vendida* [sell-out] because she is not looking after the welfare of her men.[2]

This behavior, typical of Chicano men, is a serious obstacle to women anxious to play a role in the struggle for Chicano liberation.

The oppression suffered by Chicanas is different from that suffered by most women in this country. Because Chicanas are part of an oppressed nationality, they are subjected to the racism practiced against La Raza. Since the overwhelming majority of Chicanos are workers, Chicanas are also victims of the exploitation of the working class. But in addition, Chicanas, along with the rest of women, are relegated to an inferior position because of their sex. Thus, Raza women suffer a triple form of oppression: as members of an oppressed nationality, as workers, and as women. Chicanas have no trouble understanding this. At the Houston conference 84 percent of the women surveyed felt that "there is a distinction between the problems of the Chicana and those of other women."

On the other hand, they also understand that the struggle now unfolding against the oppression of women is not only relevant to them, but is their struggle. Because sexism and male chauvinism are so deeply rooted in this society, there is a strong tendency, even within the Chicano movement to deny the basic right of Chicanas to organize around their own concrete issues. Instead they are told to stay away from the women's liberation movement because it is an "Anglo thing."

One needs only to analyze the origins of male supremacy to expose that position for what it is—a distortion of reality and false. The inferior role of women in society does not date back to the beginning of time. In fact, before the Europeans came to this part of the world women enjoyed a high position of equality with men. The submission of women, along with institutions such as the church and the patriarchy, was imported by the European colonizers, and remains to this day part of Anglo society. Machismo—which, as it is commonly used, translates in English into male chauvinism—is the one thing, if any, which should be labeled an "Anglo thing."

When Chicano men oppose the efforts of women to move against their oppression, they are actually opposing the struggle of every woman in this country aimed at changing a society in which Chicanos themselves are oppressed. They are saying to 51 percent of this country's population that we have no right to fight for our liberation.

Moreover, they are denying one half of La Raza this basic right. They are denying Raza women, who are triply oppressed, the right to struggle around their specific, real, and immediate needs.

In essence, they are doing just what the white, male rulers of this country have done. The white male rulers would want Chicanas to accept their oppression precisely because they understand that when Chicanas begin a movement demanding legal abortions, child care, and equal pay for equal work, this movement will pose a real threat to their ability to rule.

Opposition to the struggles of women to break the chains of their oppression is not in the interests of the oppressed but only in the interest of the oppressor. And that is the logic of the arguments of those who say that Chicanas do not want to or need to be liberated.

The struggle for women's liberation is the Chicana's struggle, and only a strong independent Chicana movement, as part of the general women's liberation movement and part of the movement of La Raza, can ensure its success.

NOTES

1. *Regeneración*, Vol. I, No. 10, 1971, p. 3.
2. *Las Hijas de Cuauhtémoc*, unnumbered edition, p. 9.

2

*La Chicana: Her Role in the Past and Her Search for a New Role in the Future**

BERNICE RINCÓN

Woman's struggle to become a person in her own right takes on a peculiar note for the Latin woman. If she also happens to be of Mexican descent, her battle seems almost insurmountable, and yet today the sisters are working to develop a strategy that will enable us to be women people, rather than chattels or pets; and, at the same time, not to so radically disturb the balance of the man–woman relationship that we become neuters.

*From *Regeneración*, Vol. 1, No. 10, 1971: pp. 15–18.

Many of the more enlightened Latino men in the movement are also recognizing that the status quo cannot be allowed to remain unchanged. If we speak of freedom, it must encompass all people equally, regardless of sex. These ideas are being expressed more frequently by the enlightened male leadership in the movement. The ideas are worded differently or perhaps presented in a different way, but the inevitability of change in order to establish a better society is there. César Chávez speaks of this issue to the Campesino [farm worker]. The poet, Roberto Vargas, speaks about it to teachers and college students. El Teatro Triste addresses itself to it in the barrio in its skit, "El Cuchillo" [The Knife]. The status quo must go! It is a new time and we need to make use of everybody's talent and energy.

Traditionally, Mexican culture has been male-oriented and dominated.

Family Roles

1. Paternal Role: The father wields almost unlimited power within the home. His word is usually law, and he is obeyed unquestioningly by his wife and children, especially the girls. Ordinarily, the girls may not leave the house without his express permission. If there is no father in the home, this role is usually assumed by the eldest son or male in the household. The literature and songs abound with reasons for this life style.
2. Maternal Role: Traditionally, the role of the Mexican woman is one of subordination. "She is expected to be submissive, faithful, devoted, and respectful to her husband and to take the major responsibility for rearing the children." A good wife is not expected to find fault with her husband or to be curious or jealous of what he does outside the home, nor is she supposed to share in his political, economic or social activities unless they are centered around the home.

Women are [considered by traditional Mexican culture] inferior beings, because in submitting, they open themselves up. Their inferiority is constitutional and resides in their sex, their submissiveness, which is a wound that never heals. The Mexican considers woman to be a dark and passive being. He does not attribute evil instincts to her; he even pretends she does not have any. Or, to put it more exactly, her instincts are not her own, but those of the special, because she is an incarnation of the life force, which is essentially impersonal. Thus, it is impossible for her to have a personal, private life, for if she were to be herself, if she were to be mistress of her own wishes, passions or whims, she would be unfaithful to herself. She is an undifferentiated manifestation of life; a channel for the universal appetite. In this sense, she has no desires of her own.

The falsity of this conception is obvious enough when one considers the Mexican woman's sensitivity and restlessness, but at least it does not turn her into an object, a mere thing. She is a symbol, like all women of the stability and continuity of the race. In addition to her cosmic significance she has an important social role, which is to see to it that law and order, piety and tenderness are predominant in everyday life.

This point of view is closely adhered to by both male and female members of the Mexican culture and permeates all strata of society. The head on clash of this point of view with the Anglo-American idea of the woman's role and the reasoning behind it are a direct cause of conflict and alienation in many Mexican-American homes. Most Mexicans of a low socio-economic level are from rural areas, whether they reside in the United States or in Mexico. As a result they have developed those characteristics generally common to rural people. Thus, they are reluctant to accept change, clinging tightly to those attitudes and behavior patterns which give them a feeling of security in the face of situations which tend to point up their inadequacies.

While 80% of the Mexican-American population does reside in the cities in the

United States the major part of the Mexican immigrants are from rural areas. The 1960 Census figures report 1 in 6 Mexican-Americans was employed as a farm laborer. This paper will try to relate this cultural background to the added complexities this brings to the life of Mexican-American women.

It is necessary to understand what constitutes a "bad" woman in the rural-Mexican culture as contrasted with that of the Anglo-American "bad" woman.

It is interesting to note that the image of the "mala mujer"—the "bad" woman"—is almost always accompanied by the idea of aggressive activity. She is not passive like the "self-denying mother," the "waiting sweetheart," the "hermetic idol;" she comes and goes, she looks for men and then leaves them. Her extreme mobility, through a mechanism similar to that described above, renders her invulnerable. Activity and immodesty unite to petrify her soul. The Mala is hard and impious and independent like the Macho. In her own way she also transcends her physiological weakness and closes herself off from the world. In contrast the Anglo "bad" woman is characterized by her sexually loose conduct and only peripherally by her fulfillment of other social functions. The Anglo tradition of industrial and political democracy has encouraged women to actively seek equal rights and employment outside the home. The emphasis on "getting ahead" has encouraged women to work outside the home and to seek higher education. This has been accomplished with at least the tacit approval of the men in the society. The emphasis on the nuclear family has increased the pressure on parents and children to become independent of each other. Girls are encouraged to be independent and to compete with siblings and others in the race to "get ahead." The "All American" girl is consciously pretty, clever, poised, sophisticated in the ways of society, educated, ambitious, energetic and active, adept at competing and privileged in the world of men, and is a partner in marriage, or so she has been led to believe until now.

This dichotomy in the role of females in the society places much emotional strain on the Mexican-American female who may be 90% Mexican and 10% American or the other way around. Depending on where she is in the acculturation scale she is bound to feel or be made to feel "bad," "enslaved," "wild," "submissive," "chattel," "toy," or unintelligent."

The Chicanos who are traditionalists are still tied to this ideal of Mexican womanhood. The Chicana is torn between being what her man wants her to be and what she knows she must become in order to function in today's action oriented world. She knows that there is already a population explosion, she knows that simple economic facts do not allow for unlimited propagation. She knows that she does not need to suffer and she wants to keep that maturity, that serene security, that ability to change pain to joy and lust to purity.

Traditionally we have encouraged women to stay at home and to work only when it is absolutely necessary for the survival of the family. As inflation and acculturation take place the pressure for women to work increases. Some statistics from the 1960 Census:

> Employment of Mexican-American women
>   Professional 9%
>   Clerical and Sales 30%
>   Unemployed 10%
> Education of Mexican-American women: 7.1 years
>   One year of college 6%
>   Drop-out rate is at least half of the student population.

We need to come to a decision within ourselves. Is material gain a good enough reason to become educated or go to work? If a woman is forced to work or just enjoys working how can she make an adjustment of values so that the feeling of guilt is mitigated? If a woman is going to work, how can we motivate her to aspire to professional status? When we say that a woman's place is in the home do we really mean it for all women?

In a patriarchal system the dependents are protected to a certain degree from the stress and strain of decision making. A girl who is not allowed to go out on dates unchaperoned does not have to trouble herself with wondering what she will do when her date decides to park. A woman who is not allowed to work or know about income does not need to worry about how the rent will be paid. If an error in judgment is made papa or her esposo [husband] must take responsibility if he wants to maintain his leadership; thus life in the patriarchal system has its rewards for those who function well within it. For those who do not it is prison.

In any system that advocates absolute power and authority of one person or group over another is distasteful at times to the subordinate group and the Chicana has had years to contend with this situation in that institution called Machismo as it relates to the Chicana. There are modifications that would be worth considering if we are speaking of social justice for all the people. So that question is what would we change? Perhaps listing some of the positive and negative aspects of this institution will help.

Positive

1. Bravery, loyalty
2. Pride in self as an individual
3. Responsibility of leadership in the family
4. Sacredness of the family (La Raza)
5. Human values: Love of fellows: compassion, suffering, liberty for all
6. Lack of concern for money
7. Love of music, dancing (joy of life)
8. Love of children
9. Respect for religion
10. Respect for elders
11. Modesty and reserve
12. Liberal political orientation
13. Good manners
14. Willingness to fight when needed

Negative

1. Absolute power
   a. Exploitation
   b. Self centeredness
   c. Violence used to maintain power through fear
   d. Closed aloofness
2. Women seen as a subordinate creature created to make man's lot more comfortable and pleasurable
3. Too much pride
4. Absolute power-inclination to strong man politics; Hero worship-dictatorships
5. There is a sharing of the joys of life only as man sees fit. Woman's place is home.
6. Large families (here the church has also contributed)
7. Too much responsibility placed on the male to maintain his "position"
8. Drinking, wenching, etc., seen as a sign of manhood
9. Fighting seen as a proof of masculinity
10. Too modest and reserved for survival in today's society

What is the motivation for change? Do we need to change in order to become Americans? We do not think so. We are Americans. There are some very positive good things that the Mexican culture has to offer for the improvement of life in these United States. How we go about making change will determine if we are going to be able to do it or if we will be faced with a coalition of backlashes formed of the Anglo society and our men and brothers. The basic conflict is *corazón* [heart/soul] vs. materialism and we must keep this in mind as we push for change.

La Chicana has the best of two cultures at her fingertips. Don't push her to assimilate. We have something good. Take it easy, play it cool and we will come up with something better.

Contrary to the traditional "role" there have always been those who were individuals and therefore were and are admired for their bravery and spirit. The Mexican Poetress Sor. Juana Inés de la Cruz, La Corrigadora Doña Josefa, Las Soldaderas personified by "La Adelita," Amalia Hernández of the Ballet Folklorico de México and countless "Artistas." Today, of the women active in the movement for social justice, the most well-known woman is Dolores Huerta, Vice Chairman of the Farm Workers Union (UFWOC).

We are not without role models and we have support from at least some of our men. We were most impressed by the young women of the MEChA Chicana Caucus northern region held at Stanford University in March 1970. After much discussion about the role of the Chicana in the movement the concensus of opinion was that we do not wish to join with the Anglo Woman's Liberation. We do not want to compete with men. We do want to be given the opportunity to do whatever it is that we do best in the line of work. We want to have our efforts recognized and our success rewarded with more responsibility and when feasible with financial awards. We want to have our ideas recognized and implemented with credits going to the originators. We want to be in on the decision making if we are "leaders" and to work beside our men as equals.

There is progress being made toward social change for all. I found this poem written on a poster in the Teatro Triste center:

India Es Mi Mujer

La mujer was created from the rib of man.
She was not made from his head to top him,
Nor out of his feet, to be trampled upon,
But out of his side, to be equal to him,
Under his arm, to be protected,
And under his heart to be loved.
India Era Mi Madre

3

The Woman of La Raza*

ENRIQUETA LONGEAUX Y VÁSQUEZ

While attending a Mexican-American conference in Colorado this year [1969], I went to one of the workshops that were held to discuss the role of the Chicana—The Mexican-American woman, the woman of La Raza. When the time came for the women to report to the full conference, the only thing that the workshop representative had to say was this: "It was the consensus of the group that the Chicana woman does not want to be liberated."

As a woman who has been faced with living as a member of the Mexican-American minority group, as a breadwinner and a mother raising children, living in housing projects, and having much concern for other humans plus much community involvement, I felt this as quite a blow. I could have cried. Surely we could at least have come up with something to add to that statement. I sat back and thought, Why? Why? Then I understood why the statement had been made and I realized that going along with the feelings of the men at the convention was perhaps the best thing to do at the time.

Looking at the history of the Chicana or Mexican woman, we see that her role has been a very strong one—although a silent one. When the woman has seen the suffering of her people, she has always responded bravely and as a totally committed and equal human. My mother told me of how, during the time of Pancho Villa and the revolution of Mexico [1910], she saw the men march through the village, continually for three days and then she saw the battalion of women marching for a whole day. The women carried food and supplies; also, they were fully armed and wearing loaded Carrilleras [ammunition belts]. In battle they fought alongside the men. Out of the Mexican Revolution came the revolutionary personage "Adelita," who wore her rebozo [shawl] crossed at the bosom as a symbol of the revolutionary women in Mexico.

Then we have our heroine Juana Gallo, a brave woman who led her men to battle against the government after having seen her father and other villagers hung for defending the land of the people. She and many other women fought bravely with their people. And if called upon again, they would be there alongside the men to fight to the bitter end.

Today, as we hear the call of La Raza and as the dormant, "docile," Mexican-American comes to life, we see again the stirring of the people. With that call, the Chicana woman also stirs and I am sure that she will leave her mark upon the Mexican-American movement in the Southwest.

How the Chicana woman reacts depends totally on how the macho Chicano is treated when he goes out into the "mainstream" of society. If the husband is so-called

*From *Magazín*, Vol. 1, No. 4, 1972: pp. 66–68: 35.

successful, the woman seems to become very domineering and demands more and more in material goods. I ask myself at times, why are the women so demanding? Can they not see what they make of their man? But then I realize: this is the price of owning a slave.

A woman who has no way of expressing herself and of realizing herself as a full human has nothing else to turn to but the owning of material things. She builds her entire life around these, and finds security in this way. All she has to live for is her house and family; she becomes very possessive of both. This makes her a totally dependent human. Dependent on her husband and family. Most of the Chicana women in this comfortable situation are not particularly involved in the movement. Many times it is because of the fear of censorship in general. Censorship from the husband, the family, friends, and society in general. For these reasons she is completely inactive.

Then you will find the Chicana whose husband was not able to fare so very well in society, and perhaps has had to face defeat. This is the Chicana who really suffers. Quite often the man will not fight the real source of his problems, be it discrimination or whatever, but will instead come home and take it out on his family. As this continues, his Chicana becomes the victim of his machismo and woeful are the trials and tribulations of that household.

Much of this is seen, particularly in the city. The man, being head of the household but unable to fight the system he lives in, will very likely lose face and for this reason there will often be a separation or divorce in the family. It is at this time that the Chicana faces the real test of having to confront society as one of its total victims.

1. In order to find a way to feed and clothe her family, she must find a job. Because of her suppression she has probably not been able to develop a skill. She is probably unable to find a job that will pay her a decent wage. If she is able to find a job at all, it will probably be sought only for survival. Thus she can hope just to exist; she will hardly be able to live an enjoyable life. Here one of the most difficult problems for the Chicana woman to face is that of going to work. Even if she does have a skill, she must all at once realize that she has been living in a racist society. She will have much difficulty in proving herself in any position. Her work must be three-times as good as that of the Anglo majority. Not only this, but the competitive way of the Anglo will always be there. The Anglo woman is always there with her superiority complex. The Chicana woman will be looked upon as having to prove herself even in the smallest task. She is constantly being put to the test. Not only does she suffer the oppression that the Anglo woman suffers as a woman in the market of humanity but she must also suffer the oppression of being a minority person with a different set of values. Because her existence and the livelihood of the children depend on her conforming, she tries very hard to conform. Thus she may find herself even rejecting herself as a Mexican-American. Existence itself depends on this.

2. She must find housing that she will be able to afford. She will very likely be unable to live in a decent place; it will be more the matter of finding a place that is cheap. It is likely that she will have to live in a housing project. Here she will be faced with the real problem of trying to raise children in an environment that is conducive to much suffering. The decision as to where she will live is a difficult matter, as she must come face-to-face with making decisions on her own. This, plus having to live them out, is very traumatic for her.

3. In finding a job she will be faced with working very hard during the day and coming home to an empty house and again having to work at home. Cooking, washing, ironing, mending, plus spending some time with the children. Her role changes to being both father and mother. All of this, plus being poor, is very hard to bear.

4. Child care is one of the most difficult problems for a woman to have to face alone. Not only is she tormented with having to leave the raising of her children to someone else, but she wants the best of care for them. For the amount of money that she may be able to pay from her meager wages, it is likely that she will be lucky to find anyone at all to take care of the children. The routine of the household is not normal at all. She must start her day earlier than an average worker. She must clothe and feed the children before she takes them to be cared for in someone else's home. Then too, she will have a very hard day at work, for she is constantly worrying about the children. If there are medical problems, this will only multiply her stress during the day. Not to mention the financial pressure of medical care.

5. With all of this, the fact still remains that she is a human and must have some kind of friendship and entertainment in life, and this is perhaps one of the most difficult tasks facing the Mexican-American woman alone. She can probably enjoy very little entertainment, since she can not afford a babysitter. This plus the fact that she very likely does not have the clothes, transportation, etc. As she cannot afford entertainment herself, she may very often fall prey to letting someone pay for her entertainment and this may create unwanted involvement with some friend. When she begins to keep company with men, she will meet with the disapproval of her family, and often be looked upon as having loose moral values. As quite often she is not free to remarry in the eyes of the Church, she will find more and more conflict and disapproval, and she continues to look upon herself with guilt and censorship. Thus she suffers much as a human. Everywhere she looks she seems to be rejected.

This woman has much to offer the movement of the Mexican-American. She has had to live all of the roles of her Raza. She has had to suffer the torments of her people in that she has had to go out into a racist society and be a provider as well as a mother. She has been doubly oppressed and is trying very hard to find a place. Because of all this, she is a very strong individual. She has had to become strong in order to exist against the odds.

The Mexican-American movement is not that of just adults righting the social system, but it is a total commitment of a family unit living what it believes to be a better way of life in demanding social change for the benefit of humanity. When a family is involved in a human rights movement, as is the Mexican-American family, there is little room for a woman's liberation movement alone. There is little room for having a definition of woman's role as such. Roles are for people living the examples of social change. The Mexican-American movement demands are such that, with the liberation of La Raza, we must have a total liberation. The woman must help liberate the man and the man must look upon this liberation with the woman at his side, not behind him, following, but alongside him, leading. The family must come up together. The Raza movement is based on brother and sisterhood. We must look at each other as one large family. We must look at all of the children as belonging to all of us. We must strive for the fulfillment of all as equals, with the full capability and right to develop as humans. When a man can look upon a woman as human, then, and only then, can he feel the true meaning of liberation and equality.

4

La Chicana*

Elizabeth Martínez

The history and problems of La Chicana are similar to those of Latin-American women. Although the native Indian women of the Americas was, before the Spanish conquest, far from being completely free, she often participated more fully in the life of the society than did her sister under Spanish rule. The coming of the European, with his Catholic Church and feudal social system, was a turning point. Our roots lie in the act of rape: the rape of women, the rape of an entire continent and its people.

Inside the borders of the United States, the women of La Raza lived first under Spanish rule, then Mexican rule, and beginning in 1848 under U.S. imperialist rule. That year, the process of rape was resumed. The Chicana was raped by the invading gringo both in the literal, physical sense as well as in the sense of those forms of oppression imposed on all our people, both men and women.

Today we can say that the Chicana suffers from a triple oppression. She is oppressed by the forces of racism, imperialism and sexism. This can be said of all non-white women in the United States. Her oppression by the forces of racism and imperialism is similar to that endured by our men. Oppression by sexism, however, is hers alone. (By sexism, we mean oppression based on sex just as racism is oppression based on race. Sexism includes both social structures and attitudes of male superiority that are rooted in those structures.)

The Chicana of working class origin, like her Third World sisters in the United States, is born into a life pattern that we see again and again. If she finishes her secondary education, she is lucky. The Chicana who does agricultural work is almost never able to accomplish this; she must go to work in the fields at an early age, along with other members of the family, and move with them around the country as they search for work. Eventually, the Chicana will marry and become pregnant—or simply become pregnant. After one, two or three children, it is likely that her husband will leave the home. This will not necessarily happen because he does not love the woman and children but more often because of economic pressures. He simply cannot find work to support the family. Even if he doesn't leave the home, the situation is very hard and psychological tension grows between the couple.

This tension is increased when the woman is able to find work while the man cannot. This often happens because certain kinds of jobs, such as domestic service or working in the garment industry, are available to uneducated women. One of the ugliest forms of these economic pressures arises from the U.S. welfare system. Under that system, a woman with children cannot receive financial aid if there is a man in

*From *Ideal*, September 5–20, 1972: pp. 1–2.

the house (her husband or any other). But she can receive it if there is no man. Some couples deliberately separate so that the woman and children can qualify for welfare aid. This was the case of Reies López Tijerina, leader of the land struggle in New Mexico, and his first wife María Escobar.

Despite the hard life faced by the working class Chicana—and we have barely suggested it here—she is expected to live according to attitudes and prejudices imposed by sexism. These include ideas about virginity, false definitions of femininity and the double standard (one standard of sexual behavior for women, a different standard for men). The Chicana may be working 16 hours a day to support and care for her children, but she will still be viewed as a sexual object rather than as a human being. Unless she is over the age of 35 or 40, she will be seen more as a face and body than as a fellow worker and fellow victim of oppression.

All this holds true not only for the working class Chicana—who forms the great majority of our women—but also for the Chicana of Middle Class origin. Often the spiritual growth of this Chicana is even more stunted. From birth, her life is a predestined pattern based on passing from her parents control to that of her husband. She goes through high school acquiring a strong sense of competition with other Chicanas for the attention of the boys. This is the dominant feature of her high school years. Although she is expected to become a wife and mother, the whole subject of sexual functions and physiology is treated like a dark secret. Femininity is turned into capitalist consumerism. Her womanhood is channeled into buying clothes and make-up and driving her husband to worry about making more money so that he can buy more material possessions that will give the family "status."

In the last 10 or 20 years, there has been a growing number of Chicanas from Middle Class backgrounds who go on from high school to university study and sometimes become professional workers. This group also falls prey to the values of consumerism, but some members do develop a stronger political awareness. This group has added a new element to the picture of the Chicana today.

Today—with literally thousands of Chicano women drawn into activity—there is a wide variety in positions held by Chicanas concerning their role. They might be drawn out as follows:

- The position that women should seek no change in their roles and should never challenge the status quo. This position is found among Chicanas of all classes and ages.
- The position that women are very capable, and can make important contributions as women without raising a fuss about it—in other words, without challenging the present, general situation. This position is generally held by older, working class Chicanas who often have strong individual personalities.
- The position that women must fight sexism constantly, but as an isolated phenomenon. This position is generally held by younger Chicanas, often university students.
- The position that women should and can be revolutionaries at every level of the struggle. They should struggle against sexism without fear, but within the context of our whole struggle as a people.

We will not win our liberation struggle unless the women move together with the men rather than against them. We must work to convince the men that our struggle will become stronger if women are not limited to a few, special roles. We also have the right to expect that our most enlightened men will join in the fight against sexism; it should not be our battle alone.

We have only begun to grapple with the question of La Chicana and we have much to learn.

What has been the reaction of the men to all this? In some cases, the men have seen how they themselves are oppressed by the sexist attitudes that we call "machismo." They perceive how Chicanos waste time, energy and even their lives in so-called fights over women. They perceive how our oppressor uses "machismo" against us—for example, by appealing to a Chicano's sense of supposed manhood in order to get him to kill Vietnamese. Sexism is a useful tool to the colonizer; the men are oppressed but they can beat and mistreat women, who thus serve as targets for a frustration that might otherwise become revolutionary. Some men understand very well that the full participation of women is needed if our people are to win the liberation struggle.

The truth is that we need to reexamine and redefine our culture. Some of us do not believe that in our culture, femininity has always meant: weak, passive delicate looking . . . in other words, qualities that inflate the male ego. The women of La Raza is traditionally a fighter and revolutionary. In the history of Mexico the nation closest to us, we find a long line of heroines—from the war of independence against Spain through the 1910 revolution and including the rebellions of the Yaqui Indians. The same holds true for other nations.

The woman of La Raza is also, by tradition, a worker. These are the traditions, this is the culture, that the revolutionary Chicana wants to revive. These are the traditions that a revolutionary nationalism will revive.

The revolutionary Chicana does not identify with the so-called women's liberation movement in the United States because up to now that movement has been dominated by white women of middle class background. Some of the demands of that movement have real meaning for the Chicana—such as free day-care centers for children and reform of the welfare system. But more often our demands and concerns do not meet with theirs. For example, the women's liberation movement has rejected traditional family. For us, the family has been a source of unity and our major defense against the oppressor.

Up to now, the U.S. women's liberation movement has been mainly concerned with sexism and ignored or denied the importance of racism. For the Chicana, the three types of oppression cannot be separated. They are all a part of the same system, they are three faces of the same enemy. They must all be fought with all our courage and strength. As we said earlier, the rape of our continent, our people, is historically linked. To undo the wrong, we Chicanas must understand that link, and struggle as a united force with our men and our allies.

5

A Chicana's Message*

ANONYMOUS

There was a family at the park yesterday that reminded me of my family. They were all sitting around drinking cerveza [beer], eating tacos and listening to Mexican music. Then I noticed something that bothered me. A young girl walked by the table and all the men checked her out. It looked as though the Chicanas at the table got pissed off at their husbands because the men all giggled as though one of them had been scolded for being *manoso* [conniving].

A year ago I would have thought that those *cabrones* [jerks] were cute and very easily I could have been that girl walking by. I'm so glad that I don't need to be checked out to boost my ego. That is one dependency I'm rid of. Many of my sisters are going crazy because they are no longer sex objects. That really hurts me inside because I know we have more to offer the world than our asses.

The women who were at the table were pregnant and I have gone through that torture. I have been on both sides of the fence. As women we have been pitted against each other for the big prize . . . el macho? We are constantly competing with one another, even when we walk down the street we are trying to hold our stomachs in or push our chi chi's [breasts] out. Believe me, that ain't a very comfortable way to walk, but we do it. Since we're little girls we're taught to flirt; then when we have boyfriends or get married and the men criticize us for being flirts—what do they expect? We are taught to use our bodies to get attention!

Who cares how we feel inside? Who cares about the useless feeling a woman over thirty gets because she is showing her age? Many times I have heard my mother say that she is old and stupid. What a waste of human energy for her to feel worthless at age forty. She has a lot to give, but she has such a low image of herself that she has no ambition. Christmas day I felt closer to my mother than I had in years. She kept crying about the mistakes in her life. Then I started hugging her and, of course, I cried too. Our mistakes have been very similar; one of them was trusting men. All of our lives we are taught to be dependent on men. Then when they mess us over we are supposed to remain strong and keep rolling with the punches. This is one Chicana who is sick of rolling with those punches.

As Chicanas we have a duty to ourselves as women first! We must get to know each other as hermanas [sisters] and open our hearts to each other. We must trust all women and realize that at this point in the movimiento "Chicano Power" doesn't include Chicana power!

Qué vivan las mujeres! [Long live women!]

*From *La Verdad*, January, 1972: p. 2.

6

Women of the Mexican American Movement*

JENNIE V. CHÁVEZ

As the women's liberation movement is becoming stronger, there is another women's movement that is effecting change in the American revolution of the 1970s—the Mexican-American women, las Chicanas, las mujeres.

In contrast to some of the white women of the liberation movement, who appear to encourage an isolationist method of acquiring equality, Mexican-American women want unity with their men. Here I am not negating the validity of white women's lib (as I am in support of the majority of its ideas) but am writing rather of how, as Chicanas, we are relating to the entire movement.

As Chicanas, discriminated against not only by the white dominant society, but also by our own men who have been adhering to the misinterpreted tradition of machismo, we cannot isolate ourselves from them for a simple (or complex) reason. We must rely on each other to fight the injustices of the society which is oppressing our entire ethnic group.

On May 28–30, 1971, the first national Mujeres Por La Raza Conference was held in Houston, Texas. Its being held in the "heart of Texas" struck me as being a gigantic step forward in the entire Chicano movement, as tejanos have always been considered the Mexican's main antagonists. Five hundred Latin women from states as far away as Washington, New York, Michigan and, of course, California attended.

Just six months prior to this conference I was being called a white woman for organizing a Las Chicanas group on the University of New Mexico campus. I was not only ostracized by men but by women. Some felt I would be dividing the existing Chicano group on campus (the United Mexican-American Students, UMAS), some were simply afraid of displeasing the men, some felt that I was wrong and my ideas "white" and still others felt that their contribution to La Causa or El Movimiento was in giving the men moral support from the kitchen.

It took two months of heartbreak on both sides for the organization to be recognized as valid. A handful of women supported it. These women were physically as well as intellectually beautiful, breaking the media stereotype of the women's libber. Ninety percent wore makeup, bras, didn't use four-letter words every other sentence

*From *Mademoiselle*, April, 1972; pp. 82, 150–152.

and were aware of their sex roles. I was one of the ten percent who frequently did the opposite, thus causing suspicion even amongst those women who saw the need for a Chicana organization. One mistake which caused tension and suspicion was the fact that I dressed and spoke differently from the average college Chicana. I was more into the white revolutionary rhetoric and the "hippie" lifestyle. I see now that one of the newest themes of the entire social movement, in the labor movement, in the ethnic movement, is the use of tolerance on both sides.

Previously, as one of the first members of UMAS when it got started in 1969 on the UNM [University of New Mexico] campus, I was given special attention, being fairly attractive and flirtatious. But as soon as I started expounding my own ideas the men who ran the organization would either ignore my statement or make a wisecrack about it and continue their own discussion. This continued for two years until I finally broke away because of being unable to handle the situation. I turned to student government. There I was considered a radical racist Mexican militant, yet with the Chicano radicals I was considered a sellout. I was caught in the middle, wanting to help but with neither side allowing me.

The summer of 1970, after the Cambodia crisis, I traveled extensively, "getting my head together," the result being the formation of Las Chicanas the following December. About that time I also wrote an article about Mexican-American women's liberation in the school paper and caught more shit than I knew existed from both males and females in the movement. Paradoxically, the activists were most upset, while the apolitical Mexican-American males and females on campus thought my article "great."

Now, however, because a few women were willing to stand strong against some of the macho men who ridiculed them, called them white and avoided them socially, the organization has become one of the strongest and best-known in the state. Prior to the Houston conference, Las Chicanas was being used as the work club by the other male-run Chicano organizations in the city of Albuquerque. Every time they needed maids or cooks, they'd dial-a-Chicana. Every time there was a cultural event they would call the Chicana Glee Club to sing a few songs. For three months Las Chicanas was looked upon as a joke by most of the UMAS men and some of the other Chicano organizations. Needless to say, I became very frustrated with my brain-child and left it for two months. I would not and could not set myself up as a leader as I felt I would only cause more hard feelings, so I left the women to choose their own and straighten out the new ideas in their heads.

It has taken what I consider a long time for them to realize and to speak out about the double oppression of the Mexican-American woman. But I think that after the Houston Conference they have more confidence (certainly I regained it) in speaking up for our recognition.

Chicanas, traditionally, have been tortilla-makers, baby-producers, to be touched but not heard. As the social revolution for all people's freedoms has progressed, so Chicanas have caught the essence of freedom in the air. The change occurred slowly. Mexican-American women have been reluctant to speak up, afraid they might show up the men in front of the white man—afraid that they may think our men not men.

Now, however, the Chicana is becoming as well-educated and as aware of oppression, if not more so, as the Mexican-American male. The women are now ready to activate themselves. They can no longer remain quiet and a new revolution within a revolution has begun.

The Chicana movement has produced such women as Grace Gil Olivárez, first woman law school graduate of Notre Dame who, speaking at the Houston Conference, said, "As long as we see ourselves as inferior we are collaborating in our own oppression." Olivarez never graduated from high school or college but managed to get accepted and graduated from one of the top schools of the nation. Women such as Dolores Huerta, a strong woman who has earned the right to be César Chávez's right-hand lady in California's farm worker's union movement, and Enriqueta Longeaux y Vasquez, a writer of Taos, New Mexico, who has long spoken out for the participation of the Mexican-American woman in the Chicano movement. On campuses and barrios all over the nation Chicanas are being revitalized by stories of Adelitas and Valentinas who fought beside men in the Mexican Revolution.

Women, as women's lib advocates know, are capable of great physical endurance and so it has been with women of our ethnic group. In order to someday obtain those middle-class goods (which in my eyes oppress more people than they liberate from "drudgery") our women have not only been working at slave jobs for the white society as housemaids, hotel maids and laundry workers, but have tended also to the wants of a husband and many children—many children because contraceptives have been contrary to the ethnic idea of La Familia (with all its socio-political-economic implications).

The new breed of Chicanas are changing their puritanical mode of dress, entering the professions of law, business, medicine and engineering. They are no longer afraid to show their intellect, their capabilities and their potential. More and more they oppose the Catholic Church, to which a large majority of our ethnic group belongs, challenging its sexual taboos as well as the idea that all Catholic mothers must be baby-producing factories and that contraceptives are a sin.

Out of the workshop on "Sex and La Chicana" came the following resolutions:

> (1) that Chicanas should develop a more healthy attitude toward sex and get rid of all the misconceptions about its "evil," thus allowing ourselves to be as aggressive as men; (2) that we object to the use of sex as a means of exploiting women and for commercial purposes; (3) that no religious institution should have the authority to sanction what is moral or immoral between a man and a woman.

As the new breed of Mexican-American women we have been, and probably will continue to be, ridiculed by our men for attempting the acrobatics of equality. We may well be ostracized by La Familia for being vendidos, sell-outs to the "white ideas" of late marriage, postponing or not wanting children and desiring a vocation other than tortilla-rolling, but I believe that this new breed of bronze womanhood, as all women today, will be a vanguard for world change.

Speaking for myself, I feel that Chicana women are capable of doing both and bearing children to retain the good characteristics of La Familia. We have so long endured the sufferings imposed on us by dominant white society, and the psychological and physical suppression of the men's reactions caused by their inability to cope with that oppression, that I now firmly believe that we Mexcian-American women are stronger and better prepared to accept the challenge of a liberation-within-a-liberation movement. We will have our babies when we want and also follow a responsible vocation.

My understanding of the white women in the liberation movement is that they have no other choice but to isolate themselves from what is recognizably bad—white male chauvinist bourgeois imperialists, and the other thousand revolutionary cliches. These women have no one to turn to but themselves (which may be a reason for the Gay caucuses in the women's movement.) Naturally, there are also liberated men in both the Chicano and the white groups who respect and treat women as equals, but they are so few that at this point I still have to generalize. Fortunately, Mexican-American women can work for liberation with our men and make them understand, more easily than one could a white man, the oppression women feel, because they themselves have been oppressed by the same society.

Mexican-American men, as other men of oppressed groups, have been very reluctant to give up their machismo because it has been a last retention of power in a society which dehumanizes and mechanizes them. But now they are comprehending the meaning of carnalismo (brotherhood) in the feminine gender as well.

The reincarnation of Adelitas and Valentinas throughout the Southwest leaves the men no choice but to listen to the heroines of the past revived—lest we all perish together in our struggle to change a racist society.

7

Chicana Consciousness: A New Perspective, A New Hope*

ELENA H. GARCÍA

La Raza Nueva. The new breed. Chicanismo has given young and old people of Mexican and Latin descent new hope for the future. This projects itself in demanding what is rightfully ours from the Gringo: justice and equality.

Chicana consciousness is an integral part of the new breed, the Chicano movement, chicanismo. Chicana consciousness defined is not a white woman's liberation movement nor a ladies auxiliary. We find little connection in the women's liberation movement being that we are working within a *cultural* context, a *Chicana* context. The only resemblance along these lines is that we are all women, yet women with our respective views and problems. Neither are we a ladies auxiliary in that we only want recognition in so far as "our place" is concerned, in the home, having children, and

*From *La Mujer en Pie de Lucha*, edited by Dorinda Moreno (Mexico: Espina del Norte Publications, 1973: pp. 4–5).

denial of our *self*. This is not saying we do not want this; we want it, but in its correct context!!

Chicana Consciousness can thus be defined as working within the cultural context yet not upon limitations of the self, the new Chicana self. As Chicanas we respect our men. We respect the home, the family. This is all dealing within the cultural context. Yet times are changing. You are coping with a new Chicana, a Chicana working within the college system. A Chicana who is seeing that her place need not only be in the home, with her husband and family. She is sensing her ability beyond that, yet not excluding it. She will go through the college system to get her degree and then she realizes she must go on, not stop the cycle at being a housewife. She must utilize her degree, her capacity as a Chicana woman and continue the cycle of enlightenment.

This raises serious problems. As the film "Salt of the Earth" exemplifies, once women begin to exert themselves in other than the home the men become anxious of their manliness, their machismo. They saw their women as losing respect, becoming independent, forgetting the home. Yet this is not it!! The women in their awareness of their potential, actualized their potential in active and vocal participation in the strike. They saw hope; in *helping their men, working with their men*. The husband, his machismo, refused to see this. His wife stood steadfast. She knew she was right in her beliefs. She knew that as *Chicanos* they could win the strike working together. It took time for him to see her side.

He started thinking and realized he was keeping her down the same way the Gabacho was keeping him down. Was that right? She was doing a lot of work. They were working towards the same goal weren't they? So what was he so upset about? He saw that his machismo was causing complications in bettering the situation. By seeing beyond his machismo, respecting and recognizing his woman, they won together.

This is what young Chicanas of today strive for. We are also actualizing our potential in a new way, in the college environment. We are also facing the problem of machismo. The problem that can deny the right of awareness, the right of self [determination] to the Chicana. In doing this, we would be negating the movement itself, what it strives for: a New Breed, a new perspective, a new hope.

As a Chicana I have only touched on the new awareness that is growing within our women.

Chicanas: Actualize your potential.

Chicanos: Recognize and respect this potential for the betterment of us all.

8

Our Feminist Heritage*

Marta Cotera

Because Mexican women had participated valiantly in the 1810 War for Independence and the subsequent wars for reform, they were not expressively excluded from voting and holding office by the 1857 Constitution. Unfortunately, subsequent election laws did restrict suffrage to males. Suffrage and feminist activities in Mexico in the 1880s were advocated primarily by socialists who spoke in favor of women's rights. As early as 1878 *La Internacional* published a 12-point program in which number 7 called for the emancipation, rehabilitation and education of women. In the 1880s and 1890s during the Porfirio Díaz regime Mexican women were admitted to institutions of higher learning and by the end of last century, Mexico had women professionals in law, medicine, pharmacy, and the teaching professions. The social and economic upheavals which deposed the Díaz regime and produced the 1910 revolution gave Mexican feminists yet another arena for action. Revolutionary supporters established women's organizations like the Hijas de Cuauhtémoc and newspapers like *Vesper* which helped the cause and raised women's consciousness about their own status. Juana Belen Gutiérrez de Mendoza was an outstanding feminist and journalist of the period.

In terms of women's rights, the Mexican revolution of 1910 had enormous impact. During the revolution men and women developed relationships of partnership and mutual regard very seldom seen in most societies. Through their activities as clerks, secretaries, smugglers, telegraphers, journalists, financiers, and soldiers, women had a rare opportunity to develop their potential on a large scale, beside the men, and won their respect and recognition as partners. Perhaps within the Mexican culture this phenomenon was only to be repeated in the U.S. with the Chicano farmworker and civil rights struggles of the twentieth century.

Mexicanas built on this relationship to press for more representation in the nation's public life during the revolutionary years and during the formulation of public policies following the revolution. President Francisco I. Madero, through the influence of his wife and Soledad González, his assistant, became deeply interested in women's rights. His brief term in office precluded any action on this matter.

President Venustiano Carranza had as a close aide Hermila Galindo, an early champion of women's rights in Mexico. Through various [plans] and reforms Carranza changed the legal status of women, although their political status remained unchanged. His aide, Hermila Galindo, continued to spread feminist propaganda in Veracruz, Tabasco, Campeche, Yucatán, San Luis Potosí, Coahuila, and Nuevo León. Her-

*Cotera gave this as a speech in 1973 and then published it in her anthology, *The Chicana Feminist* (Austin: Information System Development, 1977: pp. 1–7).

mila's activities no doubt also helped propagandize Carranza's Constitutionalist cause among women.

From September, 1915, to 1919 Hermila Galindo, Artemisa Saenz Rayo and other women published a feminist journal, *La Mujer Moderna*, which advocated women's rights. They also worked to organize Mexico's first International Congress of Women which was held in Merida, Yucatán, in January, 1916. This congress included more than 700 delegates nationwide. Activities included reports on the status of women on an international scale and resolutions on the protection of women and children.

Although women had sacrificed fortunes, families, and lives during the revolution, their social and political status remained unchanged when the 1917 constitution was drawn up and adopted.

There are indications that even as early as 1917 the radicals and liberals feared traditional church influence over women if women were allowed to vote in national and state elections. Feminist victories during this period included a "law concerning family relations" which gave women the right of divorce, the right to alimony, and to management and ownership of property. But again, the national election law of June, 1918, ignored women and specified that "all Mexican males 18 years of age or over if they are married and 21 years or over if they are not, who enjoy full political rights and whose names have been duly registered in their municipalities are eligible to vote."

Another feminist congress met in Mexico City in 1921 and by 1922, Yucatán passed the first of a series of state laws granting the vote to women in the state.

Mexicanas continued to press for women's rights and suffrage through a multitude of organizations such as the Mexican Y.W.C.A., the Liga Feminista, and the Asociación Panamericana.

During this period women's groups also worked towards the obliteration of poverty, the equitable distribution of land, and improvements in the lives of all women and children in Mexico.

Although states like Chiapas and San Luis Potosí provided suffrage to women, both states were forced to rescind their decisions. Women continued through the 20s and 30s to press for suffrage until 1959 when the right to vote was finally granted them.

Historians for this period and leading to 1959 indicate that during sessions of Congress, women attorneys, judges, orators, journalists, and activists showed up daily to demand the right to vote. Politicians always waved them aside for a more propitious time. But the Mexicanas did not desist until that day, July 7, 1959, when Mexican women voted for the first time.

And the sky did not fall in and no Catholic Bishop has been elected President, as the men had predicted.

Because of the human migration between borders it is difficult to separate some developments of the Mexicana's suffragist activities from Chicana history and development.

In many instances Chicana feminism followed separate but similar courses to Mexican feminism. In most instances Chicana feminist activities have been intricately interwoven with the entire fabric of the Chicano civil rights movement from 1848 to the present.

From Frances Swadesh's research on southwestern cultures we know that *mestizas* in the southwest enjoyed a very liberalized existence as compared to Mexico and other parts of the United States in the 1850s. Women like pony rider mail carrier Candelaria Mestas and "La Tules" in New Mexico blew the Chicana stereotypes. In the 1880's socialist and labor organizer Lucy Gonzales Parsons was actively organizing women workers in Chicago. Her very presence and activity as a leader in the labor movement for thirty years propelled both the feminist and labor causes.

Other feminist activities within the Chicano community included the activity of Mexicanas and Chicanas within the Partido Liberal Mexicano from 1905 to approximately 1917. Hundreds of women worked with the revolutionary exiles Enrique and Ricardo Flores Magón to achieve rights for all workers, men and women. The P.L.M. and its publication *Regeneración* became important vehicles for the espousal of women's rights in the U.S. within the Chicano community.

Other important events in Chicana feminist history include:

- The activities of Jovita Idar and Soledad Peña who advocated women's development and helped form the Liga Femenil Mexicanista on October 15, 1911, in Laredo, Texas.
- María L. Hernández' civil rights activities as early as 1923 in Texas.
- Chicana activities in labor organizing in the 1930s in the Monte Berry strike, the Pecan Shellers strike, and the concurrent national conferences. Chicanas active in the period were Emma Tenayuca, Luisa Moreno, and Manuela Sager. Many relatives of present day campesinas like Raquel Orendain were also involved.
- Isabel Malagran González' political activism in Colorado in the 1930s and 1940s and her outspoken stance on the involvement and development of Chicanas.
- The filming of *Salt of the Earth* in 1953 on the role and courage of Chicanas.

In the 1960s the historical cycle was completed and Chicanas picked up the feminist threads introduced by the radical Club Liberal de San Antonio and the autonomous Liga Mexicanista Femenil of the 1920s. Both organizations, unlike GI Forum, Ladies LULAC, and Chicana groups working within predominantly male groups, were feminist and autonomous. Chicanas had come of age. They have been willing in the seventies, as before, to participate in community and male-dominated organizations. But in addition, they recalled part of themselves, part of their energies, to participate in newly formed all-women caucuses and organizations.

The recurring rationale for this action has been expressed in Chicana feminist ideology and in position statements from coast to coast. It centers around these issues identified by Chicanas:

- Chicanas have realized that in terms of socio-economic status and prospects for improvement, they are at the bottom of the social heap in this country.
- Chicanas realize that there is always room for recruiting more women into social action and advocacy, and that women can be successfully recruited if concentrated attention is given to this matter. Chicanas welcomed the opportunity to shoulder at least 50 percent of the burden for development and improvement of the community.
- Women have some very special and unique concerns in areas such as sex education, child care, rape, Chicana studies or university and public school nonsexist ethnic studies, which they can effectively identify and clarify. In these areas, mixed groups have not always been as effective advocates as all-women organizations.
- Male-dominated organizations have provided limited opportunity for leadership experiences to women. In all-female organizations, all positions are available to women.
- Women sometimes can be more successfully involved in all-women organizations than in mixed groups. From the entry point in a woman's organization, they can be introduced to other community advocacy efforts.
- Chicanas realized that Anglo women were advocating for greater rights and privileges and prioritizing of programs on women's issues; as a good strategy, special-purpose Chicana organizations/institutions need to be instituted to benefit from the government's attention to women.

The 70s has seen an upsurge in activity and development for Chicanas without parallel. Chicanas have made enormous contributions in the fields of education, journalism, politics and labor. They have certainly added depth and new dimension to feminist philosophy and literature in this country.

Feminists within the Chicano ranks have not had an easy time, first of all because most of them received the label unintentionally for doing what they had been doing for decades and for merely reminding males that women had egos, too and needs; and secondly, because a women's movement happened to come on the scene when Chicanas were ready to take the step towards stronger development and realistic approaches to family problems.

Nevertheless, the evidence is available in Chicano journals that women have not been frightened by the challenge. They have met it head-on, and if feminism or a women's liberation movement continues its activities in this country, Chicanas seem ready to make certain it is a multicultural movement, especially in educational institutions and in the political and socio-economic arena.

9

La Visión Chicana*

ADELAIDA R. DEL CASTILLO

Encuentro Femenil

Adelaida Del Castillo is an Associated Editor of *Encuentro Femenil* and is also a linguistics major at UCLA. The journal *Encuentro Femenil* is actually the offspring of the Chicana feminist newspaper, *Hijas de Cuauhtémoc*, which was started on the college campus of Long Beach State by several consciously aware Chicana women. The publication of a journal was preferred to the publication of a newspaper when it became apparent that more in-depth specialization of subject matter was needed in order to aptly investigate those problems confronting Chicana women. *Encuentro Femenil* is distinguished as the first Chicana feminist journal ever to be published.

QUESTION: What is the Chicana Feminist Movement?
ANSWER: The Chicana Feminist Movement is part of the Chicano movement. It's a focused investigation into the problems of "la Mujer," *la mujer Mexicana* [the Mexican woman] because nobody, nobody has done any investigation into her

*From *La Gente,* March, 1974: p. 8.

situation. If it weren't for Alicia Escalante and Welfare Rights Organization which concerns mostly Mexicanas, nobody would have done anything. It took a woman to do it, and it takes specialization; like it's eventually going to take the woman to act on her behalf of her problems and it's also the responsibility of the Chicano male to support her because it's all part of the Chicano movement. This means a unified organization for improving our situation. Chicanas are part of the movement; they have problems, therefore, we deserve the support of all Chicanos and Chicanas. We're not a separate movement, that would be suicidal. We as Chicanas and Chicanos are oppressed. We're not going to ally ourselves to white feminists who are part of the oppressors. I mean, that would be a contradiction. It also hurts when Chicano men don't recognize the need for this specialization which is called "Chicana Feminism." It is a specialization, an investigation into the situation of la Mexicana. It took women to find out that in Texas, Mexicanas are used as guinea pigs. The Mexicana has found it necessary to act on her own behalf and to go out, investigate, and find the statistics. This is why the journal *Encuentro Femenil* is so important. It is the first Chicana feminist journal ever published. It will have actual data and statistics that are relevant to the problem which will put the problem into perspective. You can't obtain this kind of information anywhere else because nobody has bothered to organize and publish material dealing with the Chicana. What is unfortunate, is that since it is the first Chicana feminist journal there aren't any monies to put out the kind of quality we would like to have for a Chicana journal. We don't have the monies, so we can't print certain materials simply because we can't afford it. It's important that there be a journal, like it's important that *La Gente* [UCLA Chicano newspaper] exist so that Chicano views can be presented. If you don't have *La Gente,* what are people going to read about Chicanos? If we don't have journals which delineate the problems of Chicana women, how are people going to know that Chicana women have problems?

QUESTION: So you are saying that *La Gente* is only basically written for men because you need another magazine to express the views of the women?

ANSWER: No, I'm not. What I'm saying is that *La Gente* reflects Chicano views in general in terms of the UCLA environment or whatever community activities it gets into. It deals generally with Chicano problems. But what I'm saying is that there is a need to focus on the problems of the Chicana because her problems are very big and no one has bothered to focus on them. Women have not taken it upon themselves to say "Hey, you know what, we're in trouble and we better do something about it because no one else is doing anything about it."

QUESTION: Why don't you give me examples of the Chicana's problems and how they differ from those of Anglo women?

ANSWER: The Chicano and Anglo cultures differ significantly and because we are culturally different, there are racist attitudes practiced against us which limit us politically, economically, and socially. The differences become greater as these attitudes are used against us. So, because we are so different from the Anglos, it has tremendous consequences for us both, Chicanos and Chicanas.

QUESTION: How does the Chicana feminist differ from the white feminist?

ANSWER: It is obvious that we just differ as a group. First, we have to consider the popular white feminist movement as portrayed by the media (*Ms.* Magazine, newsreels, the burning of bras) things like that are popularly exploited. That doesn't necessarily mean that the white feminist movement is really that. They have other issues like education, employment, perhaps on the body, on how many orgasms a woman can have and whether she's getting enough. The Chicana feminist movement, as I see it is different primarily, because we are an oppressed people. Our situation necessarily becomes our responsibility as Chicana feminists to first deal with our poverty and our suppression. This includes welfare, education, child care, birth control, the law—all these issues which the white feminists are also dealing with but are entirely different. They become entirely different because, what child care means to the white woman, means an entirely different thing to the Chicana woman because she has additional considerations. For example, "is it culturally relevant," "is it bi-lingual," "is it supplying recognition of the familia." Perhaps the gringa isn't interested in the law, her issues are entirely different than ours. Is there in fact justice for us under the law considering the racist attitudes that we have to deal with? Just the other day, there was a case that illustrates my point. A Mexican woman I know is divorcing [her husband] and she went to court because he broke into her house and raped her. So, she had him thrown in jail. When she got him into court, they laughed at her. She spoke to the judge in Spanish because she could only speak Spanish (she is learning to speak English and is going to class). They all laughed at her, her lawyer laughed at her, the other lawyer laughed at her, and then the judge admonished her because she wasn't speaking English. And that is an insult. That's an insult to me as a Mexican woman and to that woman and to all Chicanos because here is a Mexican woman who is hoping that she can depend on the law, on the judge, to set this matter straight and he laughs at her in addition to which he admonished her and tells her off for not knowing English. Furthermore, he wanted her to pay him, the husband, damages when he has raped her in front of her children! So is there in fact any justice, or does racism impede justice for us? So the white woman can gripe about "Oh, there aren't enough jobs for us, and I want more advancement," but we still have to deal with the basic, serious issue of obtaining justice.

QUESTION: So then the Anglo Liberation movement is only an advancement and that's why you can't recognize it, because it's an advancement for them but only a starting point for you?

ANSWER: I think the issues are entirely different. They give us the impression of being middle-class women working for advancement. Do we as Chicanos and Chicanas want to advance and work with in this system, this capitalistic system? Does capitalism perpetrate welfare, racism, sexism? Does it perpetrate our poverty? Does it profit from it? Then because if it does, we have to start considering what alternatives are open to us.

I think we'll have to look into that eventually. We're going to have to deal with that because I was a welfare mother; as a welfare recipient, I have to settle for what they give me and it's not enough to support me, but somebody's making a profit out of it.

Well, Alicia Escalante, the organizer of the Chicana Welfare Rights organization, wrote an article for our journal, *Encuentro Femenil* that was a personal account of her experiences with the system. She discusses the fact that if you have welfare, you give jobs to certain people such as administrators, the director, and to social welfare workers. In addition there is all the paper work, the cleaning, the maintenance, and all these executive positions. Somebody's making money and it sure isn't the recipient. The ones who really need it don't get it. So there's a contradiction there. Then the government blames us for using up their money. Not only the government but the citizens, the average citizen, the working citizen, looks at the welfare recipient and says, "I'm paying for you." But one has to consider where most of the money is going to and what can be done to cut down. When Reagan [Governor Ronald Reagan] wants to cut down on the welfare programs it hurts the recipient who is already down in the dumps. He doesn't say, "I'm going to just take a couple of executives out," or "cut down on the paper work." I mean like we have to fill out 19 pages of information on both sides even to apply for welfare. It's very confusing, 38 pages! And women who don't speak English have to go through this! If she's hungry, she needs food stamps and they won't give them to her unless she has a hot plate in her house. This is the hassle we have to go through! And now every month we have to fill out a sheet indicating what kind of income we're receiving. It's degrading enough to deal with what we have to deal with.

QUESTION: Do you think that the Chicana and the Blacks could ever unite together and work besides women lib, for the movement?

ANSWER: I can see that the Black woman or any other third world woman is justified in having her own movement. It's necessary. About working together, well eventually we will have to come to that because we've got to deal with an oppressive force which is so many times bigger than us but if we can work together as Third World peoples we have a better chance of getting somewhere. At the moment, I think, there is an emphasis on focus to our particular problems so that we may learn to understand them. The situation is this: the white man or the oppressive system, uses divide and conquer tactics. Like here in school, alone when you apply for money there's a special fund for minorities, so if we want monies, we have to fight amongst each other as minorities to get that allotment of money. He knows how to control us, he knows the dynamics of keeping us apart. He has us fighting amongst each other.

QUESTION: Can the Chicana that's married also relate to these types of situations, problems, and events? Not every woman, not every Chicana that I know goes through these problems, so do you feel that the Chicana feminist movement is a movement for unmarried women?

ANSWER: I don't mean to give the impression that it is just for single women. Definitely not, it involves women of all ages. It has to. It involves the female—the Chicana female. She has occupational problems because she is at a disadvantage. If her male counterpart can't even get a job then where does she stand? Not only must she deal with racism but with sexism! Of course, Chicanos to deal with sexism in terms of this Macho attitude that people perceive he has because not only Chicanos amongst themselves have this attitude but also white people. So, they do have sexism in this way. Like white feminists have already coined the word "makismo" for machismo: "Makismo" according to them is just a chauvinistic pig, but they don't know what machismo is. So they already have this sexist attitude towards Chicano males. Also, we have to consider that a lot of women have certain attitudes towards Third World males, like Blacks and Chicanos as being incredibly potent and can perform miracles in bed. But this is not only sexist but racist as well because they are messing up the Chicano left and right. Racism and sexism work hand in hand and I think that Chicana feminism is a focus into the investigation of all Chicana problems, not just sexism.

QUESTION: We have to ask what brought on the whole interest in Chicana feminism. Why did it come about?

ANSWER: I think that a lot of Chicanas are being alienated (do I dare use this word?). A lot of Chicanas are sincerely feeling exploited if not alienated by certain organizations of the Chicano movement in the types of jobs that she is being given or relegated to.

QUESTION: Examples?

ANSWER: Like the beast of burden, she does the paperwork and if you want any food, go to her and she will cook it. She knows how to cook well! Exploited in that sense. A lot of women were finding themselves unfulfilled in just being relegated to this position of beast of burden or mere workers and not thinkers. So a lot of women were becoming upset because they couldn't use their abilities and their potentials. Chicana feminism, as I see it, recognizes the worth and potentials of all women. We recognize that all women have potential. The sad thing is that even when she does get to college, she is still seen as one who is there to support the male. If there are term papers to be typed his is first. He is to be looked up to. She is again just acting out a supportive role as in the home. The woman helps her father and serves her brothers and is there to support them. So, when she gets into the university or college she's utilized in that same way again. She's not seen as one who should actualize her own ambitions. He comes first, and then it's too late for her because she has already missed several things while helping her boyfriend achieve his own goals and realize his own potential.

QUESTION: Do you feel, then, that it should be right for a woman to totally reject her man and go about her own business?

ANSWER: We must come to the realization that we *have* to work together in order to save ourselves. If the male oppresses the female, perhaps it is because he has been oppressed. We can't turn against them, and they can't turn against us. We have to help each other. Remember, what the system wants is that the movement divide itself into small factions so that eventually it will fall apart into dust. We don't want this to happen. You are my *compañero* [brother] as a Mexicano and I am your *compañera* [sister] as a Mexicana. We're together. As Chicanos we have the responsibility to look after each other. We can't turn to anybody else. They don't understand our problems. So if we are pointing out our problems, it is so that we can begin to deal with them and achieve an understanding of them. This is why I think it's important that Chicanos speak up too, so that we can increase interaction and communication between Chicanos and Chicanas.

10

*La Chicana—Legacy of Suffering and Self-Denial**

ANNA NIETOGOMEZ

The roots of the psyche of la Chicana lies deep within the colonial period I Mexico. The conquest, the encomienda system and the colonial Catholic Church were to play a major role in forming the sexual-social roles of the Mexican woman. And the class relationship between patron and the Indian slave woman provides the historical foundation of the machismo phenomenon. Rape of the Mexican Indian women by the Spanish conquistadores was an act of conquest and marriage subsequently became a tool of colonization. Rape and marriage represented models for the Mexican male who longed to be free and strong like the conquistadores. Even the colonial Catholic church superimposed its ideology during this period and justified the oppression of conquest as something good. Marianismo, the veneration of the Virgin Mary, became the model of how to make oppression a religious obligation. This is the heritage of the Chicana.

*From *Scene,* Vol. 8, No. 1, 1995: pp. 22–24.

The veneration of the Virgin Mary defined the woman's identity as a virgin, as a saintly mother, as a wife-sex object, as a martyr. With respect to the Chicana today, Connie Nieto (an instructor at Cal State University, Long Beach) affirms the fact that Marianismo has had a tremendous impact in fostering beliefs of negative existence and self denial.

The popular image of Mexican woman is as somber-clad, long-suffering females praying in dimly-lit colonial churches. Church teachings have directed women to identify with the emotional suffering of the pure, passive bystander: the Virgin Mary. It is believed that through Her, the Chicana experiences a vicarious martyrdom in order to accept and prepare herself for her own oppressive reality. In order to be a slave or a servant, a woman cannot be assertive, independent and self-defining. She is told to act fatalistically because "all comes to those who wait." She is led to believe it is natural to be dependent psychologically and economically, and she is not to do for herself but to yield to the needs of others—the patron, her family, her father, her boyfriend, her husband, her God.

Marianismo portrayed the woman as semi-divine, morally superior and spiritually stronger than her master because of her ability to endure pain and sorrow. This pedestal of thorns also justified "men's wickedness" (passed on today as the double standard).

Today, Marriage is seen by some women as economic bondage, but marriage then was preferable to concubinage because it gave the Indian woman and her children certain economic and political rights denied to her as an "illegal" wife. As the illegal wife, she had no social, economic, or political rights or security; her children were illegitimate and denied the rights of citizenship.

Spain, in the process of "Cleansing its own race" after hundreds of years of miscegenation under Moorish rule, hoped to retain the new Mexican social and political structure through a caste system with Spanish pure-bloods at the top. Therefore, in an effort to keep New Spain in the hands of Spaniards rather than mestizos, destitute women, poor widows and women from debtor's prison were exported across the Atlantic from Spain to marry Spanish men. This new Spanish import to Mexico changed the Mexican concept of beauty, greatly affecting the position of the Indian woman who stood to lose much if she did not fit the Spanish ideal. As a result, the important of Spanish women led to the further devaluation of indigenous self-esteem. The destruction of various Mexican Indian cultures created a sense of self-rejection. Some Indian women tried to bleach their skin, but most only hoped that their children would be born white and thereby accepted as free Spaniards. Even today, many parents do not permit their children to sit in the sun for fear that they will get darker and suffer the consequences in a racist society

Marianismo forced Spanish women into acceptable sexual and social roles. The three basic images were of woman as virgin, woman as wife and woman as mother, all of which reinforced social, psychological and economic dependency for women. Some were kept secluded and under supervision; independence becoming synonymous with being out of control. For a woman to act out "su libertad" [her freedom] her independence was believed to lead to whoredom, the negative alternative to Marianismo.

The Spanish women and their children gained an indirect economic and legal social status through recognized marriage, but the indian women who lived under common law had not legal or economic protection. Thus, evolved in Mexican culture the characterization of two kinds of women, "*La Mujer Buena en La Casa Grande,*" ["The Good Woman"] and "*La Mujer Mala de la Casa Chica*" ["The Bad Woman"].

Emblematic of *La Mujer Buena*, the good, respectable woman in *La Casa Grande*, was the upper class Spanish woman, legal consort with legal heirs entitled to inherit their father's property. Her role was to stay at home, Socially and culturally, the *mujer buena* was white and segregated from social, political, and economic life. She could only go out alone to church or to visit her parents, and was totally dependent on her husband and she was expected to tolerate the man's right to use his sexual freedom.

The social station of *la mujer mala*—Indian women—was quite different. They actively participated in the religious, social and commercial life of their own people. They shared the responsibility of the household and also contributed to the economy and social life.

The different cultural and economic role of the Indian woman opposed the ideal image of Spanish women and Marianismo, and yet, unfortunately, became associated with the image of the *Mala Mujer*, the Bad Woman, the infamous one, the whore who enjoys sex in or out of marriage and entices men to "wallow in brown flesh." She left tradition and passive dependency behind. She dare to be and act independently, though, in fact, many had no choice.

Eventually, [Catholic] church ideology incorporated these differences into the concept of the ideal woman versus the tainted, despised woman, Gradually the Spanish woman became identified as the ideal and the Indian woman and her mestizo children became the pariahs of society. And instead of standing for ravaged women's economic and social rights, the church offered spiritual compensation. Marianismo bade the woman to endure.

Because culture is a remnant which mirrors people's accumulative economic adaptations in history, the social-psychological roles of Mexican men and women are the products of the economic and class conditions of 300 years of oppression.

11

*Chicanas on the Move**

BERNICE RINCÓN

> La Raza!
> Mexicana
> Española
> Latina
> Hispana
> Chicana
> or whatever I call myself,
> I look the same
> I feel the same
> I cry and sing the same . . .

*From *Regeneración,* Vol. 2, No. 4, 1975: p. 52.

This is a stanza from the epic poem "I am Joaquin" by Chicano poet Rodolfo "Corky" Gonzales. It is written in the masculine gender, so I have made an adaptation to make it more relevant to women.

Today I will speak about and to women. Mexican-American women or to the awakened *Chicana*.

La Valentina was "The Sweetheart" of the Mexican Revolution of 1910. In a recent edition of the *Magazine de Policia* the headlines read "la Valentina en la Miseria [Valentina in Misery]." She made a comment that reinforced my dedication to the struggle of equal justice for women.

"Sadly enough the destiny of many women is the same, when we are young and pretty, men are very attentive. But time does not pass without taking its toll and when that is over they abandon us as one would a piece of useless, ornamental furniture."

That was the role of many of our grandmothers, mothers, sisters, aunts, and friends. But today when a Chicana says "Power to the People" she means all of the people equally, including women.

Mexican women have always been beside their men in the struggle for justice. In the battlefield, in the vineyards, or at home with the children. The only point at issue is that this contribution has rarely been recognized by the men or even by the women themselves.

I recently purchased a book *150 Biographies of Illustrious Mexicans*. Out of 150 persons, three women were selected to represent the contribution of women to three centuries of history in Mexico. All three were relatively well educated for their day and time.

Today some Chicanas are saying *"Ya Basta!"* ["Enough!"] We are 50% or more of the Chicano population. Give us a chance. With the proper educational background, unbiased recognition and self determination we can come up with more than three outstanding citizens in three centuries of history.

We realize that it will take us a while to reach out goal. We need to build up our own self-esteem, so that we are not dependent upon men to justify our total existence. Remember La Valentina! We need to talk to our men and help them to see that this means true freedom for them too. Freedom to be themselves and not the lover Don Juan or the comic Super Macho. We propose this point of view because neither of these types make good friends or husbands for women.

We believe that the Chicana's role in the movement is to free herself from that subservient role of the past. To develop herself and her sisters, brothers, mother and father, and anyone else she comes in contact with; so that they in turn can work to see that *"La Causa"* [the Cause—the Chicano movement's struggle for justice] is a way to a better life and not just a lost *"Causa"* or a way to acquire more material goods.

There are many ways to contribute both at home and outside the home. One way is to help in voter registration and getting out the vote at election time. Every Chicano or Chicana candidate needs every vote.

Those women who work and show potential must be encouraged. Those who are leaders must be included in the front line of communication, leadership and organizational responsibility.

". . . [T]he issue of equality, freedom and self-determination of the Chicana— like the right of self-determination, equality and liberation of the Mexican community—*Is Not Negotiable*. Anyone opposing the right of women to organize into their own form of organization has no place in the leadership of the movement. *Freedom is for Everyone*. Women do not intend to argue or be diverted by engaging in wasteful

ss rhetoric on this subject. . . ." These are the words of Francisca Flores,
f Comisión Femenil Mexicana, and editor of *Regeneración* (Chicano Maga-

We realize that we cannot achieve the changes necessary to make the Chicana a
person in her own right without the support and cooperation of at least most of the
men in our lives.

We have been to many Chicana conferences and meetings and there are vey few
Chicanas who want to go along with the Anglo-American woman's movement
"women's liberation." We want justice in our daily lives and respect for the work we
do. Equal pay for equal work if it is a paid job. Equal recognition if the work is volun-
teered. These are a few of the goals of the Chicana in the movement.

Look around at the Chicanas you know who have had any degree of success
outside the home. You know that few of them could have made it without the encouragement, material help, and respect of their families; especially the fathers, brothers, husbands and sons.

The movement needs every person to be involved. In order to do this the Chicano will have to change. Change is always painful, but La Raza Cósmica is on the
move. And our contribution to the world is bearing fruit. The Chicana must be ready
for the challenge of the harvest. She must sit at the table as a person in her own right.
She must no longer be relegated to the status of serving maid at the feast that cele-
brates humanity. Viva la Causa! and equality and liberty for all the people!

12

*Chicana Feminism**

ANNA NIETOGOMEZ

I want to address myself to the common questions that come up in regard to Chicana
feminism. What is Chicana feminism? I am a Chicana feminist. I make that statement
very proudly, although there is a lot of intimidation in our community and in the society in general, against people who define themselves as Chicana feminists. It sounds
like a contradictory statement, a "*Malinche*" statement—if you're a Chicana you're on
one side, if you're a feminist, you must be on the other side. They say you can't stand

*From *Caracol*, Vol. 2, No. 5, 1976: pp. 3–5.

on both sides—which is a bunch of bull. Why? Because when you say you're Chicana, you mean you come from a particular community, one that is subject to racism and the exploitation of centuries. When you say you are a feminist you mean you're a woman who opposes the oppression of not only the group in general, but of women in particular. In fact, the statement is not contradictory at all, it is a very unified statement: I support my community and I do not ignore the women in my community (who have been long forgotten). The feminist movement is a unified front made up of both men and women—a feminist can be a man as well as a woman—it is a group of people that advocates the end of women's oppression.

People—reactionaries I call them—sometimes define a feminist as someone who hates men. Maybe this is not totally erroneous, but the label is a tactic used to keep people from listening to the issues. If somebody attacks you for being a Chicana feminist, he's diverting attention from some of the important issues at hand. What are these issues? The movement is one that supports social, economic and political issues in regard to the position of women—bettering the position of the Chicana. The Chicana is a woman and she cannot separate herself from that. One of the primary social issues is the double standard. It says that there is such a thing as male privilege and such a thing as female submission. Another issue is education—women have the right to education. When the woman was conceived it was not automatically determined that she was going to be barefoot, pregnant and tied to the stove. A third issue is child care—it's not a female duty, it is a community responsibility. Economically, the woman should have equal employment regardless of race—equal pay, equal training and an economic position which is not dependent on fathers, husbands and sons. As long as she is economically dependent she will have to allow male privilege, to compromise herself. She will always have to accept the secondary position. Politically, it means equal participation, equal representation, and inclusion of issues which address her as a woman, as a Chicana in the Raza community.

Is Feminism for Anglos?

Marta Cotera wrote an article several years ago saying that feminism is not an Anglo idea. I resent the usual remark that if you're a feminist you have somehow become an Anglo or been influenced by Anglos. That's a sexist remark, whether it comes from hermanos or hermanas. Why? Because of what it is saying—that you, as a Chicana, a Chicana woman, don't have the mentality to think for yourself! Somehow we are only supposed to be repositories—everything we say is either his idea, or the white anglo "her" idea, but not our idea. When we're confronted with these remarks about Chicana feminism, we can say, "Just a minute. Chicanas can think, too. You'd better sit down and listen to what we're thinking, because we're not only thinking it, we're doing it."

The History of Feminism

Let me prove to you that feminism is a world-wide event. It has been a world-wide event since the beginning of oppression. You can find the roots of women's struggle to end oppression of people and of themselves as far back as 200 years before the birth of Christ, in Viet Nam, in China, in Gaul, in Africa, and in the valley of Mexico. We have documentation of women who were queens, rulers, who were feminists: who addressed themselves to the needs of women in their communities, their nations. One of the most renowned feminist of the past is well known throughout the world, though she is not well known by Chicanas. Her name is Sor Juana, and she has been called one of the first feminists of the Americas (which is incorrect, because there were many pre-Columbian feminists). Several of the North American Indian societies were matriarchal and advocated the non-oppression of women—the non-oppression of anybody. Sor Juana was a seventeenth century genius. She was a genius who happened to be a woman and who therefore had only two alternatives: to marry, or to join the convent and marry God. She chose the latter because she felt it would offer her more flexibility and more opportunity to study. And she did study—she studied very hard. She was enthusiastic, to say the least, about learning. She spoke about women's hair—how the hair was a symbol of women's beauty, but if it covered an empty mind, it was nothing but a mask. She said that not until a woman's mind was equal in beauty to her long hair should she have her long hair, so in three months she would plan to read a certain amount, and if she hadn't she would cut off her hair. In three more months, if she hadn't achieved her goal of, say, three volumes, the hair was to go right back until the goal was reached. Sor Juana is famous for *Respuesta*, a letter to the bishop addressing itself to a letter he sent her praising Sor Juana for her brilliance but telling her that her duty was not to be brilliant but to serve God. The role of women was to be silent, not heard. Sor Juana very politely wrote back, "Surely you must know more than I; however, as I recall, Jesus did not say that women should be silent and not heard. You forget that the temple was a place of learning and discussion, and that women were preaching and talking to their people there, not just bowing their heads in silent prayer or absent-mindedly planning their week's activities. Jesus came into the temple and addressed himself to the people there, those who were speaking there, and those people were the women. Yes, it's my duty to be a servant of God, but how can I understand theology"—theology was a high point of learning in Mexico and in fact it still is—"how can I understand that, if I can't understand biology, geology, psychology? If the world's supposed to be a manifestation of God's great goodness, how can I understand that if I don't know anything about it? These are the prerequisites for my understanding of His great and beautiful powers." So she advocated that women have the right to education But women did not have this right until after the Revolution. During the eighteenth century they did open some convents where women could go and get educated, but the education was primarily in religious studies.

Feminism In Tejas

Here in the United Sates we have women who are very involved in the labor movement. I'm sure you know that most of the outstanding, internationally known women recognized for their efforts in the labor movement are Tejanas. Louisa González was a Tejana associated with the Haymarket Massacre. She was involved in organizing an international workers' alliance, and she advocated women's workers rights to pressure unions, to remind unions that women were working in the factories and should have their needs addressed, and that women should support the issues of the union. You have Emma Tenayuca, who was a farmworker organizer, who at the age of 18 had to support the majority of farmworkers in the pecan-shellers strike of 1938. And in El Paso you have the strike against Farah [1972], which was primarily an issue of women. Most of the workers in the factory were women, and 85% of them were Chicanas. The women who went around the nation to ask people to strike Farah Pants for Chicanas did a fantastic thing—the quiet, non-obtrusive, submissive women were coming to say, "You'd better strike Farah Pants."—Because we are workers. Because we demand workers' rights. Because as women, we demand maternity leave, because we ask for free birth control (and not false birth control), and because we ask for better working conditions for everybody. All these things are part of the history of the *Tejana*, and they are things that Chicanas all over the nation admire and identify with.

Today, What is Chicana Feminism Doing?

Today, Chicana feminism is trying to rally enough women and get them to come out from behind the doors so that everybody can hear us say, "We're a legitimate body. No one can deny that any more. Ask us about our political stance, not our validity, as women fighting for women's rights within the Chicano community." Right now, we're in the process of making the Chicano movement responsible to Chicana issues, making it support issues that involve race, welfare rights, forced sterilization—making the Chicano movement address itself to the double standard about male and female workers, and making it live up to its cry of *Carnalismo* and community responsibility. We're saying, "Prove it! Let's carry it out! Let's support child care. Children are not our individual responsibility but the responsibility of our community." We are working to get women together to build up a base, and working to get the Chicano movement to support and advocate our issues as women.

Is the Chicana Feminist Movement Different from the Anglo Women's Movement?

I myself feel that some of the distinctions made are irrelevant, but it's still very much like asking how the Chicano movement is different from the Black movement. These questions indicate that you're still fighting for recognition of your own identity, and at times I just think, "Well, I'm not here to talk about the Anglo women's movement. If you want to find out about the Anglo movement, you go and find out, and then go and find out about the Chicana movement, and compare them for yourself." Besides, the answers are obvious. The Chicana movement has to address itself to racism, and it is obvious from what Marta Cotera has written, what Evey Chapa has written, in terms of the Texas Women's Caucus (which is primarily Anglo), what you have to deal with. The issue of racism and the issue of class interest. And that class interest is not our interest. However, at the same time, I believe that not all Anglo women are middle class. It's the media that leads you to believe that, and you swallow it. What is the Anglo women's movement? First, you have to understand that it is not a unified movement. There are at least three positions. There are the liberal feminists, who say, "I want access to power. I want access to whatever men have access to. I want women's oppression to end insofar as they do not have these things." Then there are radical feminists, who say that men have the power, and that men are responsible for the oppression of women. A third position is that of women's liberationists, which says that women's oppression is one of the many oppressions in the economic system of this country, that we must understand and support that system as well as correct it and unify people to end all oppressions. Where does the Chicana women's movement stand in relation to these three positions? I do not have the authority to represent anyone in answering that, and the Chicana feminist is in the making from one place to another. But from my point of view, in my own private Los Angeles experience, the general feeling is that men do not have the power. Certainly Chicanos do not have the power, otherwise there would not be a Chicano movement. We recognize that obvious fact. At the same time, we recognize and criticize the fact that the Chicano seems to try to compensate for that lack of power with the use of "male privilege"—coming down with the double standard.

What is Male Privilege?

Here's the double standard: "If I have a meeting, you stay at the house and take care of the kids. If you have a meeting, have it at the house and take care of the kids at the same time." Male privilege is, "Let's fight for equal pay for me, and maybe later on for you." Male privilege sometimes makes the Chicano movement just like a male liberation movement. The implication is this: "Our problem is that women have to work because we are not given our economic position as men." So once the men are paid what they're due, have an economic base as workers, then women won't have to be out in the public world. When liberation comes along, everything will be hunky-dory and the women can stay at home. That says to me, "Whose liberation are you fighting for, anyway? I'm fighting for people's liberation." If the answer is, "I am fighting for people's liberation," I say, "Okay, then if you are, it means there is no 'proper place' for the Chicana except the world as a whole. There is no one place for the Chicana—just the world as a whole."

Welfare Rights

We have other issues and here's how they differ from the Anglo women's movement and the Chicano movement as it stands now. When was the last time you heard about welfare rights at a meeting? When was the last time you heard Gloria Steinem or Betty Friedan talk about welfare rights? Do you know what welfare rights are? Why don't you, if you don't? We're supposed to be poor people. One of the criticisms I have of Chicanas is that we don't use the welfare rights system, therefore we don't make it address our needs.

Race

For the last year there have been issues of race in which women have defended themselves. These were Third World women—for example, Inéz García, who suffered from rape and who retaliated. Who supported her? She was sent to jail. Where was the Chicano movement? There were people in the Chicano movement who said that Inéz García deserved it, that everybody knows that women really want to be raped, that she can enjoy it, and that rape doesn't justify the taking of human life. This is an example of a confusion in our community response to an important issue. Chai Lao is an Asian woman; she was arrested by a police officer. He said, "I'll tell you what. I won't take you in if you submit to me." She said no. He raped her; she killed him. Joanne Little is the most nationally publicized example of this. She was a woman, a prisoner. The guard said, "Do me a little favor, honey, and I might do one for you." She said no. He raped her; she killed him. Rape is an act of violent aggression, and it's something we have the right to defend ourselves against.

Child Care

Middle class women ask for more child care centers. In Los Angeles, child care costs about $150. The figure should be about a third of the rent, but it's equal to the rent. That is my rent. Chicanas ask for free child care. Chicanas ask for bilingual child care, bicultural child care.

Employment

In the middle class, the employment issue is social mobility, it's promotion, tenure. Women with Ph.D's don't want to be secretaries. The issue for the Chicana is just employment. "Give me a job. Give me a good-paying job. Let me have access to training." Again, pure class difference.

Raza Power Means an End to Colonization

These are some of the issues in Chicana feminism. We are saying something very positive. Raza power! Men, women, and children. Everybody. When we say jobs, we mean jobs for all. But something I haven't mentioned is that a lot of the things that are going to change are those things that maybe we revere and sanction and call a part of our culture. If something in our culture that is advocating oppression is unable to be criticized, evaluated and changed, this is wrong. In our culture we happen to say *"la mujer buena"* [the Good Woman] and *"la mujer mala"* [the bad woman]. And if you're active in *Raza Unida*, you're suspected of being *la mujer mala*, and in order to prove that you're not, you have to live the life of a nun. Well, I say the life of a nun is oppressive. *"la mujer buena"* and *"la mujer mala"* are historical ideas that came from the colonization of the people in Mexico. In order to assimilate and acculturate the Indians, they used to control the women by setting up two models. First, they imported poor Spanish women to marry the Spaniards. Their oppressed role was that of the woman who stays home, and the only place she goes is to church or to visit her in-laws. That was the model of the Spanish woman. The model of the Indian woman was different, a very active one. She was the business person; she was the one who controlled the market place, did the crafts, worked in the fields, participated in child care. She was the priestess of religious functions. This was a role. Don't get me wrong, I'm not saying she wasn't oppressed; I'm not saying that at all. I'm saying it was different, and comparatively speaking, it was a freer role. In order for the colonization to affect everybody, they put up these two roles. They used the concepts of the church, *Marianismo* on the one hand, Mary Magdelene on the other. The Spanish woman and the Indian woman. *La mujer buena* and *la mujer mala*. Clear who's on the top and who's on the bottom! So we perpetuate those two roles and we perpetuate our own colonized situation. We have to recognize what change will bring to this colonization, which we have unintentionally continued.

13

The Emerging "Chicana"*

SISTER TERESITA BASSO

When we are really honest with ourselves we must admit that our lives are all that really belong to us. So it is how we use our lives that determines what kind of men we are. It is my deepest belief that only by giving our lives do we find life. I am convinced that the truest act of courage, the strongest act of manliness is to sacrifice ourselves for others in a totally nonviolent struggle for justice. To be a man is to suffer for others. God help us to be men. [quote by César Chávez]

I have chosen the preceding quote by César Chávez because, for me, it epitomizes the role of the religious sister in the world today. Because I believe in the dignity of the human person, I have chosen to strive to live by this principal through service to mankind. Since I believe that giving of oneself is life-giving both for the giver and the receiver, religious life for me has been the style of life which best allows me to live out this personal conviction.

As a result of my convictions, my experiences, in religious life, and especially my Mexican-American background, I have come to realize my responsibility to that segment of society known as the Mexican-American people. The impact of this realization has led me to re-evaluate my identity as a "Chicana"† religious woman in the decades of the sixties and the seventies and my responsibility as a visible representative of the Roman Catholic Church to the Mexican-American community. As Bishop Patricio Flores of San Antonio, Texas, expressed at the first national conference of Spanish-speaking sisters on April 3, 1971:

> Tengo que saber donde esta el pueblo, donde va, y que piensa. (I have to know where the community is at, where it is going, and what it is thinking).[1]

The consequences of this re-examination have led to the following hypothesis: The identity of the Mexican-American religious woman as "Chicana" influences her response to the Mexican-American community. Of necessity this chapter will be a descriptive study rather than an empirical one since at this point in history not much has been written about the emerging Chicana religious and her influence in the Mexican-American community. I have found some information on the evolving Chicana movement and also the role of women, both in the sisterhood and outside of it, but no references that combine these two aspects.

This chapter will examine the existential conflict of identity and commitment that many Mexican-American religious women are experiencing today. This statement will be developed first, by noting how the Mexican-American religious woman

*From *Review for Religious*, Vol. 30, No. 6, 1971: pp. 1019–1028.

has had to re-evaluate her role as person and as woman in a changing society, especially how her ethnic awareness affects her self-perception in the context of religious life, and second, how this identity conflict experienced by Mexican-American religious women is affected by the emerging ethnic awareness of the Mexican-American community. To the degree that she identifies with the needs and thinking of the Mexican-American community, she will classify herself as "Chicana" or Mexican-American as these terms have been defined above. Once the Mexican-American religious woman resolves this identity conflict and declares herself "Chicana" she will want to unite with other "Chicana" sisters, forming organizations within the Church to stimulate awareness of and actions for the Mexican-American community.

Basic to the quest for self-identity are the answers to these questions: Who am I? Where am I going? What do I want out of life? What do others think of me? What is my ultimate goal? Every person, regardless of race, status, or creed, when confronted with these essentials must seek out answers that will give his or her life meaning. Every person living in a rapidly changing world, experiencing the transformations of technology, witnessing the improved self-knowledge brought on by the social sciences, is constantly called upon to re-evaluate his or her role in such a changing society.

The sister especially has had to re-examine her personal role in today's society. Is the human person of such value that no other can replace him or her? Is life more important than war? Are all people accorded the power of self-determination? Are we responsible for the poor and the needy of this world? "Does it devolve on humanity to establish a political, social, and economic order which will to an ever better extent serve man and help individuals as well as groups affirm and develop the dignity proper to them?"[2] These are the questions the religious must answer for herself, questions on which hinge her evolving role in the world today.

The Mexican-American sister can not escape this confrontation since through the varied media of television, radio, newspapers, and advertisements she is constantly being bombarded not only with the world's needy but also with her people's plight.

At present woman herself is experiencing a need to define her role in a twentieth century world. She is exploring her womanly role and potential in a male dominated society. Woman is interested in advancing in knowledge, understanding, and ability to improve herself, her lot, and her world.[3]

The social feminist movement is affecting the womn religious whether or not she is consciously aware of its effects on her life, or supports its interests. One only need look at the changing life styles within religious congregations to realize this movement's full impact within the last ten years.

> The Christian emancipation of women has a fine ring to it, but not too many know precisely what it involves. We have witnessed in comparatively recent years a rather dramatic change in the dress and life style of women. This change has opened opportunities that had long been closed. But in this liberation the Church has played little or no role. Long after secular man had agreed that women's place was not necessarily the home, clerical man reluctantly allowed that the nun's place was not necessarily the convent.
>
> Liberation from what might be called a double standard of conduct or life style has given women the freedom and the mobility to study and to practice professions hitherto reserved almost exclusively to men, including the professions of theology. . . .
>
> But the mores of life style of a culture are not always the same as the ethics or moral code of a people, and it is deliverance from a double standard of morali-

ty or code of ethics based on the inferiority of women as a person, that marks what is distinctive and radical in the Christian liberation of women.[4]

In this framework woman's search for identity is not one that seeks to supersede man-kind or supplant the male culture, but rather to take away the lopsidedness existing in our day. "If a male culture is partial and lopsided, what society can be more lopsided than the Roman Catholic-dominated as it is not only by males but by celibate males at that."[5] The woman religious is beginning to realize that she is a mystery whose powers of being are yet untapped.

The Mexican-American woman religious has an even greater struggle in exploring her womanly role in the decade of the 70s, since her strife is threefold. This triple strife consists of society's limited view of woman as housewife, bedpartner, and inferior intellectual; the Church's governing structure's condescending paternalistic view of woman as a helpless submissive creature incapable of self-determination; the Mexican-American culturally restrictive view of woman as mother, cooking and caring for the family, incapable of making decisions outside the home, or as a mistress an object of male enjoyment.[6]

If the Mexican-American sister is not conscious of those prevailing stereotypes, it may be that she has chosen to close her eyes to the realities of life or rejects the risks that a conscious awareness of such realities might make her face. The Mexican-American sisters' responses to their existential situation, needless to say, will vary in degree. If she chooses to ignore the evolving national feminist movement, National Coalition of American Nuns (NCAN), National Assembly of Women Religious Hermanas, a national organization of Spanish-speaking religious women, Chicana Sisters Organizations, regional organizations in San José and Chicago, *Hijas de Cuauhtémoc, La Conferéncia de Mujeres por La Raza,* and others, she chooses to ignore an integral part of her emerging womanly role.

In her search for identity as woman, the Mexican-American sister has to depart from her restrictive role within the Mexican-American culture. For the Mexican-American woman religious the degree of departure from this cultural characteristic depends upon its degree of influence in her life. According to some contemporary Chicanas:

> Most Chicanos have had little faith in the Chicana's ability to organize, to develop leadership, to create successful projects. Consequently no real effort has been exerted to train and educate them to become part of the movement. no real effort has been made to make our women politically aware of the general issues in the barrios. . . . Only when emergencies exist do men recognize that women can contribute to the overall causes.
>
> Once in a while, a woman decides to break this caste system. In return, she gets nothing but static. Instead of positive encouragement, she is discouraged, and obstacles are placed in her way. Chicanos . . . are afraid to develop her [Chicana] without castrating themselves.
>
> Chicanas feel that since it is the men who have the knowledge and experience, they must train women in order to strengthen the movement. We cannot have organizations that so narrowly involve and restrict the energies and capabilities of our beautiful brown women. The Chicano movement cannot hope to fight against social injustices and win at the expense of their women. *Hombres* and *mujeres* must start relating to each other in such a way that she is not always on her back being a bed partner. If the relationship between our men and our women is mediocre, the movement will also be mediocre. We are the mothers and teachers of your children. We are the ones that greatly influence them in every aspect of

life. Help us to teach them to be revolutionary Chicanos for *La Causa*. Help us to organize! Train us and develop us.[7]

The Mexican-American religious cannot escape the fact that her culture affects her self-image within the context of religious life. Her own Mexican-American value system, if it has not been totally assimilated into the dominant middle-class socio-economic culture, will continue to influence her life. "It is the exceedingly rare Mexican-American, no matter how acculturated he [she] may be to the dominant society, who does not in some degree retain more subtle characteristics of his Mexican-American heritage."[8]

Two personal characteristics of the Mexican-American which are peculiar to him is that of "being" and that termed "*carnalismo*" or "*compadrazgo*." As the Mexican-American sister redefines her role of person and woman the above mentioned characteristics will, depending upon the level of acculturation, influence her personal identity. The Mexican-American sister will hopefully place greater emphasis on the inner integrity of the person ("being") than on "role" performance. In evaluating her person greater stress will be placed on her ability to be the person she is or can become than on trying to conform to someone else's idea of who she should be.[9,10]

If she is able to retain this trait throughout her life she will be a tremendous asset to the total human community but even more so to the Mexican-American community. When she works among her own people whether nursing, teaching, or doing social work, she will be less likely to judge others on appearance. Rather she will rise above the individual's skin color, his [or her] income level, his [or her] amount of education, or other status symbols and come to the core of all relationships–the worth and honor of the human being as a person.

Another Mexican-American characteristic affecting the Mexican-American Sister to a greater or lesser degree is that termed "*carnalismo*" or "*compadrazgo*." This is the spirit of most Mexican-American people which recognizes each member without geographic borders struggling to acquire the power of self-determination. This spirit unites all members of *La Familia de La Raza*, placing ties of responsibility for the betterment of his or her people on each individual.[11] This sense of communal responsibility or close ties to certain individuals is part of the Mexican heritage.[12] The study performed by Professor Ramírez "comparing socialization practices used by Mexican-American and Anglo-American mothers of the same socio-economic class" revealed that the Mexican-American children desire to achieve more out of a sense of familial recognition than individual approval.[13] This desire to win approval from one's own and to experience a sense of belonging and "at homeness" when with other Mexican-American people are traits not too easily assimilated.

The Mexican-American woman religious recognizes that she is part of an ethnic cultural minority; to what extent she feels responsible toward the betterment of this community will depend largely on her awareness of the Mexican-American community's religious, social, and economic needs.

Upon entering religious life the Mexican-American sister just like the barrio child in the educational school system is placed in a middle-class Church oriented organization. If her background is that of a highly acculturated Mexican-American, her adjustment to and acceptance into this life style will not be as difficult as that of a less acculturated Mexican-American young woman. The latter will be placed in a situation where there is very little she can identify with. Those things of relevance in her life, such as, her family, her language, her life style, her work among her people, and her proximity to her environment are very distant in her newly acquired life style.

The Mexican-American sister, however, cannot totally divorce herself from her cultural heritage and whether she is allowed to live out her Mexican-American difference is yet another aspect of this identity conflict. Depending upon the religious congregations' attitude towards the culturally different, certain limitations will be placed on the Mexican-American sister's freedom to live out this difference.

As the Mexican-American woman religious ponders her vocation she will at some stage of her development come to realize that religious women are "women of the Church in a special way, women who have dedicated their whole lives to the *service of the Church* [italics not in the original.]"[14] Who is the Church and to whom does it minister?

> The joys and the hopes, the griefs and the anxieties of the men of this age, *especially those who are poor* [italics not in the original] or in any way afflicted, these ar the joys and hopes, the griefs and anxieties of the *followers of Christ* [italics not in the original]. Indeed, nothing genuinely human fails to raise an echo in their hearts. For theirs is a community composed of men. United in Christ, they are led by the Holy Spirit in their journey to the kingdom of their Father and they have welcomed the news of salvation which is meant for every man. That is why this community realizes that it is truly and intimately linked with mankind and its history. (15)

This affects the Mexican-American religious since it is in carrying out this Church mandate that the religious establishes herself as sister. But added to this fact is the dawning realization within the religious woman that her greatest obligation lies with those who have the greatest needs. Now it is at this point that the Mexican-American religious woman must choose whether to identify with her people as "Chicana" or remain an acculturated Mexican-American. If she chooses to be known as "Chicana" it is because she is consciously aware of herself, her power of self-determination, as well as proud of her cultural heritage and experiences. Within her religious commitment, the people of La Raza will take priority while she seeks basic institutional changes because she senses the urgency and immediacy of bringing about this change. She begins to recognize who more than her own people, La Raza, are in need of her services. She realizes as the Chicana Sisters Organization in San Jose did:

- that the Church has fallen short in our task of helping provide spiritual and material guidance for our people and that there are hundreds of thousands who need our help.
- that our Mexican-American community has been exploited over the centuries by the established community and has been treated in a paternalistic manner by the Church.
- that the poverty and degradation in which a great number of our Mexican-American population live and the despair and lack of confidence into which they are forced.
- that the demands of social justice and equal rights have not been made available to our Mexican-American population.
- that the time is late-and that it is urgent that we immediately identify ourselves with the Chicano movement.[16]

In recognizing her unique resources as a "Chicana" religious woman she realizes she is the one best able to understand her peoples' basic problems since she comes from the same culture. Necessary to the Chicana sister's reorientation is the simultaneous emerging ethnic awareness of the Mexican-American community. As the local Mexican-American communities become involved in barrio politics, the struggle for community control of health services, schools, welfare, and housing, boycotts for obtaining better wages and working conditions, and Chicano studies programs, the Chicana woman religious finds herself being affected by her people's struggles. She no longer can turn away or wait for the Church or government "structure" to meet these needs. She keenly feels deep distress and hurt at the general insensitivity of these organizations and at their lack of recognition of her peoples' plight.

As a result of this concern, the Chicana sister will find herself attending more and more grass-roots community meetings in her attempt to become aware of the local Mexican-American community's thinking on various issues. In her search for information on these local issues she will often discover that there are numerous solutions and/or resolutions to be explored. The Chicana religious will often experience at these meetings, as her people have, the perpetual rhetoric, the endless "red-tape," and the turtle-like progress towards the attainment of positive goals. But for the Chicana woman religious this is a good, since, in order to really identify with her people, she has to experience their numerous frustrations. More importantly, through all these frustrations, sufferings, and tests, she is receiving and sharing strength with each involved member of La Raza.[17]

As the Chicana sister grows weary of these countless community meetings she desires to involve herself at the grass-roots level with her people in a capacity of service and assistance. She discovers that the type of assistance and leadership she can best perform in the barrios is one of service. This type of Chicana religious has a deep commitment and concern for her people, and has worked her way up through personal dealings with her people at the grass-roots level. She should not be the type of leader who superimposes herself or who is superimposed on the community through an agency, institution, or Church.[18]

> Our barrios throughout the country suffer from the latter type of leadership. They speak about the problems of the Chicano community to their churches, obtain funds to set up "programs" to alleviate poverty and then set themselves up as leaders of those projects; a "Brown Papacy," another middle-man in our community.
>
> If we as churchmen realistically deal with the problems of poverty and powerlessness, we must support existing organizations who have been seeking and fighting for justice and/or help create new organizations which can achieve that goal without our having to set ourselves up as Chicano Martin Luther Kings.[19]

As the Chicana religious finds herself more deeply involved in working for her people and advancing their just demands as human beings, she awakens to the evolving reality that much is happening to her as a person. She is gaining confidence and strength as she becomes more capable in her work.

For the Chicana religious woman, this involvement with the Mexican-American community takes place within the context of her particular religious congregation. Here too, as in the Mexican-American community, the Chicana sister will be a great asset to her particular congregation if her community accepts her in her own culture. For the Chicana woman religious will feel much more loyalty than she would if her congregation restrained her and tried to make her something she is not. She is much more of an asset to her congregation if she feels this confidence in herself, if she feels this pride in herself, if she knows that her people need her because as Chicana she can help her people.

More and more Chicana sisters will experience an acceptance and freedom to work among their people within their various religious congregations as they make their desires known to the administrative level. The communities themselves will become more conscious of the needs of the Mexican-American community as each Chicana sister takes it upon herself to stimulate awareness among the rest of the sisters. The larger structure of the congregation needs its impetus from its individual members.

These Chicana sisters unite themselves as sisters since they realize "the strength which comes from unity will enable them to put pressure on the established community and on the Church."[20] But if they unite among themselves first it is not to become an isolated group, but rather, once united, to awaken in others the desire to serve the Mexican-American community.

The following is the rationale of Las Hermanas, a newly formed national organization of Spanish-speaking religious women, and the different approaches to be used to meet their goal.

In order to make our apostolate more effective and more relevant and in order to better meet the needs of La Raza throughout the country within our own congregations and through our own specialized work we have agreed upon the following guidelines:

First, to establish a clearing house of information; to stimulate awareness of the needs of the Spanish-speaking people in the membership as well as in the community at large.

Second, to work toward effecting social change.

Third, to establish a training force to activate leadership.

Fourth, to participate in and to contribute to the rebirth of pride in our cultural heritage.

Fifth, to identify with the leadership and the membership of the Chicanos in their demands and actions.

Sixth, to give each other moral support when the going gets rough.

Seventh, to apply pressure on the hierarchy.

Eighth, to work closer with the people in forming action groups.

Ninth, to serve as an Awareness Center to provide information for Religious Congregations concerning Chicano affairs and the role of Sisters in these affairs.

Tenth, to interest more Chicana women to choose religious life. We as a body hope to testify to the fact that Chicana religious women can be relevant and identify with La Raza in their fight for self-determination.[21]

Hopefully, as each Mexican-American womn religious begins to listen to the Mexican-American community at large, she will begin to examine her role within this community. However, this step cannot occur until each Mexican-American sister examines her own reasoning for convictions held and, in her examination, seeks out others like herself, attempting to share with them her existential conflict of identity and commitment. "All this means that today we face a time of commitment and the Chicana (Chicana sister inclusive) must make a choice. Her people wait for her, *La Familia de La Raza* need her for the building of our nation. . . . Our society needs her."[22]

I conclude that a positive identity of the Mexican-American sister with her cultural background and a personal awareness of the needs of the Mexican-American community by the religious woman will evoke a positive response of service from her for the Mexican-American people.

NOTES

†The terms Mexican-American and Chicana when referring to the sister are not used interchangeably in this chapter unless otherwise stated.

Mexican-American refers to the Spanish-speaking religious women of Mexican heritage.

Chicana in this chapter is used as it is defined in Ramon Macias' article "Evolution of the Mind and a Plan for Political Action." Chicana aspects include self-awareness, self-determination, priority of personal commitment to La Raza, active seeking of basic institutional change, and a sense of urgency and immediacy in bringing about this change.

1. Stated by Bishop Patricio Flores of San Antonio, Texas, in an address given to *Las Hermanas* National Conference at Houston, Texas, on April 3.

2. Vatican Council II, *Pastoral Constitution on the Church in the Modern World* as given in Walter M. Abbott, S.J., ed., *The Documents of Vatican II* (New York: American Press, 1966), p. 206.

3. *An Orientation to "La Conferencia de Mujeres por La Raza"*(Houston, Texas: Magnolia Park YMCA, March 1971) (mimeographed).

4. Paul E. Palmer, "Christian Breakthrough in Women's Lib," *America*, June 19, 1971, p. 634.

5. Esther Woo, "Theology Confronts Women's Liberation," *America*, March 13, 1971, p. 259.

6. "Chicanas in the movement," *La Raza*, November 1969, p. 5.

7. Ibid.

8. Celia Heller, "Chicano Is Beautiful: The Militancy and Mexican-American Identity," *Commonweal*, January 23, 1970, p. 456.

9. Manual Ramirez III, "Cultural Democracy: A New Philosophy for Educating the Mexican-American Child," *National Elementary Principal*, November 1970, p. 46.

10. Ozzie G. Simmons, "The Mutual Images and Expectations of Anglo-Americans and Mexican-Americans," *Minorities in a Changing World*, ed. Milton L. Barron (New York: Knopf, 1967), p. 300.

11. David Vásquez, "La Familia de La Raza," *El Grito del Norte*, February 28, 1971, p. 14.

12. Isidro Ramón Macías, "Evolution of the Mind and Plan for Poltiical Action," May 1969 (mimeographed).

13. Ramírez, "Cultural Democracy."

14. Sister Mary Lawrence McKenna, S.C.M.M., *Women of the Church: Role and Renewal* (New York: Kenedy, 1967), p. 3.

15. Abbott, Documents, p. 199.

16. Chicana Sisters Organization, *Guidelines* established at the first Conference in San Jose (mimeographed).

17. Enriqueta Longauex y Vásquez, "Soy Chicana Primero," *El Grito del Norte,* April 26, 1971, p. 11.

18. "Chicano Churchmen: Servitude or Support," *La Raza*, I, 4 (1971), p. 53.

19. Ibid.

20. Chicana Sisters Organization, *Guidelines*.

21. Las Hermanas National Organization, taped proceedings of the first national conference at Houston, Texas, April 2, 1971.

22. Longauex y Vásquez, "Soy Chicana," p. 14.

14

Chicana Writer Breaking Out of the Silence*

RITA SÁNCHEZ

The Chicana writer, by the fact that she is even writing in today's society, is making a revolutionary act. Embodied in the act of writing is her voice against others' definitions of who she is and what she should be. There is, in her open expression and in the very nature of this act of opening up, a refusal to submit to a quality of silence that has been imposed upon her for centuries. In the act of writing, the Chicana is saying "No," and by doing so she becomes the revolutionary, a source of change, and a real force for humanization.

By becoming a writer, the Chicana has to have already rebelled against a socialization process that would have her remain merely the silent helpmate. Everything in her society, the schools, the church, the home, has sought this goal for her: she must be sheltered from the evils, noise, confusion, from the realities of the outside world, from sex to politics, even at times from intellectual dialogue, to be considered acceptable. In short, she should make no intrusion into adult or male conversation. Now, the Chicana, by voicing her own brand of expression has rejected the latter in favor of telling anyone who wishes to read her work, hear her voice, exactly what she is not, and who she, in fact, is.

Courageously, La Chicana writer, by understanding the condition of colonization under which she was born, the images of betrayal that surround her, and the forces of racism that still exist for her, has exhibited her strength by the very denial of these impositions. By her refusal to accept the myths, misinterpretations and the stereotypes of herself as presented by another, she has transcended the bounds of tradition, made a choice to determine her own life, and finally, has become the revolutionary voice. The reality of her history reveals La Mujer Chicana as the central core and basis of Chicano struggle. The Cuban film, *Lucia*, depicts the epic struggle of an entire people, and at the center: La Mujer. The rape of a woman in this story symbolized the colonization of the country. La Mujer has suffered the violation, but has emerged as the visionary who awakens her people. The Chicana is this same woman.

In her act of self expression shared in writing with others like herself she is saying what she feels and who she is; every time she puts down on paper her words; and every time those words are read by another Chicana, she has defined further who we Chicanas truly are. Her voice, in expressing a Chicana view, comes closer to expressing a collective Chicana voice. We, her readers, through reading what she has to say,

*From *De Colores*, Vol. 3, No. 3, 1977: pp. 31–37.

through reading about her, are reading about ourselves and our own experiences. This phenomenon takes place simply because by writing she has put a name to what we have felt—a name to feelings of anger, pain, love, joy, sympathy, strength, celebration. Every poem, essay, story becomes more than a work of art in this vital combination of writer and reader. Each work becomes an expression of life. The Chicana writer, like the revolutionary, is a creator and the result is twofold. She becomes the creator of a work of art and the creator of a destiny.

Although the Chicana voice is only recently emerging in writing, her presence, like the presence of the river in [Rodolfo] Anaya's *Bless Me, Ultima*, has always surrounded us; and when this presence reveals itself, finally, as it does to the protagonist, Antonio, it is an awesome revelation, one, like life itself, to be both revered and heeded. At first, what appears to be only a silence, in reality carries with it an underlying depth, strength, and volume, constantly moving, constantly alive; it is unable to be stopped and is not to be taken lightly.

In this sense the new Chicana poet, writer, the new voice you are hearing is not new at all. It has encompassed us since time immemorial only to have revealed itself in a more profound and real way. In Dorinda Moreno's *La Mujer en Pie de Lucha*, poet Viola Correa reveals the drama and fervor of this startling reality of the Chicana presence coming to life, in her poem, "la Nueva Chicana." This voice does not come from the elite, the women with the college degrees or titles, nor is it clad like one may have expected Jesus to have been clad, with royal robes. Her grandeur is of a different kind. Her presence is clothed in the voice of *tu hermana, tu madre, tu tia* [your sister, your mother, your aunt]. And by coming to us in this way, the voice is even more real to us; it comes from midst ourselves and not from above, as poets often do. More significantly, it comes from out of our own very real struggles: the picket lines, the factories, the fields, the *barrios*, the streets, *la casa* [the home].

The Chicana voice of today is reflective of the Aztec poets long ago. It binds us to a beauty of the past. Antonia Castañeda, co-editor of *Literatura Chicana,* one of the first Chicanas to teach *"La Mujer de la Raza"* at the University of Washington, speaks of the depth of a Chicano collective voice as it comes to us from a long-ago voice of the Aztec poet, Temilotzín. Temilotzín, in his poetry, speaks not only of himself, but to all the people. *Literatura Chicana* says that his mission is to create flower and song while seeking *humanidad* [humanity] with the community. Antonia Castañeda translates, *"en prestamos los unos a los otros,"* to mean, literally, that we are on loan to one another. The Chicana presence, the Chicana voice reaffirms this concept when she speaks. In so doing, she is reaching out to all Chicanas, "with song to encircle the community."

Writing, breaking the silence, subjective as it may appear, becomes a monumental and collective act because it signifies over coming, freeing oneself from the confines and conditions of history. The collective act may not even be expressed in the words themselves, but is manifest in the act of writing down these words. Writing is the tool which allows the Chicana to implement action, critical thought, change. It signifies a voice, a dimension beyond just a presence. It allows us a voice that reaches out to yet another, spurring critical questions while creating empathy. By this process involving writer and reader, both participants are breaking out of silence, no longer are they mere presences, but instruments for change, visionaries awakening the people.

All of Chicana literature crys out to make the world, to make relationships human again. Although living in our own communities has sheltered us in a sense from the atrocities of the outside world, we are still confronted with the technocratic soci-

ety that surrounds us. And in many ways, this society is worse than the physical poverty we might have known in our communities. It is more destructive because it leaves
us spiritually poor. It attempts to strip us of those elements with which we grew up
within our communities that allowed us to hold on to our humanidad [humanity];
our language, our culture, our family unity. Our responses of anger are against such
dehumanization; they are a reaction against a kind of violence that already exists.

More and more the Chicana woman is emerging out of a traditionally imposed
silence. Her already awesome presence becomes more awesome when it speaks. It becomes the conscience of the people; from one who is a participant in history. It is the
writing process that will facilitate the goal we seek: that in writing, our effects may be
far-reaching and that it will bring each one of us to our fullest human potential.

As long as we remain silent, no voice exists. Our right to speak, to voice ourselves is stripped from us; if you do not hear us, no voice exists and no one will notice
our absence.

Verónica Cunningham through poetry admonishes our silence. If we do not
speak out, the indictment is of ourselves and we must harbor the guilt of our own
rape. If, in our silence we make no rebellion our sentence, she says, will be our own silence; in itself, the worst possible punishment. Importantly, she begins this indictment
with "I" and in so doing, her poem becomes all-encompassing. But she speaks to all
women who would remain silent: "Chicana, Black, Asian, White, any woman, any
age, child, sister, wife, aunt, or friend." As long as you are silent you are yourself guilty:

> You women are guilty of
> being victims, guilty of being raped
> And you are guilty of laying
>   yourself down
> to your courts of justice
> and your sentence has been silence . . .

Chicanas are being called upon today to put their thoughts down in writing, to
share their emotions with others, thus beginning the process, the chain reaction that
might spur others to self-expression and creativity. Our depth as Chicana women
must be shared, in fact, is urgently needed so that others might hear the prophetic
voice. This sharing is essential; it is the spirit of our people. This process creates a new
awakening, a breaking out of silence, a revolutionary act. The burden is finally on us,
on all Chicanas to break out of silence, to be present to all others who may themselves
benefit from a voice, one that is both fearless and the penetrating conscience of the
people.

II

CORE THEMES IN CHICANA FEMINIST THOUGHT

Introduction

The writings of this generation of Chicana feminists can be collected into chapters focusing on the core themes that shaped the development of Chicana feminist thought. The essays in Section One, "Chicana Feminism and the Politics of the Chicano Movement," reveal the unfolding of a feminist consciousness among Chicana writers as they challenged the problematic gender relations within the Chicano movement. Their feminist consciousness evolved as they recognized that their participation in the movement was compromised by the constraints imposed upon them by the sexism perpetuated by Chicano ethnic nationalism. Chicana feminists criticized the interpretation by Chicano cultural nationalists that reified women's roles as that of submissive nurturer and caretaker of Chicano culture. Their writings document a challenge to sexism within the Chicano movement, a need to re-evaluate the definition of "Chicano culture," and the process of redefining the role of "*La Nueva Chicana*—The New Chicana."

A second core theme in Chicana feminist ideology consisted of an analysis of the sources of oppression shaping the daily lives of Chicanas. Parallel with their critique of the politics of the Chicano movement, Chicana feminists generally agreed with the statement that would become the clarion theme of the second wave of feminism: the personal is political. These essays uncover the multiple sources of inequality that Chicanas encountered in both the public and private spheres. Moreover, Chicanas acknowledged both the individual and collective components of their feminist struggles. Their shared sense of Chicana sisterhood was based on the matrix of domination imposed by race, gender, and class. Chicana feminists identified specific areas of gender inequality while at the same time underscoring their belief in the salience of ethnic inequality. These Chicana feminist writings often displayed an uneven level of analysis based on the specific backgrounds of the writers. Overgeneralizations are sometimes evident, but can be best understood given the often polemical nature of the essay, its historical context, its intended audiences, and its general purpose of raising the consciousness of Chicanas and mobilizing them into feminist action. This theme is directly linked to a third component in Chicana feminism.

Section Three, "Mapping a Chicana Feminist Agenda," traces the further development of a Chicana feminist consciousness by documenting some of the major feminist activities undertaken by this generation of Chicana feminists. A major factor in the development of a collective protest movement, such as this Chicana feminist movement, involves the type of action shaped by the newly-emerging change in consciousness. Chicana feminists developed a feminist praxis shaped by their analysis of Chicana oppression. Such a praxis grew and matured as a direct outgrowth of the sense of efficacy experienced by Chicanas and articulated in their writings. Chicana feminist thought informed the political behavior of Chicanas that was manifested in a series of workshops, regional and national conferences, and women's organizations. The documents generated by such conferences and groups concerning organizations, agendas, conflicts and resolutions highlight the mobilization of Chicana feminists into collective feminist activities. In addition, this section uncovers the major issues debated among Chicana feminists.

One of the most emotionally charged and contentious issues that formed a core theme in Chicana feminist thinking concerned relations with the women's movement. This relationship influenced, either directly or indirectly, each of the other components of Chicana feminist discourse. Section Four, "Chicana Feminists and White Feminists: Unresolved Conflicts," examines the progression of this conflict that influenced the relationship between these two groups of feminists. As a result of the ongoing "feminist-baiting" directed at Chicana feminists by many Chicanos, a major debate in the evolution of Chicana feminism focused on their response to white feminists. Chicana feminists writings demonstrate divergent views on this relationship, ranging from a separatist position that opposed political coalitions with white feminists, to more moderate ones shaped by an emerging sense of nascent sisterhood. In either case, Chicana feminists still had to deal with the often problematic relationship between their ethnic nationalism and their feminist ideology and praxis.

Section Five, "Chicana Feminism: An Evolving Future," brings together writings published at the end of the 1970s and the first years of the 1980s as a means of providing a retrospect of this generation of Chican feminist thought and a forward look by Chicana feminists who came of political age during the struggles of the Chicana Movement. These documents assess the role of Chicana feminists in: 1. inbuing the Movement's political agenda with feminist concerns, 2. mobilizing Chicanas into feminist activities, and 3. forming what they hoped would be long-standing Chicana feminist organizations. Chicana feminists entered the decade of the 1980s with a combined sense of past accomplishment and political anxiety for the future of Chicana feminism.

CHICANA FEMINISM AND THE POLITICS OF THE CHICANO MOVEMENT

Introduction

As Chicana feminists became more alienated with the Chicano Movement, they outlined their areas of disagreement with the politics of the movement. Their criticisms of the movement as noted in the following essays revolved around the following key points: (1) the control of the leadership of the movement by men and the exclusion of women from key leadership positions including the student movement; (2) the negative role of machismo within the movement; (3) the contradiction of the movement oppressing Chicanas in the same way that the system oppressed Chicanos; (4) the contradiction of the movement seeing itself as "revolutionary" while gender relationships within the movement remained unequal; (5) the liberation of women could not wait until after the "revolution"; (6) that the movement should not give priority to some issues at the exclusion of the role of women since all issues complemented one another such as economic and gender ones; (7) and, finally, Chicana feminists criticized men in the movement for causing splits within the ranks of women due to male attacks on Chicana feminists for being "disloyal" to the Movement and of siding with white "women's libbers."

While Chicana feminists remained steadfast in their critiques of the movement, they still saw themselves as part of the movement and recognized their criticism as a way of reforming and strengthening it. Their efforts to bridge their ethnic nationalism and their feminism led them to argue that in the end their natural allies were still Chicano men within the movement. Adhering to the other goals and struggles of the movement, Chicana feminists remained committed to a multiple agenda that included gender issues instead of more narrowly focusing exclusively on gender identity.

While opposition to the politics of the Chicano movement, on the one hand, reveals the roots of Chicana alienation with particular aspects of the Movement, it, on the other hand, also reveals in retrospect a tendency on the part of Chicana feminists to essentialize or over-generalize about the role and attitudes of Chicano men. Chicana feminists pursued legitimate grievances, but often at the expense of categorizing all Chicano men as opponents of Chicana feminism. The same tendency to essentialize can be observed in the various comments in these essays regarding both the so-called "Loyalists" or Chicanas who did not side with feminists on all issues and the attitudes of so-called "*gabachas*" or white women. In these cases, Chicana feminists pro-

posed legitimate concerns, but in so doing often suggested questionable race and gen-
er binaries.

Yet, Chicana feminists were not alone in falling prey to the politics of essentialism. The Chicano movement as a whole as well as the other social movements of the
Sixties including the women's movement were all vulnerable to often rigid social
constructions of right and wrong, of black and white, of women and men, of Anglo
and Chicano. The inability to recognize the complexities and the differences within
and between social movements would be a major factor in limiting the impact of
these movements on American politics.

Chicanas at a protest rally, Los Angeles, California, mid 1970s. Courtesy Raul Ruiz, *La
Raza* magazine, Los Angeles, California.

EMPIEZA LA REVOLUCIÓN VERDADERA (1971)
[THE REAL REVOLUTION BEGINS]

The struggle is long
The struggle is much
Our men are few
Our women are few
Rigid boundaries of roles do not move
They make us separate
They make us fewer

Busily we race with the "man"
But time is too valuable to talk among ourselves,
        about ourselves
Understanding is assumed
Misunderstanding arises
Communication stops
And now we compete among ourselves,
        against ourselves
Thou shall not do
Thou dare not do

The struggle is longer
The struggle demands more
But seek the knowledge of all women
And seek the knowledge of all men
Now bring them together
Make them a union
Then we shall see the strength of la raza
Then we shall see the success of el movimiento

First,
Humanity and freedom between men and women
Only then
Empieza la revolución verdadera

                                        Anna NietoGomez

Para Un Revolucionario (1975)
[For a Revolutionay]

You speak of art
And your soul is like snow,
A soft powder raining from your
Mouth,
Covering my breasts and hair.
You speak of your love of mountains,
Freedom,
And your love for a sun
Whose warmth is like *una liberación*
Pouring down upon brown bodies.
Your books are of the souls of men,
Carnales with a spirit
That no army, pig or *ciudad*
Could ever conquer.
You speak of a new way,
A new life.

When you speak like this
I could listen forever.

Pero your choice is lost to me, *carnal,*

In the wail of *tus hijos,*
In the clatter of dishes
And the pucker of beans upon the
stove.
Your conversations come to me
De la sala where you sit,
Spreading your dream to brothers
Where you spread that dream like
damp clover
For them to trod upon.
When I stand here teaching
Para ti con manos bronces that spring
From *mi espiritu*
(for I too am raza)

Pero, it seems I can only touch you
With my body,
You lie with me
And my body es la hamaca
That spans the void between us.

Hermano raza,
I am afraid that you will lie with me
And awaken too late
To find that you have fallen

And my hands will be left groping
For you and your dream
In the midst of *la revolución.*

Lorna Dee Cervantes

Brown Berets, Los Angeles, early 1970s. Courtesy of Raul Ruiz, *La Raza* magazine, Los Angeles, California.

15

La Mujer in the Chicano Movement*

ELVIRA SARAGOZA

The role of today's Chicana is very sad because today our Chicana woman is very confused about her position in the movement.

She no longer wishes to limit her world to domesticity; making frijoles [beans], tortillas. She wants to expand to have the domestic role together with the intellectual role. She wants to be able to use her *cerebro* [mind] because she knows that she too can think, and be creative. She is not an inferior, insubordinate being and she is tired of being treated as one. She wants to develop but she is being held back. Who or what is preventing the Chicana from developing?

One factor which is most obviously suppressing the Chicana is the culturally accepted role of the woman which limits her to the house and the church. The goal of the woman is to get married and to have children. Education is seldom emphasized. To have a high school diploma is a rarity. The role here is enclosure. We must conserve our culture but our parents must realize the necessity for change. There are many pressures on the Chicana and it really hurts when her own family prevents her from developing.

The other evident and even more crucial factor which hampers the Chicana's growth is our own men. This is extremely sad because they should be the first to help the women. We women need our men. We need them to help us develop. A Chicana not only needs a man who is to love and protect her, but one who is going to treat her as a creative being. One who will push his woman to use her mind, who will give encouragement and who will tell his woman to continue although she may encounter obstacles and failures. The Chicana wants very much to communicate and to stand side by side with her man. If a woman cannot get encouragement from her own family, the man must come through.

But what is happening today? Too often our men perpetuate the Chicana's inferiority complex. He either moves up in his ladder of intelligence leaving his woman ignorant and feeling at a much lower level, or what is worse, he goes to the extreme of abandoning his beautiful brown blood and going to the white blood of a *gabacha* [white woman] for the insignificant reason that he feels a *gabacha* is at a higher level of intelligence and he can thus communicate more easily with her. This is absurd! The gabacha is not more intelligent, she is possibly more aware and nothing more. We Chicanas have beautiful minds and great potential. We just need the opportunity to develop them. Those women who have had this opportunity have proven to be exceptional women.

[Chicanas] say to our men, "Look at what you have, your Brown women." Help them! Don't abandon them because when you do *you are throwing away a great deal of yourself!*"

*From *Bronce Magazine*, Vol. 1, No. 4, June 1969.

16

The Chicanas*

ENRIQUETA "HENRI" CHÁVEZ

We are all in the liberation movement of our people and this movement should be directed by our people. It should not be directed by men only. Our struggle for our Race has placed the female (Chicanas) in direct contact with men outside of the home. We have worked together and we have marched and sung together. This has brought about a change in the concept of the Chicana. Most of us are no longer inclined to merely fill secondary positions. We want to be considered for important positions and we also want to be respected.

Mothers are educating their children to face the realities of this world. For this reason, we consider the education and participation of women to be of vital importance in the movement. We must be ready to participate in any manner in the movement that concerns the economic and cultural well being of our people. At the same time we can continue being good mothers and good wives, because in the strength of the family lies the strength of the movement. We live in a society that believes that the world is defined by contrasts. The man should be aggressive and strong and the women submissive and weak. It is understood that the man can demand yet, the woman should wait until she is offered something. This sense of inferiority is transmitted to her children.

The woman and the man must collaborate effectively without feeling humiliated. The education of women and their development both socially and politically does not mean that we wish to occupy the positions that are being filled by men in this society. We want to create more effective relations between man and woman.

> We sing and we work together
> But we are still two distinct persons.
> Don't give your heart into the care of another person
> Just because he belongs to the movement.
> A team is made up of two persons, not of one,
> And the two have to grow separately
> So that they may flower in all their splendor:
> Without possessing the other.
> It is harmony without beginning and without end.
> The earth does not give birth without the energy
> of the sun.

The two of us are capable of creating and caring for, also of taking, directing or following. One cannot separate one from the other.

*From *Regeneración*, Vol. 1, No. 10, 1971: p. 14.

17

La Chicana:
Her Role in The Movement*

ANONYMOUS

At the December 4th [1971] Raza Unida Party Conference held at San Fernando high school, there was a workshop on La Chicana and the role she would play in La Raza Unida Party. It is an understanding that Chicanos, as a whole people cannot be liberated if one sector of its whole is still in bonds. The question of La Chicana's liberation lies in the definition of this term. We are speaking of the liberation which gives the Chicana "a freedom of choice" in roles she plays within the society. She may have the freedom of choice to become a doctor, a lawyer, to run for a political office, become a Congresswoman *or* she may choose to become a housewife, a mother.

The Chicana workshop dealt with six major themes which concern all Chicanas whether she is a student, wife, mother, divorced or single. It must be realized that she could be a combination of roles mentioned and there are legitimate problems confronting Chicanas. Self-awareness and understanding of these problems can enable her to function more easily with the politics of La Raza Unida and together with the men realize the full potential strength of the party.

Creation of community controlled Child Care Centers would profit both the working mother and the child by allowing the married or divorced woman to seek employment to support herself and her child. In the area of employment there seem to be problems with working conditions, equal pay, and maternity leave. It was brought out that job counseling was needed to steer the high school Chicana into professional roles rather than as domestic help. The third theme, education, is related to the second theme by enabling the Chicana (with the proper counselling) to choose professions. In fields such as lawyers, judges, and politicians. La Chicana needs to gain a self-awareness of herself and for this she needs the creation of classes and career advisement to aid her. Fourth, there is the need for health education. There must be more Chicanas hired on the staff of organized free clinics to aid the Spanish-speaking women who need instruction on birth control, abortion and general information on the prevention of disease.

When these first four needs are met the Chicana can concentrate more heavily on politics. Women are affected directly by policy changes made by the government. We can readily see this change: higher prices in supermarkets and stores. For these reasons a Chicana should choose to hold a political office and not be discriminated against by the men in the party. La Chicana needs the representation *in* every platform decision making committees of both La Raza Unida and other government agencies.

*From *El Popo*, Vol. 4, No. 2, 1971: p. 2.

18

*Viva La Chicana and All Brave Women of La Causa**

Elizabeth Martinez

All over the country today, La Raza is in motion. A spirit of awakening runs through the big city barrios, small towns, colleges and universities, the countryside. Our people are refusing to be filled with shame any longer, they are refusing to be oppressed, they are demanding liberation and a decent life.

More and more, women are becoming involved—young, middle-aged and even elderly women like María Hernández, a 75 year old Chicana activist in San Antonio. They are working on problems like working conditions and pay, education, welfare rights, housing, child care, police brutality. They are forming groups of women with names like *Las Chicanas* and *Las Adelitas*.

At the same time we know that more Chicanas must become involved. It is our job as Chicanas to wake them up, encourage them to see that they have a responsibility larger than their immediate families—a responsibility to the whole familia of La Raza, the whole family of oppressed peoples. And a responsibility to their own unused talents, brain, energy.

We must help Chicanas to overcome feelings of inferiority that many have, or feelings that they can perform only certain kinds of work and should not be involved in making decisions outside the home. Unfortunately, these feelings are often encouraged by machos who fail to see that we need *every Chicana and Chicano* in this struggle. Because many men of El Movimiento do this, even men who call themselves "revolutionary," there has been much talk recently about *La Chicana's* role. The fact is, nothing could be more truly Chicana than the Chicana who wants to be more than a wife, mother, housekeeper. That limited concept of women did not exist under our Indian ancestors for whom the woman was a creative person in the broadest sense and central to the cultural life of the tribe. Later in Mexican history, we find that the woman has played every possible role—including that of fighter on the front lines. Any people who live close to the land, who are subject to nature's forces, know that survival is impossible without both sexes working at it in every possible way. That is the true Raza tradition, a communal tradition

In the villages of northern New Mexico, the Chicana has always done a lot of what some call "men's work." There is a tradition of strong women—women who know how to handle a gun, who have herded cattle on horseback, who have survived much physical hardship, who have had leadership roles in our struggle to win back the

*From *El Grito del Norte*, Vol. 4, No. 4–5, June 5, 1971: a–b.

land. These women draw strength from their closeness to *la tierra* [the land] and we can learn much from them.

Revolutionary Chicanas want the liberation of our people and of all oppressed peoples. We do not want to become page-girls in [President Richard] Nixon's Congress—the most recent bone tossed to "women's liberation." We know what that Congress does to people. We do not want a few Chicanas to get better jobs, higher salaries, while everyone else continues to be exploited. At the same time, we know that revolution means turning things upside down and taking another look at what is taken for granted. So revolution means new ideas about relations between men and women, too.

19

El Movimiento and the Chicana⋆

ANONYMOUS

In the movimiento [Chicano movement] Chicanas have been in the background of organizations. We have seen few Chicanas take leadership roles. *Las mujeres* [the women] have largely played the role of the secretary. When women were given leadership roles, it was mainly out of tokenism to a silent, yet potentially powerful group. This has been the very same type of tokenism that the system has used only now it's the Chicanos doing it to the *mujeres*. When a *carnala* [sister] was given a title, a definite position, it was mostly a head secretarial position. There is no denying that many organizations need an office to run smoothly, but this is where most women have remained.

At other times, there were schisms among the women themselves, that is "petty jealousies" arose. A woman who was supposedly together or in pretty much in agreement with whatever the men said would be set apart from the other women. This woman would not have to be very vocal; she did not necessarily know how to analyze a situation the organization was into. She merely had to parrot a lot of the rap that the men put out. The men would then begin to set her up as the true example of what the women's role was all about. She was symbolically put on a pedestal. She was the queen or Azteca princess of the organization. She was to be possessed, cared for like a Chicano takes care of his little sister, not equal to the men. All ideas which capitalism perpetuates. How many times would Chicanas hear, "But, you're a better worker, more together and revolutionary than the other lame chicks." This is most assuredly non-revolutionary. For being revolutionary means that you are a part of the people, you are with

⋆From *La Raza*, Vol. 1, No. 6, 1971: pp. 40–42.

the people. So, this *hermana*, [sister] having all the attention of the guys, would begin to look down on the other Chicanas. She became egotistical (another symptom of capitalism) in her total attitude in regards to the other *mujeres*. She was already a "liberated woman." She could not stoop so low as to get the other women's head straight, which is her truest revolutionary task for the liberation of an oppressed people.

The women at the Regional Conference would not deny the fact that they are in total revolution against the system. Why women are looking at Chicanas and saying that they are being used is another look into realities. There aren't very many Chicanas in the movement. This is of course ridiculous because there are two women for every man in this nation. We must realize that the U.S. System has brainwashed us in spite of all our shouts of Chicano power we still have strains of white upper class attitudes that reflect in our ideology. This is the idea that there must always be an underdog and a top dog. That there must be a rich class and a lower class because history has proved it to be that way. So in our *familias* [families], in our organizations we have vestiges of the old ideas in sex and the oppressed sex. Revolutionary ideology is an evolvement, a change in our thinking. We, Chicanas, are still unaware of our upper class attitudes. (And it's excusable at this moment for Chicanas are for the first time really looking at their role). It is in our dialogue, it is in our love relationship. It is in our organizations. Most Chicanas have been pre-conditioned (brainwashed) into the idea that they can not speak up or be smarter than their men. Now this may sound like an anglo woman's liberation thing, but the Chicana has had it in her family not to talk against the father, not to disagree with him on anything. The *Chicanita* [young Chicana] while being raised is to never question the authority, rules, or actions of her father nor of her brothers.

She is kept in a closed shell, protected from all the "evils" in the world by the men in her family. She may go either of two ways. One is that she has been so affected by male dominance that she is easily influenced by any man from there on, be it either in politics of an organization or naively falls for the guys that radicalize her pants off. The other well-protected *hermana* [sister] may go into an organization sincere in her heart to do something for her people. She is welcomed by a group of guys who try to get her into bed before she can ask "What is the Chicano movement all about?" She is basically turned off because she still has very religious ideas of virginity, *La Virgen* [Virgin Mary], St. Mary Magdalene, and the Pope.

If the *hermana* has an open mind about premarital sex, she is turned off to the *movimiento* because she values herself as a human being. She knows that she has physiological desires, but she wants to be recognized as an individual who has brains and the ability to use them. This particular type of woman is separated from all the other Chicanas and Chicanos immediately. She does not want to be used as a sexual object but does want to be involved in all aspects of the movement. This the guys don't like. They distort her actions and make foolish accusations that strong women are dikes just because she will not go to bed with him, while they mock her by stating that she tries to dominate everything.

This is about how the expression goes. These Chicanas find themselves dating few of the guys in the organization. She is socially ostracized from the group. When she brings up the issue of machismo, the other *hermanas* silently agree but do not say anything to support her.

So she is labeled a personality problem, a power hungry egotistical woman. The political and economical struggle of the Chicana is the universal question on women. The difference between the liberation of Chicana women and other Third World women is cultural. The Chicano culture has very positive effects and very bad ones. We have to fight a lot of Catholic ideas in our homes and in the movement. For example, the idea of large families is very Catholic. The Pope says no birth control, abortions, lots of kids (and make me richer). So what do the guys say in the movement, have lots of kids, keep up the traditional Chicano family. If a Chicana knows anything about sex, right away Chicanos think that she must have gone through the mill. The cultural oppression here is that Anglos have a saying that goes: A woman should be an angel in the kitchen and a devil in the bedroom. For the Chicana there is not that "double standard." She is to be a virgin before marriage and remain naive about sex through her entire married life. When a Chicana gets into an organization and doesn't go with any particular guy in that organization, the guys all become her older brothers. The Chicanos now look out for the Chicana like her father would. Who's that Tina's with? Is he ok? Like in the family the Chicana then has to argue that she has a rational mind and that she has the capacity to judge a person, and doesn't need anyone telling her who to or who not to go out with. So for a lot of Chicanas they go from the kettle into the fire, from the home into the movement.

In our movement we must work overtime on the question of the women's role. Women may have to work on separate projects or services very pertinent for changes for *las mujeres*. This will not be done to bring about jealousies, conflict, or to see which sex works better than the other nor to cause a permanent schism in the Chicano struggle for liberation and equality. This will be done for the positive evaluation of each other. To realize that in the struggle for liberation of a people, we must count the other half of the work force—the women. This will be done to realize that in order to make a successful revolution the two sexes must be completely liberated from upper class ideas, traditions and tendencies.

Hermanas should realize that we could be strong, teach each other, and help each other towards revolutionary ideals and responsibility—for what else could breakdown a revolution but women who do not understand true equality and still possess upper-class ideas of possession—property.

20

La Chicana y "El Movimiento"[*]

ELENA HERNÁNDEZ

A double standard exists because men feel that it is alright if they have relationships with various women. Society has generally accepted such a practice. However, if a woman feels that there is no need to put a limit on the number of her relationships then she is looked down upon by society. I do not agree with this type of attitude. I

*From *Chicanismo*, Vol. 3, No. 3, April 29, 1972: pp. 6–8.

believe that every man, as well as every woman should have the right to do as they wish. If a man or woman has an interest or an understanding with another person, then it is their own free choice. Society, many times is not open to accept this. The Chicana especially is not in favor of accepting this. These are things to be understood. In time each of us will resolve our own indecisiveness, because part of living is to develop our own answers.

Divorced Women

There is much to be said about the cultural taboo of the divorced woman. One ridiculous notion, shared by many, is since the divorced woman has failed as a wife she should then retreat to a convent. Another stereotyped notion of the divorced woman is "she knows the ropes." That is, because of a divorced woman's past experience it is estimated by many men that she can easily and, willingly be exploited. These notions are truly idiotic misconceptions.

There is extensive evidence to prove that one of the most instrumental contributors to the *movimiento* is the divorced Chicana. All one has to do is look around. Dolores Huerta is just one such example. Therefore, the misconceived idea that a divorced woman is a "wasted woman" must be eliminated, particularly in the Chicano movement.

Also, it would be beneficial to the *movimiento* if Chicanos would dramatize less the physical element of the woman. This is not to deny that beauty is not to be appreciated; but that a mind that is searching for the liberation of a people is true beauty.

The Movement Itself

It is about time that Chicanas rebelled against being subjected to a less assertive position in the movement. For too long have our capabilities as secretaries been taken for granted. I believe that each individual has definite assets and abilities. If a Chicana feels that she can best contribute to the movement by typing for the newspaper, or for a Chicano studies department, then her work should not be interfered with. However, if a Chicana feels she wants to go beyond the secretarial norm then she must be given the opportunity to extend her involvement. The conflict arises when a Chicana is prevented from taking positions of leadership. This prevention generally comes from the oppressive mentality of the majority of Chicanos. It is of course unjustifiable.

If a Chicana feels like, "hell, I don't want to just type. I want to be chairman of M.E.Ch.A [Movimiento Estudiantil Chicano de Aztlán]* or coordinator of a free breakfast program," it is important that this drive be recognized and the position delegated. Chicanas do not have to settle for secondary roles. We do not have to accept roles that are handed to us. If you, as a Chicana, feel you have ideas to offer, then it is your responsibility to speak up and then begin to produce. As far as people whom I really respect in the movement, Dolores Huerta is one. There are also many other revolutionary women who were and still are significant to the movement, but whom we never hear about. There is much research about such women that can be done by us, as students, because we are closer to finding leads to the sources.

I believe that there are distinct stages of development in the movement. There is

*Name of Chicano student organization (Chicano Student Movement of Aztlan) founded in the 1960s throughout the Southwest at universities and some high schools. MEChA mobilized students for mass protests aimed at educational institutions.

the point of one becoming conscious of the daily problems that confront Chicanos. This is the time that we shout "Viva La Raza" and we attend mass demonstrations, and we do the "action thing." But soon you realize that too much rhetoric and wasted energy is taking place. This is when one moves on to the more productive stage. It is important for a Chicano at this time to recognize his strongest abilities, be it education, medicine, organizing La Raza in communities, or working on the creative side, like an artist. Once a Chicano has found his or her most favorable position in which to make sound contributions to La Raza, then they should get into it and get work done!

Criticism of the Movement

One of the main criticisms that I have of the movement is "*donde esta nuestro carnalismo?*" [where is our sisterhood and brotherhood]. It is not always apparent. I am very much aware of the existence of inner turmoil, personal conflicts, breaking up of M.E.Ch.A.'s, Chicano political parties disputing over who to run as a candidate, *y me da una tristeza* [I am saddened]. Once again you see the Chicanos against themselves. This is one of the reasons why I stress to Chicana women: we cannot afford to fight against our men. Instead, it is our responsibility to develop communication and understanding within our men. In order to fight and constructively change the system we will be more effective if we work together as a people.

Each time one speaks about Chicana self-awareness there is constant opposition from the majority of Chicanos. I am sure many Chicanas have experienced situations in which they tried unsuccessfully to explain their ideas to a Chicano. I would like to share a personal experience that I had recently while I was trying to discuss the Chicana element with a friend of mine. This *carnal* [comrade] of mine is a very macho-dominant type male. Well, I told him, "these are my ideas, and this is what I think." His reply was, "It's a crock of shit." He further went on and said, "it's ridiculous, you don't know what you are talking about." What he said in essence was, "go home, go home where you belong." it was like I had nothing to say. I felt so bad, that honestly, I went home and cried. Then I started questioning myself and thought, well gee, Elena, maybe you really do not have any basis for what you said. Maybe this whole Chicana thing is a "big crock of shit." and does not make any sense, after all. I got further and further disillusioned until I hit the very bottom. Then I said to myself, "wait a minute, that is exactly what he wants me to think so that I will shut my mouth and I will not say anything." However, this has been the root of the Chicana problem. Chicanas cannot continue to live a life of apathy. We can no longer be spoken for. We cannot dismiss the Chicana issue because it carries a lot of validity. Ultimately I hope to see among La Raza relationships based on equality in which there is a respected attitude and a recognition of each other.

There is also the question of serving a man, needing a man, and being protected by a man. A woman must remember that a relationship should last only as long as she, the woman, feels comfortable and wants to do these things. The problem arises when Chicanas are put into a position where they feel they "have to serve the man." One must realize that one does not have to do anything one does not want to do.

Chicana hindrance is widespread in the movement. This is the fault of the Chicano as well as the Chicana. One thing that is very detrimental to the Chicana movement is the joking-type attitude; that there is no substance to what Chicanas have to say. I find that whenever I am in a discussion with men there is a need to practically shout so they will listen to me. Then I say maybe it is this way because I am a woman and they think I do not have any intelligence to take part in the conversation. Or perhaps it is because Chicanos are not accustomed to Chicanas speaking out. I believe that it is the latter. Chicanos are not used to Chicana self-expression. Why? Because they never allowed it before. Except now it is happening and I hope it continues with Chicanas, because it works against a person's character to put themselves in a position where they feel they cannot or should not talk. Chicanas have instrumental minds, just like everybody else.

It is also the fault of the Chicana for not fully representing herself in the movement. The reason it is part of our fault is that we have accepted the role of being subservient to the male. We sometimes think we are inferior, that we cannot take on leadership roles. This type of attitude only continues to perpetuate our present-day situation. If you think you have no capabilities then you will accomplish very little. However, if you think of yourself and your achievements positively, then you will work to make changes. I hope what I am able to do is help the Chicana understand that she has substance, that she can contribute to the movement. That you never have to take what you do not want to take.

To the Chicanas I want to stress that we must actualize our potential. As for the Chicanos, they must learn to recognize and respect the potential of the Chicanas. *"Y Chicanas, no se dejen, y Chicanos juntos no nos dejamos"* [Chicanas, don't take it anymore, and Chicanos together let's not take it anymore].

21

*La Femenista**

ANNA NIETOGOMEZ

During an era in which people have fought for their civil rights, the *femenistas* have begun to emerge as a group of minority women, the Chicanas. These *femenistas* are speaking out against the sexual racist oppression that they as Chicana women must contend with.

As minority women, the Chicanas have had to fight racism, sexism, and sexual racism. Racism oppresses the Chicana as a member of a Spanish speaking, culturally different, non-Anglo group in a society that values only one culture, and only one race as superior over all, the Anglo-Saxon race. The Chicana encounters sexism in a society that associates social and economic power, authority and superiority with

*From *Encuentro Femenil*, Vol. 1, No. 2, 1974: pp. 34–47.

male dominance and male control. It is also perpetuated by nationalists who demand that women must always be traditional and maintain the culture, in spite of their socio-economically oppressive conditions. Sexist racism is manifested by those who consider and recognize only the needs of the single, Anglo and middle class women. It is also reinforced when Anglo women are compared as more "politically active, educated," and in general superior to the non-Anglo women who in turn are viewed as passive, apolitical and illiterate beings.

The Chicana feminist has been calling attention to her socioeconomic oppression as a Chicano and as a woman since 1968. The Chicana feminist has called attention to how racism, sexism, and sexist racism are used to maintain the Chicana woman's social and economic oppression. However, it can be truthfully said that she has been ignored. The Chicana feminist has had to struggle to develop and maintain her identity in spite of the paternal and material tendencies of two social movements to absorb her into their general movements as their own rank and file.

The Chicano movement has until recently viewed the Chicana only as a member of the Chicano people in general, who are all economically oppressed as a culturally different people. It has been indifferent to the specific issues 51% of the Chicano people face as women. At the same time, the Anglo-headed popular movement has only viewed Chicanas as potential members of the ranks of women because all women are oppressed by the sexist attitudes against them. It has then ignored the issues the Chicana must contend with as a member of a minority, culturally different lower income group. In so doing, it has ignored how the Chicana's social and economic status as a woman is also severely determined by her race as well as her sex.

Instead, the Chicana feminist has been cautioned to wait and fight her cause at a later time for fear of dividing the Chicano movement. Also it has been recommended that she melt into the melting pot of femaleness rather than divide the women's movement.

In order to establish themselves as a legitimate interest group or groups, the Chicana *femenista* has continually had to justify, clarify, and educate people in the political and philosophical issues of the Chicana woman. This has not been easy. They have acted at the cost of being called "*vendidas*" (sell-outs) among their own group, the Chicanos. At the same time the femenistas have had to pressure the women's movement with little or no solid backing from the Chicano movement.

From 1968–1971 feminism was rejected by the Chicano movement as irrelevant and Anglo-inspired. Philosophical conflicts arose from those who felt that the Chicano movement did not have to deal with sexual inequities since both Chicano men as well as Chicana women were treated unequally in a racist society. They reasoned that if men oppress women it was not the men's fault but the system's fault. It is the economic structure that forced the Chicano to oppress the women because the whole world oppressed him.[1] Also, feminism was identified as an Anglo-oriented movement supporting the economically oppressive structure; consequently, the feminist movement could only disrupt and hurt the Chicano movement. Racism was seen as a greater issue of survival.[2] In general these "Loyalists" to the movement were ready to defend their men against Anglo feminist infiltration in order to survive racial-economic oppression.

> I am concerned with the direction that the Chicanas are taking in the movement. The words such as liberation, sexism [and] male chauvinism were prevalent. The terms mentioned above plus the theme of individualism is a concept of the Anglo society; terms prevalent in the Anglo woman's movement. The *familia* [family] has always been our strength in our culture. But it seems evident . . . that [you] are not concerned with the *familia*, but are influenced by the Anglo woman's movement.[3]

Femenistas were viewed by the "Loyalists" as anti-family, anti-cultural, anti-man and therefore an anti-Chicano movement. Women in search of identity, while developing a new role in society, could not be trusted. Searching for identity was an Anglo-bourgeois trip. The "Loyalists" could only see the "*Femenistas*" as ambitious, selfish women who were only concerned with themselves at the cost of everyone else.

> . . . And since when does a Chicana need identity? If you are a real Chicana then no one regardless of the degrees needs to tell you about it. The only ones who need identity are the *vendidas* [sell-outs], the *falsas* [the false ones], and the opportunists. The time has come for the Chicanas to examine the direction they wish to take. Yes, we need recognition. Our men must give this to us. But there is danger in the manner we are seeking it. . . . We are going to have to decide what we value more, the culture or the individual (as Anglos do)? I hope it's not too late.[4]

The "Loyalists" believed in the model of the unselfish Chicana. It was not important to talk about liberation from the Chicana's own particular problems.[5] This was made very clear at the First National Chicano Student Denver Conference: "It was the consensus of the group that the Chicana woman does not want to be liberated."[6]

Feminist thoughts and activities could only "divide the movement." Instead, it was important to talk about the "reality of work in the movement and the women's practical contribution to it."[7] To be associated with the women's lib movement would be helping the oppressive Anglo system and therefore treasonous to the Chicano movement.

Harassment of *femenistas* forced many Chicanas to suppress their convictions. The term "women's libber," a stigmatizing label, was used as a social label assigned to those who spoke out for women's rights in the Chicano movement." These castigated Chicanas were identified as man-haters, frustrated women, and "*agringadas*" [Anglocized]. If they spoke out against sexual inequality, they were often effectively isolated, controlled and discredited by merely becoming associated with the "taboo" Anglo women's movement, for to be associated with anything Anglo was close to being called a traitor. To gain approval, acceptance and sometimes even recognition, many Chicanas were careful not to be associated with anything considered "women's lib."

Although the advent of [the] Chicana caucus identified Chicana issues with the Chicana platform, the suppression of the women often nullified the impact of the Chicana caucus. Conventions and conferences would bring large numbers of Chicanas together to form an effective "temporary" Chicana caucus pressure group, but their diffused return to each individual organization brought few results, where numbers as well as morale were weak.[9] This prevented any whole-hearted action to internalize the Chicana platform into Chicano organizations. Marta Cotera, active member of La Raza Unida Party, describes the effects of this kind of harassment towards the women in her article "Mexicano Feminism."

> Unfortunately, the only effect that Anglo feminism has on the Chicana has been negative. Suddenly, *mujeres* [women] involved in the struggle for social justice, who have always advocated more and stronger women, and the family participation in all political activities, are suspect. They are suspected of assimilating into the feminist ideology of an alien culture that actively seeks [to continue its] domination.[10]

As a result:

> These women must retreat into more conservative stands, and in effect, retreat from certain activities that deal specifically with the special social needs of women.[11]

Therefore Marta [Cotera] warns:

> . . . Attempts to discredit women who are strongly for the development and re-
> cruitment of greater numbers of women into the political and social struggle will
> be tragic and detrimental to the cause. This will also be the case if we take "disci-
> plinarian," "purgist," or "protective" attitudes towards women attracted to femi-
> nism within our movement.[12]

To counter this suppression, many Chicanas have actively organized and spoken out
against this suppression. Yolanda Nava, First Vice President of the Comisión Femenil
Mexicana Nacional, writes in her article, "Myths, the Media, Minority Groups and
Women's Liberation: An Overview," that the women's issues must be recognized and
internalized within the movement. People believe a woman, due to the nature of her
sex, should be controlled, cared for and protected by a man because of the superior
nature of his sex. These oppressive sexual inequities contradict any cries for liberation
from a people's movement for the right to control its own destiny. In this respect,
Yolanda [Nava] reinforces that Chicanas have the responsibility to deal with the general condition of their *hermanas* [sisters].

By instructing how the media wrote off the legitimate needs of an entire group
calling them "militants," Yolanda [Nava] points out, "so do others try to nullify the legitimacy of Chicanas by making them seem insignificant or clearly a minority group
by labelling them "women's libbers." Yolanda [Nava] reminds Chicanas: we are all a
part of the woman's condition. We are all oppressed. To deny that you are oppressed
[as a woman] is to collaborate to your oppression.

Many loyalists felt that these complaints from the women were potentially destructive and could only divide the Chicano movement. If sexual inequities existed
they were an "in house" problem which could be dealt with later. However, right
then, there were more important priorities to attend to, e.g., Vietnam, *La Huelga* [the
farm workers strike], police brutality.[13]

To these people, Yolanda [Nava] emphasizes that just as "tokenism is an unacceptable price to pay for society's injustices," so it is also "unacceptable to separate
racial-sexual and economic struggle in a hierarchical list of priorities." It must be realized that it is "illogical to ask a woman to ignore and postpone her struggle as a
woman."[14]

Both Marta [Cotera] and Yolanda [Nava] agree that feminism is an added and
needed dimension of the Chicano movement. They point out that feminism has increased the number of people, politicized and organized more women into the Chicano movement. They:

> would like to see more women involved, and their development not left to chance
> or to be on a selective basis; but for all women to have equal opportunity regard-
> less of looks, availability, marital status, or economic condition. . . . Chicanas with
> Chicana points of view should be encouraged to communicate to the movement
> and to bring our needs and feelings as mothers, wives, sisters, college girls and
> "movement" women into focus for our brothers."[15]

Femenistas uphold that feminism is a very dynamic aspect of the Chicana's heritage
and not at all foreign to her nature. As Marta Cotera aptly points out "the Mexicana
has a long and wonderful history of Mexicano feminism which is not Anglo inspired,
imposed or oriented." There is a legacy of heroines and activists in social movement
and armed rebellions which Chicanas can draw from as models to emulate.[16]

It is therefore the philosophy of the *Femenistas* that in order for a movement to truly fight for justice for all its people (both men and women) must it also, from the beginning, identify and fight the economic oppression delivered through sexism as well as through racism. It is the double responsibility for both Chicanas and Chicanos to become politicized to the economic implications of sexism—sexist racism; otherwise, the issues of employment, welfare, and education as they pertain to the Chicana are not known and therefore ignored and not resolved.

Differences between the philosophies of the "loyalists" and the "*femenistas*" have indeed been controversial ones. The loyalists do not recognize sexism as a legitimate issue in the Chicano movement. *Femenistas* see sexism as an integrated part of the Chicana's struggle in conjunction with her fight against racism. This confusion and difference of attitudes towards defining the Chicana's role in the movement was turbulently visible in the first National Chicana Conference held in Houston, Texas, May 1971.

Six hundred women attended this Chicana Conference. Most were there to talk about issues concerning Chicana women; however, the fears of being associated with non-movement activities hung over the conference like a confusing and disorganizing paranoia. And it was at this conference that this paranoia catalyzed the clash between the two groups of women, the "loyalists" and the "*femenistas*."

The topics of the National Chicana Conference dealt with the topics of marriage, role of the Chicana in *La Familia*, Child Care, Sex, and the Church. In essence, the *Femenista* spoke about changing her role in the *familia* and creating a new role through the movement. "With the involvement in the movement, marriage must change. Traditional roles are, for Chicanas, no longer acceptable or applicable."[17] They agreed that women should not be the scapegoats of men's frustrations.

> Although Chicanas have a responsibility to understand that Chicanos face oppression and discrimination, this does not mean that the Chicana should be a scapegoat for the man's frustrations.[18]

However, these kinds of ideas went against the dictates of the "Loyalist" philosophy; marriage and motherhood were the very things the loyalists wanted to remain the same. Consequently, the intense feelings arising from the conflicts between the *femenistas* and the loyalists created such anxiety and confusion that the group of 600 women split up into two groups of women. Half the group "returned to the *barrio*" to officially offer feminine support to the already recognized and "legitimate" issues of the Chicano movement. The other half stayed to discuss how to support Chicanas who wanted the movement to recognize and fight the issue of sexism.

This split seems to continue to exist today. *Femenistas* still feel the pressure to justify and clarify why Chicanos have to address themselves to the sexism that affects the Chicana because she is a woman in a minority group. There is still a continuous effort on the part of Chicanas to maintain their identity and have people recognize how feminine issues have different and important facets to them when dealt with within the context of minority women, especially minority women who are Spanish-speaking and considered foreigners in their own land.

The conflict between the feminists and the loyalists is the result of not clearly defining the differences and the similarities between the Anglo and Chicana feminist movement.

The Chicana's socio-economic class as a non-Anglo, Spanish-speaking, low income Chicana woman determines her need and therefore her political position. The low-income Anglo woman does not have to deal with racism nor is she punished because she speaks another language. The middle-class Anglo woman only shares with the Chicana the fact that they are both women. But they are women of different ethnic, cultural, and class status. All these factors determine the different socio-economic needs and therefore determine the different political positions of these women.

Historical differences determine the relationship between the Anglo woman and the Chicana woman. The Anglo woman is a product of Protestant and imperialistic Anglo-European capitalism. The Chicana is a product of Catholic societies which still bear the marks of Counter-reformation feudalism and colonialism. Her Moorish, Spanish, Mexican Indian–Mestizo, Southwest heritage contribute to her cultural world view.[19] Southwest heritage contribute to her cultural world view. But it also outlines her colonized situation in an imperialistic racist country.

If the Anglo women's movement (AWM) saw itself as an independent force for social change, *las Femenistas* see their fight against sexual oppression as part of the struggle of their people. Chicana feminism shares with all women the issues that affect them as women, such as welfare, birth control, abortion, and employment. But it is in the context of the needs of the Chicano people who suffer from racism that sexual issues have a new dimension.

In providing adequate health programs, Anglo women contend with the cruel prejudice doctors have towards women patients. Chicanas must also contend with doctor's racism, insensitivity to the Chicano culture and the lack of bilingual medical staff. In addition, economics limit her choice of medical facilities to state and county health clinics which usually have inadequate health services. Depending on the availability of a bilingual volunteer among the patients, most doctors treat monolingual Spanish-speaking patients with less than adequate diagnosis. Thus women's health issues such as pregnancy, birth control, and sterilization are compounded.

Taking into consideration the dangerous combination of racism and sexism, Chicanas do realize the need to provide health programs such as birth control and abortion clinics, but they do so only if the programs can be community controlled. Hopefully, these programs will be culturally, educationally, and politically oriented to the needs of the Chicana in a Chicano community.

Specific issues of the Anglo feminist movement take on a new dimension in the context of the Chicana feminist movement. When a Chicana talks about birth control and abortion she does so in the context of understanding the cultural genocidal acts of this country. When a Chicana demands child care centers she demands that they be bilingual and bicultural. She will not settle for Mickey Mouse speaking Spanish. If she is a Chicana on welfare she may be even more adamant about being able to select the staff at the child care center so her child will not become a dropout at the age of two because of the staff's prejudices. When a Chicana works in an affirmative action program for women, she will make sure that Chicanas are not being screened according to how Anglo they look and whether they speak without an accent. In addition, she must make sure she receives equal pay between Anglo women and Chicanas as well as between men and women.

The cumulative effect of these differences between Chicana feminists and Anglo feminists finally leads to the difference in philosophy regarding the status of the Anglo women's movement as a "minority" movement in the labor market and the issues of feminism and racism.

REFERENCES

1. Longeaux y Vásquez, Enriqueta. "La Chicana," *Magazín* (San Antonio), Vol. 1, 4, April 1972:66–68.

2. De Paz, José, "Letter to the Editor," *Popo Femenil*, Chicano Student Newspaper, California State University at Northridge, February, 1974: p.3.

3. Anonymous, "Chicanas Take Wrong Direction," *Popo Femenil*, Chicano Student Newspaper, Special Edition, California State University at Northridge, May, 1974: p. 13.

4. Ibid., p. 13.

5. Borjón, Patricia, "Chicana Symposium," *La Raza Newspaper*, Dec. 1969: p.5.

6. Nieto-Gómez, Anna, "Chicanas Identify!" *Hijas de Cuauhtémoc*, Vol. 1. No. 1, 1971: p. 3.

7. Borjon, op.cit., p. 5.

8. Longeaux y Vásquez, Enriqueta. "Soy Chicana Primero," *El Grito Del Norte*, April 26, 1971: p. 11.

9. Nieto-Gómez, op. cit. p. 3.

10. Cotera, Marta, "Mexican Feminism," *Magazín*, Vol.4, No. 9, September, 1973: p. 30.

11. Ibid, p. 30.

12. Ibid, P. 31.

13. Mujeres Unidas—Chicano Studies Workshop, San Fernando, October, 1971.

14. Nava, Yolanda, "Myths, the Media, Minority Groups and Women's Liberation: An Overview," Speech presented at Santa Monica College Women's Week, March 21, 1973.

15. Cotera, op.cit., p. 32.

16. Ibid, p. 33.

17. Vidal, Mirta, "Chicanas Speak Out," Pathfinder Press, 1971: p. 5.

18. Ibid. pp. 11–12.

19. Guibert, Rita, "The New Latin Wave: Interview with Octavio Paz," *Intellectual Digest*, December, 1972

22

*Chicanas and El Movimiento**

ADALJIZA SOSA RIDDELL

The Chicano[†] movement is the all-encompassing effort to, on the one hand, articulate and intensify the Chicano existence, and, on the other hand, to articulate and alleviate the suffering which has accrued to Chicanos precisely because of that exis-

[†]The term Chicano will be used throughout this chapter in the generic sense inclusive of male and female, unless otherwise specified or used in companionship with Chicana. From *Aztlán*, vol. 5, 1974: pp. 155–166.

tence. Of the important issues it faces, that of Las Chicanas is perhaps the most problematic. Ordinarily, when the issue of Chicanas is raised, whether it be by Chicanos, Chicanas, or by those outside of the Chicano context, the concern is with the status and role of Chicanas within the Movimiento in general, within specific activist organizations, and within Chicano society. This is particularly unfortunate because expression of interest in Chicanas thus inspires a defensive attitude on the part of Chicanos included within any of those categories. These defensive Chicanos are not too different from the Mexican-Americans who, in the early days of the newly articulated Movimiento defended the status quo situation either because they had invested so much time and energy into attaining a certain status within it, or because they had reasoned, along with the Anglo social scientists, that there was something innately wrong with the Mexican culture which resulted in the conditions within which the Chicano existed in the United States.

The tragedy of this situation is simply an extension of the all-too-familiar syndrome under which Chicanos have suffered. Chicanos are induced to define and describe their very being and existence in terms of external constraints and conditions imposed upon them by their colonizers or neo-colonizers. Thus, what we have is the acceptance of certain externally-imposed stereotypes about Chicanas acting as a restraint upon actions or suggestions for changes among Chicanas; actions and changes which would not conform to the stereotypes or act to destroy the stereotypes.

Many of the stereotypes have been equated with aspects of Mexican-Chicano culture. Social scientists describe la Chicana as, "ideally submissive, unworldly, and chaste," or "at the command of the husband, who [keeps] her as he would a coveted thing, free from the contacts of the world, subject to his passions, ignorant of life."[1] Social scientists also describe "machismo" as a masculinity syndrome particularly attributable to the Latin male, and thus, by extension, to the Chicano male. These attitudes are echoed by Chicanos themselves in such contexts as in the song, "The Female of Aztlán," by the Domínquez family: "your responsibility is to love, work, pray, and help . . . the male is the leader, he is iron, not mush," and by statements such as those made at the Denver Chicano Youth Liberation Conference in 1969 emphasizing the role of la Chicana in the Movimiento was to "stand behind her man."[2] More problematic, however, are the large numbers of Chicanas and Chicanos who have come to accept these descriptions and syndromes as part of their daily lives.

Obviously these stereotypes have little meaning to those who have lived the reality of the Chicano existence. Within each of our memories there is the image of a father who worked long hours, suffered to keep his family alive, united, and who struggled to maintain his dignity. Such a man had little time for concern over his "masculinity." Certainly he did not have ten children because of his machismo, but because he was a human being, poor, and without "access" to birth control. We certainly remember mothers and sisters who worked in the fields or at menial labor in addition to doing the work required at home to survive. Submissiveness, chastity, and unworldliness are luxuries of the rich and/or nearly rich. Machismo is a myth propagated by subjugators and colonizers who take pleasure in watching their subjects strike out vainly against them in order to prove themselves still capable of action.

The term macho is not applied to the Anglo-society itself. Chicanos are faced with stereotypes of themselves which are standards they are goaded into emulating and expected to achieve in order to be accepted by the dominant society. Strenuous efforts to achieve these externally imposed goals may thus result in excesses that can then be blamed, by outsiders, on cultural traits. Conversely, failure to achieve them can result in the same syndrome, that is a view of a culture as somehow inferior and inflexible. Thus, to talk about change becomes a very real threat to Chicanos who wish to retain what they have defined as their culture. The stereotypes, the acceptance of stereotypes, and the defensive postures adopted by "culturalists" become the problems for Chicanos striving to bring about some changes, rather than the problems being defined as they more adequately could be, in terms of external forces.[3] Chicano activists, in turn, tend to define the changes they wish to see in internal terms rather than external terms so that we see articles written by Chicanas with such titles as: "*Machismo No! Igualdad Si!*" [Equality, Yes!]. The clashes thus continue unabated over Chicana roles, and the Chicana continues to feel guilty about what she is, or is not, doing for her people, to and for, her man. The important point is that Chicanos have had and continue to have, very little control over their self image, cultural awareness, and self definition.

Chicanos and Chicanas and the Movimiento must now address themselves to these realities. If Chicanos act in such a way as to ignore the condition of double-op-pression under which Chicanas suffer, we must face the fact that they are not only perpetuating the stereotypes and the conditions which those stereotypes support, but they are also guilty of intensifying those conditions and their negative results. We should articulate specific proposals and goals which relate to the Chicana and should direct ourselves to relieving some of the unique burdens which the dominant society places upon Chicanas, thus separating her from her male counterparts.

Many Chicanas find the Women's Liberation movement largely irrelevant be-cause more often than not it is a move for strictly women's rights. While women's rights advocates are asking for a parity share of the "American" pie, Chicanas (and Chicanos) are asking for something other than parity. The end which is desired by Chicanas is the restoration of control over a way of life, a culture, an existence. For a Chicana to break with this goal is to break with her past, her present, and her people. For this reason, the concerns expressed by Chicanas for their own needs within the Movimiento cannot be considered a threat to the unity of the Movimiento itself.

One of the questions to which Chicanos should be addressing themselves is what goals within the Movimiento can be constructed to relate to Chicanas in partic-ular. If we recognize the external imposition of much of what defines and delineates the conditions for Chicanas, then it is obvious there must be a special effort to remove some of these unique burdens. To end the division by including Chicanas as an inte-gral, not subordinate, part of the group we call Chicanos, is to also diminish the abili-ty of outside groups to manipulate and exploit us. This should be one of the goals of the Chicano movement.

NOTES

1. The first example is from Arthur Rubel, "The Family," in John H. Burma (ed.), *Mexican Ameri-cans in the United States*, p. 214. The second example is from Alfred White, *The Apperceptive Mass of Foreign-ers as Applied to Americanization: The Mexican Group*. Thesis. University of California, 1923, p.31.

2. The Denver Chicano Youth Liberation Conference was held in 1969 and one workshop which dealt with the question of Chicanas issued the statement that Chicanas did not want to be liberat-ed. This is akin to saying that Black slaves loved their masters and worse, saying this with pride.

3. Culturalists in this chapter are defined as those who wish to preserve certain aspects of the Chi-cano existence. Sometimes the concern with preservation of cultural characteristics becomes simply a sta-tus quo position as if cultures never change. At other times, culturalists border on traditionalists, that is, those who wish to go back to an earlier era, as if in that era "culture" was somehow pure and unadulterated by contact with Anglo society. The reality for the Chicano is that the contact has already occurred and much of what was his past was no better than his present. The Chicano, then, exists in that diversity of truths which poses a problem for analysts who would like to define once and for all what Chicano consists of.

23

The New Chicana and Machismo*

Rosalie Flores

Last summer my husband and I spent the summer working with students from the Upward Bound project and most of the girls we worked with were of Mexican descent. It occurred to me then that the question of "machismo" was brought up frequently at our rap sessions. The idea that this value was questioned at all, seems interesting since for years, this has been taken for granted as a "cultural trait" and understood as part of the Latin world. Is it really another hang-up for the Chicana to contend with? In the light of the present equality movements going on does the new Chicana have a legitimate gripe?

At present the Mexican female has an identity problem, i.e., she may be a "Mexican-American" if she is an American of Mexican parentage. She may want to be called "Spanish-American" if she is from the southwestern part of the U.S. She may prefer to be a "Chicana" if she identifies with the NOW people of La Raza. It may be she finds the term of Mexican American does not describe the woman activist within la raza, aware of her cultural heritage and of herself.

Though she may be an American (born in the United States), she is reluctant to say so because she must be prepared to be questioned about it, if she is "foreign" looking. She feels she must defend her status even though her ancestors predate the pilgrims. She faces questions like "what race are you" (the human race?) or what nationality are you, and better yet, "what *are* you?" This can be particularly frustrating especially when you face the problem starting at five or six years of age, one learns quickly to be on the defensive and sensitive to how you are being accepted. She also learns that the quicker she assimilates (and if she is light enough) she can escape the hassle.

The new Chicana does not necessarily want to assimilate; she is proud of the heritage that makes her "different." A third generation Chicana finds herself reared by traditionally oriented parents, educated by middle class standards, thrown into a society whose values she is familiar with but they may go against her upbringing. She is often not educationally nor economically prepared to cope with this society. A Chicana finds she has to compete with her more liberated sisters for jobs, dates, and recognition on other levels and is further hampered by male "machismo," a phenomenon of the Latin world. She is reluctant to give up traditional folkways and Mexican values and yet, if she is to actively participate in society, she must assert herself.

Machismo is an elusive Mexican value, inbred and fostered by parental anxiety for the males in the family to show manliness, virility, honor, and courage, all honorable traits in any culture. However, when this is coupled by self doubts because of in-

*From *Regeneración*, Vol. 2, No. 4, 1975: p. 10.

equalities in our system that has the Chicano constantly having to "prove" their manhood, it is inwardly defeating. By denying Chicanos jobs, dignity and a sense of worth, it often manifests into aggressiveness and male "watchfulness" over his female counterpart. It is this that is resented by the modern Chicana. It leads to a situation where girls are "watched" over and escorted on dates. Where they can go to dances but are protected from certain people. Wives may be taken for granted and expected to wait on their spouses and sisters on their brothers. In many homes daughters are not allowed to date at all, and with modern day temptations and old country values, it is not realistic. They are left to resort to clandestine affairs, an added frustration for the Chicana female. If a female shows aggression or if she has definite opinions, she is somehow stepping into the male realm of masculinity.

Aside from not being healthy for her, it breeds generations of timid, submissive women that harbor unvented resentments. Consider the possibilities of el movimiento if it could be strengthened by energetic Chicanas asserting themselves as liberated women everywhere are doing. How refreshingly different this would be from sullen, resentful women.

It is my view that the macho male is truly a larger man if he can free his sister from the petty hang-ups and attack the real issues. He can liberate his female and still remain "macho"—for that desirous trait lies within oneself and his self esteem. If he is secure and his self-respect is not threatened, he doesn't need to prove anything. Indeed, the more liberated a woman is, the more helpful she can be to him, thus enabling him to assert his masculinity and arriving at the same end. I am not sure, if we reexamine the concept that machismo is not working against the Chicano. Take, for example, this passage from a recent book: ". . . Historically, the Mexican-Americans have been a suspect 'foreign' minority—like the Japanese Americans, during World War II they have been under great pressure to prove loyalty to the United States."[1]

When la raza makes up 10% of the total population [of the Southwest] and 20% of our boys on the front lines in Vietnam have Spanish surnames, can it be that officials know too well that "cultural trait" of machismo and make it work for them, too? The already impressive record of heroism in time of war by Mexican males speaks for itself, from the same publication: "War deaths by branch of service indicate that a great number of Mexican-Americans choose high risk duty. For example, during the first period 23.3% of all southwest Marine Corps casualties had distinctive Spanish surnames."[2]

To the free thinking Chicana, may I encourage you to assert yourself for the good of everyone "involved" and in particular la raza. It is a fact that Chicanos comprise the second largest minority in the country, and if we can stop being disengaged and apathetic about our affairs, Chicanos could create an impressive voting bloc that would upset the present situation in education and public social policy on all levels. We need to make our people aware of our community resources. Our women need to be involved in our educational system to correct gross inequities. Bi-lingual education should be stressed so that children who speak Spanish are considered exceptional instead of handicapped. Farm workers need day care centers, nurseries, and medical centers. Needed farm legislation is languishing for want of support. We can write letters to our representatives to stop the use of pesticides on the fields while our people are working. If you choose to assert yourself at home instead, do it by keeping alive your culture, language, and home arts. Teach your children; to speak Spanish well, so it does not become obsolete like the Indian languages have. You as a Chicana, are in a unique position of having two and possibly more diverse cultures at your fingertips. You can glean the best of each. You can function easily, keeping both feet firmly planted in both worlds, becoming a more versatile and interesting woman. If we let ourselves be submissive and if it is not our nature, surely this smacks of sadism and/or masochism on our part. The truly tragic part of our silence is that many of our women fail to vote, because traditionally, politics was left to the men. Most of all, we need to get rid of our guilt feelings, and fears. We do not aspire to revolution, only social change. With eighty per cent of the people affluent, we can only effect social change.

The new Chicana is into the people thing herself, she does not necessarily admire machismo, nor does she see it in the same light as her sister of Mexico. Machismo does not need to be a problem to her, it only needs a different interpretation, so that we can get to the business at hand, which is social change. Together and organized we can. Believe it!

NOTES

1. Wayne Moquin, *A Documentary of the Mexican-American* (New York: Praeger), p.373.
2. Ibid. p. 372.

24

*Sexism in the Movimiento**

ANNA NIETOGOMEZ

What is sexism? Sexism is part of the capitalist ideology which advocates male supremacist values. These values define the nature of women and men in respect to being superior or inferior. Men are defined as "naturally" stronger, more logical, and able to economically provide for others. Women are defined as "naturally" dependent, childlike, and therefore always in need of authority. Her primary functions are to secure others as a wife and a mother since her primary abilities are to conceive, procreate and nurture. Therefore, man is defined "naturally" superior to women since man is independent and aggressive, and women are dependent and passive.

Racism

The psychology of racism works in a similar manner. Racism is also a part of capitalist ideology. This set of values supports white supremacy. White supremacy measures su-

*From *La Gente de Aztlán*, Vol. 6, No. 4, 1976: p. 10.

periority according to the color and culture of people. White people are defined as more superior because they (1) are a source of authority, (2) they are wealthier, and (3) they are more aggressive. People of color, which includes both men and women, are regarded as inferior because: (1) they play subordinate roles in society, (2) they are economically dependent and constantly poor, (3) they are considered childlike, and in need of authority, and are passive. It is assumed people of color are not able to determine for themselves: "their primary ability is to have sexual intercourse, and to procreate."

Racism–Sexism

Both the Chicano and Chicana experience is affected by these two ideologies. In fact both the Chicano and Chicana experience racist-sexism. Colonized men of color are considered as inferior as women since colonized men do not have the power or authority to rule, provide economically and protect the family. Thus racist sexism considers Mexican males as either effeminate, or a "Macho," overcompensating because of his powerless position in his society.

The colonized women of color are considered more passive, dependent, and childlike than women of the superior race. Therefore white women's relationship with women of color is paternalistic and stratified.

The sexual role of the colonized woman is intensified. Her skills and abilities are centered around her sexual prowess, and procreation. It is the assumption of racist sexism that the mental ability of women of color has atrophied. Thus it is justified that "those who know better" should make decisions for her. Therefore doctors decide how many children a poor Chicana may have, hence continuing the practice of forced sterilization.

Since the colonized woman is placed in a dependent state, her primary source of support hopefully will come from her children and/or husband. But this support is sporadic, since all involved are in a social-economic and political state of dependency.

Capitalist Ideology

All institutions in a Capitalistic society perpetuate these myths of racism and sexism. The educational institution reinforce the division between people of different races, cultures, sex, and class, and define these divisions as natural.

In respect to sexism, educational, institutions reinforce the capitalistic ideology of male supremacy. Role models reinforce men acting, participating, initiating and creating. Verbs and adjectives describe women as pathetic, observing, receiving and preserving.

Male supremacy dictates that women depend on men. Therefore women must compete with other women towards developing their economic futures for better jobs, rich husbands, or poor husbands. Individualism and male superiority as opposed to collective unity are within the interests of increasing profits for the capitalists.

In many places within the Chicano movement, sexism has not been considered a valid issue. In fact often times there is conflict between Chicana feminists and cultural nationalists or so-called "marxists" who do not recognize the woman question.

Chicana feminism is in various stages of development. However, in general Chicana feminism is the recognition that women are oppressed as a group and are exploited as part of la Raza people. It is a direction to be responsible to identify and act upon the issues and needs of Chicana women. Chicana feminists are involved in understanding the nature of women's oppression in respect to such issues as child care, reproduction, economic stability, welfare rights, forced sterilization and prostitution. The Chicana feminist is involved in research analysis in order to understand how women's oppression is related to the oppression of other groups. Finally, Chicana feminism is involved in developing and initiating a means to end the oppression of women and all people.

Unfortunately, a Chicana feminist is discredited by associating her with "white" women. This sexist racism implies: (1) only white women can initiate and create change, and (2) all women who speak out against sexism have the same analysis as to the cause and resolution of the issue. This is far from true. Feminist women's politics represent conservative, liberal, radical, and leftist politics. It is clear that this ignorant criticism encourages lack of support to Chicanas in their struggle for liberation. Thus, an effort to integrate the issues of Chicanas with the established "legitimate" people's issues are thwarted. Ironically women are accused of dividing the movement when their goals are to fight the effects of sexism and unite with everyone.

In organizations where cultural nationalism is extremely strong, Chicana feminists experience intense harassment and ostracism.

Very generally, cultural nationalism advocates group survival through group solidarity, revival of the culture and the resurgence of the pride and worth of people belonging to a particular group. In the case of Chicano nationalism racism is identified as the issue and cause of oppression. The economic system of capitalism is not always addressed as the focus of change.

Acknowledging a conspiracy of white supremacy to control and exploit the people, group survival is defined by preserving the language, music, folklore, folk medicine, customs, and history. In addition an effort is directed to increasing their political and social participation to all institutions in order to increase economic and educational opportunities. The base of attack to end oppression is to attack racism. Chicano representation in all socio-economic classes seems to be the goal.

The Chicana feminist comes into conflict if she feels the movement is an effort to secure male privilege for men. She cannot support male privilege at the same time. All privileges must be eradicated. Otherwise it would seem in her interest to fight for female privilege. However, the Chicana feminist does not want to oppress, therefore she is forced to investigate beyond racism and sexism in order to understand the nature of the internal struggle within the movement. Marxist-Leninist ideology and women's history of socialist countries offer a clear analysis as to the function and division of the sex roles and of racism. However, the struggle to make a clear analysis has just begun. The Chicana must apply this analysis to her conditions. If there is not sufficient data to provide a historical perspective then the struggle to develop becomes more intense.

At the same time, some cultural nationalists criticize Chicanas' activities as divisive. Three priorities are constantly emphasized. Support "your" men, maintain traditional roles, and preserve the culture. This is offered as a formula for unity and success within the movement. Women are told to wait until the revolution is over before they deal with the women's question.

Many times cultural nationalism promotes paternalism. In return for services and support people are reminded to be grateful for the progress made.

Criticism and new ideas are controlled and suppressed for fear of losing existing benefits. Eventually red baiting tactics are used to preserve group unity. An appeal to the emotions, fears, prejudices, and lack of information, is used to rally threatened isolated groups. Issues or people are discredited in associating them with something undesirable.

In respect to Chicana feminists, the credibility is reduced when they are associated with white women. They are called reactionaries and therefore a threat to the group's survival.

For example, if Chicana classes and feminism are defined as reactionary elements in Chicano Studies, students will not take the classes and continue to remain ignorant on the women's question.

Feminists are harassed and ridiculed as man-haters and degenerates. Many times these women become alienated from the group. Rather than relying on emotion in order to do the right thing, a continual process of investigation, research, discussion, and analysis should be a means of defining positions and action. Conflict should be seen as a struggle to develop.

In the last seven years women involved in discussing and applying the women's question have been ostracized, isolated, and ignored. It is time to evaluate this historical trend. It is time for all to study the women's question and to develop an analysis which is applicable to the Chicana and Chicano. Therefore, if there are any criticisms in respect to this presentation, do not hold it against me. Instead, let us study the issues together—criticism can be a seed to growth.

25

*The Role of the Chicana within the Student Movement**

SONIA A. LÓPEZ

Introduction

Women have traditionally been confined to the home to maintain the family structure. This does not negate that at the same time women have also been part of the labor force. But, their role as laborers has simply been considered a supplement to that of men. Yet whether in the fields or factories, professional or skilled occupations, women have worked by the side of their husbands and sons. And just as their contribution to the labor force has been neglected, their importance in other social organizations has also been, as a general rule, minimized.

Within the Chicano movement, women have also participated in the struggle

*From *Essays on La Mujer* (Los Angeles: UCLA. Chicano Studies Center, 1977: pp. 16–29).

alongside the men. However, Chicanas were active from the inception of the movement, they were generally relegated to traditional roles played by women in society. It was the realization of this oppressive situation and their secondary roles within the movement which led many Chicanas to initiate a process by which they could begin to resolve the inconsistencies between male/female roles.

To examine the political development of Chicanas within the Chicano student movement and the subsequent formation of Chicana groups and organizations throughout the Southwest, is the intent of this paper. But to understand the historical content it is essential that we first review briefly the historical development of the Chicano student movement itself, before proceeding with the specific analysis.

The Chicano Movement

Throughout the 1960s the Chicano population, as the second largest minority within the United States, continued to provide the main source of cheap labor in the Southwest, not only in the urban centers where Chicanos worked in factories and canneries, but also in agribusiness. The relative prosperity created by the production of war material in the middle of the 1960s brought more comforts to the middle class, and deepened the sharp contrasting differences between middle class neighborhoods and the barrios and ghettos of Chicanos, Blacks, and other minorities.

The stimulus of militancy within the black movement in the United States, together with the socioeconomic and political factors, provided conditions which gave rise to the Chicano movement. Though the phenomenon of Chicano organizations was not new, the Chicano movement of the 1960s represented a break with the traditional approach towards resolving the problems facing Chicanos. At this time, confrontation tactics and direct action were substituted for the integrationist politics of the 1940s and 1950s.

The Chicano student movement, inspired by the militancy of the black movement and political activities of Chicanos in the barrios and agriculture fields, directed their political activity towards forming student organizations. Some of the these were: MASC, MAYA, united Mexican-American students, Mexican-American youth organization and PASO. The issues they raised were basically of the same nature as those of Chicano community groups and politicians. They centered around police brutality, poor housing, unemployment, poor health care services and substandard education. However, their main emphasis was on education for Chicanos, and their activity revolved around the institutionalization of Chicano studies and supportive service programs for Chicano college students.

A major turning point in the Chicano student movement in California came in the Spring of 1969 with the convocation of a statewide student conference in Santa Barbara. At this conference, Chicano students, faculty, administrators, and community representatives formulated *El Plan de Santa Bárbara*, a plan based on unity of will to demand and implement programs necessary for Chicanos in institutions of higher education. According to *El Plan de Santa Bárbara*, these programs would begin the process of self-determination and liberation for the Chicano.

In retrospect, though cultural nationalism resulted from the general denial of the Chicano's historical and cultural heritage contributions, it becomes a common base for Chicano groups and organizations with diverse goals and objectives. It succeeded in obtaining some concessions in school integration and affirmative action programs. But cultural nationalism, with its limited analysis, also led to the containment and cooptation of the movement.

Thus, the years 1968 to 1970 can be viewed as the "peak" years of the Chicano student movement due to many activities occurring at that time. Conferences, marches, sit-ins, demonstrations, development of Chicano studies departments, and other services for Chicanos at the colleges and universities were on the upswing. However, certain questions are posed as the objectives and outcome of these activities and the concessions given, both in the educational institutions and in the barrios. Were these programs initiated to bring about concrete changes in the economic status of Chicanos? Did they push class consciousness and prepare the way for genuine revolutionary change? To what degree have they succeeded in solving the problems within the Chicano communities? Were these activities a liberating force within the community and university? What kinds of changes were they designed for?

It is true that at the time many involved in the Chicano student movement viewed it as revolutionary. Chicanos thought self-determination could be achieved by understanding institutionalized racism and taking systematic steps to combat it. However, under close examination and by keeping the precious questions in mind, several points can be seen. Though some changes did occur in the areas of awareness of racism among the general public and the revival of cultural pride for certain sectors of the Chicano community, these activities and programs, local, state, or federally-funded, have been successful in appeasing the Chicano community, especially the one-time militant element, by creating token social service programs and a few high-paying jobs. Mexican communities still have a high rate of drug abuse, poverty, unemployment, low quality health care, low educational achievement, and no political power.

As with other subordinate groups in the country, Chicanos are burdened with racist policies. Like racism, sex too has been used as a basis for dividing working class men and women; for example, women have traditionally received lower pay than men for doing the same job. Women have been channeled into the domestic sphere, where they serve as laborers. During the industrial revolution, women were incorporated into the industrial labor force, often times performing the same type of work they performed in the home. These included work in food-processing, clothing, and textile manufacturing. But minority women, because of their sex and ethnic origin, are the lowest paid sector of the working class.

As active participants of the Chicano movement, on campuses Chicanas also became involved in the struggles for programs and recruitment of Chicano students, faculty, and staff. However, within movement activities and responsibilities, Chicanas generally continued to fill the traditional roles assigned them within the Mexican culture and the American-Anglo society. A woman's role has traditionally been defined in terms of her biological reproduction capacity, which is also the reproduction of the labor force, her role in the education and care of children and her role in the care of the sick and the elderly.

The ideal women within the Mexican culture has been defined as faithful, passive and obedient. Because these traditionally defined female roles continued to exist, Chicano student organizations were male dominated. Meetings were conducted as if the goal of ending oppression of Chicanos could only be initiated and carried out by men.

The lack of Chicana participation in leadership roles has its origin in a socialization process which asserts that men are "naturally" superior to women. Being exposed to the same socialization process both men and women give credibility to this belief system, until experience lead to the realization of the mutual oppressiveness of the situation. This idea is reinforced and perpetuated by either formal or informal institutions in this society, and are divided into the following areas:

1. The family structure in the traditional Chicano household is headed by the husband, who exercises authority. He is the main provider in the family, consequently, the economic situation of the woman is directly related to her dependency on him. In Mexican culture, the role of the Mexicana/Chicana, whether single or married, has been to serve her family, particularly the men: her father, brothers, husband, and sons. In short, the role of Chicana *abuelitas* [grandmothers] mothers, and *tías* [aunts], with few exceptions, has been to bear children, rear them, and be good wives.
2. Religious institutions and Christian ideology, with its tales of Adam and Eve, the Virgin Mary and reference to sex roles in the Bible, has served to maintain and perpetuate women's inferior position. The Catholic Church, in particular, has been influential in cultivating this aspect of the Mexican culture and accordingly has relegated women to an inferior status.
3. In educational institutions women have historically been geared towards "feminine study courses," home economics and clerical or secretarial classes, which prepare women for domestic and subservient work; professional careers are stressed for men. These attitudes manifest themselves in the Mexican culture in such common sayings as the following: "*Para que quieres educarte si de nada te va a servir cuando te cases.*" ["Why do you want to educate yourself if it won't be any use to you when you get married?"]
4. In legal institutions women have been and continue to be discriminated against in property ownership, divorce, employment, and welfare laws.

These concepts and attitudes concerning the roles of women, and particularly Chicanas, prevailed and were reinforced in the Chicano student movement. In the organizing of conferences, symposiums, meetings, and publications of newspapers, and magazines, Chicanas usually provided their invisible labor by being the cooks, secretaries, and janitors. Oftentimes a Chicana's recognition was established by being the wife, girlfriend, or party mate of a "heavy." But as Chicanas became more politically aware, they began to question assigned roles on the basis of sexuality in the Mexican culture and in the movement.

As early as the Spring of 1969, at the Chicano Youth Conference held in Denver, Colorado, a few vocal Chicana activists raised the issue of the traditional role of the Chicana in the Movement and how it limited her capabilities and her development. However, the majority of the Chicanas participating in the workshop which discussed the role of the Chicana, did not feel the same. One Chicana observed that, "when the time came for the workshop report to the full conference, the only thing that the representative had to say was this—"It was the consensus of the group that the Chicana woman does not want to be liberated."[1]

This outcome can be viewed in two ways; either the majority of Chicanas attending the conference did not see or understand the contradiction of the sexual roles between Chicanas and Chicanos, or they simply did not want to alienate the men.

This blatant internal contradiction, between the professed goal of liberation from oppression and the fact that within the Chicano student movement Chicanas were relegated to traditional roles, became more obvious. A lack of Chicana leadership existed in student organizations, Chicano studies departments, and in administration of Raza programs. Their assignments were clerical in nature in the organizations, and domestic in the household of movement men.

By 1970, Chicanas began to form groups on campuses in order to analyze, and propose solutions to the problems they encountered as women involved in a political movement. Such groups as "la Chicanas" from San Diego State University, and "*Hijas de Cuauhtémoc*" from Long Beach State University, were among the first groups to appear. Not all Chicanas on the campuses nor in the Movimiento Estudiantil Chicano de Aztlán (M.E.Ch.A) participated in these groups. This may be attributed to the following factors:

1. Lack of political awareness to perceive the oppressed status of Chicanas and the working class women as a distinct group within the social, economic and political structure;
2. Fear of being labeled a "*vendida*" [sell-out] if she rejected the traditional role of the Mexicana;
3. The idea that supporting the "women's movement," which consisted mainly of white middle-class women, meant supporting a separatist and reformist movement which saw "men" as the enemy, and had as its main goal becoming part of the system, to gain equality in jobs;
4. Reaction of many men in the movement towards Chicana groups was that they, the Chicanas, were trying to divide the movement.

The contradictions of the role of "la mujer" in the movement, were crystallized at the First National Chicana Conference held in Houston, Texas in May 1971, where more than 600 Chicanas from 23 states participated. After two days of forums and dialogue, the four main workshops produced the following resolutions:

1. Sex and the Chicana—That free legal abortions and birth control in the Chicano community be provided and controlled by Chicanas and that double standards be eliminated.
2. Choices for Chicanas in education and occupation—That educational institutions encourage Chicanas towards pursuing higher education.
3. Marriage, Chicana Style—That the traditional role of the Chicana within the marriage context no longer be acceptable due to her involvement in the movement. In order to facilitate and encourage Chicana involvement and provide services for working Chicanas, child care centers should be promoted and established in the Chicano communities.
4. Religion—That as *mujeres de la Raza* [women of the Raza], Chicanas recognize the Catholic Church as an oppressive institutions and oppose any institutionalized religion.[2]

The purpose of these resolutions was to serve as guidelines for workshops, seminars, groups, and organizations relevant to the immediate needs of Chicanas. However, about half the women involved in the conference did not support the resolutions. This group felt that Chicanas had no business sponsoring a Chicana conference with the help of the Young Women's Christian Association (YWCA), considered by them to be a racist organization, or discussing "Chicanos oppressing Chicanas." They felt that emphasis should be placed on issues which revealed that "our enemy is the "gavacho" [whites] and not the "macho" and stressed work in prison, protesting the Vietnam War, denouncement of immigration laws, and works with the farm workers' struggle. Accordingly they said, if Chicanas are to be politically involved, this involvement must not detract from their family commitment. Chicanas must then make an extra effort to do both jobs, in the home and in the movement. This culminated in a split with half the women that opposed the resolutions leaving the conference to meet in a nearby park.

The differences that developed at the First National Chicanas Conference were indicative of those evolving in the Chicano student movement as a whole, but not yet clearly defined. Although there were many Chicanos and Chicanas who prioritized issues such as prison reform and immigration, there were also those who gave more importance to taking a critical and analytical look at the internal contradictions of the Chicano movement. Those contradictions which were becoming more obvious were:

1. Unclear objectives and goals—some groups were pushing for institutional changes while others were advocating separate institutions for and by Chicanos. This was an outgrowth of having only a superficial analysis of problems facing Chicanos which made it impossible to create concrete alternative measures consistent to a given political direction. It became clear that the Chicano student movement was willing to deal with problems, events, and issues spontaneously. It would attack problems without analyzing the interrelated factors of the situation and its implications.
2. Lack of practice in community involvement although spoken of frequently. Practice is the involvement of an individual or a group of individuals in direct action to change given objective conditions.
3. Present was the romantic notion in the Chicano student movement, as expressed in an idealization of colleges and universities as places of revolutionary activity. This was a contradiction in reality, given the oppressive nature of the institutions themselves.
4. Opportunism became prevalent in cases where Chicanos used the movement for their own socioeconomic and political advancement.
5. Existence of a hierarchy within the movement which gave Chicano men superior status over Chicana women, while at the same time espousing liberation rhetoric.

Because the Chicana was involved in the Chicano student movement from the beginning, even though she was not visible and little credited for her efforts at that point, we cannot isolate her political development from that of the Chicano student movement itself. Two trends in her development were evident as early as 1971. The split was between those Chicanas who did not see the importance of dealing with sexual contradictions as they existed between Chicanas and Chicanos in the movement. Rather, they concerned themselves with "movement issues," and in maintaining and perpetuating the traditional roles, such as seeking approval from males and being passive. These attitudes connote the "ideal Chicana."

The other Chicanas saw the need to organize Chicana groups due to the inconsistencies between liberation rhetoric of the movement and the reality as it existed for Chicanas within the movement—that of being exploited by their own people for their labor and sexuality.

The Chicanas who voiced their discontent with the organizations and with male leadership were often labeled as "women's libbers," and "lesbians." This served to isolate and discredit them, a method practiced both covertly and overtly. In the more politically advanced M.E.Ch.A. organizations, lip service to Chicana demands and needs were given, and a "selected few" Chicanas were given leadership positions in organizations, boards, and committees. Yet in practice the men continued to be the "*jefes*" [bosses] in decision making policies and political direction. Chicanas who belonged to Chicana groups came to be seen as a clique by those Chicanas who were not involved in any type of Chicana awareness process. This division, more often than not, was used by those men who felt their "machismo" threatened, pitting one group against the other. This situation often created a breakdown of communication among women in the organizations. It hindered their working together as *compañeras* [sisters]. A saying, "*Las Chicanas con pantalones*," [The Chicanas with pants] was often used to ridicule and tease Chicana activists. Often, even though they contributed much of their time and labor, these Chicanas were not fully accepted into organizations. This caused many Chicanas to drop out of the M.E.Ch.A. organizations. The formation of Chicana groups, therefore, became the only vehicle through which some Chicana activists could receive moral and political support. At Long Beach State University, for example, a Chicana group by the name of Hijas de Cuauthémoc, separated from the M.E.Ch.A. organization. They not only created support for Chicana activists, but also organized other Chicanas in the struggle of their people. In this particular case, some of the male members of the M.E.Ch.A. organization reacted to the formation of the women's organization by conducting a symbolic funeral to make their dissatisfaction known.

The period 1970 to 1972 can be considered the years in which Chicana awareness emerged. This resulted not only in Chicana campus groups, such as those formed at Fresno State College, San Diego State University, Long Beach State University, and Stanford University, but also Community based groups and organizations. Some of these were Comisión Femenil Mexicana Nacional, National Chicana Political Caucus, and MARA (Chicana organization at California Institute for Women). These groups and organizations were instrumental in organizing and sponsoring local, regional, statewide, and national meetings and conferences. These conferences included the First National Chicanas Conference held in the Spring of 1971 in Houston, Texas; the Chicana Regional Conference held in the Fall of 1972 at Whittier, California; La Conferencia Femenil held in the Spring of 1972 in Sacramento, California; and a few programs and projects for barrio women, such as the Chicana Service Action Center in Los Angeles.

In looking at the development of Chicana awareness, one must keep in mind that this phenomenon occurred mainly among a small percentage of the Chicana women who were involved in the Chicano student movement. It was their direct participation in the movement that made them aware of the Chicanas' double oppression. Chicana activists channeled their efforts in working towards educational reform, such as establishing Chicana classes, Chicana counselors and Chicana teachers. It was felt that if Chicana women had the proper role models and classroom courses, eventual solutions to many of the socioeconomic problems confronting them could be found. Chicana activists, therefore, failed to direct their energies in educating and organizing the sector of Chicanas most oppressed and exploited; those Chicanas in the fields, factories, and service jobs. This is not to say that the need for Chicana models and classes is not important, as is the need for Chicano Studies and bilingual-bicultural education. But these innovations in themselves did not change the social conditions for Chicanos.

If Chicanas are committed to bringing about social change not only for their people, but for all oppressed people in a class society, they must begin to analyze objectively existing conditions that give rise to exploitation, poverty, and misery. To do this they need to see class society as the basic problem. They need to do a great deal of political studying together, in groups, in order to develop the political understanding necessary to correctly guide organizing in their work places and communities.

NOTES

1. Enriqueta Longeaux y Vásquez, in *Sisterhood is Powerful* (New York: Vintage Book, 1970), p. 379.
2. *La Verdad*, "National Chicanas Conference," (San Diego, 1971) p. 15

ANALYZING THE DYNAMICS OF CHICANA OPPRESSION

Introduction

In addition to issues related to sexism that Chicana feminists faced both within Mexican-American culture and within the Chicano Movement, they also had to contend with a variety of additional gender-related issues as the following essays illustrate.

These documents note, for example, that Chicanas as a whole bore the brunt of family life including the school problems of their children. Due to language differences, Chicanas often encountered particular problems and obstacles with institutions such as the welfare system and the legal system. Moreover, Chicanas faced physical problems such as high mortality rates during childbirth and in some cases were subjected without their knowledge to experiments in birth control such as nonconsensual sterilizations. Caught between a traditional Mexican-American culture and the lack of proper health care, Chicanas possessed little control over their own bodies.

As these essays indicate, Chicanas faced these particular problems at the same time that many of them confronted additional ones at the workplace. Despite prevailing stereotypes that suggested that Mexican-American women were predominately bound to the home, in fact many of them worked in the paid labor force to increase the family income. Although in the labor force, Chicanas received lower wages than Chicano men and were restricted to limited employment opportunities usually within the service sector. Chicanas also experienced higher rates of unemployment and less access to education.

Yet women often had little choice but to work as the number of female-headed households increased as did the poverty rates associated with such households. Employment discrimination, as Linda Aquilar stresses in her essay, made it extremely difficult for Chicanas to escape a cycle of low-paying menial jobs. According to Aquilar, although no data is cited, Chicano employers were even more likely to discriminate against Chicana employees because, Aquilar alleged, Chicano employers were more culturally threatened by Chicanas being in the labor force.

In their struggle to overcome the particular problems faced by Mexican-American women, Chicana feminists sought encouragement and inspiration from a history and tradition of strong women in their culture including that of the Pre-Columbian past. Revising history and mythology to suit contemporary ideological needs, Chicana feminists such as Adelaida R. Del Castillo proposed that Chicanas identify with historical figures such as Doña Marina (La Malinche) the native princess who assisted Hernán Cortés in his conquest of the Aztec Empire. Rather than the traitor that she is portrayed as in Mexican history, Doña Marina should now be appropriated or resignified as an assertive and independent female figure who herself was struggling against Aztec tyranny.

Besides revising history, Chicanas also sought a voice in the movement whereby they could articulate their own issues. One way of gaining a voice was by publishing their own newspapers and newsletters as well as instituting classes in Chicano Studies programs concerning Chicanas.

Crusade for Justice, Denver Youth Conference, early 1970s. Courtesy Raul Ruiz, *La Verdad* magazine, Los Angeles, California.

Mujer (1971)

Mujer, piel canela, ojos negros,
Mujer, que eres México,
Mujer, madre, esposa, trabajadora,
Mujer que has sufrido a las manos del
      gabacho, y peor, a las manos de tu hombre.
Mujer, valiente y luchadora que nunca has
      dejado el lado de tu hombre,
Mujer Chicana, eres tu la espina de nuestra
Raza,
Mujer Chicana has perdurado las injusticias
de
      los hombres,
!Despierta!
Despierta mujer, y lucha por tu libertad.

Leticia Hernández

Mujer (1972)

Mujer, since I can remember you have suffered with eight muchachos
You have cooked day in and day out. You know no peace.
Your older muchachos go out and leave you with the chiquitos.
You have lost weight. The shine in you hair is gone. You smile
      no more.
You were cheated out of life since your hombre was taken to the
cold
      war overseas.
Mujer you never complained: you never even once raised your
      voice in protest.
Why then, do you weep in silence?

Mary Helen Vigil

26

¡Despierten Hermanas!
The Women of La Raza—Part II*

ENRIQUETA LONGEAUX VASQUEZ

When we look at and talk about the Raza woman, we have to really think seriously and realize that we are dealing with a real mixed-up side of the social battle. We must know that we again have a fairy tale to live with. How many times have we heard reference made to the "squaw" of the family? The woman has been stereotyped as a servant to the man and the Raza has come to accept this as a great *tradition*.

Well, Compadre after doing some thinking and reading, I'll have to blow up that little dream bubble for us. It seems that before the Europeans came to the Americas, our highly cultured Indian woman usually held an honored position in the "primitive" society in which she lived. She was mistress of the home and took full part in tribal elections. The position of the woman was not only free, but honorable. She was a strong laborer, a good mechanic, a good craftsman, a trapper, a doctor, a preacher and, if need be, a leader. It seems that among the so-called *savage* people of this continent, women held a degree of political influence never equalled in any *civilized* nation. The woman of the Aztecs was far superior to that of Spain, then and now. And in Oaxaca, Mexico, the Mayan woman to this day is equal to her man. As a matter of fact if there is some political issue at hand, it is the woman you will see *protesting*. They won't take anything lying down. They even tell the government where to go.

So, after all of this, it looks to me as if this continent had a highly *civilized* way of life (and that is probably why the European could not live up to it). The Europeans certainly *destroyed* a good thing. ¿Que no? And now we talk of the tradition of the woman and say, "No, we must not change the role of the woman, the woman must remain totally dominated in order to keep this tradition." Let's take another look at this family "tradition" the men say we have.

Remember we are Mestizos, a people of Spanish fathers and Indian mothers. Male domination over the woman is a thing of Spain and Europe. Destroying the Indian woman's freedom was necessary in order to conquer and destroy the Indian. It was also a tool used to make subject-wives of the Indian woman, who would have to submit to a European way of life.

When we look at all of this and see our real history and heritage, we come to realize that a strong Raza woman is inevitable. If our Raza is to survive and endure, it seems that we have to prepare the woman once again to live a strong role in relation to her people. We can expect to see the Raza woman stand up and take more and

*From *El Grito del Norte*, Vol. 2, No. 10, July 26, 1969: p. 3.

more action in matters, for it is in doing this that she will be fulfilling the deep thirst of our Indian blood. Our Raza woman will take her place in the social and cultural struggle and this will be nothing new to her, it will be as natural as giving birth.

The woman of the Raza is becoming more and more aware and has been learning in her silent way. She has been watching her people suffer. She is watching her culture being raped. We see that our families are being destroyed, not only as families but also because our children are growing up without the human values we know are ours. We see many a Raza woman having to confront the Anglo world alone and trying to raise a family. She hasn't quite figured it out, but she knows that something is wrong.

Look at the Reform Schools

And why should we be concerned? In order to see just one of the problems of our young people, we have but to look at the reform schools. For example, in the state of Colorado where the Raza is 10% of the population, three reformatories have an average of 62% Raza. That's way over our population percentage, no? The biggest percentage of the youths there come from broken homes. This alone, *hermanos*, means that there is a problem and that, my dear sisters, we are bearing the brunt of raising our families in a barbarous society.

One of the things that we Raza women must do is to see just what it is that our families have to contend with, and what we can do to prepare them for facing up to life. We must make them strong and unafraid in today's world. We must first talk to our children and examine just what it is that they are learning in school. I believe that one of the big problems we will find is the racism in education. We know that in school they are not given a culture that they can identify with. They are not taught who they are. Our way of thinking and our human values are, as a matter of fact, discouraged. Our own children are wandering away from Raza culture and this is mostly because they have been educated to feel inferior. Our own history books in the schools tend to wipe us out as a people. Our children don't know themselves. It is our obligation and responsibility to teach and show them who and what they really are. We must realize that when educators speak of equality, it is in law and in writing, but not in practice. And worse yet, what is being taught to our children is that the Americano as well as their history is superior and infallible. This is totally inhuman, and if you really want to see what this attitude does to people, just go to a foreign country and see the behavior of the American wherever he goes. And listen to what people from other countries feel about the *gringo*.

Teach the Children to Question

At home we do not only have to learn what the family is being taught, we must teach them to question these things in order to learn. We have to teach them to discuss things, not just sit in the classrooms and accept everything as the "ulitmate truth." They have to learn to relate to the teachers as fellow humans, humans who also have to learn. And we as women have to support our children in the classroom, go to school and question too. Remember the teachers and schools are there to *serve* you. You tell them what you think should be taught. Everywhere that our families walk the path of life, we must question the things of man. The only thing in life that we have to accept and take our place in harmony with is *nature* and its *creator*.

Justice is another thing that we have to deal with when raising our families. Go to the courtrooms with the family now and then, and see what really goes on. You are bound to learn that if you have money, there is very little that you can't pay your way out of. The poor Raza can't afford to get himself [herself] out of trouble. There are double standards in our laws and don't you for one minute doubt it. Raza is the loser. Jails and other penal institutions swell with Raza and we don't even question *why*.

These are but a few of the things that we have to contend with in the matter of raising the family. Now Chicanos, we must look at the things that are going to give us strength in raising our families. If we are to teach our families something of what is *really* going on with the Raza, we have to look around and hope to find a strong and lasting bond for our people. We must look and see what is going on with the people. We have to start thinking about the land grant struggle. The Alianza [New Mexico Land Grant Organization] has been in existence for many many years. Let's look at some of its claims and see what they are. The Crusade for Justice in Denver is confronting the educational system, the court system, the politicians and all the establishment and making them answer some questions. They are teaching old schools some things they can't seem to find in books. How to *think* for instance.

Let's Talk to Each Other

And what about César Chávez in California? What's the history of the campesino and what is he fighting for? These are our people too. And in Texas our brothers and sisters have a struggle. Just what is this all about? What is happening to our people? We feel what is happening, let's learn about it and let's start speaking up. Let's talk to each other and let's not be afraid to be heard.

We women must learn to function again like full humans, as did our ancestors. We are the ones that feel the deep *amor y dolor [love and pain]* for our people. I know many women who would give their lives for their Raza. Let's look around and see where we can give the most and where we are needed. And then let's plunge right into action. Let's hold our head high and proud and walk in beauty.

27

*Introduction to Encuentro Femenil**

THE EDITORS

Over the years (350) there has been an acute absence of literature concerning the Chicana woman. This vacuum of literature has perpetuated myths and in effect led people to believe that Chicanas have played no significant role in society other than the impression that the Mexican woman has nothing to say and/or she does not care to participate in society. Like most assumptions, these implications are not true. The search for Chicana ideas has created a great demand for information on the Chicana question, but mass publication and distribution of her ideas has not occurred.

Over the past three years there has been a continuous effort to maintain some means of communication about Chicana women. Special editions of Chicano press newspapers, magazines, and radio programs have dealt with the Chicana question sporadically.

The most outstanding of these special Chicana publications have been *El Grito Del Norte* and *La Regeneración*. *El Grito Del Norte* from Española, New Mexico, was organized by Pepita Martínez. Her newspaper was one of the first to report what Chicanas were doing in the areas of welfare, *las pintas* [prisoners], historical Mexican feminism, birth control and the politics of male oriented consumerism. *Regeneración*, a journal organized by Francisca Flores, has devoted two important issues to the Chicana question. In *Regeneración*, an up and coming writer, Ms. Sylvia Delgado, has given valuable insight to the question of abortion and mutual sexual responsibility towards birth control. This publication also documents the controversial National Chicana Conference in Houston (1971), the Farah [El Paso Texas, 1972-74] strikers as well as focusing on child care, employment and welfare.

Two newsletters, the *Comisión Femenil Mexicana (CFM)* and the *Chicana Service Action Center (CSAC)* Newsletter were used as instruments to describe what Chicanas are doing in Los Angeles and to inform women about their employment situation. The Chicana Service Action Center (CSAC) is a first time employment referral and counseling center for Spanish Speaking women. The Chicana Service Action Center is sponsored by the Comisión Femenil Mexicana (CFM), a National Chicana/Mexicana organization. The Center publishes and disseminates the *CSAC Newsletter*, which primarily contains information on employment related issues such as: child care, status of the Chicana in the labor market, job opportunities, legislation and related publications. The *CFM Newsletter* (Comisión Femenil Mexicana) is primarily a chronological historical description of the development of the first statewide Chicana organization, Comisión Femenil Mexicana Nacional. Information also deals with em-

*From *Encuentro Femenil*, Vol. 1, No. 2, 1973: pp. 3–7.

ployment related issues such as child care, status of the Chicana in job-openings, legislation and women's publications.

Dorinda Moreno Gladden and the Raza Women's class at California State University at San Francisco has compiled a book of articles, *La Mujer En Pie de La Lucha*. The articles include Luchadoras, Political prisoners, Guerrilleras, and historical liberation movement mujeres, with an overview of women involved in present day community issues.

Another student group, Hijas de Cuauhtémoc, initiated and implemented one of the first feminist newspapers focusing on "la Chicana." Realizing the only alternatives available to most of the women were jobs as clerical workers, hostesses, and cooks for fundraisers, the *Hijas de Cuauhtémoc Newspaper* served as a vehicle to help make Chicanas aware of their leadership potential.

Critical that only one-third of the college recruitment of Chicanas were women in 1969 and 1970, because more than half of these women dropped out before their junior year in college, "las Mujeres" decided to investigate into the low retention rate of Chicanas in higher education. They discovered two important facts related to the drop-out rate of Chicanas on the college campus. First, Chicanas did not fail because of academic deficiencies; in fact, Chicanas reflected high grade point average over-all. Second, nebulous support from faculty, peer group, counselors, as well as from the family, provided little psychological reinforcement for the Chicana to stay in college. The new Chicana advocates felt is was their mutual responsibility to provide a strong positive reinforcement to stay in school. Finally, pregnancy, welfare, motherhood, marriage, and social pressure were identified as the major reasons given for dropping out of school. If people believed that motherhood was the Chicana's main purpose in life they would encourage her to marry an educated Chicano, but not to necessarily educate herself. And pregnancy does not always lead to financial security. However, lack of education, pregnancy, and financial insecurity do lead most women to low paying jobs and/or to the welfare department.

In 1969, there was a great eagerness to experience the first Chicano studies classes. The women were very excited to learn about their heritage both as Chicanos and as mujeres. However, the women were very disappointed to discover that neither Chicano history, Mexican history, nor Chicano literature included any measurable material on the mujer. La mujer either had a baby in her arms or a rifle in her hand or both. But few dealt with the identity of la mujer in the family, or even really knew who was "La Adelita." They were merely symbols for her to look towards, and if she was any Chicana at all, the spirit of either model was expected to appear instinctively.

Stumbling over some Mexican history books in search of knowledge about the women, the Chicanas discovered that women's suffrage was not a social phenomenon unique to the Anglo women of the United States. There were actually many groups of women involved in what was identified as "Mexican Feminism." Inspired and reassured that "speaking out" was not alien to the Chicana's culture, las Mujeres de Longo [Long Beach] named themselves after a Mexican feminist press organization, active in the Revolution of 1910, Hijas de Cuauhtémoc.

The goal of Hijas de Cuauhtémoc was to inform the Chicana about herself through history, by reporting Chicanas' political activities in the communities, and by educating her to the socioeconomic condition that she must deal with as a woman in a minority culture of an oppressive society. In addition, the newspaper reflected an unrecognized resource-Chicana minds, Chicana creativity, Chicana art, Chicana action, and Chicana obligations. In other words, the newspaper would become a concrete and positive example of combining women's ability and Chicano know-how—Chicana style or more appropriately described as *Chicana power*!

In March, 1971, the first issue of *Hijas de Cuauhtémoc* was received with mixed feelings. Locally most people from the different campuses ignored twelve pages of hard work and focused negatively on a provocative article called "Macho Attitudes." The other three-fourths of the newspaper concerned Chicana history, Chicana education, Chicanas in the *Pinta* [prison], Chicana activists in the community, Chicana poetry, and socio-sexual problems in Chicano organizations and in the family. The over-all response nationally to the newspaper seemed to indicate that other Chicanas were excited to know their hermanas were speaking out and becoming visible.

The second issue of *Hijas de Cuauhtémoc* was designed to report the ideas of Chicanas of 1970. Sponsoring the Los Angeles Regional Chicana Conference, Hijas were able to document Chicanas' attitudes towards religion, the feelings about the men's role in the Chicano movement, and changing ideas towards the value of sex. It was the feeling of Hijas that Chicanas all over the U.S. were desperate to know what these Chicanas were saying. And it was the intention of Hijas De Cuauhtémoc to bring as many Chicana ideas from California to the first National Chicana Conference held in Houston, May 1971.

Of all the ideas which came out of the National Chicana Conference, three impressed Hijas most. Chicanas expressed a dire need to establish a national means of communication among women. This communication system would strengthen a new feeling of *"Hermanidad"* (sisterhood) among Chicanas. This communication system and the new philosophy of *hermanidad* would motivate Chicanas to identify, understand and work against the racist and sexist economic problems adversely affecting the Chicana and her people. Reflecting the spirit of the Conference, the third issue of *Hijas De Cuauhtémoc* presented the "Philosophy of *Hermanidad*." Other topics presented in the same issue included Chicana identity in the Chicano movement, Chicana Studies and its responsibilities to the Chicana, and a biography of Sor Juana Inez de la Cruz. In addition to these topics, *Hijas* provided a referral guide directing Chicanas to different kinds of social services for women in the community.

The women of *Hijas De Cuauhtémoc Newspaper* realized the demand to develop more information concerning the Chicanas was so vital that a more in-depth means of writing needed to be developed. As more and more Chicanas became very involved in the Chicano movement, they seemed to search more intensively for greater encompassing identity. Everyone seemed to be anxiously thirsty to know what Chicanas were thinking and doing. They wanted to know how Chicanas were different from other women.

As a result, Hijas de Cuauhtémoc created a Chicana publishing organization, designed to relate the Chicana feminist experience through the journal, *Encuentro Femenil*.

Encuentro Femenil is distinguished for being the first Chicana feminist journal ever to be published. As a feminist journal it respects and acknowledges the need for the self-realization of the worth and potentials of all women. As a Chicana feminist journal, it recognized the fact that the Chicana feminists' struggle is necessarily distinct from that of the Anglo woman's popular feminist movement, although we may indeed have many similarities. Realizing that our economic struggle is racial as well as sexual, in representing Raza women, the journal could in no way fight for feminism without it also being an effort on behalf of all of la Raza.

In the areas of health, education and welfare, the Chicana feminist struggle incorporates racial and sexual issues as they affect one group: *las mujeres*. For example, Chicanas have the second highest mortality rate during childbirth; Chicanas do not receive proper gynecological care because there is a predominance of non-Spanish speaking, culturally insensitive, sexist and racist doctors; Chicanas are victims of birth control experimentations rather than health education; pregnant Chicanas fail to receive their welfare checks because they cannot speak English; poor Chicana mothers fail to seek welfare when they fear they will be labeled foreigners in their own land and sent to the immigration office. Chicanas fail to receive proper counseling and education because this society perpetuates the myth that Chicanas only want to nurture families; unfortunately, Chicanas can only obtain "traditional feminine" jobs if they pass for Anglo-Saxon and speak without an accent. All this and more happens every day-sexism works together with racism in this capitalistic society to negatively affect the daily lives of Chicanas. Here and now.

Encuentro Femenil is very proud to express that is has begun to examine the dynamics of sexism and racism as they apply to the Chicana woman. The first issue of this feminist journal deals with the areas of welfare, employment, counseling and education. In it Alicia Escalante makes a very personal and sensitive account of her experiences with the welfare system. A lucid presentation of the Talmadge Amendment is also included in this issue, carefully explaining the threats and disadvantages such an amendment presents to the welfare mother and to all seeking aid. The other articles explore new alternatives as a basis for Chicana education. Causes and solutions are aptly discussed in relation to employment, counseling, job training, school curriculum, sex discrimination, and education.

This issue has a historical theme as its basis. The topics of the second *Encuentro Femenil* issue are: Malinche and the image of the Mexican woman; sexual stereotypes of the Chicana in literature will also be presented as well as an anlysis of the Chicana feminist movement between 1968 and 1971.

History and literature have distorted and abused the story of an Aztec Indian slave named Malinche, the interpreter for Cortez. She has been blamed as the ultimate traitor to Mexico and she has also been used to symbolize the total negative essence of the Mexican woman. However, "Malintzín Tenepal" begins to correct and clarify the real story of Doña Marina. In an effort to focus attention to the general stereotypes of the Chicana, "sexual stereotypes of the Chicana" continues to delve into treatment of the Mexican woman in literature.

"The feminista" is an attempt to identify the socioeconomical and philosophical conflicts surrounding the issue of the Chicana question and women's lib and their effect on the Chicano movement.

In addition to these historical topics, identity, welfare and employment continue to be explored. The initial awareness of womanhood, Chicana welfare rights and the Chicana's position in the labor force explain and justify Chicana feminism.

As you can see, *Encuentro Femenil* is probably the first of its kind. It is unique in that it is one of the first Chicano press media to be made up solely of women working to develop a means of exchange for Chicana ideas and to provide a platform to clarify women's issues as they pertain to the Chicana.

28

Macho Attitudes*

Nancy Nieto

When a freshman male comes to MECHA, he is approached and welcomed. He is taught by observation that the Chicanas are only useful in areas of clerical and sexual activities. When something must be done there is always a Chicana there to do the work. "It is her place and duty to stand behind and back up her Macho!" This is the attitude of a great many "heavies" in a Chicano organization and it greatly influences the rest of the Chicanos.

If the Chicanas were not in these organizations, who would do the work? If all Chicanas boycotted typing, filing, and all the other duties of a female, what would happen?

What would have happened during the last student elections, if the Chicanas had not worked like dogs on the campaign, speeches and platforms while the "heavies" were out getting loaded? Why is it that these people can't perceive that a Chicana can do the same for the movement, if not more, than a male. Chicanos are alienating many Chicanas by calling some work inferior and some superior, and thereby really not working together.

Deep Macho hangups are the reasons for the Chicanas having certain beliefs as: "Men are supposed to be leaders, to fight and to protect." When these Chicanos see their women becoming educated, they jump back! When their women stand up for themselves and really begin to contribute to the movement, they react and shout "women's lib, women's lib"!!

Many of the Chicanos have sadly mistaken the idea that, women are only good to make love to; women should stay at home and clean the house; and women don't talk as heavy as men. They refuse to believe that Chicanas have intelligence and that the women could actually have sincere feelings for "*el movimiento.*"

Another aspect of the MACHO attitude is their lack of respect for Chicanas. They play their games, plotting girl against girl for their own benefit. (Both women and men play this very unrevolutionary game). They use the movement and Chicanismo to take her into bed. And when she refuses, she is a *vendida* because she is not looking after the welfare of her men. How much lower can Chicanos go, to use the movimiento for their own ends?

Chicanos take the credit for the suggestions, the work, and even the pride of a Chicana product. They take the credit without even a thank you to the workers.

Chicanas are getting fed up with being told when to jump, and how high. They are tired of being coerced to stay in their place or pay the price of losing a so-called boyfriend.

Chicanas must be allowed to express themselves, to work for the movement and most of all, to accomplish something.

*From *Hijas de Cuauhtémoc*, Vol. 1, No. 1, 1971.

29

*The Adelitas' Role in El Movimiento**

ANONYMOUS

Chicanas have always been involved in every *movimiento*, every Revolution our Raza has had.

You know it was a Mejicana who helped start the Mexican Revolution [Independence Movement] in 1810. The first person hung in Califas or should we say lynched, was a Chicana who killed a gavacho who had raped her.

So you can see our Raza has always needed Chicanas and we are needed even more in this Revolution. Chicanas are needed to stand by their men; to encourage them, and at times where it calls for, physically assist them.

But the girls in the Brown Beret movement, have they been given the opportunity of working for their Raza instead of just working for the Beret guys? It is true that the most logical of anyone in the organization to do work such as washing dishes, cooking, etc., are the girls but this shouldn't be the only reason why girls are to be allowed to join. The girls dedicate their lives for their Raza just as much as the guys do. As our Prime Minister, David Sánchez, has stated, in his work, "The Chicano-Gringo War": "The women and children can educate the not yet educated people as to the critical need for the defense of La Raza. . . .The women can support the Brown Berets in every way possible. The women can fight just as good as a man, if she wishes." But like we said they should not only be allowed to support but also to participate. There are many ways a woman can participate actively in the organization. David points out one when he states that "women can fight just as good as men," which is very true. Women can also be given the responsibilities of organizing and keeping up offices, taking care of financial matters, working with the community, etc. With these areas already taken care of by the women, men can get down to business. But one thing that should be *enforced* this time so that another incident does not take place such as the one that occurred with the girl Berets in the Los Angeles chapter and the free clinic is discipline. Discipline applies to every Beret in the organization regardless of whether you're a man or a woman. If a rule is broken the person responsible for breaking that rule should be disciplined.

Another thing that should be impressed or if possible stamped in the minds of every guy Beret is *RESPECT*. The guys are expected to respect the women as Berets and as women. As mentioned in the Brown Beret 8 Points of Attention #7, "do not take liberties with women." This includes Beret women.

We would again like to quote someone whom we respect and admire greatly: "It is necessary that you talk to every potential Chicano who crosses your path. Every

*From *Hijas de Cuauhtémoc*, Vol. 1, No. 1, 1971, p. 9.

Chicano that you might miss is a potential enemy."You are alienating many Chicanas and are making a lot of enemies by refusing them the honor of working for their Raza. Think about it *machos!*

The Chicanas in the Berets and outside the Berets are the Adelitas [female revolutionaries during the Mexican Revolution of 1910] of this Revolution. And in order to have a successful Revolution you must have full involvement from both the Chicanos and Chicanas. Like we said before there are certain things women can do, and be effective that guy's can't. For example its going to be up to the Adelitas to get ourselves together. Adelitas can be a great Asset not only to the Berets but the Revolution as a whole.

There are many things that can be said about this subject. But before we get too far into this article we'd like to try to abolish the stereotypes of Brown Women and what they're supposed to be good for. Such stereotypes include: the feeling that,

1. "A woman is only good for making love to."
2. "All women should do is stay home, wash dishes, cook and clean the house."
3. "Women don't rap as good as men; they aren't as heavy regarding the movement, and they don't command the respect of their peers."
4. "Women shouldn't be allowed to do community work; the work should be done by men."

These stereotypes are the by-products of deep-macho hang-ups. They refuse to believe that women have the intelligence to do community work, to organize Chicano organizations, just as good as, if not better, than men.

We really don't blame Chicanos for feeling that women are inferior. The Chicano family structure teaches the men to be the leaders while the women are taught how to do household chores and to think in terms of the day when they will be married.

And we're not talking about women's liberation because, like that's not ours—that's a white thing—we're talking about our Raza's Liberation and in order to get our Raza liberated we all have to work together within our Raza.

VIVA LA REVOLUCIÓN
Orange County Brown Berets

30

Chicanas and Abortion*

BEVERLY PADILLA

Chicana Liberation: "Cultural Disruptment? No! Cultural Evolvement."

The above quotation is taken from the text of a speech that was made by a Chicana, Chulita Devis, at a rally [for repeal of anti-abortion laws] in San Francisco recently.

Her speech aroused much sentiment among the Chicanas who were present, including myself. Chulita addressed not only the issue of abortion, but also aspects of our Chicano movement (of which she is an active part) and our Chicano cultural heritage (of which she is an obvious part).

Chicanas along with Chicanos suffer from lack of education, poor health care . . . job discrimination, along with all the other intrinsic results of oppression that capitalism exerts on its working class members and members of ethnic and racial minorities. But Chicanas also suffer as women within their culture. Octavio Paz, in his book *Labyrinth of Solitude* states: "Mexican women are inferior beings because, in submitting, they open themselves up. Their inferiority is constitutional and resides in their sex, their submissiveness is a wound that never heals."

Although today very few Chicanos would openly state this, the submissiveness of the Chicana to "her man" is very real. Chicanas have been victims of this submissiveness so long that many pride themselves as being less than "her man." As Chulita says, "Many Chicanos feel that Chicanas are needed right there behind her *macho*. But like the Chicano answers to the gringo, we also answer, no more *behind*, but *beside* and at times leading and guiding the revolutionary struggle."

The Chicano movement has organized around and glorified the stoicism and quiet strength "*que nuestras madres tenían* [that our mothers had]." There is no doubt of this strength, but a Chicana has had no choice but to bear the burdens of a life role that was selected for her. To be a good mother and a good wife has been her *only* acceptable role. All other ouside activites she might have chosen have had to remain within the domestic "domain." All Chicanas are asking for is a choice whether or not to be a wife or mother, to be given a chance to choose their life roles. Just as our Chicano men are no longer being silent about their subservient position in society, so too the Chicana can no longer be silent about her subservient role in her culture as well as in society.

Many feel that the issue of "right to abortion" and "control of one's own body" is a white women's-liberation hang-up. Like hell; it is not a white woman's hang-up exclusively! For years Chicanas, just as all woman, have been bearing children that

*From *The Militant*, February 18, 1972: p. 4.

they didn't want. For years they have suffered and died from self-induced and illegal abortions. For years they have been ridiculed and scorned for becoming pregnant out of marriage. As I speak with *viejitas* [elderly women] they confess of tales long ago spoken by their mothers and *tías* [aunts]. Talks of rapping sessions, quiet and secret discussions with other *señoras* [women] on how to have a miscarriage (spontaneous abortion by sitting in hot tubs of water, sitting on smoke, drinking and eating many types of potions).

Ms. Enriqueta Longeaux y Vásquez states in her discussion entitled "*Soy Chicana Primero* [I Am A Chicana First]," "Many of our *viejitas* know of moon-cycle birth control and have practiced it. (This has been scientifically affirmed in Czechoslovakia, by the way.) This birth control predated the pill and its dangers to women. And as for abortion, this was and can be done by herbs, that's right, no knife, and we as a poor people have had abortions among us for many decades. Each woman can deal with her own problems and conscience in this area of womanhood. The knowledge of womanhood is ancient and highly cultural among Raza. We are working in the movement to value it highly in order to retain and seek out this knowledge. It is a strong part of our cultural roots."

What I must respond to is that *hermana* [sister] Enriqueta's romanticizing has blinded her vision of reality. Control of one's own body and mind is *not* up to each indivual woman at this stage of reality—it is a collective problem; we live socially, it is our problem. Sex and abortion, contraception and pregnancy, are things Enriqueta feels are personal; that is because our Raza has never spoken of it. Our experiences have remained isolated (and to our detriment).

The moon-cycle birth control method that our *viejitas* knew about may be well and good, but . . . how many Chicanas have known or know about this method? . . . how good is it as a sure contraception method? Can we depend on it? What I am saying is that we are living today's realitites—like women dying in emergency rooms with post-self-abortive infections. We cannot find all our answers to problems in this difficult life by saying "it's a strong part of our culture."

To further quote Chulita, "When the Chicano man denies the Chicana her basic right to organize against her special forms of oppression like the abortion laws, he is denying her control of her own life, he is helping maintain the same status quo which keeps *him* down. He is acting in the best interest of his oppressor. That is the real Anglo thing. It is our oppressor that benefits most when Chicanas are down. What would happen if our women would realize their full potential? The flowering of the women means the rising of the race. When men realize the need and appreciate the power of Chicanas in action, our Raza will be in a position to win our struggle for freedom."

"Still there are those Chicanos who feel that when we as Chicanas seek to make our power felt, we disrupt our movement. They claim we are talking disunity in our cultural heritage. Like one of my *hermanas* puts it, "cultural hell," that's what we are trying to disrupt. This is not cultural disruptment, it's cultural evolvement. Disunity is the result of the fear of [those] whose status is being threatened, whose age-old privileges are being denied. . . ."

No more can we allow Chicanas to be restricted only to the cleaning, the cooking, the office, the bedroom. No longer can we allow freedom to be the privilege of one class or one race, like the white man has done in America . . . and no longer can we allow freedom to be the privilege of one sex. Freedom, we say, is for everyone. *Qué viva mi Raza!* [Long live my people!].

31

Malintzín Tenepal:
A Preliminary Look into a New Perspective[*]

ADELAIDA R. DEL CASTILLO

Introduction

History, literature, and popular belief normally introduce us to the story and image of Doña Marina, La Malinche, in either of three ways: (1) the woman is often times presented very simply and insignificantly as just another part of the necessary backdrop to Cortés' triumphant conquest or, as is more commonly done, (2) her portrayal assumes synonymity with destruction when she is singled out as the sole cause of the fall of the "patria" and becomes the scapegoat for all Mexican perdition thereafter while, on the other hand, (3)romanticists find themselves almost instinctively driven to depicting Doña Marina as the misguided and exploited victim of the tragic love affair which is said to have taken place between herself and Hernán Cortés.

The above approaches for depiction of Doña Marina do no justice to the image of this Mexican woman in that the following historical aspects are not taken into full consideration:

1. Quetzalcoatl—the prophet and his religion;
2. Aztec religion—in particular, the works of Tlacaelel;
3. The political milieu of the Aztec empire at the time of the conquest;
4. The situation of the Indian peoples under Aztec rule;
5. Marina's personal life;
6. Her actual deeds in the conquest of Mexico, and finally;
7. Speculation based on all of the above concerning Doña Marina's motives for having involved herself in the conquest.

Only after all of the above historical aspects have been carefully considered can a comprehensive account of Doña Marina's behavior be given, for her actions were contingent upon the historical events of her time.

Doña Marina is significant in that she embodies effective, decisive action in the feminine form, and most important, because her own actions syncretized two conflicting worlds causing the emergence of a new one—my own. Here, woman acts not as a goddess in some mythology, but as an actual force in the making of history.

[*]From *Encuentro Femenil*, Vol. 1, No. 2, 1974: pp. 58–77.

The Story

Malintzín Tenepal was born in the Aztec province of Coatzacoalcos around the year 1505. Her father and mother were both of noble birth; in fact, her father was cacique [tribal leader] of the entire province of Coatzacoalcos and, as such, Malintzín was born into Aztec nobility, making her inheritance a sacred matter. It is not surprising, then, that when the Spaniards baptized her she was christened with an appropriate Spanish title denoting her nobility—namely, that of "Don/Doña" a title by which not even Cortés himself was addressed until after the conquest.

It is known that when Malintzín was still a child, her father died, leaving behind a still very young and beautiful widow. Eventually, Cimatle, Malintzín's mother, re-married and from this second marriage she bore a son. It was then that Malintzín's childhood was shattered. It occurred to both Cimatl and her new husband that Malintzín's inheritance, as sacred as it was, should be secured for their newborn son. It is believed that Cimatle then sent for Malintzín to be taken out of school (her noble birthright dictated that she be educated according to her status) and brought home to live so that Cimatl could begin the implementation of her heartless plan.

That night, Cimatl stealthily took the child to some itinerate Mayan merchants of Xicalango and sold her to them. Malintzín's mother then feigned that the child had died and made use of another child's corpse (it so happened that Cimatl had a servant whose child had actually died) to execute the mock funeral and obituaries that were accorded Malintzín's status. It is now that we can begin to understand that la Malinche, the young Aztec princess, was, in fact, betrayed, dethroned, and sold into slavery by her own mother—it all had the simplicity of an evil fairy tale. From here on, we know nothing of Malintzín's life up until her first encounter with the Spaniards; one can only speculate as to what she experienced as a Mayan slave and what effect these experiences had on her character.

With this in mind, I should like to offer a fourth alternative to our understanding of Doña Marina's role in the conquest of Mexico. This fourth alternative entails that Doña Marina should not be portrayed as negative, insignificant or foolish, but instead be perceived as a woman who was able to act beyond her prescribed societal function, namely, that of being a mere concubine and servant, and perform as one who was willing to make great sacrifices for what she believed to be a philanthropic conviction. As such, my depiction of this woman is not intended as an historical narrative per se, instead it is intended to be more of a mystical interpretation of a historical role. The interpretation is necessarily mystical because it involves what I've come to understand as Doña Marina's faith in a supernatural force (God), and those spiritual obligations to which she commits herself.

The Young Woman

To be sure, it must have been a very painful, traumatic and confusing experience to have gone from the drastic transition of Aztec princess to a Mayan slave. One naturally would suspect that the young child would at least have grown up with revenge in her heart, if not hatred for her mother. However, written accounts tell us differently.

Bernal Díaz del Castillo, Spanish conquistador and later candid chronicler of the conquest of Mexico, knew Doña Marina well. In his *Historia Verdadera de la Conquista de la Nueva España*, he tells us of her gentle consideration for both indios and Spaniards alike. Bernal himself was present on the day that Doña Marina, years later, finally met up with both her mother and brother. The encounter demonstrated to all present how Malintzín was prepared to deal with the cruelty and misery her own mother had bestowed upon her.

Similar accounts seem to indicate that Doña Marina was indeed a sensitive and loving woman. She sincerely cared for people and continued to love those who had caused her the most pain and, as such, it is not surprising to read that both indios and Spaniards alike loved her dearly. Among the conquistadores, she was known as "the angel of the expedition" primarily because she had saved their lives many times. The indios at first took her for a *diosa* [goddess] because she could speak their language fluently and because her communication served to mitigate violence between themselves and the white strangers. Indeed, it was the love and care of both indio and Spaniard that saved Doña Marina's life the time of "la noche triste," [the tragic night] Cortés' desperate escape from the city of Mexico: she perpetually merged their efforts and finally their worlds.

Malintzín Tenepal, the Aztec princess, must have devoted much of her time to learning. How else can one explain the vast knowledge this girl had by the time of the conquest? She was approximately fourteen years old when she first met up with Hernán Cortés and already she was fluent in many Indian dialects and managed to learn Spanish in a matter of weeks! She was just as politcially alert and astute as was the thirty-four year old Cortés; it was her astuteness which saved his life and secured their victory.

To be sure, religion must have been one of those fields of education in which she was diligently instructed for being a child of noble birth. And perhaps it was the contradictions of her religious education and the reality of the military Aztec state which determined the future actions of Malintzín.

The Arrival

It was the Aztec priests themselves who had recorded the expected date of Quetzalcoatl's return. Quetzalcoatl had prophesied: "On the day One Reed [April 21st] and the year One Reed [1519] I shall return. I will come from the east like the Morning Star." On a Thursday afternoon of April 21st, 1519, Hernán Cortés and his Spanish expedition landed on the island of San Juan de Ulua. No sooner had they done so when , out of nowhere, Mexica (Aztec) ambassadors sent by the great Motecuhzoma [usually spelled Moctezuma] himself welcomed the white strangers by presenting them with the Treasure of Quetzalcoatl. The Mexicas had now acknowledged Quetzalcoatl's return. Ironically, Christianity (the Spanish faith), as stated in Revelations 22:16, proclaimed: "I, Jesus, have sent mine angel to testify unto you these things in the churches. I am the root and the offspring of David and the bright and Morning Star." The Morning Star had indeed returned and his coming had been heralded among the Indian world by the revival of old superstitions and the observation of omen in the sky, in the water and on earth.

Just before his arrival at San Juan de Ulua, Cortés had fought a tenacious battle with the indios of Tabasco who, in the end, finally surrendered to him. Soon after, several Tabascan indios approached the Spanish camp and presented Cortés with many gifts of gold and women, one of whom was Malintzín Tenepal herself.

Malintzín not only made communication between the two worlds possible, she made it meaningful as well. The indios recognized that this woman was also Indian and that she was in a position to help them through her direct influence on and contact with the Conquistador himself. In fact, the extent to which the indios recognized the dual leadership of both Cortés and Malintzín can be better understood when we learn that the indios referred to both as "Malinche."

When the indios realized through their own defeat that Cortés was indeed a powerful force, they came to seek his help, but spoke with Doña Marina directly. They complained to them of the cruelties they were subjected to under Aztec dominance. They described how the Mexicans pillaged their settlements and raped their daughters in front of them. They told them of how the Aztecs took victims en masse for their bloody sacrifices and of how they were expected to pay tribute in heavy taxes. Many Indian peoples could no longer endure these injustices so that occurrences of rebellious outbreaks were not unusual. But, because the Aztec empire was more of a loose confederation (perhaps not even that) of Indian nations ruled more for fiscal than for political purposes, the conquered peoples were able to retain much of their own political and cultural autonomy as nations. Unlike the Romans, the Aztecs made no attempt to "Aztecize" or integrate those conquered into the empire. They were simply used as a resource for exploitation. Aztec political thought had no conception of anything beyond the city. Similar to the Greek "polis," the Aztecs saw the "*altepetl*" (city) as the fundamental autonomous unit.

In effect, when Doña Marina is accused of being "una traidora a la patria," [a traitor to her nation] one wrongly assumes that there was a "patria" (similar to the patrias of today). The fact is, there were many Indian nations within the Aztec Empire and these nations were always attempting, through one rebellion of another, to regain their former independence.

It was not unusual for Indian nations to resist Aztec dominance by refusing to pay them tribute and by sometimes even resorting to killing the calpixqui and whatever men accompanied him. For instance, when the province of Cuetlaxlan on the Gulf of Mexico, rebelled, the Cuetlaxtecs forced the Mexican tax-collectors into a house and quickly set fire to it.

It is willful to forget that the concept of Mexican nationalism (la patria) was introduced only long after the conquest of Mexico and *not* before. Nationalism might have been easier to implement after the conquest since, by this time, many Indian nations had already encountered the viability of allying themselves and working together as one political force.

Again, we cannot accuse Doña Marina of having betrayed the Indian peoples as a whole for it was they who had decided it would be to their advantage to help free themselves from the yoke of Aztec dominance. In effect, the whole nature of the Aztec Empire decreed its own self-destruction in that it was the subjected peoples of the empire who eventually joined together to make its downfall a reality.

The Outcome

Because history is notorious for depicting the female as being one of the the main causes for man's failures, it's extremely important that we understand the ethics with which historians, most of whom have been men in the past, distribute blame and justice. Apparently, what seems to be involved here is an unconscious acceptance of morals which blindly depict the male force as one which generally strives to do good in spite of the ever-present influence of the opposite sex. Woman is perceived as being one whose innately negative nature only serves to stagnate man, if not corrupt him entirely. So just as Eve was chosen long ago by misogynistic men to represent the embodiment of "the root of all evil" for western man, Mexico's first and most exceptional heroine, Doña Marina "la Malinche" now embodies female negativity (*traición*) [betrayal] for our Mexican culture. Yet, why is Doña Marina demeaned and obscured in history?

I believe that her negative portrayal in history and, thereby, in popular belief, can be attributed to two things: (1) misinterpretation of her role in the conquest of Mexico and (2) an unconscious, if not intentional, misogynistic attitude towards women in general, especially towards self-assertive women, on the part of western society as a whole.

32

*Chicanas in the Labor Force**

Anna NietoGomez

Although the Chicana is thought to be outside of the labor market, 57% of Chicanas 14 years and older were income recipients in 1971. According to the national census in March 1972, 544,000 Chicanas (34%) were in the labor force. This approaches the national work force rate for women in general (40%). The 1970 statistics on employment indicate that the work participation rates of Chicanas in California (40%) and in Los Angeles (30%) were proportionately equal to the total work force of all women in California and Los Angeles.

At the same time, however, the Chicana has a two percent higher rate of unemployment. The unemployment rate for the Chicana nationally was 9.4%, 9.6% for the state of California, and 14.5% for Los Angeles. But the total unemployment rate of women in general is 7% nationally, 7.0% for the state of California and 12.1% for Los Angeles.

Because the Chicana may suffer from sex discrimination as well as from racial discrimination, the Chicana's income is at the bottom of the economic ladder. Although both Chicanos and Chicanas have an average of 9.5 years of education, the median income of the Chicano ($5100) is almost three times as much as the median income of the Chicana ($1800). In fact, 54% of the Chicanas had incomes below $2000, but only 20.5% of Chicanos had comparable incomes. 82% of the Chicanas

*From *Encuentro Femenil*, Vol. 1, No. 2, 1974: pp. 28–33.

earned less than $3,999 as compared to 40% of the Chicanos' earnings. At the same time, 16% Chicanos and 8% of the Chicanas earned between $5-6,999.

Assuming that sex discrimination (ascription of work according to sex) determines that women compete with women, we find a racial-sexual hierarchy within the traditional occupations for women. This imbalance is noted when representation of Chicanas in high paying jobs is inversely proportionate to women in the general population. Therefore, the Chicana is primarily a poorly paid worker, with little or no job opportunities.

The largest job category of working women in general is clerical (35%). This is consistent with the major job category for both whites and Chicanas; however, there are more white women (37%) in clerical occupations than there are Chicanas (27%).

The second largest category of occupations for the general women's working population is service work (17%). However, there is almost twice as many Chicanas service workers (25%) as there are white women service workers (15%).

The third largest job category of women in general is the professional and technical worker (15%). This category is predominantly composed of white women (16.3%) and white men, since only 5% of Chicanas and Chicanos enter into this category. In fact, the third largest occupation represented by Chicanas is operatives (22%) or semiskilled workers. However, 14% of both the general female working population and white female working population are represented in semiskilled jobs.

Another aspect of racial-sexist discrimination seems to be that there are more Anglo women in white-collar, and professional jobs than either Chicanos or Chicanas. This would imply that the Anglo woman is hired more often and preferred over either the Chicano or the Chicana in jobs which offer more social status and better pay.

The male's earning power and the women's marital status greatly influence whether or not women work. It is assumed Chicanas were more likely to work because the median income of the Chicano ($5100) for an average family of 4.1 persons was only $1423 above the poverty income (annual income which separates poor from the non-poor is $4137). Another interesting factor which influences Chicanas to work is that 44% of the Chicanas 14 years and over are not living with a husband present in the home. Seventeen percent of these women are female heads of household with an average of 3.6 persons living in the family. It is interesting to note that although 36% of the female heads of household were married, the spouse was not living in the house. Widowhood (29%) and divorce (23%) were also other characteristics of the Spanish Chicana head of households.

The experience of the Chicana Service Action Center parallels the national findings of the Chicana in employment. 53% of the Chicanas were found in low status, low paying jobs such as domestic workers, cleaning, laundry and food service, in addition to factory work. This low occupational status of the Chicana was reflective of the fact that 42.1% of the Mexican-American families headed by women were living at poverty level or under in the county of Los Angeles.

At the Chicana Service Action Center of Los Angeles, 50% of the Chicanas looking for work are unskilled and untrained women under the age of 30 years. Most of the women coming to the center are women who have dropped out of high school, are single and/or are mothers. Older women between the ages of 31 and 41 are looking for an up-grading job and higher pay. Women over 45 can no longer do heavy factory service jobs and are in search of light service jobs. Older women who find themselves head of household (because of being abandoned, divorced, separated, widowed or with a disabled husband) are handicapped because their age and their lack of job experience and training reduce their competitive appeal to prospective employers.

Experience has taught us that the majority of the Mexican-American women have many obstacles to overcome. They are usually unprepared to enter the labor market. A lack of skills, vocational and communication skills in addition to racist, sexist and age discriminatory stereotyping contribute to her unemployed status.

Three major factors seriously affect the Chicana woman from securing and maintaining job placement. They are communication barriers, lack of oral knowledge concerning interviewing techniques (i.e., application interviews and oral interviews) and lack of competitive entry level skills.

A significant disqualifying factor which the Chicana faces is inadequate preparation in communication skills. Regardless of occupation skills, if the applicant is unable to express herself in the interview or on the job, she will not be hired. For the monolingual or marginal English speaking Chicana, opportunities in the labor market are primarily menial and found only where large number of people in the same position are employed, i.e., canneries, run-a-ways, garment factories. Consequently, better paying job opportunities or job training placement is rare because there are no bilingual training programs. English as a second language training (ESL) does help many of these women, as they must have some degree of knowledge of English before they can understand the instructions.

In the past, educational and vocational training programs have not been necessarily oriented to the needs of the Chicana. Unsuccessful reading and writing programs have failed to prepare the Chicana for vocational hiring or job opportunities. The low retention of Chicanas in the secondary schools, 70% drop out before the tenth grade, inadvertently fails to make available to the Chicana even the traditionally oriented feminine curriculum, i.e., typing, business English, shorthand, which are offered in the 10th, 11th and 12th grades.

In addition, the Chicana Service Action Center has discovered that the nature of Chicana-oriented college retention programs also tends to deliver the college drop out, or even the college graduate at the same door step, as the high school drop out and high school graduate respectively. Neither obtained the employable skills or job experience to qualify for good paying jobs. Therefore, when they are thrown into the labor market, they compete for jobs such as nurse's aide, waitress, office clerk, and factory worker.

Racist sexual stereotypes also work as social barriers. From the educational system to the employment force, the image of the Chicana is still that of nurturing, passive and submissive woman. These false stereotypes influence counselors and educators to offer nonsupport to the Chicana to continue school. Thus the women enter the labor market ill prepared. Employers culminatively contribute to the Chicana's economic situation when they selectively "cue" the women according to how closely they fit the image of the Anglo woman prototype.

Unfortunately, there are insufficient data fully delving into the employment and educational picture of the Chicana. To date, further statistical breakdowns about women only reflect Anglo and Black women. This assumes that other minority women have an employment picture comparable to Black women. However, this is not true. For example, the largest job category for Black women is service workers (25%); the second is clerical (21%); the third is private household workers (18%); fourth is operatives (16%); and fifth is professional (11%). As stated prevsiouly this is much different than either the Anglo or the Chicana profile of women in employment.

Furthermore, if the employment picture includes only the general category of Spanish speaking, it ignores the specific trends and therefore the priority of employment needs for women from each of the Mexican, Puerto Rican and Cuban cultures. The general category of Spanish speaking in essence distorts the real needs of these women. For example: the largest job category of the Spanish Speaking women is operatives (30%); the second is clerical work (26%); the third is service work (20%); and the fourth is professional (7%). This picture substantially distorts the employment picture for those who want to know specific data on the Chicana. In addition this picture is substantially different from either the Chicana, Anglo or Black women. Therefore, it is also important to continue to further develop the demographic data about women from each of the different cultures who are lumped together as the Spanish speaking women.

In view of the general occupational picture, the Chicana Service Action Center is calling attention to the educational training needs of the Chicana in order to better her economic opportunities in the job market and in education. We feel it is vitally important that educators, woman-manpower experts, and employers become more aware of the real socio-economic picture of the Mexican-American woman in order to more adequately serve her.

Statistics are taken from:

1. March 1972 census for the Spanish Speaking Population, U.S. Dept. of Commerce.
2. Hand Book on Women Workers, page 139, Women's Bureau.
3. We the American Women, U.S. Dept. of Human Resources.
4. Women in California, California State Dept. of Human Resources.
5. Employers for the City of Los Angeles, Mayor's Office, L.A.
6. Chicana Action Report for Los Angeles County, 1973.

Chicanas at anti-Vietnam War march in Los Angeles carrying crosses with the names of Chicanos killed in Vietnam. Courtesy Raul Ruiz, *La Verdad* magazine, Los Angeles, California.

33

The Chicana—Perspectives for Education*

ANNA NIETOGOMEZ

In trying to deal with the problems of the Chicana today, one must understand the socioeconomic, historical, and psychological context in which the woman has always lived. However, most information on the woman, especially the Chicana, is speculation, and prejudiced by a male and racist oriented society.

Classes concerning the Chicana would create a new sense of identity for her, and also enable everyone to understand and accept her new roles in society. Classes concerning the Chicana and cultural change in education, her relationship with the law, her role in religion, and her history throughout the ages are needed not only to create a new identity for the woman, but also to give her a new position in society, a position which recognizes the full potential of the Chicana.

A. *The Chicana in Education* would delve into how the impact of education and the issue of sexual inequality have affected the socioeconomic position of the Chicana society. It would also try to understand how education has affected the traditional role of the Chicana and how it can be used by her in an emerging culture.

B. *The History of the Chicana* would identify the heroines and the social roles of the past. Marina [Malinche] may be given a new interpretation as a positive symbol for the mestizo. Sor Juana de la Cruz will be given recognition for literary contributions to the world. *La Respuesta* [written by Sor Juana] may become the symbol of the right of every Mexicana and Chicana to education and the fulfillment of her potential. Women will know that in 1911, Hijas de Cuauhtémoc issued a feminist manifesto calling for "Political enfranchisement and full emancipation of Mexican women in their economic, physical, intellectual and moral struggles." And Señora Licenciada Aurora Jiménez de Palacios will be known as the first woman member of the Mexican in congress in 1954.

C. *The Chicana and the Law* will not only deal with the effects of the 1964 Civil Rights Bill, and welfare, it will also delve into how Moslem Law, Spanish Colonial Law and different Indian Laws of Mexico, as well as the English Common Law, have determined the woman's role in society.

D. *Religion and la Mujer* would include a study of the Indian Goddesses in Mexico, and the queen of heaven. This may give new insights in explaining the meaning and the mystery of women seen as the magic vessels of life and death for their people. Witch craft, the *Curandera*, [woman healer] and the Lady of Pain may explain all the fears that man has had of woman since the beginning of time.

*From *Encuentro Fermenil*, Vol. 1, No. 1, 1973, pp. 34–61.

E. *The Cultural-Psycho-Physiological Realities De La Mujer Y El Hombre.* There will be three goals which this class will try to achieve. First, it will identify and explain the myths and the truths concerning differences in the sexuality of the man and woman. In reaching this understanding, one will study how these myths and truths have influenced the roles of each sex in our culture. Hopefully, this understanding will extend into how these ideas have influenced the kind of relationships which exist between the different institutions and each sex; i.e., attitudes of doctors towards Chicanas.

Another goal is to identify the different physiological and psychological changes which are a part of the maturation of the body of a man and woman in one lifetime due to the symbiotic relationship of the body and the mind.

Last, this study will delve into the cultural factors influencing attitudes towards menstruation, menopause, pelvic exams, Pap smears, impotency, sterility, virility, contraception, feminine and male hygiene, and prenatal/postnatal care.

This kind of understanding will lead to an effective medical program in the Chicano community.

Epilogue

During a Chicano Studies—Mecha conference at the California State University at Northridge, the mujer workshop proposed that not only a curriculum be established relevant to La Mujer, but that requirements for all Chicano Studies Majors should include at least one class on La Mujer for graduation. This proposal recognizes the need to lift the veil of the Virgin's face to show a real woman who is not exempt from the trials of life. In order to truly understand the needs and problems of La Raza, we must include the Chicana in our study.

34

Women's Rights and the Mexican-American Woman*

Elizabeth Olivárez

Because the basis of discrimination is the same for sex, race or national origin the same political, psychological and economic issues must be considered by the Mexican-American woman as are being considered by her Black and Anglo counterparts.

*From *Regeneración*, Vol. 2, No. 4, 1974: pp. 40–42.

Beyond these basic considerations, there are distinct issues peculiar to the Mexican-American woman which must be resolved or clarified in the process of pursuing her rights as a woman or perhaps even before she feels she is able to pursue her rights as a woman.

The Mexican-American women in La Conferencia de Mujeres Por la Raza held in Houston, Texas in late May 1971 clearly indicated that they too wanted liberation and equal opportunity but that their manner of liberation could not and would not be like their Anglo counterparts. The obvious reasons given for this were the cultural considerations and the political ties to the Mexican-American movement, but also some women felt that the Anglo women's liberation groups in the main had their origin in the leisure time that comes with the luxury of being fashionable, middle-class, materialistic and competitive.

They thought that some of the solutions or goals pushed by the Anglo women's liberation groups were no real solutions. For example, the day-care center was not only viewed as an economic necessity, a view similarly held by Anglo women's liberation groups, but also as being based on the cultural concept of family unity, still a strong force in the Mexican-American family. Therefore the destruction of the nuclear family unit was not considered an acceptable solution, and thus the rationale for the day-care center as urged by some women's liberation groups also was not acceptable.

Essentially, the main issue before the Mexican-American woman is that of identity. While the fact of discrimination against her within her own cultural structure could not be denied, she still maintains loyalties to her culture which are based in part on the reality that her raza is not yet liberated. Furthermore, she could not deny the fact that the discrimination against her within her culture in many instances took the same form as with her Anglo and black counterparts and, in some instances, took a more oppressive form as a consequence of certain contributing factors.

Some of these factors additionally contributing to the oppression are the continuing strength of the Catholic religion, the persistence of discrimination against the Mexican-American male in education and economic opportunities, the continuing lack of national unity and national leaders within the movement, the lack of identity of some Mexican-Americans with their movement—indeed a basic issue. Out of the necessity for recognizing the need for liberation within the women's ranks comes the necessity for recognizing that this liberation will not come about without changes in the culture and without the liberation of her people, economically, politically, psychologically and socially.

What, then, are those specific areas of discrimination which take the same form for the Mexican-American woman as for the Anglo and the Black woman? Generally it may be said that these specific areas are defined in terms of basic individual needs, common to all women.

Individual Identity

Her identity as an individual is defined in terms of how well she serves her husband or boyfriend or in terms of the role her husband or boyfriend defines it to be. If, for example, she is not only a homemaker but she is also allowed to be active within the community, her identity is still defined in terms of the credit it brings to him, not her.

For the Mexican-American woman this issue of identity is twofold, but it is also critical as with her black counterpart. It is not just a question of individual self-determination, but also a question of self-determination within the context of the Mexican-American Movement or the Black Movement.

Human Psychological Damage Coming from the Loss of Identity

The concern is for women who have lost the ability to recognize certain existing choices as relevant to their lives. In fact, the loss of identity or lack of its development may be so profound in some women that they may come to deny the existence of choice or alternatives in their lives.

How real is any existing choice to the woman who is not able to grasp the relevancy of such a choice for her? But this question of recognizing relevancy is two-fold again for the Mexican-American woman, as well as her black counterpart. For the former, the choices are less meaningful as long as they are also not within the reach of her raza. As these choices come within the realistic grasp of the Mexican-American male, so too is the Mexican-American woman able to grasp them as her choices.

The Need to Redefine Changes in Familial Responsibilities and their Role in the Home

The problems common to all women in this area are the lack of shared responsibility in raising the children, the lack of authority commensurate with the woman's responsibilities in the home and simply the opportunity to engage in activities outside the home—activities which may enrich everyone's life within the family.

For the Mexican-American woman this also means contending with the cultural concept of family unity and humanism. While she realizes that her self-determination cannot be realized without changing or modifying the concept of family unity which places the main responsibilities on her, she also realizes that the humanism and personal ties that are part of this unity must not be destroyed.

One of the resolutions coming out of the Houston Conference dealing with this subject aims at urging the Mexican-American woman to re-educate her husband and her sons to understand and respect her desires as an individual. This cannot be done without close personal ties. Thus, instead of declaring the man as the enemy, the humanism of the culture may be the driving force for communication of both sexes. This remains to be seen.

Equal Economic Opportunities in all Phases of Employment from Recruitment to Promotion

This is the area of women's rights most easily understood by men and the less liberated among the women. While many Mexican-American women are participants in the labor force of this country, many are still trying to assert their rights to participate. It is interesting to note what one woman said at the Conference: "The Mexican-American woman is equal when it comes to working in the fields alongside her husband but not when it comes to making decisions."

It is also interesting to note how many of the minority poverty programs perpetuate employment discrimination against black and brown women, a demoralizing situation for the qualified minority woman.

Political Rights

Not only is the Mexican-American woman concerned with preserving or furthering the rights of her people in the political processes, but she is especially concerned with pursuing her rights as an individual within the context of the Mexican-American movement. She realizes that it is necessary to establish an individual pride as a means necessary to further the cause, but also as a means to enable her to participate fully in achieving the goals of la raza.

A resolution coming out of the Conference recognizes the need for encouraging Mexican-American women to run for policy-making offices within the structure of their organizations and the women designated as candidates be truly responsive to the needs of the other women within these organizations. Paramount in this resolution is the assumption that there is nothing wrong with being aggressive and that, in fact, it is very necessary to be so.

What is significant is not so much that the Mexican-American woman should run for policy-making offices but that the women encouraging her or selecting her for the office rate her according to her qualifications and to her responsiveness to themselves, not according to how she is rated by the men. It goes without saying that you can have a female president of UMAS who may not be responsive to the needs of the women and in the end do nothing to further their rights within an organization.

In this respect it is easy to see how a Mexican-American woman running for or holding office within a Mexican-American organization could be labeled a "*vendida*" or sell-out to her *hermanas* [sisters] if she isn't responsive to their needs. Perhaps an hermanidad or sisterhood among Mexican-American women ought to be established in order to give each other active support, as was suggested in another resolution. Whether this *hermanidad* should be formal or informal is another matter to consider.

Sex And Religious Considerations

For the Mexican-American woman the Catholic Church is still a strong force, both in terms of maintaining the family structure and of maintaining the sexual roles. The role of the Catholic Church must be redefined and reconciled with the concepts involving women's rights.

A resolution coming out of the Conference urged women to form local discussion or sensitivity groups to communicate and, or re-educate women on these issues. Specifically, some of these issues are the guilt, extreme fears and resulting oppression created and perpetuated by the Catholic Church. By emphasizing those parts of the Bible which were written by male supremacists and which place women in an inferior position, the Catholic Church has played an active role in "putting a woman in her place," the inferior one. The Catholic Church has even gone beyond this by essentially justifying through the Bible the inferior role of women.

This form of oppression is devastating when viewed from the point that many women truly come to accept their role as inherently and spiritually inferior. The assumption inherent in the view that some Bible passages were written by male supremacists is that these passages are basically contradictory to the teachings of Christ which assume that we bear our moral responsibilities as individuals. This is why Mexican-American women were urged to read and interpret the Bible for what it is.

Other religious and sex questions which should be considered in local sensitivity groups are: the need for birth control and information, legal abortion for the women who choose it, attitudes towards sex and the sexual role of women as aggressors. Finally, a religious issue, not directly related to the sex issues and which was introduced by some of the older Mexican-American women, was that we should throw out the idea of "let things be and God will take care of them."

While in the process of liberating ourselves, it becomes necessary to recognize how this concept has had a stifling effect on Mexican-Americans. Although there are other religious concepts that are not stifling, it was generally recognized that Mexican-Americans should not feel guilty about taking a more aggressive role in shaping their future and asserting their rights.

Education

In this area there is no substantial distinction between the ways Mexican-American women and other women are discriminated against. Therefore the solutions are the same. Mexican-Americans should assert their rights to receive higher education and should work toward achieving equal pay for equal work, especially at the university level. Part of the problem of equal pay for equal work is that women with equivalent education and educational experience are not accorded commensurate academic status.

What then is the significance of equality, unity and liberation for the Mexican-American woman? Equality to most women liberationists does not mean being treated like a man, but obviously it means having equal opportunity as an individual. It doesn't mean being slapped on the shoulder and told, "Well, buddy, you're one of us," because, let's face it, men aren't liberated either and often times are placed in degrading positions and situations in this society. Equality is especially meaningful for the Mexican-American woman and for the Black woman who ironically in working to achieve equal rights for their people, find that these rights are not accorded them within the ranks of their respective organizations.

This brings us to the issue of unity. Blacks and Mexican-Americans, as well as other minorities, have long recognized the need for unity if goals are to be realized. Diversity in the Mexican-American movement has been one reason for the lack of unity. Lack of identity with the movement through psychological brainwashing against the image of Mexican-Americans is yet another reason for the lack of unity.

Therefore racial and ethnic minorities have long recognized the need for unity, the cause of disunity and the need to present a united image in spite of disunity within the ranks. Of course, this is where women's liberation is having its biggest problems, and perhaps where its biggest problem will be throughout the life of this movement. Unity within the women's liberation movement will not come easy and will not come soon from the Mexican-American woman. It will be some time before the majority of the latter recognizes that some basic needs are common to all women. Why? Like her Black counterpart she should define where the changes must occur, but she maintains loyalties to her culture and the Mexican-American movement.

What then does liberation mean to the Mexican-American woman? The term liberation is most commonly used by women liberationists to mean the purging of oneself of conscious and unconscious sex or role "hang-ups." Its broader meaning includes liberating ourselves from political, social and economic discrimination. Liberation, for the Mexican-American woman, not only means liberating herself but this in conjunction with liberating her people. The psychological reality which we must all recognize is that no one is liberated. There is no such thing as a liberated woman unless the people who surround her are liberated.

Finally, this article could not possibly cover all of the issues which are in essence human rights or human liberation, but something must be said about the separation of the sexes. First let us proceed from the assumption, not held by many of the "enlightened" males, that the women's rights movement is as legitimate and valid as the Black and Mexican-American movements because the basis of discrimination is the same for sex, race or national origin (the first words beginning this article). The anal-

ogy begins that many—not all—Mexican-Americans have, in the process of liberating
their people, come to the realization that they cannot do it without working with Anglo Americans or the predominant majority. The analogy continues that women's liberation will not occur without working with the men. The analogy ends with this
question: Will the sophistication acquired by the black and brown women working
within their respective movements be such that it will permit them to assert their
rights as women without separating themselves from the men?

We have black supremacists, white supremacists, brown supremacists, male supremacists and female supremacists. How much more separation can we tolerate? But,
more important, who among men and women will have the courage to truly communicate on the changes that are so desperately needed?

35

Unequal Opportunity
and the Chicana*

LINDA AQUILAR

The position of the female in American society poses a particularly difficult struggle
for the Mexican-American woman.

The traditional role of the Mexican-American female or Chicana, has been that
of housewife and mother whose primary purpose in life is to serve and assist her man,
the Chicano. This is no longer true. The Chicana has stepped out of the kitchen into
the world to become a visible force for change and the elimination of discrimination.
Therefore, it is understandable when the general public assumes that the Mexican-
American woman who has become very vocal and assertive is part of the current
"women's libertion movement" sweeping the country, or has at least been inspired by
its efforts.

Actually, emergence of the Chicana as a strong motivating force within the
Spanish-speaking community has been in conjunction with that of the Chicano. For
this reason, her struggle cannot be paralleled with the Anglo woman's fight for rights

*From *Regeneración*, Vol. 2, No. 4, 1975: p. 45.

against the Anglo male. Chicanas have fought side by side with their men in the struggle fo equal opportunity in all areas of American life. Unfortunately, because the major emphasis has always been on opening doors of opportunity for the Mexican America male, the female in essence . . . fights the battle, but does not share in the spoils.

Much has been written on the problem of lack of equal opportunity for Chicanos in the various areas of employment. Practically no one has ventured to write about employment discrimination directed at Chicanas not only from Anglo male employers, but potential Chicano employers as well. I say potential because from my experience if she seeks any type of administrative position, a Chicana has a better chance of being employed by an Anglo than by a Chicano.

One can see that part of the reason for this is that the Anglo administrator does not feel that his masculinity is threatened by the Chicana. Rather, he finds it enhanced, if he even vaguely falls for the stereotype of the Mexican-American female—Mexican women are said to be for the most part hot blooded, primitives interested only in sexual gratification and grateful for any attention from Anglo males. This image is constantly reinforced by the various media, television, movies and publications. Rare is the film that does not depict the Chicana as a loose, wanton woman.

The Chicano Revolution has brought about great changes in the Mexican-American community and family structure. The Mexican-American female has taken on some characteristics of what has been described as a *Macho*. She may be very vocal, aggressive, and an effective community organizer. She may prefer to pursue interests outside the home and reject homemaking as the total fulfillment in her life.

This is the new image for some Mexican-American females. The docility and submissiveness are evidently dwindling and although the Chicano views her with interest, this interest is not totally absent of fear, wonder, and suspicion. Fear, because Mexican-American women always have been expected totally to be submissive to males. Wonder, because Chicanas are now demonstrating abilities the Chicano thought them incapable of. Lastly, suspicion, because one is always suspicious of something one does not understand. Chicanas who have grouped together for strength and unity of purpose are at best tolerated, more often ostracized and ridiculed by Chicanos.

Women have stepped out of the background into the spotlight as spokesmen at various public meetings. School boards, commissions, and city councils, to name a few, have felt the sting of the verbal slaps from irate Mexican-American women. Chicanas have shown themselves to be alert, forceful, and intelligent and they have proved to be a major catalyst in the Chicano community. The aggression on the part of the Chicana towards the Anglo has not only been condoned but encouraged by the Mexican-American male. The results have been good. Capable and competent Chicanos have been hired into decent positions of administration by a reluctant Anglo community.

The problem begins. The same forceful Chicana that berated the Anglo looks to the Chicano for employment. She has been forced into a leadership role in the community but finds that with the Chicano employer, the outmoded man/woman relationship that existed in the home has not changed. In the book *A Forgotten American* Luis Hernández writes: "Traditionally all men (Chicanos) are considered to be superior to women (Chicanas), a girl looks forward to the day she will fulfill her role as a woman . . . where her first duty is to serve her husband."

As far as the Chicano is concerned, the role of the Chicana has not really changed. It has merely been transferred from the home to the office. If a Chicana seeks employment above clerical help status, her fiercest opposition comes from the Chicano. The reprieve from the kitchen has been temporary, or more realistically, not a reprieve at all, for although a Chicana is encouraged to "stand up" to an Anglo, deference to the Chicano is still mandatory. In his book *Pensamientos*, Elius Carranza states, "Chicanos have exposed with a little bit of honesty the big lie that we are all free, we are all equal . . . " Perhaps the time has come for Chicanas to also expose "with a little bit of honesty" the big lie that we are all free, we are all equal. In our own San Jose, California community the number of Spanish surname females employed by the city is 21, out of a work force of 2,575. In a special program, the Emergency Employment Act (EEA), the number employed is 20 out of 288. These numbers do not mean that 41 Chicanas are employed by San Jose City. Some of these women are Anglo females married to Mexican-American males. In addition, the majority of these positions are non-supervisory.

Equality in employment for Chicanas is simply not a reality although the Chicano family organization is certainly changing. Chicanas, through divorce, separation, or other factors, are assuming the role of family breadwinner. In these families headed by women two-thirds of the incomes in the Los Angeles area alone are below the poverty level.

Chicana at protest rally, Los Angeles, early 1970s. Courtesy Raul Ruiz, *La Verdad* magazine, Los Angeles, California.

MAPPING A CHICANA FEMINIST AGENDA

Introduction

Chicana feminists transformed their ideological discourse into feminist praxis during the Chicano movement by organizing various types of conferences, symposiums, and workshops at the local, regional, and national levels. Chicana feminists also participated in general Chicano movement conferences, particularly meetings of the La Raza Unida Party. In addition, Chicana feminists attended national and international women's conferences. Section Three includes the writings by some of the key Chicana feminists such as Evey Chapa, Marta Cotera, Francisca Flores, and Anna Nieto-Gómez, who were present at some of the major conferences of this period and who reported their analysis in Chicano newspapers and their own Chicana feminist publications. Selections included in this section provide historical documentation that will allow future scholars of feminist movements in the United States and the Chicano movement of the late 1960s and 1970s to place Chicana feminist discourse and activity in its proper historical context.

In general, the participation of Chicana feminists in these political activities demonstrated a growing awareness of the need for Chicanas to collectively formulate their most salient issues and concerns and, in addition, discuss the formation of a feminist organizational structure to deal with their feminist agenda. This process uncovered persistent sources of tension among Chicana feminists as they voiced a diversity of ideological perspectives. Significant sources of tension involved social class differences, political orientation, their views on the white women's feminist movement, their relationship with other women of color in the United States, their affinity with Third World women, specifically Latin American women and, inevitably, their role as feminists within the Chicano movement. The outcomes of such conflicts produced ideological splits that often manifested themselves in groups of Chicana feminists walking out of a conference or boycotting it altogether. The 1971 National Chicana Conference held in Houston, Texas represented a classic case study of internal political struggles. Essays by Marta Cotera, Francisca Flores, Elma Barrera and Anna Nieto-Gómez provide insightful discussions of this first national conference of Chicana feminists.

Such internal disputes notwithstanding, Chicana feminists did produce a feminist agenda that consisted of their most pressing demands. Based on their continued disillusionment with the sexism of the Chicano movement, Chicana feminists emphasized the need to redefine the role of Chicanas at all levels. They organized numerous workshops on the "New Chicana" and "Liberation Chicana Style." Similarly, a Chicana feminist agenda focused on the general topic of equal opportunities and social justice for Chicanas in the areas of education, employment, income, child care, reproductive rights, and political representation in Chicano organizations. Chicana feminists worked diligently to revise existing by-laws and platforms of political organizations such as La Raza Unida Party, in order to institutionalize their feminist concerns. The formation of Chicana organization also witnessed the on-going political cleavages among Chicana feminists. The issue of reproductive rights with a specific focus on abortion rights produced intense disagreement among Chicanas. During the pre-Roe v. Wade years, several conferences and workshops included debates over the support for the legalization of abortion. Such factors as forced sterilization of Chicanas and Latinas, a religious tradition of Catholicism, and the belief that abortion represented cultural genocide for Chicano communities, all contributed to the debate over abortion rights. Nevertheless, resolutions passed by some of the major conferences did included support for the legalization of abortion. Still, Chicana feminists qualified such support by calling for low-cost, community controlled abortion clinics with bilingual staff.

The issue of Chicana feminist lesbians began to surface in the last years of the 1970s. The hostility usually encountered by Chicana feminist lesbians made it difficult, but not impossible, to raise this issue. Records show, nevertheless, that feminist conferences did address this issue. Lesbian concerns were usually only incorporated into conference structures at the insistence of lesbians. It was not until the mid-1980s and the 1990s, that the concerns of Chicana feminist lesbians became directly addressed within the context of such organized Chicana feminist activities.

Chicana feminists also began to push for the participation of Chicanas in electoral politics at the local and state levels. Articles by Evey Chapa and Cecilia Burciaga called for Chicana organizations to encourage and support Chicana feminists as political candidates. Paradoxically, the essay by Dolores Prida supported the efforts of Chicana political candidates and their supporters yet Prida also raised a cautionary reminder to Chicana feminists regarding the nature of the political system. Prida argued that a basic political lesson involved the fate of social movements, like the Chicana feminist movement, that turn to electoral politics. Such a development, Prida stressed, risked curbing, if not eliminating altogether, the movement's role as an oppositional political force.

Hijas de Cuauhtémoc (1971)

Hijas de Cuauhtémoc
son las flores de nuestra nación,
dieron luz a nuestra gente Azteca,
fueron sacrificadas al Dios Huitzilopochtli,
fueron violadas por los españoles y
dieron luz a nuestra gente mestiza.
Hijas de las Adelitas de la revolución,
Luchadoras por la libertad.
Les damos gracias a ustedes, nuestras madres,
que nos han dado el sagrado privilegio
de ser también, Hijas de Cuauhtémoc,
luchadoras por la libertad no solo
para nuestra Raza, pero libertad para
nosotros, las Hijas de Cuauhtémoc que
somos las reinas y madres de nuestra nación.

Leticia Hernández

Let Justice Be Done (1970)

On a bed in a shack a brown child lies
He tosses in anguish and restlessly sighs
His mother sits by him and helplessly cries
His father is broken, he knows his son dies
He must be in Calcutta, Ceylon or Bombay
No, he's in San Antonio, Texas, USA.
In the land of the free and the home of the brave
He is dying of hunger, he cannot be saved
Come brothers and sisters and weep by his grave
This child is our child, we are all one
La Raza Unida—Let Justice be done.

Joanne González

36

*Chicana Conferences and Seminars, 1970–1975**

MARTA COTERA

Chicana Workshop, Denver Youth Liberation Conference. March 1969. (Held at the Crusade for Justice in Denver, Colorado, well known because the women supposedly indicated they did not want to be "liberated," which more than likely meant that they were not ready to take a stand on the issue of Anglo feminism; Enriqueta Vasquez of Española, New Mexico, has written extensively on this workshop.)

Raza Unida Conference in Austin, Texas, July 1970. (An informal Chicana caucus led by Marta Cotera, who spoke of presenting women's needs at the next statewide meeting.)

Women's Workshop of the Mexican-American National Issues Conference, October 10, 1970, Sacramento, California. (This workshop was organized by Francisca Flores and Simmie Romero Goldsmith and resulted in the creation of the Comisión Femenil Mexicana.)

Women's Caucus, Raza Unida Conference, Houston, Texas, winter 1970. (Informal session among Texan Chicanas; discussion on the fact that there were no women speakers or workshop leaders; among those present were Yolanda Birdwell, Carmen Lomas Garza, Gloria Guardiola, Marta Cotera, Alma Canales.)

Chicana Regional Conference, May 8, 1971, Los Angeles, California.

La Conferencia de Mujeres Por la Raza, May 28–30, 1971, Houston, Texas, YMCA. (This conference is sometimes referred to as the National Chicana Conference and is historical because, as far as it is known, it is the first national conference ever held for and by Chicanas in the United States. It was organized by Elma Barrera and the staff of the Magnolia Park Branch YWCA. Speakers and workshop leaders included the most active Chicanas in the nation. Keynote speakers were Grace Olivarez, lawyer, and Julie Ruiz, School of Social Work, Arizona State University.)

HEW Women's Action Program, Research Recommendations, July 1–2, 1971. Washington, D.C. (mostly Chicanas). (A conference organized by Lupe Anguiano for the purpose of establishing research and program priorities for Chicanas. Some of the women present included educators Cecilia Suárez, Gracia Molina de Pick, Mirian

---

*Partial listing of conferences compiled by Cotera and published in 1980. (*Twice a Minority*. St. Louis: Mosby, 1980: pp. 228–231.)

Ojeda, Teresa Aragón de Shepro, Vera Martínez, sociologist Deluvina Hernández, and community persons Paulina Jacobs, Esther Martínez, and Marta Cotera. This group organized the National Chicana Foundation.)

Spanish-Speaking Coalition Conference, Women's Caucus, October 23–24, 1971.

Eastern Region National Spanish-Speaking Women's Caucus, December 15, 1971, New York City.

Midwest Region "Mi Raza Primero," Women's Caucus, February 22–23, 1972, Muskegan, Michigan. (Some of the organizers were Olga Villa, Jane González, and Rhea Mojica Hammer.)

Southwest Meeting, February 22, 1972, San Diego, California (mostly Chicanas).

Washington, D.C., Spanish-speaking women employed in various federal and non-federal agencies, February 23, 1972, Washington, D.C.

League of United Latin American Citizens, Women's Affairs Committee, March 11–12, 1972, Phoenix, Arizona.

Chicana Caucus, National Chicano Political conference, San Jose, California, April 21–23, 1972.

Midwest Spanish-Speaking Women's Political Conference, May 6, 1972, Notre Dame, Indiana.

Chicano Studies/MECHA Conference, California State University, Northridge, California, May 1972. (This conference supported a resolution introduced by Chicanas to require all Chicano studies majors to include at least one course on la Mujer [Chicanas].)

Women's Auxiliary, American G.I. Forum, July 26–29, 1972, Washington, D.C. (special women's meeting).

National Chicana Caucus, National Women's Political Caucus (NWPC), Houston, Texas, February 9–11, 1973. [Over 100 Chicanas from all states in the United States gathered to strategize and pass resolutions on issues relating to the Chicana. Among those in attendance were Alicia Escalante, Rhea Mojica Hammer (who won a national office with NWPC), Lupe Anguiano, Maria Cárdenas, Evey Chapa, Lydia Serrata, and Marta Cotera). Many Anglo women like Sally Andrade and Jeanette Lizcano were part of the caucus and helped in the floor maneuverings.]

Chicana Curriculum Workshop, University of California, Los Angeles, California, June 18–22, 1973. (This workshop, headed by the best-known Chicana academicians, resulted in the first Chicana curriculum adequate for colleges and universities and adoptable for high schools, entitled *New Directions in Education: Estudios Femeniles de la Chicana,* edited by Anna Nieto-Gómez.)

Mujeres Pro-Raza Unida Statewide Conference, San Antonio, Texas, August 4, 1973. [Organized by women active in Texas RUP (Raza Unida Party) politics—Irma Mireles, Juanita Luera, Ino Álvarez, Evey Chapa, Chelo Ávila, and Marta Cotera—the conference resolved to work for the development of women within the party.]

Institute to Prepare Chicanas in Administration, Washington, D.C., July–August 1973. (This institute was headed by Corine Sánchez and involved women from throughout the nation; courses of study included the curriculum previously developed at U.C.L.A.)

Chicana Educational Conference, Austin, Texas, at St. Edwards University, February 23, 1974. (Sponsored by Olga de León and Imelda Ramos, the conference was statewide and issues included bilingual education, employment, day care, welfare, rape, and revenue sharing.)

Mexican-American Business and Professional Women of Austin, Steering Committee and Organizational Meeting, Austin, Texas, March 1974. First annual meeting was held in June 1974. (Organized by Austin Chicanas including Annabelle Valle, Amalia Mendoza and Marta Cotera to work locally on Chicana issues.)

Chicana Symposium, Texas Southern University, TSU Week, Houston, Texas, April 22, 1974.

Conferencia Chicana Estatal, José Antonio School, Montezuma, New Mexico, August 23–25, 1974. (Purpose of the conference was to involve more barrio women in the movement, and to focus on women's issues, food stamps, child care, school systems, housing, and sex discrimination.)

Chicana Symposium held during Chicana Month, University of Texas at El Paso, October 4, 1974.

Chicana Seminar, University of Notre Dame, Notre Dame, Indiana, spring 1975. [Participants and workshop leaders included Olga Villa (Midwest), Lydia Espinosa (Texas), Evey Chapa (Texas), Gracia Molina de Pick (California), and Gloria Gutiérrez Roland (Texas).]

Chicana Week Seminar, University of Texas, Austin, Texas, May 1975.

Mexican-American Business and Professional Women of El Paso, Texas Conference, August 1975.

National Chicana Foundation Meeting, Tucson, Arizona, August 8, 1975.

National Chicana Foundation Meeting, Los Angeles, California, October 15, 1975.

Chicana Identity Conference, University of Houston, Houston, Texas, November 15, 1975. (Organized by Mujeres Unidas de Houston, Texas, including Luisa Vallejo, Chris Vásquez, and others. This conference was statewide in scope and topics were both academic and community oriented with history, education, labor, and politics as main concerns. Keynote speakers were Anna Nieto-Gómez, Northridge, California, and Marta P. Cotera, Austin, Texas.)

Formation of Mexican-American Women's National Association, Washington, D.C., 1976.

Chicana Advisory Committee for International Women's Year, a statewide advisory committee organized in Texas, which reached 2,000 Chicanas about the IWY activities; also coordinated activities with other states, 1977.

37

*Chicana Symposium**

ANONYMOUS

The "Corazón de Aztlán" symposium at UCLA was announced by MECHA for November 25, and the more worldly Chicanos breathed deeply and said, "about time." There were enough disparaging remarks too. But the fact that some Chicanos were involved in the creation of the symposium has to mean that perhaps the novelty of women's liberation will soon wear out, and we can get down to business.

That over 1,000 Chicanos and Chicanas participated in the symposium shows that many more Chicanas are seeing themselves as capable of contributing much more creatively than in the past. The degree of her participation, as well as the areas of her activity will be more thoughtfully selected. She will choose more, and cease sitting on the shelf waiting to act as a temporary stop gap, or emergency secretary.

Active Chicanas in the Southwest composed the panel. They discussed the activity of their organizations, as well as its ideology. This was not too different from any other rap given by panelists at any other conference. But there was more. Their own particular role as women (first in the context of their own organizations, and then in the greater Chicano movement) was the thing that directed us back to the topic of liberation. Here the panelists could have come out a little heavier. There was not enough discussion on the reality of where the liberation movement for the Chicana goes from here.

All this has made some Chicanas uptight. This is not entirely a bad thing. There is no reason for anyone to get uptight. The attempt is to bring up the other end of the circle, to create a whole unit—the Chicano movement. For example, the speakers themselves are very important contributing factors to their organizations.

Again in terms of units composing wholes, the age level of the symposium panelists alone would give us the impression that liberated Chicanas are generally over 30. Yet, the symposium was sponsored by young students, and the majority of those in attendance were young [women].

The generality that could be drawn from this is that the older Chicanas are living liberation, while the younger ones are still planning their move towards it. Chicana liberation is on its way, and in order to prevent stagnation, the Chicanas from the barrio, the campus, from fifteen years old to fifty years old must direct it together.

The reason for having conferences and symposiums is not to sit around talking about the liberation movement in terms of the Chicanas' own particular problems, but rather to discuss the *reality of work* in the movement, or the "what" of our practical contribution. But besides the usual differences in ideology, the Chicana must contend

*From *La Raza*, Vol. 2, No. 10, December, 1969.

with social problems involving her and the Chicano. One outstanding example is the issue of anglo chicks and brown dudes. Chicanas have never dug it, and now they are protesting loudly. The dudes have always rationalized it away from any meaningful discussion. Emotions ran extra high at the symposium when this and its related subject of anglo involvement in the [Chicano] movement were discussed. Both of these are very heated topics around today.

Comments from the panelists on the question of Anglo participation in the movement ranged from liberal to ultra-nationalistic. Of course, their frame of reference was from their own particular organizations and sections of the country, and no attempt was made by them to impose their positions on anyone. The conclusion was that to define the Anglo's role in the movement throughout the entire Southwest is simply ridiculous.

All in all, the symposium brought about some interesting and vital discussion, and is one more important step toward crushing the notion of the liberation movement as a mere novelty and then concentrating on it as a necessity.

It is beneath the dignity of the Chicana to quibble about where her place is. She is where she best serves the movement. There must be respect for her ability to decide. There is no room for patronizing males. We must be *Compañeros en la lucha. Mano en Mano* [Comrades in the struggle. Hand in Hand]. *Adelante!* [*Onward!*]

38

*Resolutions from the Chicana Workshop**

ANONYMOUS

[*La Verdad* Editor's Note: One of the most important and controversial workshops that developed during the Denver Conference [1969] last March was the Chicana Workshop. The following is a statement put out by the workshop and a list of the resolutions that grew out of it.

*From *La Verdad*, June, 1970: p. 9.

The Chicano Women Resolve Not to Separate but to Strengthen Aztlán, the Family of the Raza.

With the grave responsibility of the re-birth and forming of our Nation of Aztlán the women have come to realize that they must begin to develop and function as complete human beings. We have reached a point in our struggle for the liberation of La Raza where the growth of our women is repressed as a great potential for strength and knowledge. We must through education develop a full consciousness and awareness of the woman to the revolution and of the revolution to the women. This is the beginning for women to free themselves psychologically of thinking of themselves as inferior beings and to educate themselves so that they too can implement the Plan de Aztlán. In order to implement the Plan, we must understand all of the things that it calls for.

With the preceding things kept in mind, we *resolve* the following:

1. All women must participate according to their capability in all levels of the struggle.

2. We encourage all Chicanas to meet in their own groups for the purpose of education and discussion.

3. Self-determination of the women in terms of how they will implement their goal of becoming full human beings and participants [in the Chicano movement].

4. We must change the concept of the alienated family where the woman assumes total responsibility for the care of the home and the raising of the children to the concept of La Raza as the united family. With the basis being brotherhood, La Raza, both men and women, young and old, must assume the responsibility for the love, care, education, and orientation of all the children of Aztlán.

5. All of the preceding ideas must be included in the ideology of the La Raza Independent Political Party so that everyone, men and women will work consciously towards the goal of total liberation of our people. For the purpose of unity and direction, the women of La Raza have set up communication in the form of a newsletter to be shared by all women active in the struggle for the liberation of our people.

We resolve not to separate but to strengthen and free our nation of Aztlán, women, men, and children.

39

Chicana Service Action Center *

Anna NietoGomez

The Chicana Service Action Center [CSAC] is one of the largest employment programs in Los Angeles. Leadership and inspiration is provided by Francisca Flores, the Executive Director of CSAC. Chicana leadership, advocacy for women's issues, as well as employment for low-income women are the focus of women activists at the Center.

Women Search for Work

The purpose of CSAC is to ultimately place women into jobs which will lead to upgrading and advancement. The women who come to the center vary in age, ethnicity, and education, but they share the need for employment. Social issues such as child care, legal aid, welfare rights, and housing are endemic to the lower social economic experience. Social services are directed towards relieving these problems in order to free women to work.

The Chicana Service Action Center is an environment where Chicanas are working together to serve women. A sense of moral support and spiritual strength is experienced by the women when they realize that they are not the only ones trying to escape the dependence and hopelessness of welfare.

Opportunities for job preparation, work experience, on-the-job training and nontraditional training programs for women create new alternatives for self-development and a renewed hope for a brighter future for the low income women.

The seedlings for the establishment of a center to serve Chicanas were planted almost ten years ago. Manuela Banda, Francisca Flores, Simmie Goldsmith, Jo Valdez, Bernice Rincón and many others, planned the first Chicana workshop held for the 1970 Mexican-American National Issues Conference in Sacramento. This workshop was the grandmother of the Chicana Service Action Center.

The Chicana Workshop at the 1970 Mexican-American Issues Conference

Approximately 40 women attended the workshop. Most of them had been married, workers, and political activists. Reports were given by Lilia Aceves, Bernice Rincón and Frances Bojórquez. Francisca Flores chaired the workshop. The reports stimulated

*This essay discusses 1970 Chicana Workshop at the Mexican-American Issues Conference. From *Somos*, July–August, 1979: pp. 12–15.

148

many questions. The women addressed the issues of abortion, birth control, child care, stereotypes of the Chicana, machismo, and Chicana leadership.

Resolutions

In general, the Chicana Workshop at the 1970 Mexican-American National Issues Conference was a success. Chicanas agreed to act on the issues facing them.

They recognized child care centers were crucial to the advancement of the Chicana, and planned to support and organize bilingual, bicultural, 16-hour child care centers. Birth control was identified as an important aspect in women achieving control of their destiny. Legalized abortion was considered within the interest of the general welfare of Chicanas.

Chicanas were victims of stereotypes, and did not have respect or credibility in their community. Although most of the women attending the workshop had worked in the community for years, they regretted that they were not generally accepted as part of the leadership in the Chicano movement. Machismo and negative stereotypes of the Chicana demoralized the women and stunted their development. The creation of a women's organization was the only alternative in the face of unequal representation of women in community organizations and the general lack of respect for their abilities.

A women's organization could promote positive images of the Chicana, develop leadership, increase their credibility, and win the respect of the community. It could advocate constructive changes for the Chicana in education, employment, health, and welfare. At the same time, it could extend its support and unity to women in the world-wide movements.

A unanimous vote came from a Chicana Organization, Comisión Femenil Mexicana, whose members would organize and train women to assume leadership in the community. It would disseminate news and information regarding the work and achievement of Chicanas. And most important, it would focus on the problems and solutions of the Chicana. It was at this time that Francisca Flores was elected President of the organization, which eventually gave birth to the Chicana Service Action Center.

By 1978, the Chicana Service Action Center combined social action with employment services. A battered women's shelter was established in East Los Angeles to help women who were victims of domestic violence.

Women and their children find themselves trapped in relationships with violent men. Although they are forced to leave their home for their own protection, they do not have a place to go. Women without marketable skills have few economic resources at their disposal to support themselves after they have left home. A few are lucky if they locate emergency shelter at a mission or a "skid row" motel. The CSAC Shelter provided another alternative for desperate victims of family violence.

The CSAC Shelter is maintained strictly by volunteer help. Funds for food, and keeping the facility open are totally dependent on fund-raising efforts of the CSAC volunteers. Since the State had not made domestic violence a priority, only six shelters were funded by the State of California in 1978. At present, the survival and future of the CSAC Shelter is dependent on the dedication of women helping women. And the Chicana Service Action Center continues to trail blaze new paths for the Chicana's struggle for equal opportunity.

40

*Comisión Femenil Mexicana**

FRANCISCA FLORES

More often than not, when the issue of women enters a conversation . . . all of the defenses go up. The women become defensive because they do not want to be considered anti-men and the men immediately feel challenged. The composition of the group does not matter; lower economic or professional, the scene is the same. And yet, in all fairness to the more enlightened men, it must be said that there is a growing army of those who understand, those who appreciate what women bring into a movement. Women too: more Chicanas are fighting for their own identity, and they do not care who does not like it. Women must learn to say what they think and feel, and free to state it without apologizing or prefacing every statement to reassure men that they are not competing with them.

The Comisión Femenil Mexicana was organized [1970] to provide a platform for women to use for thinking out their problems, to deal with issues not customarily taken up in regular organizations, and to develop programs around home and family needs. This it has done. One of the fringe benefits women have experienced as a result of this effort has been more sensitivity on the part of men they work with in the community. It has also infused more humor into their work. Now, they can laugh as well as cry about personal problems. A means to discuss anxieties, fears, ask questions that could never be asked of others is available through members of the organization. The women can discuss abortions without having to first discuss the emotional question of moral issue. Few women raise this question when dealing with pregnancy. Women who seek abortion do not first get into a discussion of moral issue. The need to end the pregnancy is present, urgent and the quicker they can address themselves to that issue the better.

Abortion is a fact of life. Long before more moderate laws were introduced, women were engaged in aborting pregnancies, many times endangering their health. Some in desperation going to quick abortion mills or to unscrupulous medical men bent on making a fast buck. Abortion, in our opinion, is a personal decision. The women must be allowed to make it without legal restrictions.

*From *Regeneración*, Vol. 2, No. 1, 1971: pp. 6–7.

41

Chicanas Attend Vancouver Conference*

ANONYMOUS

Women from many countries and U.S. states came together in Vancouver, British Columbia on April first [1971] to take part in an international women's conference that would go on through April sixth. This was the second women's conference in Vancouver organized by The Voice of Women/Women Strike for Peace, for the purpose of peace. At the first conference in 1967, the Indochinese women asked that there be a second conference to include third world women since none of the participants there were third world. The conference in April of this year was set up expressly for the purpose of having third world women participate in a conference dealing with the wars in Indochina.

Some of us Chicanas who went to the conference have been asked why we went to a white women's thing. Well, if the Vancouver Conference had been a white women's thing we would have gone to learn from the experience and to make it a Chicana thing, because the war in Viet Nam is affecting Chicano people too. We have also been asked why it was a women's conference since men and women could join together to end the war. Yes, men and women would be more effective if they joined together to end the war, but the truth is that men and women are not together on a lot of things and the reason for this is that men aren't together with themselves and women aren't together with themselves either. We as women want to get together on every level including a political level. We have been brought up with the ideas that men take leading roles and women aren't political. This conference was mainly a political experience for women. The conference was divided into four parts. On April first the Indochinese women met with the Voice of Women/Women Strike for Peace. On April second the Indochinese women had an open session with the public. On April third and fourth the Indochinese women met with third world women. On April fifth and sixth the Indochinese women met with the women's liberation, which included the poor white women, lesbians, etc.

During the third world session of the historical conference, political, and cultural presentations were given by women from different states, regions, and countries. The Indochinese women responded to these and sang a couple of songs after our cultural presentation. Many things happened during the third world session—the poor white women gave a very brief and sincere presentation, and we were confronted by individual lesbians. Two very important things happened that need to be brought out. First, white women and some third world women asked if it were not true that we were being racist by not allowing the white women to come in and observe at our

*From *La Verdad,* No. 28, May, 1971: p. 14.

meetings with the Indochinese. Many points were brought up. One opinion was that we were discriminating solely on the basis of color since some girls were allowed simply because they were the right color. In other words, white women are oppressed yet they were not allowed. Another point brought up was that we should let the Anglo women observe so that they could learn. Also brought up was the point that we were discriminating at the expense of the time and comfort of the Indochinese since they would also have to allocate time and energy to meet with the white women. On the other hand it was brought up that it had been the decision of the Indochinese women to meet with us exclusively. Self-determination was brought up in that just as women had decided this would be a women's conference, third world women should be able to say that the sessions would be for third world women. Another point brought up was that although white women were always "observing" they never seemed to understand what we said. It was decided that the third world sessions with the Indochinese would be for third world women but the question still stands—[are] we being racist?

Another very important thing came up. At the conference there was a group of Chicanas who expressed the feeling that they wanted the Chicanas to get together as a group to talk about the conference, to get to know each other, or just to bring our feelings and ideas. Another group of Chicanas were entirely against this. They argued that this would be against the concept of the third world. The meeting was attempted but it did not succeed. From this experience we began to ask ourselves "What exactly is the third world concept" and knowing that we are both Chicanas and third world women, when are we third world women first and when are we Chicanas first?

Those of us Chicanas who went from San Diego decided that we learned one main thing at the Vancouver Conference. This was that we heard how not just Blacks and Chicanos, but Hawaiians, Canadians, Indians, Eskimos, North American Indians—people of the sun—had been deprived of their land and exploited, because they had different values, different concepts of the land, of time, and of life, than the conquering Europeans. Once their land was taken away and their values and morals belittled the people of color also lost their dignity and their spirit. This is what the Vietnamese are fighting—they won't give up their land, their dignity, or their spirit—they will not be a conquered people.

Women *can* get together on an international scale for a worthwhile thing. All the women who went to the conference can say that they learned by observing, or participating, even though most of us were observers, few of us actually participated. The Chicanas who went from San Diego feel that we could have learned much more if we had balanced participation with observation. This experience has taught us that in all future conferences relating to the Chicano, Chicanas should go and they should go knowing that they are going to observe *and* participate.

42

*Chicana Regional Conference**

SANDRA UGARTE

The Chicana Regional Conference was held May 8th at Los Angeles State College. The conference was sponsored by the Chicanas at Cal. State L.A., Los Angeles City College, and Long Beach State. There was an estimated 200 participants and it was looked upon as very successful. The conference covered such topics as philosophy, the *pinta* [prison], political education, the community, education and communication. Here we have some of the results and proposals as submitted by women up and down the state of California.

Philosophy Workshop

The philosophy workshop of *la Chicana nueva* [the new Chicana] covered such topics as the relationship between men and women, the Chicana and the family, the Chicano and the family, the oppression of the Church, and the oppression of society.

The Struggle Between Men and Women

The historic division between man and woman was recognized. These barriers are a carryover from historic oppressive institutions.

There were many approaches in attacking these problems. Many felt that Chicanos and Chicanas must first recognize that problems exists between them, and then they must define these problems; thus they will be able to work on solutions to actually strive for self-determination. Men and women must understand themselves before they can successfully change the system.

In order to recognize the problems, we must educate ourselves as to the different types of oppression, and how it has divided us.

We do not want to have one revolution against one oppressor and one-hundred years later fight a revolution against another oppressor.

We want liberation for all people.

Separation of La Familia y El Movimiento [*the Chicano family and the Chicano movement*]

These are some of the opinions in regard to problems of the relationship to the *familia y el movimiento*.

*From *Hijas de Cuahtémoc*, Vol. 1, No. 1, 1971: pp. 1–3.

1. The movement is an escape for *el hombre* [man] to get out of the house. Traditionally the *cantina* [the bar] was his escape. Now the movement has become his substitute.
2. The family often had to compete with the movement.
3. It was a divisive attitude for those men who felt that the movement came before the family, and that the family should not restrict or interfere with his involvement.
4. Marriages are breaking up because of the movement.
5. Children turn off to the movement because they hold the movement responsible for the breakup of their home.
6. Teacher and student relationships are perpetuating *la casa chica* [refers to the practice of a man keeping a mistress] standard.
7. In the absence of the man from *la familia*, the woman is to make decisions concerning the family by herself.

Achieve New Family Concepts

The family relationship and involvement with the movement should not be separate. *Chicanas y hombres* [women and men] must work together and try to educate themselves to new roles in order to meet the responsibility of building a nation.

The mother was often criticized for spoiling the men. Thus the mother must teach her son not to oppress another human being and also work for a new opening for the future of her daughter.

It is also the man's responsibility to keep the house organized.

Church and Family

The Church has worked to hinder and oppress the woman in many ways. It has taught the woman that she must suffer in order to get closer to God. Everytime *el hombre* walked out she became a martyr. Thus she accepted such things as *la casa chica*.

The Church has oppressed her by defining and limiting her role. The Church has supported the necessity to keep the woman ignorant, barefoot, and pregnant by condemning legal abortions and birth control.

It can be recognized that birth control can be used as genocide against people, but the Chicana has the right to have control over the destiny of her own body. In addition, abortion is not a new concept to La Chicana. Many Chicanas with large families risk their lives every day by trying to abort themselves or by having another do it for them.

Chicanas want to be able to say how many children they want and when. They no longer want to irresponsibly have a family through ignorance.

A young Chicana sixteen years old should have some alternative to turn to. Otherwise, if she becomes pregnant she is just a child having another child.

It must be understood that the Chicana is not condemning the past, but she is trying to strengthen the family.

The Chicana and Women's Liberation

It was recognized that few Chicanas really had information on the women's liberation movement. Therefore, she must investigate into what it is if only to reduce her paranoia whenever anyone accuses her of being women's Lib. Even so, there were definite feelings about the women's liberation movement. The Chicanas pointed out that there is a difference in oppression between middle class and lower class peoples. With Chicanas, it is a cultural, environmental, class, and racial oppression as well as an economic oppression.

And as Chicanas, self-determination is not identified with the white middle class Anglo woman.

Woman's Role, Historically

Historically, women of all nationalities have played a major role in all movements; however, the woman's role has not been heard of. Thus, by keeping both men and women ignorant of the important and various historic roles in societies, the system has used this ignorance as a divisive tool to keep men and women apart.

Societal Perspective of Oppression

We are in a struggle for the liberation of our people. In this struggle, we must recognize that there are many forms of oppression.

There is class, race, and women's oppression, which is tied into the same thing—capitalism. We cannot just separate these types of oppression and leave them separated. If we analyze it, we have to see how each form of oppression ties into the struggle as a whole.

We must start with the oppression of the Chicana woman and develop it to see how it ties into the Chicano movement. We must also realize how the Chicano movement ties into the struggle of all oppressed people.

43

La Conferencia De Mujeres Por La Raza*: Houston, Texas, 1971

MARTA COTERA

About 500 Chicanas attended a national conference in Houston, Texas, May 28–30, 1971. Approximately 80% of the women were in the 18–23 age bracket from various universities across the United States. The main theme covered throughout the confer-

*Conference also known as National Chicana Conference. From *Profile on the Mexican American Woman*, Austin: National Educational Laboratory Publishers, 1976: pp. 224–227.

ence was that of clarifying the women's role as Chicanas and in the [Chicano] movement, mainly eliminating the passive role (home and motherhood) the Chicana has always played.

Among one of the main speakers was Julia Ruiz, an assistant professor of social work at Arizona State University. Her topic was "The Mexican-American Women's Public and Self-Image." Central to the speech was the idea that "togetherness can liberate Chicanas." The only choice in this society for Chicana women has been the home and motherhood. Chicanas have to fight together for liberation so that they will have a choice. Chicana women can change the society that places inferior sexist and racist labels on them. Too much hatred has been stamped on Chicana women and it has to be shed.

Workshops were held on identity and movimiento issues. Topics ranged from "marriage Chicana style" to "religion," and "militancy or conservatism—which way is forward?" to "exploitation of women—the Chicana perspective."

A resolution was easily passed that the conference join others from San Antonio in speaking out against the use of "dummy" birth control pills in an experiment conducted on Chicana women, which resulted in ten unwanted babies.

Other resolutions, some of which met controversy, were: "We as *mujeres de la Raza* [women of la Raza] recognize the Catholic Church as an oppressive institution and do hereby resolve to break away and not go to them to bless our unions, and [give our] support for free and legal abortions for all women who want and need them."

Throughout the whole conference, in the workshops, in group sessions, a lot of personal differences were brought out. By Sunday, on the whole, the conference had divided into two groups. One group staged a walk-out because the conference was being held in a "Gringo" [white] institution [YWCA] and should have been in the "barrio" where the people were. They went to a nearby "barrio" park to finish up their evaluations and resolutions. The other group decided to stay in the YWCA and finish up the conference, making evaluations and resolutions. Last-minute workshops on "strategies for [the future]" were cancelled because of this reason. Two sets of final resolutions and evaluations were finally presented.

La Conferencia de Mujeres por la Raza

Complaints were presented by Group I that no "barrio" people were represented at the conference. Group II remarked that they were, but when they (barrio residents) talked, attention, and respect, were not given to them.

Key Points

1. Chicana women not only want to support the men in the [Chicano] movement, but also want to participate.

2. With further involvement in the movement, marriages have changed; traditional roles for Chicanas are not acceptable or applicable anymore.

3. Chicanas want Chicano and public recognition as a major facilitator in the movement.

4. Education and career opportunities are wanted for Chicanas.

5. There is a tremendous amount of personal and group differences among

Chicana women. Some will react, others respond rationally, others just rap a lot and still, no action. We feel, along with other Chicana women at the conference, that it makes no difference how many differences there are between what we think. The most important thing is to look at common problems, to get ourselves together, and even more important [to decide] what we're going to do.

44

Conference of Mexican Women in Houston—Un Remolino [*A Whirlwind*]*

FRANCISCA FLORES

The Conferencia de Mujeres Por La Raza held in Houston, Texas over Memorial Day weekend was the beginning of a *chubasco* [storm] to say the least. Like the *chubascos* that threaten La Paz from time to time, the women's conference represented such force and potential for a breakthrough against existing stumbling blocks and obstacles in the women's struggle for equality . . . that persons within the movement who disagreed with this direction, urged and supported some women to form a flank within the groundswell of the conference in order to break it.

Close to 600 women participated in the workshops held at the Magnolia Branch of the Houston YWCA. Some of the workshops held on Saturday were so large that only the most vocal and most aggressive could be heard discussing issues that interest women but which are shaking the men who feel threatened by women in action, women in leadership roles, women who are literally out of reach of the masculine dictum.

The three workshops which received the greatest and the hottest discussion were: Sex and the Chicana—Noun and Verb; Marriage: Chicana Style; and the Feminist Movement: Do We Have a Place in It? In these workshops the question of the role of women in relation to men, and to the Anglo society were raised. The waves

*From *Regeneración*, Vol. 1, No. 10, 1971: pp. 1–5.

raised by these issues split over into the afternoon workshops and the discussion and controversies which developed continued through the night. By Sunday morning the women who believed that women in the Chicano community must submit to the dominance of the men walked out. Much of their rationale was superficial . . . charging that the YWCA was using the women to further their own program to wipe out racism . . . that women of the barrio were not invited . . . that men were not allowed to attend, although there were "gringas" present.

Scratch the Surface

Beneath the rhetoric, such as so many people use these days, and which the most out-spoken participants engaged in, were the fundamental issues of: the right of self-determination by Mexican women over questions affecting their bodies. The issue of birth control, abortions, information on sex and the pill are considered "white" women's lib issues and should be rejected by Chicanas according to the Chicano philosophy that believes that the Chicana women's place is in the home and that her role is that of a mother with a large family. Women who do not accept this philosophy are charged with betrayal of "our culture and heritage." *Our culture, hell!* Many of the women who insist that the woman's place is in the home are college students or graduates.

Mexican women who bear (large) families beyond the economic ability to support them, suffer the tortures of damnation when their children die of malnutrition, of tuberculosis and other illnesses which wipe out families in poverty stricken or marginal communities in the Southwest. The young people, as well as others, who promote such theoretical absurdities do not know what they are saying. *If a woman wants a large family . . . no one will interfere with her right to have one . . .* even if they cannot personally afford it . . . that is their right. However, to stipulate this right as a tenet of *la causa* for all women of la Raza is to play a dangerous game with the movement. It means—stripped of its intellectual romanticism—that Chicanas are being condemned to wash diapers and stay home all of their youth . . . something that the girls in college are not doing, although some of them are the ones insisting that their *hermanas de raza* [sisters] do so because this "is their role."

They are some strong women who can handle a family and a career at the same time. Some can make motherhood a career by giving birth to many children in an equal number of years. However, most women cannot. In the course of many pregnancies many mothers and children do not make it. The toll in human life is very great. If the promulgators of the "Chicana's role is in the home having large families" also projects concern with the health problems of abnormal or self-induced abortions and still born births, we might accept their contentions as a basis for discussion. As it stands, however, we have to conclude that their belief on the role of the Mexican women is based on erroneous cultural and historical understanding of what is meant by "our cultural heritage," as it relates to the family.

What We Say

As stated before, the question of large families is the choice each person or family will make for themselves. That is their inalienable right. A woman who wants a large family should not be denied. What we are saying is that the woman should have the right to participate in making that decision. And if she chooses to have a large family she should enjoy all of the protection and benefits necessary for her and her children's health and economic well being. This means that the health and well being of her husband is very important . . . otherwise, the family is jeopardized . . . if they are left to shift for themselves economically. It can devastate a family. In East Los Angeles, CA, it is estimated that 20% of the heads of family are women. This is 1/5 of all Mexican households. The men, formerly heads of these families, have real problems. And these problems must be taken into account when discussing the role of individuals in a family. The cry of machismo will not answer these problems.

The women who advocate that the woman's place is in the home and that they should raise large families should contemplate long and seriously the ramifications of their theory and develop a program to fit the needs of women who stay home and raise large families. These needs cannot be filled with rhetorical abstracts—stripped of its verbage—which means continued inequality and suppression of women. Further, those who promote backward and reactionary theories cannot cleanse themselves by engaging in diversionary tactics . . . blaming all who do not agree with them—as being *women's lib!* The tactics of reaction used to be red-baiting . . . now we have women-baiting. Women's lib, *indeed!*

A Weekend Long to Be Remembered

The influence and impact of the Houston Conference of Mujeres Por la Raza may not be fully realized for many years to come. It has given greater impulse to discussion on the role of Mexican women which has been going on for the last two or three years. There have been numerous attempts, on the part of women, in general Chicano organizations to express themselves as a group. However, men have been mildly interested and amused by their efforts. A couple of years ago, the women attending the Denver Youth Conference [1969] met in a workshop to discuss their role within this movement . . . however, they returned to report: "It was the consensus of the group that the Chicana woman does not want to be liberated."

Last year, the women in MAPA, Mexican-American Political Association, attempted to establish a women's caucus at their annual convention. The caucus only functioned during the course of the convention. Women attending the Latino Conference held in Wisconsin, last year, also held a workshop on women. One of the proposals voted out was that one-third of the leadership of the organization be made up of women. It is not known if their organizational efforts continue in effect or if they have become lost in the general policy that the women's first responsibility is to the men and to keep the family together.

Other organizations have dealt with women. Some have auxiliaries which meet separately but function together on issues of over-all concern. Women in these types of organizations usually do the housekeeping tasks of the men's organizations. Last year, the Mexican-American National Issues Conference [1970], meeting in Sacramento, included a workshop on women. This workshop voted to become the *Comisión Femenil Mexicana* and functions as an independent organization affiliated to the Mexican-American National Issues Conference. (Femenil, for those who do not understand Spanish, means feminine or womanly).

Resolution

The effort and work of Chicana/Mexican women in the Chicano movement is generally obscured because women are not accepted as community leaders either by the Chicano movement or by the Anglo establishment.

The existing myopic attitude does not, however, prove that women are not capable or willing to participate. It does not prove that women are not active, indispensible (representing over 50% of the population), experienced, and knowledgable in organizing tactics and strategy of a people's movement.

Therefore, in order to terminate exclusion of female leadership in the Chicano/Mexican movement and in the community, be it *resolved* that a Chicana/Mexican women's commission be established at this Conference which will represent women, in all areas where Mexicans prevail, and;

That this commission be known as the Comisión Femenil Mexicana, and;

That the Comisión direct its efforts to organizing women to assume leadership positions within the Chicano movement and in community life, and;

That the Comisión disseminate news and information regarding the work and achievement of Mexican/Chicana women, and;

That the Comisión concern itself in promoting programs which specifically lend themselves to help, assist and promote solutions to female type problems and problems confronting the Mexican family, and;

That the Comisión spell out issues to support and explore ways to establish relationship with other women's organizations and movements.

VIVA LA RAZA!

Women on the Move

The women will have a lot to say from now on. Not only on those questions which affect them personally, such as abortions, the pill, sex information, child care, well being of the family, relationship to other women's organizations, education, equality, etc., but also issues of interest to the whole group, such as peace, prison reform, law enforcement. And this includes the welfare of the men.

Mexican women do have strong opinions on the inferior position to which they are relegated. At the Houston Conference a mini survey was taken on eight general and two specific questions. This survey indicated overwhelming agreement that women are considered second class citizens and that they are, basically, expected to be *amas de casa* [housewives]; 84% felt that they were not encouraged to seek professional careers and that higher education is not considered important for Mexican women. Only 68% thought that women were not given on the job training in industry or upgraded to skilled and semi-skilled positions, however, 84% agreed that women do not receive equal pay for equal work.

On one question, they were unanimous. When asked: Are married women and mothers who attend school expected to also do the housework, be responsible for child care, cook and do the laundry while going to school . . . 100% voted yes. 88% agreed that a social double standard exists.

The last two questions were very specific: 1. Is there a distinction between the problems of the Chicana and those of other women. 84% felt that there was. However, most did not state how. 2. This question was asked to find out if the women felt that there was discrimination towards them within la Raza. 72% said yes, none said no and 28% voiced no opinion.

There is no doubt that discussion will continue and controversies develop over methods of approach and exactly what the role of women within the Mexican movement is. However, those women who wish to continue playing a secondary role will do so, but it is hoped that they will respect the right of others who view solutions to problems faced by women are best served by their own effort through their own organizations within the total movement. Such organization of women will strengthen and complement the movement as a whole. Women, like any minority, have personal problems which many do not feel can be, or will be, discussed in general meetings of men. Women must have an avenue open to them, to deal with these issues so that they can project them for support of the whole movement of *la causa*.

What is Reality?

The phrase, "It is not our cultural heritage," used to reject issues or philosophies we do not agree with, is being used more and more these days. Presently, with the greater interest and action by Mexican women in *la causa* and the greater degree of attention being paid by the media on the "women's liberation movement," it is being used to cover many sins. Primarily, it is being advanced to reject the white middle class dogma of social values, however, it also serves to keep hidden some very important problems being faced by our young women.

Rationale

All rationale [and] rhetoric being given for opposing a movement for women's rights must be exposed, in order to allow for needed change in attitudes. Otherwise, the youth are going to pay heavily in mental and physical health.

Graciela Olivarez, in her speech at the Houston conference of *mujeres mexicanas* pointed out that the real problem faced by women (and men) in relation to machismo is that they both suffer from a "virgin image and a mother complex." "The young men," she pointed out, "look up to their mothers as saints, as virgins (all women worthy of marriage must be virgins). The mother is placed on a pedestal. The young man cannot face the fact that his mother had to have intercourse with his father in order to give birth to him." Therefore, the Mexican woman . . . *lindísima mujer* [beautiful woman] . . . in the mind of the male, must be a virgin when he marries her. The family, the church, but most important, the attitude of the men, and the girl's own sense of guilt does not allow her to face the reality. Sexual involement requires preventative measures, if unwanted pregnancies are to be avoided. Abortion may seem the way out for these young women, but the price they will have to pay later, may be fatal. All because we insist that "our cultural heritage" implies that the woman must be placed on a pedestal, without examining the reason for this attitude, it's inevitable consequences and it's effect on the youth. We must bring this issue out into the open . . . discuss it and its psychological implications upon our community. Only in this way will it be possible to lift the burden it is placing on our women.

45

Chicana Encounter*

ANNA NIETOGOMEZ AND ELMA BARRERA

The convention [National Chicana Conference, Houston 1971] was organized by a very small group of women working at the YWCA. The YWCA was located in the middle of the six Houston barrios. The convention could have been organized from any center of organization. But we had the facilities and the promises of money from the "Y" people. Plus we had the woman power, actually the power that comes from any nucleus. We hoped this small group would generate more women, more leadership in the movement

We started developing the conference with all the hopes and good intentions imaginable. How could we have deluded ourselves into thinking it would work out? It turned into a fiasco, with so many accusations directed to us. At first there was bewilderment and bitterness. It still is difficult to erase the hurt and disappointment today. We really had no idea that women, Chicanas, could be so misinformed about one another.

"*El pleito es con el gavacho no con el macho,*" they said: We're no man haters, not against Chicanos or Chicanas, not against anything that stands for betterment of the movement, and in this case, not against the Chicana women. You see, *we were, and we are from the barrio.*

More than 600 Chicanas arrived that last weekend in May. But less than half let us know they were coming. Although, most were happy to be together, the groupies used our inexperience in conference organization to disrupt. How did we know more than 300 women would feel the need to come? "We have no place to go, give us transportation." Like rude guests, they began to treat us like servants: "I have no money to register." "Why should I pay?" "This is an irrelevant women's lib conference anyway." "Give us gas fares, and plane fares, we want to go home." "Feed me." "Power to the people."

And the workshops began: "With involvement in the movement, marriages must change." "Traditional roles for Chicanas are not acceptable or applicable." "Sex is good and healthy." "Free legal abortions and birthcontrol for Chicanas" "No sexual experiments on Chicanas." "24-hour daycare facilities for Chicano communities." "Religion and culture do not control our sexual lives." "No double standard between the sexes."

We are, from the barrio, *we are the barrio.*

They said it would happen—"Women's Lib." "Chicanas you are thinking of yourself first—that's an Anglo trip." "You're changing too fast where there should be

*From *Regeneración*, Vol. 2, No. 4, 1975: pp. 49–51.

no change." "What are the *real* political issues?" "Where is your allegiance to the movement." Like prodigals, 300 "returned to the barrio."

At the park they sang support of all the issues our people had fought for: "No Vietnam, No Chicano Political Prisoners, Viva La Huelga." Ashamed of flying a middle class jet to Houston, they proved their Chicano patriotism. They cleansed themselves of the guilt of confusion born of the problems of womankind. With each day, many became more indignant to each other. Disruptors attempted to stop the speech of Julie Ruiz. But the disruptors were insulted in their failure, for Julie merely turned her back and proceeded on. She spoke appropriately on the Mexican-American women's public and self image. The next day, someone sold *The Militant* newspaper. And they called us Socialists. There was a book display of Marxist ideology concerning the history of the family, and they called us communists. Others called us middle class, because we looked not like barrio women: But you see, *we were and we are from the barrio!*

I remember you standing on the platform, tears in your eyes. Pleading with the women to stay together, saying "This happens every time." I gathered at that time, this was the usual kind of thing. I had had no previous experience. I'm talking about the kind of experience convention groupies acquire. How to criticize, protest, demand, take over, and more than anything, condemn each other. You see, the movement is different here. We don't fight or bicker for power. We don't give fiery speeches. We don't have shoot outs, everything is much more subtle. This is the way we operate—right or wrong. This is the way we do things. And this is the way the conference, for some women, failed. We were too conservative.

You see, *we were and we are from the barrio!!*

Our only grave mistake was that we didn't have that convention groupie experience. Which so many of our Chicanas developed before they came to Houston. And so we didn't know, we couldn't understand why, we didn't have the defense that other women had built up. In short, we remained silent during the screaming and raging "We are the people del barrio?" We remained silent when a woman pushed one of our women away from the microphone. They pushed Berta. But it was her, the protestors demanded to see, but couldn't see. They, the college students, the government workers—Berta—who filled all the requirements of a stereotype barrio woman. Poor, broken English, no education. Short, dark and with lots of real suffering behind her. Yet she was pushed around because there were no barrio women. Or because we served hot dogs instead of mole. Or because the "Y" was airconditioned in the middle of May I still don't know why. *[Si supieran esas mujeres la agonia que nos causaron]* [If those women only knew the anguish that they caused us.] But I don't believe anyone will know

We were, *we are from, we are the barrio.*

They demanded to see people of the barrio. I had only hoped that they had come from the barrio. It was only barrio women that organized that conference. Marta Moreno still lives in the barrio down the street from the "Y." Lucy Moreno, her sister in law, married to Marta's brother, very active in community work, very Chicana, always working her ass off for the cause. Stella Borrego, a social worker, devoting most of her time in programs for the poor. She works at Ripley House, the barrio right next to Magnolia, where people don't make much over 4–5 thousand a year for a family of 6 or 7 kids. Me, born in West Texas, *cuando andaban mis padres en las piscas en el West* [when my parents worked in the fields in the West]. I could have been born in California, where they also migrated to pick peaches. Raised mostly in trucks and cotton fields. Berta Hernández, a welfare rights organizer, a real hell raiser. Probably stems from the years of beating from her husband, whom she finally left. Now she works with those who live in the same misery.

But you see it doesn't really matter that Marta has devoted most her life to la Raza. Neither she nor any of us looked the part of barrio women. To the eyes blurred with confusion, confrontation, and condemnation.

What happened at the conference? *Si pudiera contestar esa pregunta, posiblemente hubiera podido prevenir lo que paso aquel trágico fin de semana.* [If she could only answer that question, she could possibly have prevented what happened that tragic weekend.] The conference meant so much to the few that organized it. Its failure, and many do call it a failure, changed some lives. One woman dropped completely out. Although she was a main organizer, she has never been to another meeting, anytime, anywhere, since. *Otras* [others] have become *mas cerradas* [more withdrawn] within themselves, not caring quite as much for "community work" organization. *No quiero decir que cualquiera cosa las desanimaría.* [I don't want to imply that any small thing could have disillusioned them.] *Sinó que no conocen las cosas* [they don't understand the things] which kept the movement going. Too complicated. Today I can only say that I lived through it, and so did all the other women. It had a profound effect on some, it didn't faze others. But that weekend was only one week-end in our lives. A weekend no one will remember 10–15 years from now. Sounds a little bitter, but really, I'm not sorry we put it on. I'm sorry things happened as they did. It didn't turn out nice and orderly like we all thought it would, but I think it taught us more than we ever imagined. We learned about us, about *mujeres* [women] in the movement, about how some of us operate, right or wrong, like you, ever constant and courageous, *Cuando se Debe de ser* [when it is necessary to be].

We know, *we were and we are the women del barrio*!

46

*CCHE Conference**

ANONYMOUS

The CCHE (Chicano Committee on Higher Education) held in San Diego, March 19–20 was a historical policy-making weekend for the Chicana.

The electrifying atmosphere created by 19 state colleges assembling with the common objective of statewide unity came to a climax when it was unanimously re-

*From *Hijas de Cuauhtémoc*, Vol. 1, No. 1, 1971: p. 4.

solved that El Plan de Santa Barbara (the bible of CCHE and other higher education policy-making organizations) be revised to include the Chicana and her vital role in el movimiento. Equally important were the amendments that followed after Cal State College Long Beach's initial motion which included:

1. That no form of policy be made without adequate Chicana representation.
2. That Chicanas be recruited into significant faculty and administrative positions.
3. That all Chicano Studies Programs initiate and implement coursework on the Chicana.
4. That the cover of El Plan should recognize the Chicana and her movimiento input.

Chicana AD HOC Committee was derived with the objectives of setting up intrastate communications of las Chicanas del movimiento through a newsletter, exchange of papers and research projects on la Chicana, the publication of journals and an anthology on women, propose classes on the Chicana and start community groups to aid in bringing la "*mujer*" [women] into the forefront of involvement in determining our destinies. The ad-hoc committee is comprised of approximately 35 Chicanas from the universities, colleges, junior colleges, private schools and high schools who attended the CCHE Conference in San Diego.

It was in this summer that CCHE set as one of its priorities the development of awareness, leadership and recognition of the Chicana in order to make the movimiento truly the total Chicano struggle *para justicia* [for justice].

Venceremos!
[We shall overcome!]

47

*Party Platform on Chicanas 1971**

LA RAZA UNIDA PARTY OF NORTHERN CALIFORNIA

In many parts of the country, Chicanos are getting together under the banner of the Raza Unida party—a new, independent party of and for Chicanos. The Raza Unida Party of Northern California adopted a platform this spring with a section on Raza women. Below is the platform and some of the introduction to it.

*From *El Grito del Norte*, Vol. IV, No. 4/5, June 5, 1971: pp. J–K.

We feel that the importance of the Raza Unida Party will be determined by the measure to which it takes into account the needs of la Raza *as a whole*, and by the measure to which it actively works to meet those needs and to eradicate every form of exploitation which burdens us.

For our women . . . there exists a triple exploitation, a triple degradation; they are exploited as women, as people of la Raza, and they suffer from the poverty that straitjackets all of la Raza. We feel that without the recognition by all of la Raza of this special form of oppression that our women suffer, our movement will greatly suffer.

Bearing this in mind and recognizing that a people as a whole can never be liberated if an entire sector of that people remains in bondage, we of the Raza Unida party state our position as follows:

A. We shall respect the right of self-determination for our women to state what their specific needs and problems are, and how they feel that these needs can be met and these problems can be eliminated, as a basic principle of our party.

B. The party encourages la Raza women to meet in Raza women's groups wherever the movement is functioning, in order to enable the women to discuss the direction that their participation is taking, and the particular needs that Raza women they feel must be acted upon. . . .

C. The party will include Raza women in all decision-making meetings . . .

D. Raza men and women both will cooperate fully, in this party and at home, in the very difficult task we have before us of freeing our women and encouraging them in every way we can, at all times, to become involved in every level of the struggle, and in working actively towards the elimination of all attitudes and practices that have relegated our women to the unquestionably bondaged positions they are now in.

Child Care

A. Child-care centers controlled by Raza must be made available for Raza in schools, workplaces, and neighborhoods, totally free of charge, wherever our people are found.

B. These child-care centers will be open 24 hours a day and must accommodate children from the age of 45 days through the preschool ages.

C. Medical attention will be made available for the children, and facilities will be available for children who may be sick, with the necessary medicine, free of charge.

D. These centers will function as educational centers as well as child-care centers.

Work

A. An end to inequality in pay because of sex or race. Statistics show that for the same job, women do not get paid half the wages earned by men. The poorest suffer from this the most. Raza women as a group are paid even less than their underpaid Raza male counterparts.

B. Fifty percent of Raza women who work, work as domestics. We want job openings in all areas of work for Raza women, specifically in full-time employment with salaries to meet the standard of living no matter what it may be and no matter how much it increases. All Raza women who apply for jobs, no matter what area, must be accepted. If training is needed, it should be given with pay.

C. Maternity and paternity leave with pay and with a guarantee of a job on return.

Birth Control

A. Clinics and agencies within our communities that distribute any birth-control information and/or abortion counseling and information and clinics and agencies that pass out birth-control devices and perform abortions *must* be community-controlled, and a woman who is counseled must be thoroughly informed about all the dangers and possible side effects of any devices or operations.

B. No forced abortions or sterilizations on our women.

C. The ultimate decision whether to have a child or not should be left up to the woman.

Education

A. Intensive recruitment of Raza women into the schools, with Raza counselors and tutors to help the women stay in school and to encourage them to enter all areas of study.

B. Guaranteed jobs for all Raza women upon graduation in whatever field the women choose.

C. Part of the education of our women will be dedicated to the study of the history of the oppression of women within the framework of our background, and to the study of the role that Raza women have played in the history of our people.

48

*Party Platform on Chicanas, 1972**

LA RAZA UNIDA PARTY OF TEXAS

La Mujer

Second-class citizenship exists within the social, political and economic structure of this society. The existence of second-class citizenship manifests itself in the form of the denial, overtly and covertly, of equal rights for all citizens. This manifestation is perpetuated because many people are and will continue to remain powerless.

The position of second-class citizenship is shared by many—Chicanos, Blacks,

*From *Profile on the Mexican American Woman*. Austin: National Educational Laboratory Publishers, 1976: pp. 232–236.

poor Whites, and other minorities. However, women have now emerged as one of those groups clamoring for equal rights as first-class citizens. The minority woman finds herself in an unusual position when faced with the new movement for equal rights for women. Minority women cannot speak of greater political participation, equal pay for equal work, or even control of their own bodies, since all of these are denied in practice to all members of minority groups, male and female. This means that the minority woman does not have the luxury of dealing exclusively with feminism and fighting male chauvinism, as racism plays an even bigger role in suppressing peoples in the State of Texas.

A. *La Mujer* and the Raza Unida Party

The Raza Unida Party came into existence because the powerless must unite with one voice to demand what belongs to them by law and to change those laws that ignore or suppress them as individuals. The cry of the Raza Unida Party has been the same one heard in the women's movement: equal legal rights, equal educational and economic opportunities, equal political participation, and respect of the individual's rights to control his/her own future without legal obstruction.

The Raza Unida Party has been fighting to end the existence of second class citizenship through full political participation of all peoples. To be suppressed is not a novelty to those who are organizing the Party throughout the State, therefore, all people are encouraged and urged to participate in all stages of development of the Raza Unida Party.

The statistics of the political participation of women in the Raza Unida Party indicate that they are actively involved:

- Fifteen percent of the candidates running for state offices under the Raza Unida banner are women. These positions include Lieutenant Governor.
- Thirty-six percent of those holding the position of County Chairmen are women.
- Twenty percent of those holding the position of Precinct Chairmen are women.

B. *La familia y* la Raza Unida

The women, men, and youth of the Raza Unida Party join their sisters in the women's movement in demanding equal rights for all peoples, but more importantly, in assuring that human rights are guaranteed to all citizens. The Raza Unida Party will work for this by fighting to ensure that everyone, regardless of age, socioeconomic status, or sex group, will have a voice in changing those things that control their lives: schools, courts, employment, and government.

The Raza Unida Party is taking a strong stand on justice to ensure equal legal rights; on economics, to ensure equal economic opportunities; on education, to ensure equal educational opportunities; and on politics to insure full political participation of all citizens. The Raza Unida Party does not feel that a separate stand on the rights of women is necessary, as it is explicit that women are included in the fight for equal rights. The Raza Unida Party believes that the strength of unity begins with the family. Only through full participation of all members of the family can a strong force be developed to deal with the problems that face la Raza.

This total family involvement is the basic foundation of the Raza Unida Party—men, women and youth working together for a common cause. However, acting in good faith and realizing that women, as a group, are suppressed, the Raza Unida Party resolves that:

1. The amendment to the U.S. Constitution providing equal protection under the law for women be endorsed and supported;
2. All laws that maintain a double standard such as the "protective legislation" be repealed or amended to give women equality;
3. All resolutions referring to equal rights or a group representation included in the Raza Unida Party platform apply to women whether they be working mothers, career women, or housewives;
4. And that the participation of women, to include the decision-making positions of the Raza Unida Party, be actively continued through political education and recruitment of women.

49

National Chicano Political Conference, 1972*

ANONYMOUS

We, as Chicanas, are a vital part of the Chicano community. We are workers, unemployed, welfare recipients, housewives, students; therefore, we demand that we be heard and the following resolutions be accepted at the Raza Unida Statewide Conference on July 1, 1972 [resolutions presented April 21–23, San Jose, California].

Be it resolved that we as Chicanas will promote "*la Hermanidad*"[sisterhood] concept in organizing Chicanas. As Hermanas [sisters], we have a responsibility to help each other in problems that are common among all of us. We recognize that the oldest example of divide and conquer has been to promote competition and envy among our men and especially women. Therefore, in order to reduce rivalry, we must disseminate our knowledge and develop strong communications.

Be it also resolved, that we as Raza must not condone, accept, or transfer the oppression of la Chicana.

*From *La Mujer en Pie de Lucha*. Mexico City: Espina del Norte Publications, 1973: pp. 263–268.

That Chicanas be in on all policy-making and decision-making concerning la Raza [Unida Party].

All la Raza literature should include articles, poems, etc. written by Chicanas. Chicanas should also be encouraged to publish more, to relate the Chicana perspective in the Chicano movement.

In *La Raza Unida* [political party] that:

a. Chicanas be represented in all levels of the *Partido* [Party] (leadership, decision-making, organizing, and representation).
b. Chicanas be run as LRUP candidates in all general, primary and local elections.

California Social Welfare Board

Whereas the concept of the importance of *la Madre en la familia* [the mother in the family] is a real fact in the stability of Chicano children, and,

Whereas research has established that children brought up in institutions are irreparably damaged by this experience,

Be it resolved that this conference as Chicanas will go on record to write the California Social Service Welfare Board in opposition to their stated position of seizing children from all mothers under the age of 16; children born out of wedlock; and the third child of any unwed mothers on welfare over 16 years of age.

Community Controlled Clinics

We resolve that more Chicano clinics (self-supporting), be implemented to service the Chicano community as the door for

1. Education of medical services available to the [community], i.e. birth control, abortion, etc.
2. A tool for further education of Chicana personnel into medical areas, returning to the barrios, and
3. As a political education to our people in view of the contracting bandaid programs now in existence.

Childcare Centers

In order for women to leave their children in the hands of someone they trust and know will understand the cultural ways of their children, be it resolved that Raza child-care programs be established in our barrios. This will allow time for women to become actively involved in the solving of our Chicano problems and time to solve some of their own problems. In order that she will not be deceived by these programs, be it further resolved that these programs should be run and controlled by "*nuestra raza*" [our people].

Chicana classes educating the Chicana, Chicano, and the community in educational growth together be implemented on all campuses. That these classes be established, controlled, and taught by Chicanas. The classes should deal with existing problems faced by the Chicana as a wife, mother, worker, and as a member of "la Raza," also historical research should also be done by the classes on the discrimination of Chicana women.

Interpreters

Whereas many la Raza women do not speak English, and whereas this poses a problem in her support of her minor child, be it resolved that juvenile justice courts be petitioned to provide interpreters for Spanish-speaking mothers, and be it further resolved that Chicanos make a committee to offer time and moral support to mother and child who are involved in juvenile justice court action.

Vietnam

Whereas the Vietnam War has victimized and perpetuated the genocide of la Raza and has been used as a vehicle of division within our community and *familia*, be it resolved, that we as Chicanas demand the immediate halt of bombing and a withdrawal from Vietnam.

Be it resolved that:

A. Chicanas receive equal pay for equal work.
B. That working conditions, particularly in the garment factory sweatshops be improved (shorter hours).
C. Chicanas join unions and hold leadership positions within these unions.
D. Chicanas be given the opportunity for promotions and that they be given free training to improve their skills.
E. That there be maternity leaves with pay.

Abortions

Whereas we, as Chicanas, have been subjected to legal, dehumanizing and unsafe abortions, let it be resolved that we endorse legalized medical abortions in order to protect the human right of self-determination. Be it also resolved that Chicanas are to control the process to its completion. In addition, we feel that the sterilization process must never be administered without full knowledge and consent of the individual involved.

50

Third World Women Meet*

Enriqueta Longeaux Vasquez

There was the strong feeling of human insight in attending the Third World Women's Conference held in San Anselmo, California in November 1972. The conference was sponsored by the Division of Church and Race of the United Presbyterian Church and was a first, in the history of the Church.

The purpose of the conference was to develop communication between Third World women as well as to increase participation in the struggles of our people here and throughout the world. Also, to include women at decision-making levels as well as to heighten and explore third world concerns and build solidarity between third world women and men.

The Presbyterian Church is a Chicano resource that has a La Raza Churchmen group in Los Angeles who fortunately has a dedicated Raza Churchwoman, Josephine Granados Alemán. Josephine is not only concerned with the welfare of La Raza community but is very much aware of the extreme importance of a strong Chicana as being a need that affects the whole of the community. Any of us who have lived in projects, barrios, and ghettos and have had to raise families alone know the urgency of "la Chicana." With this well in mind, seven of us made up the Chicana Caucus. We presented our mestizo history as to the Chicano nation of Aztlán and we learned of other views and struggles. To learn of other struggles and peoples was no threat to our Chicanismo but a reaffirmation of our struggle and what is yet to come. We came together aware of our differences, but with the realization of what bought us together; *a deep concern for the necessity of unity within the issues of humanity on a long term world basis*. There was a welding and respect to recognize dedication and concern for the struggles within the U.S. to be meted with world struggles.

Probably one of the lessons one feels in blending with other people is to live a humanity under the skin. How stirring to feel the strength of a Japanese who lived in a concentration camp; the endurance of a Chinese and Phillipino whose cheap labors were imported to the U.S.; the stoic quiet of a Korean whose land and genetic family has been torn by politics; the consistent spirit of the Native-American and the vitality of blacks, the cradle of humanity.

To meet with people from other struggles makes one aware of the meaning and the affects of the systemic genocide, personally as well as within our descendant family trees. It makes one further aware of the meaning of the sufferings and turmoil of Vietnam, Angola, Puerto Rico, Latin America and the whole of Asia. Also to take a stand against genocide is to refuse one's share of the guilt of bloodshed. It was a living

*From *El Grito del Norte*, Vol. 4, No. 1, January–February, 1973: p. 12.

experience of José Vasconsuelos' Raza Cósmica, la Raza de Colores [Cosmic Race, Race of Colors], which tells us of Raza being elements of the whole of humanity and its colors—white, black, yellow, red, and brown.

To see and speak with these women of the third world was to see oneself. There were blacks who looked like me. There were Indians who looked like me. There were Asians with traces of me. All were pieces of struggles; pieces of reality; pieces of flesh. All were pieces of me.

What is The Third World?

An important purpose of the third world conference was to adopt a definition of "third world," and to heighten and explore third world consciousness and concerns, and to strengthen the work of individual caucuses by building solidarity between third world women and men. Also, to develop communication between third world women and to encourage women to participate in the overall struggles of peoples and be included at decision making levels.

Third world means the colonized and formerly colonized countries of the world.

It includes nations and peoples of Asia, Africa, Latin America, and Aztlán, all having been oppressed by colonialist European powers and the U.S.

The first world is—the United States, the weakened European nations built on "free enterprise" (England, France, Germany). Native-Americans and Chicanos became foreigners in their own lands, left with only broken treaties.

Within the U.S., the third world consists of colonized peoples from Las Americas, the Caribbean, Africa, and Asia. The third world idea can not be used to adopt an attitude "neutrality"; the fact remains that there is no middle road. We know that to combat international enemies (expansionism in the name of God and "free enterprise"), international cooperation is needed. There is a need for world unity of all peoples suffering exploitation and colonial oppression here in the U.S., the most wealthy, powerful, expansionist country in the world, to identify ourselves as third world peoples in order to end this economic and political expansion.

We must realize that nations and people can be part of the third world and still be oppressors and exploiters. (Japan is an example of this, together with other nations run by puppets of neo-colonization such as Chiang Kai Shek, Mobutu, Governor Ferre, etc.) Third world is not an ideology unto itself. It describes oppressed and exploited lands and peoples who suffer internal and external colonialism. Through imperialist expansion and oppression of peoples of the third world, the international nature of the oppressor has been exposed.

Commitment to liberation is wherever struggles may be, and struggles must interlock to obtain effective results. The third world has suffered under the yoke of white racism and economic pillage by expansionist powers. We are concerned with the long-range results of our struggles; we have a common oppressor, we hope to achieve a society free from racism, exploitation of human by human, nation by nation, and woman by man.

In spite of cultural differences, historical oppression unites us in the struggle to eradicate these evils. We occupy a unique place, located within the most expansionist country in the world at a critical time in the history of humanity. Many third world nations have spoken against U.S. power policies (Latin America, Indochina, Africa) to no avail. Third world people in the United States must identify our exploitative history in order to end this economic and political expansion.

51

*Report from the National Women's Political Caucus**

Evey Chapa

The experience of the members of the Chicana Caucus at the National Women's Political Caucus Convention [1973] left many of us with mixed emotions ranging from pride in the *mujeres* [women] of the Chicana Caucus to frustration with the actions of the women at the convention. The goals of the *mujeres* of the Chicana Caucus were aimed towards including the needs of the *mujeres* of La Raza in any political action the National Women's Political Caucus might undertake. It was hard for many of the other women at the convention to understand what we were trying to accomplish. Even the newsmedia accounts did not make clear the Chicanas' beliefs and feelings. In fact, many of the newspaper and magazine articles reported our views in a biased manner and in a negative perspective.

The *mujeres* of the Chicana Caucus believe that if the National Women's Political Caucus is to function, it must include the point of view of the Chicana. As women within a minority group, Chicanas confront special problems in their efforts to develop socially, educationally, economically, and politically in this country. Chicanas are affected by similar sex discrimination factors that other women are struggling against. These factors, however, are multiplied because of our minority and socio-economic status. Chicanas are hindered in their development by the biases that exist against language and cultural differences. Our cultural values are either mistakenly viewed as glorifying passivity or non-involvement. This misconception is often used as an excuse to continue to exclude Chicanas from participation in decision-making roles. The Chicanas' struggle for cultural pluralism, their desire and determination to identify with desirable Chicana values are ignored or rejected simply because they are different or because Chicanas seem reluctant to assimilate into the dominant culture. Because of the uniqueness of the problems of the Chicana, we can not allow anyone or any group to speak for us. We must make the decisions concerning the solutions to our problems. It is also this uniqueness that is a barrier to the understanding which is so slow in coming from other women and from the newsmedia.

Despite the other women's lack of understanding, we knew we had to act together to decide what actions we would take at the convention to assure that the other women would take action with us against our problems. The Chicana Caucus which consisted of sixty *mujeres* from seven states—California, Texas, New Mexico, Illinois, Washington, DC, Louisiana, and one other state—met several times during the

*From *Magazín*, Vol. 1, No. 9, September 1973: 37–39.

convention to discuss the resolutions we wanted to present on the floor of the convention. Each time we met more discussion was held concerning problems faced by the Chicanas and each discussion fell into four categories: employment, education, welfare, and politics. As the discussion narrowed into definite problem areas, each Chicana decided which area most interested her and we split into groups to assure that everyone would be able to have a say in what went into the resolution concerning the different problem areas we discussed. We worked as a united group, with all Chicanas present in agreement, to decide upon and formulate the resolutions that went to the general Convention from the Chicana Caucus. Although there are many problems that we face as *mujeres* de la Raza, we decided on seven resolutions dealing with *los problemas de la Chicana en* [the problems of the Chicana . . .] strike, en *educación* [in education], *en* welfare, *en la política y en el* [in politics and in the] Women's Political Caucus.

"Los Problemas de la Chicana en Strike"

We realized it would be impossible to touch on every problem Chicanas face in employment. However, the support of two situations in which Chicanas are involved for better working conditions through nation-wide strikes seemed the best manner to involve the women of the National Caucus in assisting Chicanas. We decided that positive action which is directed toward the good of the working Chicana would be a way in which the women of the National Caucus could commit themselves to the betterment of the working Chicana. We drafted two resolutions in support of the Farah and Lettuce boycotts. The following resolutions were presented by the Chicana Caucus:

Whereas for the past ten months, our Chicana sisters at Farah Manufacturing Company in Texas and New Mexico have been on strike in a struggle to win their right to union representation and some measure of control over their working lives, let us therefore reach out our hands to these Chicana women who are taking positive action to bring the purpose of the National Women's Political Caucus as drafted in July 1971, to fruition;

Therefore be it resolved that the National Women's Political Caucus endorses the Farah Boycott and urges all local caucuses to enter into the Farah boycott.

Whereas the Agricultural working woman is the most exploited in this country; and,

Whereas the United Farm Workers Organizing Committee has successfully alleviated many of the problems facing Agricultural workers in this country; and,

Whereas the lettuce boycott is a viable means for the National Women's Political Caucus to become involved in supporting Agricultural working women;

Therefore be it resolved that the National Women's Political Caucus actively endorses the lettuce boycott to indicate our full support of the just struggle of all working people for a decent wage and working conditions through an organization of their own choice.

"Los Problemas de la Chicana en Educación"

The problems we experience in trying to attain a higher education or even a high school education seemed to the Chicana Caucus to be a very important issue. This was especially true since we had learned that the National Women's Political Caucus was supporting the Women's Education Act of 1973 and no Chicana had been consulted to see if the Chicanas had special needs which were being ignored by this Act. The difficulties we as Chicanas face in trying to graduate from high school or go to college could never be understood by the majority of the women in the National Caucus so we decided that we needed a definite commitment from the National Caucus that the Chicanas would no longer be ignored if the National Caucus is to work for the needs of women in education. The following resolution was presented by the Chicana Caucus:

Whereas the Chicano community is the most neglected in educational opportunities and;

Whereas women within the community are even more needy of educational development;

Therefore be it resolved that educational legislative efforts supported by the National Women's Political Caucus such as the Women's Education Act of 1973, include the following:

1. Concerned efforts to research educational needs of Chicanas.
2. Chicana recruitment for higher education and into the careers and continuing education programs.
3. Active, realistic financial support for the education of Chicanas at all educational levels.
4. Chicana oriented tutorial and counseling programs.
5. Incorporation of Chicana culture into educational systems and textbooks.
6. Active support of Spanish/English, bilingual/bicultural education programs.
7. Inclusion of Chicanas in all affirmative action activity.

Los Problemas de la Chicana en la Política

The *mujeres* of the Chicana Caucus were in general agreement that the Democratic and Republican Parties had done little to involve Chicanas in politics. This is attested to by the fact that there are very few Chicanos much less Chicanas with decision making powers involved in either of these two parties. Because of the tremendous success the Raza Unida Party has had in involving so many Chicanas in politics on all levels, the Chicana Caucus fully supported and endorsed the Raza Unida Party. In an effort to make the women of the National Women's Political Caucus aware of the affirmative action the Raza Unida Party has accomplished in the involvement of Chicanas in politics; the following resolution was presented by the Chicana Caucus;

Whereas a democracy cannot succeed without full participation of all the people it purports to respresent; and,

Whereas Chicanas and other disenfranchised women have not successfully found political expression in the established two party system of this country; and,

Whereas the main objective of the National Women's Political Caucus is to encourage the participation of all women in the political process; and,

Whereas the Raza Unida Party is a recognized innovative means whereby Chicanas have found effective political expression and participation;

Therefore be it resolved that the National Women's Political Caucus recognizes the Raza Unida Party as an innovative means of political expression for Chicanas and other disenfranchised people, and be it further resolved that the name of the Raza Unida Party be included in all official and promotional materials which cite the Democratic and Republican Parties.

Los Problemas de la Chicana in the National Women's Political Caucus

Las mujeres of the Chicana Caucus had decided that many of our women were having trouble dealing with the Women's Caucus, as it existed. We felt that many Chicanas were being excluded because they were not being recruited to join the Women's Caucus, from many areas, e.g. South Texas. Racism is such an integral part of everyday life that Anglo women would not even consider involving Chicanas. The proof that Chicanas were being excluded from participation in the Women's Caucus was in fact that of the 60 Chicanas in the Caucus, only one had heard about the Convention by direct line; the others were contacted by Chicanas who had written letters of announcement. It was through the efforts of Chicanas themselves, that so many Chicanas were present and participating. We felt that there were still many barriers that would prevent *las mujeres del barrio* from being a part of such a Convention.

It was with these collective feelings that the Chicana Caucus decided that they should provide alternative methods of involving Chicanas into political action. We felt that by forming separate Chicana Caucuses [they] would offer more opportunity for Chicanas to participate in the political reality of their own communities; and that these women would hold a major role in setting priorities that would focus on the *barrios* of the nation.

We had trouble trying to communicate this reasoning to the women of the convention. The resolution concerning this ideas was not accepted by the Resolution Committee because they felt it was a question of structure; and that therefore it should be handled by the "Structure Committee." The Structure Committee would not accept the resolution; they did not know how to handle the idea. Determined to have our views heard, we presented the following resolution on the floor of the Convention:

Resolution 7.

Whereas the Chicana has specific political priorities, unique to the Chicano experience in the United States: Therefore, be it resolved that in those states where Chicanos reside, that Chicano Political Caucuses be established and maintained, on an equal basis with the other State Caucuses.

This resolution had to be presented out of Committee, therefore it had to be an amendment to the suggestions that had come from the Structure Committee. Many women of the Caucus took our suggestion like a slap in the face. They refused to understand why we felt this move was necessary. After much debate and bickering, our resolution passed and we will now be able to recruit Chicanas into Chicano Caucuses to carry out political action for the good of the people *en los barrios* [in the barrios].

52

Mujeres Por La Raza Unida * *(1974)*

Evey Chapa

[*Mujeres por la Raza Unida* were born out of a need to give a working political knowledge to *la mujer envuelta en el partido de la Raza Unida,* and to involve more women in our efforts to develop a viable political alternative in the State of Texas. The history of the efforts to develop an organization for the purpose of providing concerted, planned political education activities for *las mujeres del partido* involves many, many Chicanas throughout the state, and this is dedicated to them. E.C.]

Mujeres have always been active in La Raza Unida Party, providing the human-power to complete the tasks which are essential to political organizing: door-to-door canvasing, office procedures, fund raising, and various other supportive activities. But we were few and we lacked the political sophistication which is demanded by confusing and misleading election laws and by the *movidas* [preplanned political moves] of the other two parties against our people. Even at the beginning stages, however, the Raza Unida Party offered the Chicana a chance to show what she could do; for the overriding rule in our experiences has been that the *partido* [Raza Unida Party] belongs to those who will work for it and who believe in it.

During 1971, in the formative stages of the development of the Raza Unida Party as an official party, a phenomenal event took place for *mujeres.* La Raza Unida Party was the only political party which included in its platform a section devoted to *la mujer.* The precedent set by this fact has had, and will continue to have, a tremendous effect in involving more *mujeres* in la Raza Unida Party.

Summarizing the section of the platform entitled "La Mujer":

The Raza Unida Party declares the belief in the family structure as the basis of development, but also clearly states that it must be a *total* development of the family—men, women, and children. La Raza Unida Party resolves in this section of the Platform de la mujer, that equal rights includes *mujeres,* no matter what their status in life. In addition, the Raza Unida Party resolves "that the participation of women, to include the decision-making positions of the Raza Unida Party, be actively continued through political education and recruitment of women."

Our success as Chicanas in the Raza Unida Party continued as we developed the 1972 campaign; some Chicanas had the opportunity to run for political office:

O Alma Canales ran for Lt. Governor, the first Chicana to run for statewide office in Texas;
O Marta Cotera ran for State Board of Education, and she ran a formidable campaign, continuing her professional and familial responsibilities as well as traveling a sixteen-county area with little or no money; and

*From *Caracol,*Vol. 1, No. 2, 1974: pp. 3–5.

O Elena Díaz ran for County Commissioner in Zavala County and *won*, the first time la
   Raza Unida Party was on the ballot as an official statewide party, a woman was elected to a position as high as County Commissioner.

In addition, during the same year, (36%) of those holding the positions of County
Chair were women and (20%) of those holding positions of Precinct Chair were
women. It was clear that the County Chairwomen of the Raza Unida Party were not
in token positions because they were in such important counties as Zavala County,
the birthplace of the Raza Unida Party; Travis County, the Capital City; and El Paso,
Harris and Dallas Counties, all urban areas that present difficult tasks in developing
the Raza Unida Party. If that was not enough, a Chicana feminist was elected as State
Committeewoman [Evey Chapa].

We used the already evident commitment of many *mujeres* to the Raza Unida
Party, the Platform commitment to *mujeres*, implement the strategies for the development of Mujeres por La Raza Unida. In January of 1973, a mini-meeting was in
Cristal (Crystal City, Texas) attended by those who felt that words are not enough,
that action is the only possible recourse. We formulated a strategy to discuss and survey the *mujer* [woman] issue with *mujeres* [women] themselves. We canvassed opinions
throughout the state for five months and by the summer of 1973, the idea of a *conferencia* [conference] to start this organized effort had been conceived. This coincided
with the statewide Raza Unida Party meeting which was held in San Antonio. At this
meeting (50%) of the participants were *mujeres*, and this was not by chance for they
had been notified by the organizers of Mujeres por La Raza Unida that the meeting
was taking place. Those who had not voiced their concern about the formation of
Mujeres por La Raza Unida were consulted. As had been our experience for the last
five months, not one woman objected and all said they would participate.

On August 4, 1973, in San Antonio, Texas, the first Conferencia de Mujeres por
La Raza Unida was held. It was attended by almost 200 women from 20 different
counties. Chicanas attended all the way from Fort Worth and Dallas to Brownsville,
from Houston to El Paso and from San Angelo to Corpus Christi. The experience
was phenomenal. The variety of life styles and ages represented were unique: high
school students, college women, professional women, grassroots women, 18 to 80
years of age, attended. In fact, the Conferencia began with an inspiring *bienvenida*
[welcoming] by the woman who is considered the oldest member of the Raza Unida
Party, María L. Hernández from Lytle, Texas. The women who implemented the
workshops represented nearly all geographic areas of the state and the experiences and
expertise they demonstrated left no doubt; the *Conferencia* was a success. Virginia
Músquiz from Cristal closed the *Conferencia* with an eloquent plea for all of us to continue our efforts to develop Raza Unida Party throughout the state.

The Chicanas who participated in the *Conferencia* came to share their experiences in their local areas and to learn from the experiences of others. They left with a
firm commitment to support Chicanas as candidates and as party officers; and to continue to politically educate, on a regional basis, more Chicanas to actively participate
in the Raza Unida Party. In short, the Chicanas who participated in the first Conferencia de Mujeres por La Raza Unida demonstrated that the Chicano movement is
stronger because *mujeres* are actively involved, and further, making decisions.

We feel that these efforts of Mujeres por La Raza Unida begin to fulfill our
commitment to *la mujer* as an active participant and supporter of our own political
expressions in the Raza Unida Party, and allows us to develop our own philosophies
as women within a minority group—as *Chicanas*.

53

Presentation by Chicanas of La Raza Unida Party*

ANONYMOUS

Chicanas of La Raza Unida Party in the United States send special greetings to all the united national delegates in the historic International Women's Year Conference [held in Mexico City, June 19, 1975].

The full participation of women in society is a goal, a dream yet to be realized by every country and every culture world-wide today. As Raza Unida Party delegates to this conference we would like to share with you our views of what women's liberation means to Chicanas in the United States.

First of all we believe that liberation can be obtained only after a group succeeds in reaching a true analysis of its reality. Root causes of sexism, oppression and discrimination must be eliminated if true human liberation is to be lasting and not simply an occassion for one group to become the next oppressor. A solid historical framework and an analysis of a group's economic, political, and social status is a process that helps a group reach the conclusions of much-sought reality. It is within this context that La Raza Unida Chicanas in the United States are zealously working for their liberation.

Political: The history of our people, our economic, and social conditions lay a strong argument and reason for La Raza Unida Party, an independent party in the United States that seeks a Chicano/Chicana political vehicle for gaining control of our own communities, our lives, our humanity.

The two party system has never served the interests of our people. Life experience has taught us that "our needs as a people can only be resolved by us," because only we understand what those needs are. La Raza Unida Party seeks to create social, political, economic, and ethnic insitutions that will break the cycle of Chicano repression in the United States. These institutions must develop political and educational reforms, a sense of ethnic identity, and equitable distribution of economic goods and resources.

La Raza Unida Party does not seek power as an entree into Mainstream American Society—in fact, we reject assimilation into a racist system—but, rather, as a way to safeguard our cultural distinctiveness.

Chicanas comprise close to 50% of La Raza Unida Party leadership. At the National Convention of the eighteen States participating, six were led by women.

Many of our efforts to establish a multilingual–multicultural society where we are free to express our humanity—where we can feel free to speak Spanish (our language) and not be punished—to live according to our value system that is based on

*From *La Comunidad,* August, 1975: pp. 5–6.

respect for human dignity—and to live without being ridiculed and labeled as unciv-ilized [and] clannish.

Because the Chicana understands well the mind of the colonizer, we would like to suggest that this conference change the term development to liberation. We have learned from personal experience that development has been used by colonizers to impose upon, to organize, and grow from a pattern already set by them (the Coloniz-ers). If we are to work as women for the liberation of all world women, we must do this from a premise of mutual respect for language and cultural variations. We must be ready to support the expression of a woman's humanity in her own language and cul-ture.

54

A Chicana's Look at the International Women's Year Conference*

Yolanda M. López

The United Nations has declared 1975 as "International Women's Year," (IWY). On June 19, 1975 the conference was held in Mexico City "to seek mutual understanding and appropriate strategies for reaching IWY goals."

In actuality the conference was called to finalize and approve the adoption of the "IWY Plan of Action" which had been drafted in committee before the confer-ence.

Two conferences were concurrently held in Mexico City. The main conference was the governmental conference that official delegates from nations attended.

Security at the conference carefully monitored attendance to only officially cre-dentialed persons. This was the body that approved and amended the "IWY Plan of Action."

The second IWY Conference was called the "Tribune." Participation at this conference was open to all non-Mexicans who could get themselves to Mexico City. Participation strangely enough, was severely limited to interested Mexican women who wished to attend. The Tribune's only power was to make recommendations to the "official IWY Conference," who in turn could consider or totally ignore these suggestions.

An example of the unity of ideas at the IWY Conference can be seen in the of-

*From *Chicano Federation Newsletter,* August, 1975: pp. 2–4.

ficial acceptance of a 40 page "IWY Plan of Action" that was finally approved after 894 amendments were proposed.

The IWY World Plan of Action is probably a fine document. What it means to us here in San Diego and specifically to me as a woman and a Chicana, can best be discussed in terms of the U.N.'s power of implementation. The U.N.'s power in the World Food Conference, the World Population Conference, etc., these "Plans of Action" are recommendations—sincere sounding rhetoric—that must go into some gigantic file cabinet in the U.N.'s basement filed under "Good Intentions."

The official U.S. Delegation was made up of four spokespersons and several alternate representatives and advisors. The two co-heads of the delegation were Patricia Hutar, representative on the commission on the status of women of the economic and social council of the U.N. Her partner was Daniel Parker, administrator for the Agency for International Development (AID), a reputed CIA front and one of the most despised U.S. agencies in international world affairs; AID, it has been alleged, used American technology and $$$ to support totalitarian dictatorships favorable to American exploitation.

The U.S. delegation was in a sense a true representation of U.S. policy and our international posture—but in no way is it a true representation of American women.

Because official delegations from other nations were also people chosen to carefully reflect their country's national policy and not chosen as "women's representatives," what we had in Mexico City was a microcosm of international world politics and all its stalemates. Delegates had their assigned roles.

The benefit of these conferences comes from the exchange of ideas and addresses the lower echelon participants. It is these women who paid their own way, who are vitally concerned without benefit of official status who are the fundamental material of change.

About 200 San Diegans went to the IWY Tribune. Most of us went uninvited and generally uninformed about what to expect.

The 42 women and one man who went on the bus, arranged by the Chicano Federation, were a mixed bag of people with a wide range of concerns and political savvy.

An attempt was made to coalesce Chicanas at the Tribune. These Chicanas formed a coalition with black women from CORE and Latin American women from different countries. This coalition came to be known for its brief life as "The Coalition of Unrepresented Women."

The Americans in the coalition drafted a series of five demands protesting the make-up of the U.S. delegation and the total fraudulent operation of the Tribune conference.

An attempt was made by the coalition to be heard at a press conference in the U.S. Embassy. What resulted was a general disruption of the press conference and a cathartic out pouring of dissatisfaction by women who were not part of the coalition, but frustrated by the conference. The minority women had struck a nerve.

Chicanas came together again, this time with other Tribune women to protest the selective exclusion of Mexican women attending the conference. Some concessions were made on the day of the picket and Mexicanas were allowed in the building. The next day, the restricted policy continued.

Because Mexico's highest ranking law enforcement officer, Attorney General Pedro Ojeda Paullada was made head of the Mexican delegation, Mexican feminists boycotted the conference. Many delegates from other nations were visibly dismayed when Señor Paullada was also selected as President of the IWY Conference.

Paradoxically, the person who perhaps crystalized the major problems facing the conference delegates as individuals and as citizens of nation states was Mrs. María Esther Zuño de Echeverria, the wife of the President of Mexico.

In her inaugural statement to the IWY Conference Señora Echeverria called for a new international economic order.

In her own words: "Fundamentally the prejudices that domination over women is based on are the same as those forming the basis for every other kind of discrimination and injustice. In combating racism, colonialism, inequitable social systems, and underdevelopment, women are fighting for their own liberation. It requires an authentic transformation of the economic and social structures of a world shaped by men. I am convinced that the new order of collaboration in the family and social spheres without distinction based on sex, age, race, or beliefs will not progress beyond the stage of good intentions unless it is supplemented by a new international economic order."

Clearly, the struggle for the liberation of women is tied with our situation as Chicanas. We face not only the ugly facts of sexism but its shameless twin, racism.

Mexico City hammered home again the idea that our liberation is intimately tied to our actions as Americans and as world citizens. The treatment of women and Chicanos is a fair reflection of our political, educational, and economic institutions and our treatment of "underdeveloped" nations.

Attending to our liberation as Chicanas we must consider an analysis of American institutions and values.

55

The 1977 National Women's Conference in Houston*

CECILIA P. BURCIAGA

The National Women's Conference in Houston, Texas in November of 1977 signaled several gains, but also revealed several disappointments for the Hispanic women of this country.

As one of the three presidentially appointed Commissioners on the National Commission on the Observance of International Women's Year, I have several perspectives and I welcome the opportunity to share them with the readers of *La Luz*.

*From *La Luz*, November 1978: pp. 8–9.

I will present the outcomes of the Women's conference not only as a single event but also as an analysis of the dynamics that were, and are, currently operating in the Women's Movement vis-a-vis Hispanic women in general and Chicanas in particular.

The Houston Conference began its evolution long before 1977; its roots were in the United Nations International Women's Year Conference in Mexico City [1975]. Many Chicanas went to Mexico and found themselves disenfranchised and unrepresented from the official delegation that was selected by our government. It was that sentiment of no voice and no consensus among American women that stimulated congresswomen like Bella Abzug to come home and begin to architect a plan for having the diverse population of women in this country meet, on a national basis, to decide our own issues and priorities. Thus, after much political resistance Public Law 94–167 was passed by Congress in 1975 and mandated funds to organize and convene a National Women's Conference. By Executive Order, President Carter established and charged 45 appointees to serve on that Commission.

As with all legislation and federal mandates, the true road to implementation lies with the staff members in the organization. Though Hispanic women held none of the executive level positions in that Commission, we were fortunate to have some Hispanic women provide much of the negotiation, recruiting, research, and articulation for our concerns on that staff.

It is important to note that one of the key ground-rules of the law was that of aggressive affirmative action. The law stated that "The conference shall be composed of . . . members of the general public, with special emphasis on the representation of low-income women, members of diverse racial, ethnic, and religious groups, and women of all ages." Hispanic women were important advocates and guardians of that legal goal.

Each state of the union had a coordinating committee that was charged with the organizational and fiscal responsibilities of their state meetings. The members of these committees were appointed by rather vague guidelines and that established an understandably unfortunate sense of resentment on the part of those women who were not selected. Many Chicanas who had long been active in feminist and political struggles were absent from the committee and thus for them, this created an early feeling of distrust and disengagement from the rest of the activities. For those of us who participated in these committee meetings, the process of attempting to reach consensus in highly complex political, social, and economic arenas was clearly instructive and we paid the price of emotional and physical exhaustion.

The state meetings themselves were the crucial determinator of the delegation that was to go to Houston. The process of election was often brutal and Chicanas quickly perceived that the rule of the game was fierce and unrelenting competition. There are countless stories of how Chicanas in states like Washington, Colorado, California, Arizona, Texas and New Mexico met and reached agreement on how to present a united front. That, in and of itself, was an important experience and one that will serve us emminently well in current and future local state and national Hispanic issues. We were in many cases, Chicanas who had never met one another. We were poor and rich, old and young, blue and white collar workers, and married or single. We had many differences to resolve and, to a great extent, we dismissed superficial distances and joined one another in the spirit of our cultural heritage. We truly understood that unity would mean strength and that a loud voice would be essential in order to represent a much larger constituency before the public eye.

Houston provided yet other important lessons. Clearly many Chicanas were profoundly dissatisfied with the global minority women's resolution that had been written prior to the conference. Chicanas wanted specific issues of bilingual education, immigration, media, health, farmworkers and employment to be written into the follow-up report; but it was unclear what avenues we were going to use to insure inclusion of these concerns. In addition, Chicana delegates had several roles they had to serve: as part of their own state delegations, as promoters of their own issues, and as members of a national Chicana constituency.

I see the following gains as having been made. We gained important networks both in our states, nationally and internationally and we must continue to use and build them in a effective way. We were the ones who could best relate to the international aspects of the conference because of bilingual and bicultural skills. . . . We gained proficiency in the art of negotiation, coalition building, political participation, representation of a consituency and reaching consensus. We were able to define our own global concerns. We strengthened the bonds and goals of each of our organizations. We learned that our geographical locations were a non-existent barrier. We saw our excellence, our numbers, our diverse talents and we celebrated our sense of collectivity during the communion moment of the passage of the minority women's resolution. In a real sense, we "legitimized" the women's movement because without our participation, the movement would have been judged as exclusionary and elite. We respected our identities as Chicanas, Puerto Ricans, Cubans, etc. and yet coalesced under the identity of Hispanic women.

Some of our disappointments are also sources of lessons so I do not translate them in a totally negative fashion.

It is clear that we, in the collective sense, have not yet made lasting inroads into the leadership of the women's movement. (That "rainbow of women" that was shown in *Time* magazine after the conference, failed to display our color in any crucial frontstage setting.) While some of our people question whether we should even be involved with women's issues I believe that it is an undeniable fact that the women's movement has been internalized in the social economic and political fabric of this country. It is also undeniable that *Hispanas* are doubly oppressed by both sexist and racist issues. I contend that we must, for survival reason, be involved because we must keep the women's movement honest and on course towards elimination of racism and sexism and create a new tomorrow governed by principles of humanism and equality. Without our participation in the leadership positions which confirm our ethnic identity and strengths, we run the risk of having the previous all white male power structure simply replaced by an all white female power structure. In essence, we stand in danger of gaining a new oppressor.

We are still somewhat plagued by the *"envidia"* [jealousy] syndrome. It has been said that a phenomenon of women is that they tend to denegrate other strong women while men tend to down-grade other weak males. An old Spanish saying reinforces that we all want to be generals and none of us wants to be a foot soldier. I have often found it difficult to point to our own women leaders who rise without being attacked on very personal levels. This too happened in Houston. We must get beyond the mode of challenging, dismissing and "trashing" our own women and recognize that each of us is contributing to our own community in our own unique way. We must respect and acknowledge that we have too many battles to fight and that each individual contributes to his or her own battleground.

We still lack a national network. While Houston gathered many assertive and

strong Chicanas in organizations like Comisión Femenil, Cara, Mana, Mujeres
Unidas, Mexican–American business and professional women, we have failed to form
a national coalition of organizations that can serve as instant catalysts and mobilizers
on issues that concern us on every social, political, legislative, and economic front. I
see the information of this national coalition as an essential tool that must be forged
and used in effective participation on every political front.

56

*Looking for Room of One's Own**

DOLORES PRIDA

"Girls! Girls! $.25 $.25." Every day on the way to work I pass the porno shops and
movie houses of 42nd Street, their tacky neon signs flickering on and off in the middle of the morning. At the corner, a young Latino in tennis shoes hands a passerby
colorful brochures of naked women. Muttering in sing-song (sing-song?), he chirps,
"Check it out! Check it out!" With time, one becomes immune to the scene, much as
one becomes inured to the news of young women raped in subway trains while people in the next passenger car do nothing to help. It is appalling to admit, but these
things do not really register anymore. So many variations of them are played over and
over in every level of a woman's life.

   Without realizing it, one tends to accept certain things as a matter of course.
Take this *NUESTRO* issue on women, for instance. It has created more attention and
more involvement from the editorial staff (mostly male) than if we were doing the
Watergate story all over again. One is overwhelmed by the stream of names that
should be named, statements that should be quoted, angles to be explored–as if this
was the one and only "serious" women's piece this magazine will ever run. And how
about the sisters out there? Ah, they expect that *the truth* be herein revealed, that the
brothers be enlightened, the funding increased, the federal appointments multiplied,
and that, of course, I list their titles and affiliations correctly. Then you sit at the typewriter, and what comes rushing at you are lines from T.S. Eliot: "That's not it at all.
That's not what I meant at all. . . ."

   What I meant was to hear the rattle of windows and doors being opened, the
deafening peal of a thousand bells, the roar of an avalanche of things to come. Perhaps

*From *Nuestro*, Vol. 3, No. 5, June–July, 1979: pp. 24, 26, 28, 30.

I meant to put my ear to the ground and hear the mad beating of a heart pumping out new life. But idealized expectations always lead to disappointment. What I hear is the clicking of a few typewriters, the ringing of a few phones and the complacent hum–humming of "maybes" and "tomorrows" being carefully filed away in alphabetical order. Yet, in the distance, I hear the definitive voices of some women. And they are saying something. I don't know who is listening.

What is happening? A few years back, some hardy optimists spoke of a shining promise of new blood and leadership that women would bring to the Latino community. Although there are a much greater number of Latinas in prominent positions, that large promise has not been fulfilled. After almost a decade of struggles, where are Latinas at today? Everywhere and nowhere—depending on which Latinas you are talking about. Twenty Latina attorneys, forty-five GS-15 federal employees, three bank presidents and one golf champ are the exceptions who are proving the rule.

And the rule still is that Latinas are grinding away in the factories, watching the Spanish soap operas, standing in humiliation at the welfare lines. And the saddest part of all, is that young Latinas, *las mujeres de mañana* [the women of the future] are being left to fend for themselves, sweating at the disco, dropping out of high school, entering beauty contests and making the same mistakes many of us made 20 years ago.

No doubt there have been impressive changes in some areas, and many Latinas have reached a level of consciousness and activism that offers hope for a better future, however distant it may be. To follow the established order of change-federally approved-hundreds of Latinas, mostly professionals, now cluster around a number of national and local women's organizations. This, to be sure, is a significant advance. I remember, back in 1970, three other Latinas and I formed the first Latina feminist organization in New York City. We called a meeting, and nobody came.

Many meetings—perhaps far too many—are called today, and hundreds of women come. Now it is safe and O.K. Now even the government gives money to hold women's conferences. In fact, a new breed of "conference attenders" has emerged that gives considerable business to the nation's airlines. Ten years ago, Latinas were afraid to join feminist organizations because they might be called bra-burners, or worse yet—*ay, Vírgen!*—lesbians. And besides, argued the men, it was "divisive" in terms of the Latino movement. "Women's liberation is a white women's issue," they said.

Well, plenty of troubled waters have passed under the bridge since. Nowadays, no aware Latino would dare mouth any such platitudes. Today it is more along the lines of "Some of my best friends are feminists." Today even men join some of these organizations and are guest speakers at their annual conventions, exchanging over the roast beef well-intentioned jokes about castrating females.

There is no question about the oppression of women, both as members of an ethnic minority and as victims of the roles and double standards dictated by our own culture. No one argues with the rights of women to fight for themselves and the need of society at large to eliminate the inequalities that afflict half the population. There is no need to discuss that any longer. Now the emphasis is on action, on developing skills, survival know-how in a new world of activism. And that seems to be the orientation of the major Latina groups. Although few of them can truthfully be called feminists, they play an important role, serve, at least in name, as useful lobbying tools and are a training ground on how to deal with the system.

NACOPRW (National Conference of Puerto Rican Women) was founded in 1972 and became one of the earliest established national Latina groups. With chapters in seven Eastern and Midwestern states, it plans to open an office in Washington this year. Angela Cabrera, its national president, sees many worthy projects ahead. "The Washington office will also serve as a training and education center," she says. The training and educating are to be mainly in terms of how to handle meetings, parliamentary procedures, public speaking, lobbying. "We also plan to start a Puerto Rican women's library and a scholarship fund," adds Ms. Cabrera, who is deputy director of the Women's Division of the State of New York and active in the Democratic Party.

A sister organization is MANA (Mexican-American Women's Organization), which already has offices in Washington, where most of its members reside and work. Established in 1974, it has members in 16 states and publishes a monthly newsletter crammed with information on women's issues and news of who is doing what where. MANA's national president is Elisa Sánchez, vice-president for special programs at the National Council of La Raza. Sánchez is articulate, enthusiastic—and realistic—about the issues confronting Latinas today. "Latinas are still hesitant to join women's organizations because they tend to see them as extensions of the total feminist movement. MANA has a unique Hispanic perspective," she says. "We have said to the feminists, 'Look, there are issues where we agree, such as the ERA ratification, but there are issues on which we don't agree and can't work together.' For example, the National Organization for Women has not supported federal regulation of sterilization. MANA is in favor of regulation, because the Latina's right to choose has been abused so many times in this area."

The National Association of Cuban-American Women (NACAW)is the least woman-oriented of all. Although it supports ERA and other women's issues, it is mainly a service organization on a very limted level. Its most active chapter is in Fort Wayne, IN., where it runs an educational center which offers counseling, guidance, employment referral, a lending library and even runs a local radio program. Its national president and founder, Dr. Ana María Perera, is a program officer for the Women's Educational Equity Program at H.E.W.'s Office of Education. Asked about the lack of programs geared to women, Dr. Perera says, "Issues are asexual." (That of course, is debatable; imagine abortion being an asexual issue.) Surprisingly, NACAW does not have any programs in Miami, capital of the Cuban community in the U.S.

And there is plenty to worry about in that city. A paper presented by José Szapocznik and Carroll Truss at the last COSSMHO conference reports that there is widespread abuse of tranquilizers by Cuban women in Miami to combat the stress placed upon them by an alien social and cultural environment, particularly in regards to their roles as mothers. Heavy stuff, this. And there seem to be many more such heavy problems than there are Latina organizations with the will and resources to cope with them.

Nonetheless, a few are trying-the Chicana Rights Project of the Mexican-American Legal Defense and Education Fund, for example. With support from a Ford Foundation grant, the project was launched in 1974. It has brought suits dealing with discrimination in CETA programs and day care legislation, and it has conducted research on Chicana inmates. Today, the project is fighting court battles on several fronts. One is to get more Latinas into nontraditional jobs (such as construction). Another combats sexual harassment in employment situations, and others strive to guarantee the education of undocumented children. The list is long.

Pat Vásquez, a San Antonio attorney and director of the project, has her finger on just about every legal action relating to women that MALDEF tackles. For example, three or four years ago, no one talked about battered wives, as if that did not happen among Latinos. "In the last two years," says Vásquez, "there has been a great deal of focus on domestic violence. We did some research and found that 50%–60% of women served by shelters for abused wives are Latinas. And here in Texas, there is no legislation on domestic violence. Irma Rangel, a Chicana state representative, is now co-sponsoring three bills dealing with domestic violence." Vásquez, points out that it is not that more husbands are beating their wives nowadays, but "that more women are coming out and saying it."

The Comisión Femenil Mexicana of California, perhaps the most feminist-oriented of the Latina organizations, has chapters in 10 Western and Southwestern states. The Comisión also runs several Chicano action centers and bilingual/bicultural child-care operations. "Each chapter has different programs, according to the needs of the membership and the community," says Sandy Serrano, the Comisión's president. "But as a national organization, we support such issues as reproductive freedom and sexual preferences," which other groups such as MANA downplay.

Then there are the Horacias Algers of the Chicana Forum, a non-profit, economic development, "go-get-it" type of organization based in Washington. "The biggest problem women have is money," says Sharleen Maldonado Hemmings, Chicana Forum's chairwoman. "Women are very naive; we are embarrassed to want money. I am of the philosophy that you can go after the dollar and still have a good heart." One unfortunate example of the problem Maldonado Hemmings cites is the fact that many of the women's organizations are limited in their operations by the lack of funds. They are all nonprofit and still have much to learn about grantsmanship, which is really the name of the game."

The Chicana Forum is acting on its own philosophy and has just bought a $1.5 million commercial property in downtown El Paso. It will house several Chicana-run businesses in its shopping mall, and the profits of this venture will go into a re-investment fund which will help other women get into business. Monies for the purchase of the property came from the Economic Development Agency and private investments. "The Chicana Forum will not get into any project that will not produce income," says Maldonado Hemmings, using a hardline capitalistic approach that will surely raise a few eyebrows. "Let me tell you, César Chávez is not my hero; 80% of Latinos live in cities where we have to struggle with urban problems. I would like a Latino hero who sits on the board of directors of IBM."

Sure, and the moon, too. Women should be able to be whatever they want to be. Women come in all political colors and have as varied aspirations as anyone else. But still, in the view of many women, having 200 Latinas in top positions is not the solution. I ask Elisa Sánchez whether this would make a difference if it were to happen tomorrow. "I hope so, but I cannot guarantee it," she says.

Why should that be? Perhaps it is because the attorneys and the executives and the lobbyists and the IBM board members can only address problems of the external kind. The kind that can be legislated, fought over in court, discussed in committees. But the kind of human problems that only the heart and the mind can legislate, the battles that are fought deep within our inner selves, where no Roberts' Rules of Order can possibly apply-those are waged alone and unannounced. It is the old story of dealing with the effects and not with the causes, of concerning ourselves with the flesh and not with the spirit.

Latinas who themselves have not dealt with those latter problems will not be able to effect significant changes on behalf of other Latinas. At this point, what may be most needed are such unquantifiable undertakings as delving more thoroughly into the Latina's self-image; exploring her dreams and aspirations, examining the roles that are prescribed and self-assigned, defining her place in the sun, and most of all, searching out the right place in her own mind.

"For too long," says Sánchez, "we have been involved in the bread-and-butter issues of our community; they need to be addressed, for sure. But I have the fear that we don't really know where we are going, don't really know the consequences of the activities we are pursuing. We have to re-assess where we, as people, are, and where it is we are going, when no opinions are available to half our population. This is easily misunderstood. People think we want to change our culture, to be less Latina. See, we define our culture in terms of our country of origin, but we are here, and thus we should re-assess our culture of origin in light of here and now. It doesn't mean you have to become Anglo. But we have to be more aware of the possible influences that this society has in our culture, in ourselves."

"Feminism here," says Mercedes Sabio, a Venezuelan-born television assistant producer in Boston, "has become mostly a competition for jobs, trying to get the same privileges men have. In very few instances do you see an analysis of women as women, by women; discussions of our new possibilities as human beings does not take place. We have been co-opted with *puestitos en* [jobs] Washington." The Comisión's Serrano agrees that "we have been caught up in the glamour of being activists. I think in many ways we are failing."

And nowhere is evidence clearer than in the way Latinas are failing the young. Not nearly enough is being done for them. Yes, some of the organizations are gearing some activities toward them. Comisión Femenil has "big sister" programs in some of the California chapters; MANA is planning an internship program to bring young Chicanas to live and work in Washington for periods of two weeks; and the Chicana Forum is negotiating to obtain historical Bryant House in Washington to be used as a guest house for young Latinas. But these are token gestures. "The truth is that the young women don't see themselves in the leadership," says NACOPRW's Cabrera. "They see the same faces all the time."

The depressing message that young Latinas see in the too familiar faces is that what has been, will be. It is hard for many women, no matter how much their collective consciousness has been raised, to break away from the past. "The worst enemy of a Latina is herself, in terms of everything she has internalized, in terms of our culture, education, and the media," says Mercedes Sabio. Perhaps then, it is time to face the enemy within. Many agree that it is no longer the fault of the men or the "system" alone. Machismo has by now been glamorized and commercialized, and Madison Avenue can have it.

Instead, the main problem is ourselves and what we are going to do about ourselves. "We have to create an atmosphere," says Serrano, "establish our own priorities. We should discuss our sexuality, analyze how we are going to live our own lives, be supportive of each other." Adds Vásquez, "The Latina needs to develop herself more as a person." Going further, Sánchez expresses concern about the narrowness of many women's objectives and thinks that "we have to encourage our researchers, philosophers, thinkers, artists, to look at the situation of Latinas vis-a-vis our culture and then try to get exposure for their works."

See, our mothers were right all along. A woman's work is never done. And now the work is more complex, infinitely more difficult. And there are no electrical appliances to help us do what has to be done, to undo what has been done. It is not enough to have a room of one's own. In acquiring such a room, many women have crammed it with files and reports and with the same old cultural trappings in deceptive new wrappings. The room we need now is room to pace and think, to roam and dance, to jump and then run wherever it is we choose to go. We have to be able to guarantee that women who reach the top make a difference to those who will not. We have to assume that, as Sánchez puts it, "they bring with them the special type of sensitivity and understanding that we should have learned by virtue of the position we have occupied in this society"—a position that *las mujeres de mañana* need to never occupy again.

Chicana—a portrait—Los Angeles, early 1970s. Courtesy Raul Ruiz, *La Verdad* magazine, Los Angeles, California.

CHICANA FEMINISTS AND WHITE FEMINISTS: UNRESOLVED CONFLICTS

Introduction

Chicana feminists not only had to contend with the politics of the Chicano movement, but also with the politics of the women's movement. As the following essays point out, Chicana feminists chose not to identify with nor integrate themselves completely within the women's movement. Chicana feminists believed that key differences existed between themselves and white feminists. These differences included a sense that their true identity was with the Chicano movement or "*la familia*." They believed that white feminists focused too narrowly on men as the enemy. Chicana feminists believed that it was the system and the colonization of all Chicanos that was the real problem. Chicana feminists further believed that racism was stronger than sexism. In any case, unlike white feminists, Chicanas were faced with a double or even triple oppression if class differences were considered. Some Chicana feminists, moreover, believed that some of the goals promoted by the women's movement, such as access to more upper-middle class and executive positions, did not make much sense to Chicanas who represented a predominantly working-class population.

Other differences included the charge that white feminists practiced class discrimination against Chicanas, that white feminists were essentially opportunists, and that white feminists were insensitive to the history and particular experiences of Chicanas. Finally, as Consuelo Nieto notes in her essay, Chicana feminists had to first define themselves and their agenda before they could even consider participating in the women's movement and then it would have to be on the basis of white feminists' respect for Chicanas.

These differences with white feminists did not mean, as one Chicana writer pointed out, that Chicanas did not face major problems with Chicano men in the movement. However, despite these problems, Chicana feminists continued to maintain that ethnic and cultural bonds between men and women still represented the basis for a common struggle. Machismo, some Chicana feminists proposed, had been highly exaggerated, especially by white feminists, as it pertained to Chicano men and that this constituted an example of white feminists racializing sexism with respect to Chicano men.

In their discourse concerning white feminists, Chicana feminists tended at times to overly simplify the state of these relationships. Velia Hancock, for example, criticized without any data the negative effects of exogamous marriages between Chicanos and Anglos. According to Hancock, such marriages led to the loss of Chicano cultural identity. On the other hand, some of the writers in this chapter did suggest a more complicated relationship between Chicana and white feminists. Even Hancock noted that Chicana and white feminists were in agreement with respect to achieving equal rights and equal opportunities. Corrine Gutiérrez in her essay observed that Chicana feminists themselves were not monolithic and in her call for a coalition between Chicana, black, and white feminists, she questioned the use of strict ethnic/race categories. Yolanda Orozco in her essay differentiated between white liberal feminists and white radical feminists and agreed with Martha Cotera that radical feminists or socialist feminists appeared to be more sensitive and supportive of a Chicana feminist agenda.

THE BROWN WOMEN (1975)

The Brown woman
She waves her banner,
And cries out liberation for the women,
As all other women today
She proclaims, "sisters unite—unite and
     together we
Shall all survive."
Survive the struggle for equality that is
     rightfully ours.
Rightfully ours, as all other human beings.
The Brown woman
She waves her banner,
And cries out liberation for our people,
The Brown people of the world,
Liberation for my brothers
And sisters who have fought so long,
Every day of our lives,
When will that equality arrive?
Our Brown fathers who sweated like hell,
For that equality to be ours,
Our Brown brothers, husbands and
     sweethearts,
They fought in wars so that we
Would have those rights,
Our Brown mothers, those precious
     long suffering
In silence Brown mothers,
While they saw their families divide—
They stood back and cried, silently
     they cried.
Their sons were sent off to fight—
Wars to save their country
Some sent off to die, for what?
For the ground that would never be theirs
But instead belong to the affluent
     white folks,
The ones who stayed back because
     supposedly they had
The brains to be deffered.
The Brown woman
She wonders what the hell is meant
When the white women say "we're all alike"
The Brown women ask the white women
     "were you
Denied to go to school because you
     were misunderstood
Were you made to feel ashamed because
     you ate a different food,

Did you have to run and hide
To eat so as not to be made fun of."
She asks the white women, "Were you
   to become silent and withdrawn
Because you spoke different
And when you did you were punished
By the so-called educators?"
She asks the white women "Were you
   made to feel ashamed because you
Were poor and instead of a house
   you lived in a shack or perhaps
A tent under a tree?"
That is the difference between our
   Brown mothers.
Who said "Poor them, they do those things
Because they really don't understand"
For sure that is the difference between
   them and us.
The Brown women of today.
"The Chicana Women"
God bless her strength and her courage,
Today the Brown women declare,
"No, we are not alike, you the white women
Have never felt the pain that we have
Endured and suffered. You the white women
Have never been discriminated as we have,
You the white women have never been
   denied
What we the Brown have known that we
Should never seek.
We the Brown women say,
"Yes, Unite, Sisters, Unite!"
But damn the white woman if
   she discriminates
Against our race, and damn the
White woman if she thinks we will
Discriminate our race,
For we shall unite in Sisterhood, but never
   at the expense of the Brown people,
Man and Woman alike,
God bless the strength and courage of the
Chicana of today,
We make no bones about it,
Do not, we do not nor shall we ever accept
Racism to be a friend to you,
   to be your sister,
It is too much of an expense,
At age three we fell to our knees,
   but we have since stood up,
And shall never live on our knees again,

To no white woman, to no white man, nor to
Any other human being,
Viva La Brown Woman
Viva La Chicana
Viva Todo mi Raza.

Anita Sarah Duarte

57

*¡Soy Chicana Primero!**

Enriqueta Longeaux Vasquez

The Chicana today is becoming very serious and observant. On one hand she watch-
es and evaluates the white women's liberation movement and on the other hand she
hears the echoes of the "Chicano" movement, "Viva La Raza," the radical raps and
rhetoric. For some it becomes fashionable, while for many of us it becomes survival
itself. Some of our own Chicanas may be attracted to the white woman's liberation
movement, but we really don't feel comfortable there. We want to be a Chicana
primero, we want to walk hand in hand with the Chicano brothers, with our children,
our *viejitos* [elders], our Familia de La Raza.

Then too we hear the whisper that if you are a radical Chicana you lose some of
your femininity as a woman. And we question this as we look at the world struggles
and know that this accusation as to femininity doesn't make sense. After all, we have
seen the Vietnamese woman fight for survival with a gun in one hand and a child
sucking on her breast on the other arm. She is certainly feminine. Our own people
that fought in the revolution [Mexican Revolution of 1910] were brave and beautiful,
even more human because of the struggles we fought for.

So we begin to see what our people are up against as we take very seriously our
responsibility to our people, and to our children; as we sense the raging battle for cultural survival. We know that this means we have hardships to endure and we wish to
strengthen our endurance in order that we may further strengthen the endurance of
our coming generations. Nuestros hijos [our children] that are here and those that are
yet to come. Our people would often say when they saw a strong spirited woman,
vienen de buen barro (she comes from a good clay). Thus we now must make our children strong with the realization that they too, "vienen de buen barro."

When we discuss the Chicana, we have to be informed and know how we relate
to the white women's liberation movement in order to come up with some of our
own answers. This requires a basic analysis, not just a lot of static. Looking at the issues
of the women's lib movement it is easy to relate to the struggle itself as a struggle. We
can understand this because the Raza people are no newcomers to struggles, we can
sympathize with many basic struggles. However, it is not our business as Chicanas to
identify with the white women's liberation movement as a home base for working for
our people. We couldn't lead our people there, could we? Remember Raza is our
home ground and family and we have strong basic issues and grievances *as a people.*

In looking at women's lib we see issues that are relevant to that materialistic,
competitive society of the Gringo. This society is only able to function through the

*From *El Cuaderno,* Vol. 1, No. 2, 1971: pp. 17–22.

sharpening of wits and development of the human instinct of rivalry. For this same dominant society and mentality to arrive at a point where there is now a white women's liberation movement is *dangerous* and *cruel* in that social structure has reached the point of fracture and competition of the male and female. This competitive thought pattern can lead to the conclusion that the man is the enemy and thus create conflict of the sexes.

Now we, Raza, are a colonized people (we have been a colony of New Spain, we have been Mexico, and have only a veneer of U.S. of A. rule—since 1848, just 100 years) and an oppressed people. We must have a clearer vision of our plight and certainly we can not blame our men for oppression of the woman. Our men are not the power structure that oppresses us as a whole. We know who stole our lands: we know who discriminates against us; we know who came in (our parents still remember), threw out our Spanish books and brought in new, fresh-written history books and we know who wrote those books for us to read. In other words, we know where we hurt and why. And even more important, we can not afford to fight within and among ourselves anymore, much less male pitted against female.

When our man is beaten down by society, in employment, housing or whatever, he should no longer come home and beat his wife and family; and when the woman doesn't have all she needs at home or she perhaps has a family to raise alone, she should not turn around and hate her husband or men for it. Both the man and the woman have to realize where we hurt, we have to figure out why we hurt and why these things are happening to us. And more important, through all of these sufferings and tests we have to receive and share strength from each other and together fight the social system that is destroying us and our families, that is eating away at us, little by little. And we have to build a social system of our own.

One of the greatest strengths of Raza is that of our understanding and obedience to nature and its balance and creation. This same awareness makes us realize that there can't be total fulfillment without the other. Life requires both in order for it to go on, to reproduce. This same basic need of each other is the total fulfillment of beauty in its most creative form. Now the reason that we discuss this is that we must also think of life generally, without the BAD and TABOO connotation that has been placed on our basic human functions. We can not allow negative attitudes in regard to our physical capacities, because when we allow this kind of control on ourselves, we are allowing ourselves to be castrated, controlled, and destroyed at our very basic, essential level. This can affect generations to come.

In working for our people, a woman becomes more and more capable; this Raza woman gains confidence, pride and strength and this strength is both personal and as a people. She gains independence, security, and more human strength because she is working in a familiar area, one in which she puts her *corazón* [heart] and love. When a man sees this kind of spirit and strength, the Chicana may be misunderstood as having lost her femininity. A man may misinterpret this and feel it as a threat. But he, too, must stop and evaluate this. He should not react against her because this is a great source of strength for him, for her, for our children, for the Familia de La Raza. This is the kind of spirit and strength that builds and holds firm La Familia de La Raza. This is love, my Raza; we can not compete with "el barro" that has held us firm for so long. This is total *respect* and equality in loving ourselves, our men, our elders, our children. It is this force that has allowed us to endure through the centuries and it is the strength that carries on the struggle of our people, the demand for justice.

With this kind of strength, how can we possibly question the femininity of the Chicana? Femininity is something more than the outer shell . . . stereotyping of women seems like a materialistic attitude. That kind of judgment should not be placed on our women.

Many Raza women relate to the earth [*La Tierra*]—we have worked in the fields, as migrants and campesinos. We are not afraid of the sweet smell of sweat from our bodies . . . our mother wearing coveralls with knee patches, thinning beets . . . who would dare to say this woman is not feminine?

The Chicana must not choose white woman's liberation. . . . To be a Chicana PRIMERO (first), to stand by her people, will make her stronger for the struggle and endurance of her people. The Raza movement needs "La Chicana" very, very much. Today we face a time of commitment, LA FAMILIA DE LA RAZA needs her for the building of our *nación* de Aztlán [our nation of Aztlán]

58

*La Chicana, Chicano Movement and Women's Liberation**

VELIA GARCIA

There are major philosophical and tactical differences between Chicanas and white women's liberation groups. Neither of the two factions of the women's movement addresses itself totally to the issues central to the concern of the Chicana. The most obvious discrepancy lies in the very concept of a women's movement as an independent force for social change. In the United States there is no qualitative difference between the social experience of the Chicana and the Chicano. That is not true in the case of white women and white men. In American society, white men have a distinct advantage and have used that advantage to limit and shape the lives of women with the same apparent lack of conscience with which they oppress racial minorities. It makes sense for white women to struggle against the controlling influence of white men just as it makes sense for Chicanos and Chicanas to struggle together against the forces of racism and economic exploitation that deny them the basic human right to self-determination.

*From *Chicano Studies Newsletter,* University of California–Berkeley, February and March, 1977: pp. 1, 6.

This is not to say Chicanas cannot identify with some aspects of the white women's struggle for equality. They can and do. Educational and professional freedom is a major issue among the more moderate faction of the white women's movement. Likewise, most Chicanas will tell you women should have equal access to higher education in whatever field of endeavor that interests them. That means that if women want to become architects, engineers, or neurosurgeons, they should not in any way be blocked or discouraged in that pursuit. At the same time, Chicanas understand that most Chicanos spend no more than eight years in school. Educational opportunity has been systematically denied to all of our people, not just our women. None of the predominantly white, middle-class, professional women's groups have come to grips with racism in American society or the deliberate role of the government in the oppression of Chicano people educationally and in every other way. These women are reformists in the liberal tradition. As a force for change, they are basically irrelevant to the Chicano people and therefore to Chicanas.

The radical faction of Women's Liberation does address itself precisely to the social, economic, and political conditions that happen to oppress white women in some of the ways Third World people have been oppressed ever since white men and women set foot on the Americas. Unfortunately, many of these women focus on the maleness of our present social system as though, by implication, a female-dominated white American would have taken a more reasonable course. Chicanas have no more faith in white women than in white men. We aren't oppressed by Chicanos, we're oppressed by a system that serves white power and depends upon a white majority for its survival and perpetuation. In our struggle we identify our men, not white women, as our natural allies.

That we have decided as Chicanas that our place is beside our men and with each other does not mean there are no problems between us or that we as women are completely satisfied in our relationship to our men. Many Chicanas feel a deep sense of frustration over the fact that so many Chicanos perceive us in roles limited more by romantic conceptions of the past and of our grandmothers before us than by historical reality. In fact, the women of La Raza have always shared the lot of their men, and since the time of first contact with this western society, that lot has been a difficult one demanding the sacrifices of our women as well as our men. The struggle we face today will require no less.

Certainly there are some traditionally feminine aspects to our role as Chicanas. We enjoy relating to our men as women in all of the traditional ways. The problems arises when the perverted, stereotyped notions of machismo, used by Anglo society to ridicule the Chicano people, infect our own minds and threaten the working relationships we are trying to develop with one another.

Because many Chicanos seem uncomfortable with the prospect of actively involved Chicanas, both our married and our single women must spend valuable time and energy trying to resolve this conflict to their own satisfaction and to the satisfaction of the men who are important to them. Sometimes the result is the loss of the support and service of valuable Chicanas. While being good wives and mothers in the tradition of our people, married Chicanas also want to use their education, skills, and strength for the benefit of La Raza. This poses a serious dilemma that will require the cooperation and commitment of both Chicanos and Chicanas if it is to be resolved. While that resolution cannot be effected here for all Chicanos, two points for consideration can be offered:

(1) The white, middle-class, nuclear family model must be recognized as the basic unit of North American society and the foundation of social life. It is ideally de-

signed for socialization leading to the maintenance and perpetuation of the social, economic, and political system in the U.S.

(2) Historically, we are a communal people who have lived and worked together in extended family and friendship units and in village cooperatives. As Chicanos we still place considerable value on cooperative, interpersonal relationships.

Does it, perhaps, follow that one way out of our present dilemma might be to draw upon our history to begin redefining our concept of the family. We often refer to all Chicanos on campus or in the southwest as "la familia" [the family]. When Chicanos complain about the coldness and isolation of the university campus, they frame their complaints in concepts of "la familia." We are still a family-oriented people. Our children are precious not just because they are ours but also because they are an expression of our people and valuable to our struggle for social justice in the U.S. Everything we know about human behavior suggests that the healthiest human beings are those who grow up with a clear sense of identity and purpose. In the case of Chicanos, is this even possible within the context of the nuclear family and a child's 24-hour relationship with his mother?

The major dilemma for single Chicanas seems to be that posed by interracial dating and marriage. Most Chicanas would probably agree that whenever possible it is preferable for Chicanas and Chicanos to marry each other. Racial integrity has always been desirable to different groups during different periods of history. Indeed, in Anglo-American society it has always had a high priority. For many Chicanos, it is not the mingling of the bloods that is of greatest concern. No other people in the world have the blood of so many racial strains. What seems to be of principal concern to Chicanos is that intermarriage often results in a weakening of ties and a declining sense of responsibility and commitment to La Raza. Intermarriage is not going to disappear among Chicanos. In Los Angeles county in 1963, 40% of all Chicano marriages were intermarriages. Whether this rate rises or falls will depend on how well Chicanas and Chicanos come to terms with each other over the nature of their relationships in contemporary society and within the Chicano movement. It is unlikely that the college-educated Chicana will be satisfied confining her talents to the kitchen. This is neither an accurate reflection of our role in the history of our people nor an appropriate expenditure of our present-day resources. It is up to Chicanos to break away from the Anglo stereotype of the sex-crazed, hard-drinking, oppressive, authoritarian macho and to encourage Chicanas to fully develop as human beings capable of struggling, like our grandmothers before us, for the benefit of all our people.

White women's liberation movements are a positive force for social change. It provides one more front for struggle toward social justice for all people. That it does not attract a majority of Chicanas does not lessen its importance or mean that Chicanas do not approve. What it does mean is that Chicanas understand the nature of the struggle for the Chicano people and we choose to struggle alongside our men.

59

Feminism As We See It[*]

MARTA COTERA

It was suggested to me that the topic of my presentation be the role of the women in the Chicano movement politics, and perhaps to give some background on the development of women in the struggle. Like many of my sisters, I pretty much typify this development.

It began with the Kennedy campaign in 1960, continued with social and economic issues in the mid-sixties, and then on to reform in the educational system in the late sixties. Further on, we moved into political participation in 1970 and to the founding of the Raza Unida Party. As to the nature of the Chicanas involved with this conference [Texas Women's Political caucus, 1972], you have a group of polished, battle-scarred veterans of a social movement.

Naturally, the achievement of cooperation among us is going to be a long, tedious process. We are Chicanas and women. We have nothing now because of these two factors. And we can "go for broke." We certainly can't do worse than we are doing now with the present system. However, since we are seeking all possibilities for the development of Chicanos, we are willing to devote some time and effort keeping up with the women's movement to provide the necessary input and, of course, receive the benefits gained by all. We are completely aware that the condition—if you want to call it that—of Anglo women can't help but affect us, since Anglo women teach our children and provide most of the input for all media in this society. In other words, if you're screwed, we're screwed, figuratively speaking of course. In fact, we do know that our own basic condition and culture is changing in the Southwest because of this influence. Therefore, help you we must.

Now, here are some major pitfalls we want to avoid in order to operate our political union smoothly.

The Anglo woman's chauvinistic attitude is: "Look, we are achieving political status and we're going to liberate ourselves and then liberate Chicanas, Blacks, and all the women in the world." They always assume that the minority woman's plight is worse. In terms of personal status, the minority woman is usually ahead; she is more likely to be head of a household or a working woman with plenty of experience as to "what is what in life." If she shares the economic burden with her husband, she'll usually enjoy a much stronger position at home and have a stronger base from which to spring into action than a "kept woman." In the case of the Chicana—although I am no psychologist or anthropologist—I'll tell you, we are way ahead. We share with the

[*]Marta Cotera delivered this speech to the Texas Women's Political Caucus in March 1972 and then published it in her anthology, *The Chicana Feminist,* in 1977 (pp. 17–20).

women of the world the usual "role" dominance, but our economic and social development plus technological changes will take care of that. The important element is that our domination is physical, not intellectual. In other words, Anglo women move around more and think less, and we stay close to home—but if we want to forge ahead intellectually, Chicanos will adjust to it and even encourage it. Again, let me state that Anglo social scientists have done a lot to change Chicanos, so this is becoming extinct in our educated class. But in our grassroots movement, a woman who thinks and acts on community issues is respected and does assume posts of responsibility. In Crystal City, for example, we have Chicanas as City Commission members, and in all administrative boards which make local decisions. I can cite hundreds of examples.

Another attitude which might create problems is basic racism of the mind. It is a disease. What is stronger: racism or sexism? I believe racism. Anglo women must analyze their emotions and intellect and think clearly on this. Is the women's movement a move to place just another layer of racist Anglo dominance over minority peoples? Look at it through our peepholes. Minorities are working hard, pressuring the system for equal opportunity. Suddenly, the hereto silent Anglo woman emerges, clamoring for her poetical, social, and economic rights. She, who has reaped the physical comforts, the physical pampering, suddenly is unhappy at the whole situation. So she wants equal opportunity. And is her cry one for intellectual liberation? No! It's 90 percent for political opportunity so she can have economic opportunity. This looks very, very suspicious to us. Priorities are shifted, programs opened up. Women will be heard above the minorities! Women—white women—the wives, lovers and mothers of those in power, of course, will be heard above the clamor of male and female minorities. Of course, I'm not saying to all sincere women activists and politicians, "Please watch your women—and please make certain your motives and your moves with minority backing will be above reproach." We are saying, "Put yourselves on the line against racism. Don't become accessory to it in your fight against sexism. If you are for women, then you will support candidates like myself despite male-imposed party affiliation."

This brings us down to the political level and ways that we can cooperate politically to improve the total societal picture. I hear that we, as women, are ready to explode all the myths, abolish all institutions and otherwise change the world. No institution or practice—be it the job, the school, the home, or the bed—is beyond our grasp in this effort. But when it comes to the American political party system, I have heard hardly a peep. I have seen women bend over backwards attempting to infiltrate these systems. Yet, we have the power, the numbers, the energy, and the money to take to wherever and whomever will provide the most in return. "Political reality" is what we hear. But the reality is that we have everything I've mentioned. And "political reality" is "using what you've got to get what you want." Unless reality has changed lately! A strong reality, to me, would be to form a women's political party and quit playing hostesses and auxiliaries to the national parties. This, women, is anarchy. Another reality is to shift our support wherever women's participation is the strongest and make this support meaningful, not token, especially if the inclusion of women is done on a realistic level.

Now we have new parties which can stand analyzing, such as the Raza Unida Party in Texas, Kansas, the Midwest, and the West. In looking over the recent Midwest Convention, I saw that the top organizers and dignitaries were women. This is true, also, of the Texas party where the party convention included significant women's representation and participation. The most important Raza Unida Party County,

Zavala, has women precinct chairmen and the County Chairman is a tremendous woman, Virginia Musquiz. Again, as an example, Raza Unida Party knows where Chicano voting strength and organization comes from and because of this, it is supporting women candidates in the statewide races—Alma Canales for Lt. Governor and me for State Board of Education for Congressional District 23. For me, reality within the present limits means I'll be eighty by the time I might be given the opportunity to run. Or, reality is I'm getting the opportunity here and now and when I'm young enough to be effective, if elected. And for all of us as a group, political reality should be using our tremendous strengths to support all women candidates for statewide races, and to begin turning intelligently to all political possibilities available to us as a group of organized, intelligent women.

60

*Chicana Liberation**

ALICIA SANDOVAL

Numerous magazines and newspapers in the past few months have featured articles on the effect of the white middle-class woman's liberation movement on the black woman and the Negro community. Unfortunately, little or no coverage has been given to the impact the feminist cause has had on the Chicana or Mexican-American community. Since the history of the Chicana has been distinctly different from that of both the white and black woman, it is sometimes difficult to draw parallels between these three highly significant but unique social happenings.

Locally [Los Angeles], the formation in 1971 of the Comisión Femenil under the leadership of such outstanding women as Francisca Flores, Josephine Valdéz de Banda, Dr. Raquel Montenegro, and others became the catalyst for the Chicana liberation movement as it is now known in the Los Angeles area. As a result of the Women's Commission (or Comisión Femenil), the Chicana Service Action Center, located in Boyle Heights, came into being last year. It's main function has been to provide counseling to grassroots Spanish-speaking women regarding employment and educational opportunities. In addition to this, however, like all feminist centers it uti-

*From "Chicana Liberation." (*Los Angeles Free Press,* Nov. 30, 1973: p. 23).

lizes rap sessions, consciousness-raising techniques, workshops, and conferences in an overall humanistic effort to liberate the Mexican-American woman from sexism as well as racism—a two-front battle she shares in common with the black woman.

The right of a woman to have complete control over her own body (that is, be free to have an abortion or use contraceptives) has been a major issue among Anglo feminists. It has, nevertheless, been less pronounced among Mexican-American women, most of whom are Catholic and therefore find it harder to internalize these basically WASP (White, Anglo-Saxon, Protestant) concepts: specifically, birth control and sexual freedom. Right now, Mexican-Americans have the highest birth rate in the nation, according to the U.S. Census Bureau; and like some black nationalists, who believe the zero population drive among ethnic minorities is a white conspiracy to eliminate them, many Chicano activists are also highly suspicious of family planning efforts. Furthermore, as part of Latin cultural heritage, many Chicano men have been led to believe that the major way for them to validate their manhood is to father children.

Unwittingly, Anglo women's rights advocates have done a great disservice to the entire Spanish-surnamed community through the improper use of the words "macho" and "machismo" to describe male chauvinist pigs. Within the actual Mexican-American family structure, which is not as patriarchal as many Anglo sociologists think it to be, the woman has traditionally been treated with great deference and respect; even to the point of being indulged in by overprotective husbands, brothers, and sons. Most Latin males, for instance, are very fond of their mothers and often put them on pedestals. This is probably why the Chicano still enjoys the extended family setup, although a rising divorce rate along with the women's liberation movement is having somewhat of a detrimental effect on this familial institution.

Contrary to popular opinion, Chicano male activists in particular have been amazingly receptive of most of the tenets of the women's liberation movement and of late have encouraged Chicanas to accept leadership positions in organizations such as MAPA (Mexican-American Political Association), La Raza Unida Party, etc. Many of these men, having suffered from racial discrimination, can understand the frustrations of feminists who have been discriminated against because of their sex. Also, most leaders in the Chicano civil rights movement realize that the self-actualized woman can only be an asset to them in their fight against racism and, therefore, they are anxious to see more Chicanas go on to college and become more involved in the community.

Although it is not quite the same as either the white woman's or black woman's feminist movements, all three causes, however, do share the same ultimate goal, which is "humanism," the doctrine that asserts the dignity and worth of both men and women via their innate capacity for fulfilling inborn abilities.

61

The Chicana and the Women's Rights Movement*

CONSUELO NIETO

Like the Adelitas who fought with their men in the Mexican Revolution [1910], Chicanas have joined their brothers to fight for social justice. The Chicana cannot forget the oppression of her people, her *raza*—male and female alike. She fights to preserve her culture and demands the right to be unique in America. Her vision is one of a multicultural society in which one need not surrender to a filtering process and thus melt away to nothingness.

Who is the Chicana? She cannot be defined in precise terms. Her diversity springs from the heritage of the *indio*, the *español*, and the *mestizo*.

The heterogeneous background of her people defies the stereotyping. Her roots were planted in this land before the Pilgrims ever boarded the Mayflower. As a bicultural person, she participates in two worlds, integrating her Mexican heritage with that of the majority society. The Chicana seeks to affirm her identity as a Mexican-American and a woman and to define her role within this context.

How does her definition relate to women's rights? How does the women's rights movement affect a Chicana's life? The Chicana shares with all women the universal victimhood of sexism. Yet the Chicana's struggle for personhood must be analyzed with great care and sensitivity. Hers is a struggle against sexism within the context of a racist society. Ignore this factor and it is impossible to understand the Chicana's struggle.

The task facing the Chicana is monumental. On the one hand, she struggles to maintain her identity as a Chicana. On the other hand, her demands for equity as a woman involve fundamental cultural change.

The Chicana shares with all women basic needs that cut across ethnic lines. Yet she has distinctive priorities and approaches, for the Chicana is distinct from the Anglo woman. The Chicana's world, culture, and values do not always parallel those of the Anglo woman.

Many Chicanas support the women's movement as it relates to equity in pay and job opportunities, for instance. Yet for some, particularly the non-activists, the closer the movement comes to their personal lives, the more difficult it becomes to tear themselves away from the kinds of roles they have filled.

The lifestyles of Chicanas span a broad and varied continuum. Education, geography, and socioeconomic living conditions are but a few of the variables which make

*From *Civil Rights Digest*, Vol. 6, No. 3, Spring 1974: pp. 36–42.

a difference. The urban, educated middle-class Chicana usually has more alternatives, sophisticated skills, and greater mobility than her sisters in the barrios or the fields.

In the worlds of the barrio and *el campo* [the fields], with their limited social options, the role of the woman is often strictly defined. Fewer choices exist. Yet among all groups one finds women who are strong and who have endured.

Traditionally, the Chicana's strength has been exercised in the home where she has been the pillar of family life. It is just this role that has brought her leadership and her abilities to the larger community. The Chicano family is oftentimes an extended one, including grandparents, aunts and uncles, cousins (of all degrees), as well as relatives of spiritual affinity, such as godparents and in-laws.

Chicanas, collectively and individually, have cared for that family. It is the Chicana who goes to her children's school to ask why Juanito cannot read. It is the Chicana who makes the long trip to the social security office to obtain the support needed to keep *viejecita* Carmen going in her one-room apartment when taking in ironing will not do it.

It is *la Chicana* who fights the welfare bureaucracy for her neighbor's family. It is *la Chicana* who, by herself and with her sisters, is developing ways in which the youth of her community can be better cared for when their mothers must leave home to work.

Because life in the poorer barrios is a struggle for survival, the man cannot always participate in such community activities unless they pay a salary. He must provide the material support for his family. This is the tradition. It is in his heart, his conscience.

Chicanas owe much of their freedom to work for their communities to their men. It is the Chicana who often gains and develops those skills and attitudes that provide the basis for the transition of her culture into that of the modern United States. A transition, and yes, even a transformation—but not at the price of dissolving that culture.

Last year I taught an adult education class that included some mothers from the barrio. I'm sure they were not aware of the women's movement per se, but I was amazed at their high degree of interest and concern with the question, "How can I help my daughters so that when they get married they will be able to do things that my husband won't allow me to do?"

None of them thought of trying to change their own lives, because they knew that it was a dead end for them. They would say, "He loves me and I love him. I will accept things as they are for me, but I don't want that for my daughter."

It's not that they didn't view change as personally attractive, but that to demand it would place their family and their home in too much jeopardy. It would mean pulling away from their husbands in a manner that could not be reconciled. And they will not pay that price.

Other women who wanted to enroll in my class could not, because their husbands would not permit them to go out at night or allow them to get involved in activities outside the home during the day. This is not surprising—some Chicanas have many facets of their lives more tightly controlled by their husbands than do their Anglo sisters. For some women of the barrio, their hope is to achieve that measure of control over their own lives that many Anglo women already have.

Similarly, some Chicano men will state that they are fighting for their women, but not for that kind of status and position that would give women equal footing. They are fighting to be able to provide for their women the social and economic status and position that Anglo men have been able to give Anglo women.

The Church

The role of the Catholic Church in the history of the Chicana is an important one. Not all Chicanos are Catholic, and among those who belong to the Church, not all participate actively. But since the arrival of the Spanish, the values, traditions, and social patterns of the Church have been tightly interwoven in Chicano family life.

The respect accorded the Church by many Chicanos must not be shrugged aside. Many will support or oppose a particular issue simply on the basis of "the Church's position." For these people it is very difficult to assess a "moral" issue outside the pale of Church authority and legitimacy.

For the most part, the Church has assumed a traditional stance toward women. It has clearly defined the woman's role as that of wife and mother, requiring obedience to one's husband.

The words of the apostle Paul have been used to justify this attitude: "As Christ is head of the Church and saves the whole body, so is a husband the head of his wife, and as the Church submits to Christ, so should wives submit to their husbands in everything."

Also: "A man certainly should not cover his head, since he is the image of God and reflects God's glory; but woman is the reflection of man's glory. For man did not come from woman; no, woman came from man; and man was not created for the sake of woman, but woman was created for the sake of man."

Marianismo (veneration of the Virgin Mary) has had tremendous impact upon the development of the Chicana. Within many Chicano homes, *La Virgen*—under various titles, but especially as *La Virgen de Guadalupe*—has been the ultimate role model for the Chicano woman.

Mary draws her worth and nobility from her relationship to her son, Jesus Christ. She is extolled as mother, as nurturer. She is praised for her endurance of pain and sorrow, her willingness to serve, and her role as teacher of her son's word. She is Queen of the Church.

Some Chicanas are similarly praised as they emulate the sanctified example set by Mary. The woman par excellence is mother and wife. She is to love and support her husband and to nurture and teach her children. Thus may she gain fulfillment as a woman.

For a Chicana bent upon fulfillment of her personhood, this restricted perspective of her role as a woman is not only inadequate but crippling.

Some Chicanas further question the Church's prerogative to make basic decisions unilaterally about women's lives. When the Church speaks out on issues such as divorce, remarriage, and birth control, those Chicanas wonder, "Who can really make these decisions for me? Upon what basis should such choices be made?"

Many Chicanas still have a strong affiliation with the Church and seek its leadership and support as they attempt to work out their lives. Others try to establish their identity as women on their own, yet choose not to break with Church mandates.

Still others find this middle road too difficult. They choose not to work within Church structure and seek their independence totally outside the folds of religion. Chicanas find that to advocate feminist positions frowned upon by the Church often evokes family criticism and pressure. Thus some compromise personal values and feign conformity for the sake of peace within the family.

Concerned leaders within the Church do speak out in behalf of the Chicana's struggle for equity. But this is not the norm. While the Church supports equal pay and better working conditions, it would find it most difficult to deal with the sexism expressed in its own hierarchy or within the family model.

Brothers and Sisters

Chicanos often question the goals of the women's movement. Some see it as an "Anglo woman's trip," divisive to the cause of *el movimiento* [The Chicano movement]. These men assert the need to respect women, but women's liberation . . . ? "That deals with trivia, minutiae—we all must concentrate on the battle for social justice."

Many of our brothers see the women's movement as another force which will divert support from *la causa*. On a list of priorities, many Chicanos fail to see how the plight of *la mujer* can be of major concern within the context of la raza's problems. They see the women's movement as a vehicle to entrench and strengthen the majority of culture's dominance. They are concerned that their sister may be deceived and manipulated. They warn her never to be used as a pawn against her own people.

Yet the Chicana may sometimes ask, "Is it your real fear, my brother, that I be used against our movement? Or is it that I will assume a position, a stance, that you are neither prepared nor willing to deal with?"

Other Chicanos may be more sensitive and try to help their sisters achieve a higher status, but the fact that they, too, usually limit the aspirations of their sisters is soon evident. They would open the doors to new roles and new alternatives, but on a selective basis. Some support upward mobility for their sisters in the professions, but reneg when it comes to equality at home.

A good number of Chicanos fear that in embracing the women's movement their sisters will negate the very heritage they both seek to preserve. The Chicana would ask her brother, "To be a Chicana—proud and strong in my culture—must I be a static being? Does not the role of women change as life changes?"

Dealing with Contradictions

Participation within organizations of the women's rights movement can bring to the Chicana a painful sense of alienation from some women of the majority culture. The Chicana may often feel like a marginal figure. Her Anglo sisters assure her that their struggle unequivocally includes her within its folds.

Yet as she listens carefully, certain contradictions will soon emerge. The Anglo women will help the Chicana by providing a model, a system to emulate. The Anglo will help the Chicana erase those "differences" that separate them. Hence, "We will all be united under the banner of Woman. This will be our first and primary source of identity."

For a Chicana allied with the struggle of her people, such a simplistic approach to her identity is not acceptable. Furthermore, it is difficult for the Chicana to forget that some Anglo women have oppressed her people within this society, and are still not sensitive to minorities or their needs. With Anglo women the Chicana may share a commitment to equality, yet it is very seldom that she will find with them the camaraderie, the understanding, the sensitivity that she finds with her own people.

Anglo women sensitive to Chicanas as members of a minority must guard against a very basic conceptual mistake. All minorities are not alike. To understand the black woman is not to understand the Chicana. To espouse the cause of minority women, Anglos must recognize our distinctiveness as separate ethnic groups.

For example, in dealing with sex role stereotyping in schools, a multicultural approach should be used. Materials must encompass all groups of women. Women's studies courses should not exclude the unique history of minority women from the curriculum.

And the inclusion of one minority group is not enough. Chicanas know only too well the pain of negation that comes from omission. The affront of exclusion may not be intentional, but to the victim that doesn't matter. The result is the same.

What does it mean to be a Chicana? This question the Chicana alone must answer. Chicanas must not allow their brothers or other women to define their identity. Our brothers are often only too ready to tell us "who" we are as Chicanas.

Conversely, some Chicanas seeking fulfillment in *la causa* do not question or challenge the parameters set down for them by Chicanos—or more basically, they do not challenge the male's right to such authority.

Similarly, a woman who has never shared our culture and history cannot fully grasp the measure of our life experiences. She will be unable to set goals, priorities, and expectations for Chicanas.

Chicanas must raise their own level of awareness. Too many do not recognize their repression and the extent of it. Many have come to accept it as the norm rather than as a deviance.

Chicanas also need to deal with their men openly. Perhaps the Chicana has been overly protective of her brothers. Hers is a difficult role. She must be sensitive to his struggle, but not at the cost of her own identity. She must support him as he strives to attain the equality too long denied him, but she too must no longer be denied. To fight and provide for the fulfillment of the Chicano while denying equality to women does not serve the true aims of *la causa*, and will not liberate our people in the real sense.

What must the Chicana do? First, she must work with her own sisters to define clearly her role, her goals, and her strategies. This, I would suggest, can be done by involvement in one of the many Chicana feminist organizations that are currently emerging.

Second, she must be involved with Chicanos in the Chicano movement. Here the Chicana must sensitize the male to the fact that she, as a woman, is oppressed and that he is a part of that oppression. She must reinforce the *carnalismo* (spirit of fraternity) that is theirs, but point out that as long as his status as a man is earned at her expense, he is not truly free.

The Chicana must tell her brother, "I am not here to emasculate you; I am here to fight with you shoulder to shoulder as an equal. If you can only be free when I take second place to you, then you are not truly free—and I want freedom for you as well as for me."

A third mandate I would give the Chicana is to participate in the mainstream of the women's rights movement. She is needed here to provide the Chicana perspective as well as to provide support for the activities designed to help all women. Moreover, her unique role as a liaison person is crucial. How tragic it would be if all women did not promote and participate in a valid working coalition to advance our common cause?

Chicanas must avoid a polarization that isolates them from Chicanos as well as other women. They must carefully analyze each situation, as well as the means to reconcile differences. This is not easy—it requires a reservoir of understanding, patience, and commitment. Yet unless it is done, success will not be ours.

Finally, the Chicana must demand that dignity and respect within the women's rights movement that allows her to practice feminism within the context of her own culture. The timing and the choices must be hers. Her models and those of her daughters will be an Alicia Escalante and a Dolores Huerta. Her approaches to feminism must be drawn from her own world, and not be shadowy replicas drawn from Anglo society. The Chicana will fight for her right to uniqueness; she will not be absorbed.

For some it is sufficient to say, "I am woman." For me it must be, "I am Chicana."

62

The Progress of the Chicana Woman*

CORRINE J. GUTIÉRREZ

When I was called upon to present some facts about the progress the Chicana woman has made in Kansas, I had no idea how depressing it was going to be. I'll give you a few figures as to our status, but I refuse to call it "progress."

First of all, according to the 1970 census, there are 22,500 Spanish-speaking Chicanas in the State of Kansas, with half of them employed outside the home. 35% work in low-pay, low-status service positions; 24% work in the clerical field; and only 11% work in professional fields. However, we do not stand alone, for I found these figures compare very closely to women of other races as well.

As to the educational status of Chicanas, national figures show that only 5% have completed four or more years of college. From that, only 1% are earning more than $10,000 a year. I'd like to repeat that—*1% are earning more than $10,000 a year.* 1 is the lowest number in our numerical system and that's where we're at. I have to laugh at the Virginia Slim's advertisement that says, "You've come a long way, baby." Maybe she's come a long way, but we've only just begun and we have a very, very long way to go if we're ever to become economically independent women.

If you're wondering how the Chicana feels about the women's movement as a whole, I can't answer that. You cannot put the feelings of the Chicana in one big pot

*Speech given at Woman's Day Rally, State Capitol Grounds, Topeka, Kansas, August 26, 1975. From *Adelante*, October 19, 1975: p. 9.

and say, "This is how we feel!" More than anything, I detest the stereotyping of people just because their skin happens to be brown, or black, or even white. We are all individuals with our own individual beliefs and we have to be treated as such. Chicanas may *all* agree that we are being discriminated against and that something has to be done about it, but we will not *all* agree as to what to do and how to go about doing it.

If it seems to you that Chicana women are not interested in the fight for equality for women, you are mistaken. We have been involved for many years in working for human rights, fighting side by side with our men for equal opportunity for the Mexican-American. But although our fight for human rights may have made things easier for the Chicano male, it is becoming increasingly clear that the Chicana woman somehow did not qualify as a "human" because she is not reaping the same opportunities.

It gives me great pleasure to find that Chicana women are finally awakening and are beginning to organize in attempting to do something about their problems. And in finding solutions to her problems, she has one added cross to bear—that of being discriminated against as a minority, as well as being a woman.

But I feel this added burden can be lessened by combining our efforts with our sisters—and I don't mean just her Chicana sisters, but her black, and white sisters as well. Not only *should* we work together, but we *must*, if we ever expect to gain any ground in what I consider to be a mutual and common cause. I see the woman's movement as being an ideal avenue for bridging the gaps between different ethnic groups and promoting a better understanding among ourselves. A chance to come together and share our backgrounds and ultimately becoming aware that those differences that we supposedly have are not so different after all. And more than anything, a chance to see ourselves as individuals instead of being categorized as a "Mexican-American," a "Black," an "Indian," or even as an "Anglo." This doesn't mean that we have to give up our own unique culture. It simply means that we have two cultures—the one we were born with and the one we're living in. But the culture we're living in now is what we have to learn to deal with if we have any desire for making a better future for ourselves and our children. The time for isolating ourselves in our own little ethnic corner is past and we all have to work together if we are ever to raise ourselves from the status of second class citizens as women, to first class citizens as people, as it should be.

But more than that, only by working together can we make sure that our cause will benefit *all* women and not just the white, middle-class working woman. We need to ask ourselves, how the woman's movement can help the minority woman? What can it offer the woman who has chosen to be a housewife and not employed outside her home? How can it benefit the low-income woman, as well? These are basic questions we'll all have to deal with and answer in order to make our fight worthwhile.

And in our fight for human rights, we cannot forget the male attitude. And one of our Chicanas, Enriqueta [Longeaux y] Vásquez said it better than I ever could when she said, "We must strive for the fulfillment of all as equals with the full capability and right to develop as humans. When the man can look upon "his" woman as *human* and with the love of brotherhood and equality, then and only then, can he feel the true meaning of liberation and equality himself."

63

Among the Feminists: Racist Classist Issues—1976*

MARTA COTERA

It is really fitting for me to preface my comments on racism, sexism, and classism with a quote from the type of Anglo feminist who has often worked most successfully with minority women, the radical feminist.

The *Radical Woman's Position Paper on Race and Sex* positions the ideal situation for race, sex, and class interaction, succinctly. "The essential interaction of women's liberation with human liberation must become a guideline for every women's liberationist in the daily life and in her intervention into every area of political and community action."

Many of us have worried about the speedy abandonment of the term "women's liberation" by many feminists when they were pressured to do so for reasons of image and political expediency. Somehow, along with the term seems to have gone our efforts to reach the point of *concientización* or consciousness about principles of liberation so essential to the survival of feminism. Along with this move has gone the fragile respect we had for each other's differences. We also stand to lose the incentive to work together, despite our race and class differences, for a common goal, the liberation of women and men from the system that has exploited and dehumanized us.

I am not going to lay on anyone the usual guilt trip about the racism and classism that Blacks, Chicanas, and poor women face every day from feminists in the name of feminism. But we do need to share information about the power dynamics that are generated openly, daily among women in communities throughout the Untied States. Unfortunately, many feminists who are now experts at these games engage in them in the name of feminism and liberation. It behooves the rest of us to become conscious of the fact that these persons haven't the dimmest notion about the meaning of either term. Otherwise, instead of playing destructive games we would all be involved creatively in effective humanistic-oriented strategies which could develop coalition-building among us. In all fairness, it may be said that often gross errors are made by feminists out of ignorance rather than malice, and these feminists might look over what we have to say, check themselves, and hopefully work constructively for change.

Before any coalition-building can take place, we should be aware that, like it or

*Marta Cotera delivered this speech at the Feminism and the Law Conference held in Denver in October, 1976 and then pubished it in her anthology, *The Chicana Feminist*, in 1977. (Austin: Information Systems Development, 1977: pp. 33–47.)

not, Anglo women are going to have to accept certain obvious facts. Within our society there are hierarchies of need because there have been hierarchies of oppression. If minority women, specifically Chicanas, scream loudly, it is because we have been doubly oppressed. Because of this, we do often demand priority for our needs. It is often painful to recall that majority women, through passive acquiescence or active discrimination, have been accessories to our oppression. Beverly Hawkins, in *Woman is Not Just a Female*, supports this position:

> The fact that ethnic minority women have had a different cultural, social and economic experience than white women makes it imperative that the diversities between minority and non-minority women be realized, accepted, and dealt with in the appropriate manner—the manner that will assume the most equitable results for all of us. (Hawkins, p. 1)

Hawkins srongly states that there is insufficient research to prove that the impact of sexism is more severe than the impact of racism.

> The visible ethnic minority groups—the Asians, Chicanos, Native Americans, and Blacks—have had a unique history in America. They have been exploited, abused, dehumanized, and killed because of the color of their skin. America expressed its repugnance for the above-mentioned minority groups, while simultaneously exploiting them as a cheap labor source. Racism and oppression have traditionally been synonymous with good business practice for America. (Hawkins, p. 2)

No one can deny that we are all women, but neither can we deny that we are not the same; that many of us have not shared in the gains made in the name of "Woman" in this country. Chicanas share with the Blacks and other visible minority women many gaps in benefits enjoyed as a matter of course by white women.

Politics

Like the Blacks, Chicanas did not necessarily benefit from suffrage legislation giving women the vote during this century. If Chicanas could not afford the poll tax, they couldn't vote. If they could cross the tracks to the Anglo part of town only to work as domestics, they couldn't vote; if they were U.S. citizens, but had no documents, they couldn't vote. If they were not physically able to resist the Sheriff's threats and blows, they couldn't vote. Finally, if the polling place was in a private home (a common practice in Texas) and if the homeowner did not allow Mexicans in, they couldn't vote. Chicanas who couldn't vote couldn't help elect Chicanas or Chicanos to office.

In the Southwest, the Chicanas' right to vote was not protected effectively until 1976 when Barbara Jordan, a Texas Black legislator, introduced and ramrodded through the U.S. Congress an Extension to the Voting Rights Act of 1965 to cover Mexican-Americans.

Herstories and Images

Another tragic aspect of our relationship with Anglo women is that it is difficult to forget that Anglo women pioneers like Susan Magoffin were among the first to fix strong, repulsive stereotypes about Chicanas, when they first came to the Southwest in the 1840's and 1850's. These myths and stereotypes are not being addressed in the current crop of "herstory" textbooks. Rather, their disregard for our contributions on the development of feminism, the arts, politics, civil rights, labor, and countless other areas, will condemn us to live with Susan Magoffin's assessment.

Time and time again small, struggling publications have pointed out to the well-funded, well-heeled women's projects that Chicanas and their families made many of the labor unions; that our educational gains and progress have followed more than a century of arduous work and struggle; that Chicanas have died and been deported for principles that the majority community takes for granted: a minimum wage and freedom of speech.

In every movement and every effort, Chicanas and Chicanos have paid a "harsh price" for their involvement; often with little or no support from Anglo colleagues. Chicano and Chicana socialist and labor activists in Texas, California, and the midwest suffered long prison terms and deportation for their activities. Chicanas in Texas have certainly paid their dues for their liberation work, culminating in 1953 with the deportation of Luisa Moreno, labor activist, who had given twenty years of her life to the development of our community in the United States.

To begin my documentation of case studies, so we can be aware of racist practices among women, let me repeat that currently all white women's "herstory" publications have been severely criticized for being blatant in their disregard for the pluralistic aspects of our society. Unfortunately, this has forced us to separatism in documenting history out of self-protection and need. Needless to say, everyone—saint, socialist, radical, conservative, feminist, or non-feminist—has an ego and a self-concept to nurture. And in this respect many "herstory" historians have ignored our egos. It is very destructive to take "herstory" texts and to call them women's histories by merely replacing Anglo male heroes with Anglo heroines. It is even worse to put in Anglo labor women organizers who were largely ignored and detested by the Chicana workers they were trying to organize, and to try to give them to us as our models and heroines. It is bad form to exclude the Luisa Morenos, Emma Tenayucas, and Manuela Sagers who were deported or silenced forever. One ploy commonly used by "herstory" projects is to approach minority women and say "We have $100,000 or $248,000 for a curriculum project, but it is barely enough for us. We realize there are ethnic materials out there but we can't pay you for books, or to compile materials. If you want us to incorporate Chicana (or Black, or Asian, etc.) history into our project, do it on your own time, and at our convenience." For example, though a book on women in Texas politics had been in progress for some time, Chicanas were given five days in which to come up with a chapter on Chicanas in politics.

In terms of documenting contemporary history, not much has changed from feminism in 1910. Needless to say, 1910 Anglo feminists did not document the Chicanas' feminist activities with the civil rights movement, then or in the Partido Liberal Mexicano. In 1911, at the Congreso Mexicanista in Laredo, prominent Texas Chicanos and women advocates like Soledad Pena organized and spoke eloquently about women's roles and activism. Likewise, in the Partido Liberal Mexicano unionizing activities, Chicanas from Texas to California took the lead organizing rallies and mobilizing other women and entire communities for the rights of workers and women.

Our own activism for women's rights in the 1960's and 1970's is being ignored even by people who mean well. Nancy Seifer, in her publication *Where Feminism and Ethnicity Intersect: The Impact of Parallel Movements*, credits the white middle-class professional women with "spawning" the women's movement. This is a recurring theme through contemporary movement history. There is total silence about Chicanas' sustained efforts for women's rights within the Chicano movement ranks and often in coalition with Anglo feminist groups from at least 1905 on.

In the *Chronology of the Women's Movement in the U.S. 1961–1975*, published by the U.S. National Commission on the Observance of International Women's Year

1975, the major Chicana feminist activities in the 1960's and 1970's are ignored. Activities such as the 1969 Chicano Liberation Conference, Woman's Caucus, the 1971 National Chicana Conference and the formation of Concilio Mujeres, Concilio Femenil, the National Chicana Institute, and the National Chicana Foundation are ignored. If the "herstory" documentation of the last six years is any example of what lies ahead for us, we are going to suffer the same fate as our Chicana feminists in 1905: oblivion and lack of credit at least as far as the Anglo community is concerned.

This doesn't worry adult women too much. We know who we are and what we've done, but "herstory" books are getting to our schools and are just as destructive to our children's self-concept as the all-male Anglo texts have been. It also doesn't help our relationship with borderline racist and classist feminists who can always write us off, since as far as their literature is concerned, we have never done anything anyway. Obviously, another area where Chicanas are being blatantly excluded is in the women's studies courses and departments. I know a few courses where Chicanas and Blacks [materials on] will be [covered in] one or two lectures a semester. I know of many courses in which Anglo women are allowed to teach courses that are supposed to teach [survey courses on] all women, but if a Chicana is hired for such a course, she is supposed to know and teach only about Chicanas.

Institution Building

This is also a very critical area as far as our development is concerned. There is much in social services funding earmarked for women's institutions. Women's Centers flourish that claim to speak for and to service all women. Their boards might include one or two choice Chicanas, if the Center considers itself liberal. But for the most part, these centers merely replace male institutions that have used minority and poor women in the past to learn a profession and earn a professional salary. We have been "clients" of white male institutions for generations. Now we are becoming "clients" of Anglo professional women's institutions, since they are the ones who get the funds and the jobs.

I can cite several examples of typical "moves" in the area of institution-building by liberal white women or feminists.

O Hire a white director and professional staff, and at least one Chicana or Black secretary or clerk.
O Start in the Anglo side of town and expand the minority community to "service minority women."
O Use the Anglo woman's power and influence to convince politicians that Chicanas' institutions could not serve the entire community and that if they attempt to serve the Chicana they only would be duplicating your efforts.
O If you get hassled by the minorities, make up an advisory committee of "safe" Chicanas to oversee the project. But make certain the funding and salary money is going to Anglo pocketbooks.

We're still wondering what would happen if a group of Blacks or Chicanos were to approach a city council and propose a woman's project for the Anglo side of town. Even among real feminists, there are some racist attitudes, which in the spirit of liberation should be documented, worked on, and obliterated. Although they might seem minor or trivial, when the minority women are the target for these attitudes and actions day after day, the time comes when they're ready to explode with rage. Some of these attitudes are racist and classist. Most of them are so ingrained in our feminists' culture and psyche that they're second nature to them. Work on them, please. Anglo feminist committee women or women elected officials constantly say to Chicanas, "I'm so proud of you," or, "I'm so impressed with you." (Upon your initiating an enormous feat or completing a superb job that is nothing to you.) The Chicana feminist would like to say, "Who the hell cares what you think? By whose standards are you judging me? Have I come up to your standards? Don't you think I have a brain? Am I the little train on the hill?" Next time an Anglo tells us this, accompanied by a pat on the shoulder or head, we're going to pull this one on them and watch the reaction.

Another comment is "many Chicanas would never do this or say this," or, "our Chicanas on the Board agree with this concept." One always gets the picture of our women on the auction block, bought lock, stock, and mind by these majority women so adept with personal pronouns. Come to think of it, I've never heard them say, "my lesbians," although they would come close to it.

- "But you know I love you all and sympathize with you. (I may not be able to vote with you, but my love and appreciation is more than enough for the likes of you.)" This is a common reply when Chicanas lobby Anglo women, whom they have supported politically.
- The good old double standard: "We can't set a numbers quota, you know, because it would be reverse discrimination." (When you've asked to assure adequate representation for the state-wide international Woman's Year conference.) Then, again,
- "We've given you people all you asked for; what more do you want?" (Very common attitude especially when funding and questions of proportional services are concerned.) Minority women are looked on by non-minority women as a nuisance when issues of quality and quantity services are introduced. Also, women project directors, like their male counterparts, forget very fast that we, too, are taxpayers and that we get nothing free. Forget sisterhood; that's the first thing that flies out the window.

Within all these attitudes, statements and gestures are several basic problems. Many Anglo women, including feminists simply cannot accept the fact that there are minority women with brains and status. They seem unable to realize, possibly because of gross ignorance of minority history, that we have a strong history of involvement, achievement and guts, since we've had to fight not only the issue of sexism but the issue of racism. In terms of human dynamics, we're usually knowledgeable and aware since we are operating on two planes: the racism inherent in White–Brown relations and sexism.

The strongest feeling that becomes evident is that minority women are not active participants in the woman's movement, but mere observers. Very often the most visible or most vocal among us will be invited to a woman's function to "have our say" or for the media's sake. There is never any real intent to incorporate our bodies and our needs into the feminist activities. Consequently, we have proceeded to act as observers, often without being aware that we're doing so. With the entire I.W.Y. state conference activities throughout the nation, minority women have swum against the current to become incorporated beyond the "observer status."

Classism in the Ranks

The issue of classism in the feminist ranks hit us square in the face. One fine day, we realized that Anglo feminists who were pulling certain "movidas" (moves) on us were not operating at the racist level. What they were doing was bewildering since it really did not resemble the racist attitudes of their men.

We realized that a certain air of arrogance, insensitivity to the needs or incomprehension of needs of poor women, regardless of race, come from another source. We realized that these feminists see all minority women as members of a certain class, mainly lower class.

It is immaterial that they don't realize they're dealing with minority women from diverse socio-economic situations and backgrounds. To them, all minorities are the same. I cannot attempt to do here the superb analysis that Charlotte Bunch and Nancy Myron accomplished in their *Class and Feminism*. They indicate that a

> middle class cop-out on class issues has been to claim that as women we are powerless. We did not create class society which is patriarchal to its core. However, upper and middle class women do get privileges from that system and do behave in ways that oppress women. (Bunch and Myron, p. 11)

Most minority women would agree with Charlotte Bunch in her assessment of class behavior among some white women who call themselves feminists. That classist behavior is rooted in the idea of class supremacy, that the individuals of the upper and middle classes are superior to those of the lower classes. Bunch says, "No one in our movement would say that she believes that she is better than her working class sisters, yet her behavior says it over and over again." (Bunch and Myron, p. 72) Certain beliefs and attitudes underlie the middle class movement woman's relationship with women who she believes are lower class:

- The belief that lower class women are less together, personally, politically
- That they are not as "articulate"
- That they tend to be hostile and emotional so their judgement can't be trusted
- Unlike us, they can't check their emotions, be reasonable
- That they don't have what I have because they haven't worked for it

I can't speak of our experiences with classist behavior in the feminist ranks without speaking of volunteerism and how it has affected our lives and relationships with some Anglos who call themselves feminists; I don't question the value of red-blooded American volunteerism. And I applaud the move to get employers to recognize and credit volunteer work as work experience for women. However, this is an area in which minority women are at a disadvantage with Anglo women. First of all, in coalition organization work, Anglo women will not recognize the fact that Chicanas work long hours at non-feminist Chicano community work. This has no value to them, so they constantly reproach Chicanas about all the work they can get done that is "volunteer" work. Often, too, Anglo feminists, like "herstorians," get their part of their activities done with paid labor and when it comes to outreach to Chicanas or services to them, they'll say the institution is there; if they want the services they can do them on a volunteer basis. With the Texas I.W.Y. Conference in 1977, for example, Anglo involved women were reached through paid staff help. Although the federal government supplied $100,000 in funding to reach all women, Chicanas had to do all their planning and outreach on a volunteer basis.

The "movida" of volunteerism also hurts the poor woman and the minority woman in competition for jobs. A middle-class woman may be able to afford to volunteer for a while at a job while a Black or Chicana or poor woman has to work at nickels and dimes until she can land a better job. For the middle-class volunteer, there is always the chance that an opening will occur right where she is volunteering (or that a job will be created for her). And she has got herself a good job.

As I said before, we might kill ourselves at a voter registration project or Chicano health clinic or forming a large organization, but if it isn't something that these women in power recognize, they will not believe minority women ever do anything. Ultimately, the most maddening classist behavior with the feminists in power is what Bunch calls their "privileged passivity."

In this whole issue of class, which we believe has arisen as a more damaging issue than race in feminism, we believe Anglo women are harder to deal with than men. With Anglo men, we had to fight the sexist racist issue. If they discriminated on race, we sensitized, trained, and sued. However, at least most of them had been around working people of different classes enough to realize that minorities did come from diverse class groups. Also, classism in the professions and working groups is a more hidden issue because you have other factors such as knowledge experience, and the natural propensity to push your career aggressively regardless of your class background.

With Anglo women feminists, it's different. They haven't had the same professional exposure to class differences as the males. Many of them are entering the job market for the first time. Many of them have been stuck in suburban homes, protected from the somewhat more democratic processes in the job market. Whereas they have been taught that racism is not nice, no one has ever told them that they have to put up with poor people, or at least people whom they think ought to be poor, like minorities. So once they open up a conference to all minorities, they see nothing wrong in imposing fees and exorbitant rates which they know will exclude the poor. They simply cannot successfully hide their classism and have not even learned to recognize it yet.

Sexism vs. Racism

Not much has been documented to refute the Anglo women's position that sexism has been more destructive than racism. Beverly Hawkins very dramatically points to the Japanese American women who were incarcerated during World War II, not because they were women but because they were Japanese American. Chicanas, too can cite examples of deprivations that Chicanas have suffered as an ethnic group, not because they were women but because they are Mexican or brown.

Hawkins cites that particularly in the subject of employment discrimination, many feminists have drawn analogies concerning the experiences of racism and sexism. In this respect they compare themselves to ethnic minorities and the discrimination they have faced and are currently encountering in the labor market. To illustrate her point, Hawkins indicates that although Anglo women do suffer from lower wages than Anglo males, their position is superior to that of minority women and this despite their inconsistent status in the labor force. By contrast, Black women consistently stay in the labor force and reap meager results.

We should realize that the problem of race, class, liberation and power dynamics is complex and that most of us will shrug and say that we are not like that at all; that women who do those awful things are opportunists who also hurt other white women. And I can honestly concede that a lot of this is true and that the more radical Anglo woman has been more responsive to minority needs. However, to a large degree all of us share the responsibility of raising the consciousness of every woman who is not aware. Hopefully, we are all involved in developing coalitions which will help all women develop and I think minority women are sincerely committed to this. Further, I think that even the barrier of "cultural diversity" could be lowered, if we trusted each other more. If this barrier could be removed, we could reach more of the women who need to be helped out from "under the floor." To do this, Anglo feminists would have to work in earnest to eradicate their racism and classism, which breed the tendency to deny minority women their self-determination.

Unfortunately, our "cultural context" feelings and expressions will continue to be the barrier used by us in coalition building as long as we feel that our daughters and ours sons need to survive and need protection, not only from sex discrimination but from race and class discrimination. Like you, we cannot separate our race and sex identity. Neither can we prioritize our need to survive with both intact. We must continue to face both issues together, as long as most white men and women refuse to face up to their racism and classism.

Particularly, I would alert sincere feminists and radicals to evaluate all new organizations, collectives and institutions that this is where the new feminist racism and classism is flexing its muscle against minority women. I could go on all week about the daily dynamics that take place in our community, and the many manifestations of residual and new racism and the destructive classist practices against all poor women.

Am I bitter? Are we bitter? Not bitter enough to quit the struggle. Actually, no minority person of any race or sex thinks that racism, like sexism, will disappear by wishing it so, or by assuming that all feminists are truly liberated human beings. Racism, classism, and sexism will disappear when we accept differences and if we continue to resist loudly and clearly all racist, classist, and sexist efforts on the part of other persons to enslave Black, white, lesbian, heterosexual, male, or female. Maybe then the level of consciousness will be raised, if not through goodness, at least through our resistance and unity.

64

La Chicana and "Women's Liberation"*

YOLANDA OROZCO

Lately, many Chicanas have made efforts to more clearly define our position within "el movimiento." Chicanas have been organizing around issues arising out of our particular needs and problems. These issues are seldom treated within the context of the women's liberation movement. Yet, it is often the case that as soon as Chicanas begin to assert themselves in a particular situation we are labeled as "women's libbers." The implication being that we are followers of a women's movement and therefore we can be dismissed for all intents and purposes. How invalid the arbitrary application of such a label becomes evident upon a brief examination of what the women's liberation movement is all about.

The women's movement has in recent years evolved into a multifaceted political movement wherein exist diverse factions that often are in conflict with each other. Jo Freeman in *The Politics of Women's Liberation* divides the women's movement into two major groups. One, the "older group," consists mainly of women employed by the government who initiated the first task forces to examine the status of women in government agencies, and the founders of the National Organization for Women (NOW). The "younger group" is comprised of more "radical women," those who participate in the civil rights movement or as members of the New Left.

The major distinction between the two groups is at once obvious. The former is characterized by a conservative approach; their goals have been to institute legislative reform and to have new laws passed with the hope that these in turn will effect changes in policy and create equality for women. The more progressive sectors of the women's movement recognize that true equality for women is not possible within this capitalistic structure that exploits not only women but also Third World people and members of the working class.

So whereas the conservative element of the women's movement has shown some political clout as evidenced in the passage of various pieces of legislation to end sex discrimination in employment, provide maternity benefits, and the most recent struggle to have the Constitution amended by the Equal Rights Amendment the question concerning us is if, in fact, such legislation will benefit Chicanas. The answer is an unequivocal NO! While the women's movement can struggle and agitate for career and professional advancement, more facility in securing credit and property, the reality is that such demands are inconsequential to us. Many Chicanas do not even

*From *Voz Fronteriza*, Vol. 1, No. 1, Jan. 5, 1976: pp. 6, 13.

graduate from high school, fewer yet attend college. And although a majority of Chicanas are employed, they are relegated to the lower-paying jobs, as are Chicanos. The oppression of Chicanas cannot be divorced from the exploitation of La Raza, for to do so would be to fall prey to the system's divide and conquer tactics.

This is not to say that the women's movement has not had any effect on Chicanas at all. In a survey conducted at this campus dealing specifically with the Chicana and the women's movement, an overwhelming response was that the women's movement had affected their role as women in some way. The majority of Chicanas responding to the survey saw the movement as being a "consciousness raising one" resulting in more "self-confidence" and "assertiveness." The respondents also readily identified with certain issues raised by the women's movement, especially the right to legal abortions on demand and ready access to birth control. So it is that the women's movement struggle for the right of women to have control over their bodies is an issue that has influenced Chicanas. However, it is important only in so far as there is freedom of choice. For many Chicanas as well as for Black and Puerto Rican women who have been victims of forced sterilizations or who have served as guinea pigs for testing new methods of birth control, this freedom to choose is lacking.

Even through the majority of Chicanas responding to the survey could relate to certain issues of the women's movement, for the most part they saw it as being an elitist movement comprised of white middle-class women who see the oppressor as the males of this society. Their struggle becomes one of attempting to achieve relative equality with white males. But as Emily F. Gibson, a black writer, wrote in the *L.A. Times*: "Equality of opportunity with men simply loses its luster when survival is the dominant drive or when 'to be equal' to a black man still means to be discriminated against." Thus, for Chicanas to demand equality with Chicanos is to ignore that together we are fighting for political and economic survival as an ethnic group and as a class.

It needs to be pointed out that if the women's movement has ignored the needs and priorities of Chicanas and therefore excluded us, then to some extent so has the Chicano movement that often confines Chicanas to stereotyping sex roles-in the kitchen or at the typewriter.

Sylvia Gonzales, professor at Sacramento State College, writes in an article in the *L.A. Times:* ". . . for the Chicana, the awakening of consciousness has also been prompted in part by the 'machismo' she encounters within the Chicano Freedom Movement itself."

Of course, it must be recognized that often Chicanas, as well as Chicanos, perpetuate traditional social roles through our attitudes and actions. It is imperative that Chicanas and Chicanos recognize that sexist attitudes do exist on both sides. Out of this recognition should evolve a consciousness that will enable a restructuring of traditional male–female responsibilities and roles.

It is understood that we are necessarily reflections of the political and economic system that envelopes us. Nonetheless, where attitudes exist that divide Chicanas and Chicanos and as a result hinder our struggle, they must be eradicated at the individual level. Barbara Ehrenreich, in a speech given at the National Socialist Feminist Conference, illuminates this point well.

> . . . socialism means much more than a redistribution of wealth or a change in the ownership of the means of production. The revolution is not just something you read about in the newspapers; it is not just something which occurs in the realm of political economy. The revolution process extends into all aspects of life—including those which have been defined as "personal" and not "political." And the

revolutionary transformation of the entire fabric of social relationships . . . socialist feminist thinking is characterized by an emphasis on the importance of subjective factors in revolutionary change. That is, we don't have to wait until "after the revolution" to transform ourselves as people—we know that transforming ourselves is part of making the revolution. From this point of view, the task of "consciousness raising"—uprooting deeply entrenched bourgeois, racist, and sexist attitudes—is central to political struggle.

65

Feminism: The Chicano and Anglo Versions—A Historical Analysis*

Marta Cotera

The relationship of the Chicana to the women's movement, including the suffrage movement in the United States, has been marked by complex factors affecting the development of both groups from 1848 to the present.

There is evidence that a relationship between Chicanas and the women's movement has existed at least for the past 80 years. There is evidence, too, that this relationship has been affected by the same factors affecting women's interaction with black women, white ethnic women, and working-class women, because the Chicana is a minority woman and is considered an immigrant. In addition, a great percentage of Chicanas are in the working-class at the lowest occupational scale.

Chicanas' involvement with the women's movement in the 1890 to 1920 period was limited by the barriers that impeded all women with similar backgrounds: the antilabor, antiminority attitudes of the leadership of the women's movement. They were affected also by the antisocialist and anticommunist attitudes of the movement in the early twentieth century, since many Chicana workers and leaders were ardent socialists.

The greatest victory for the women's movement was not victory for minority women. The suffrage amendment did not enfranchise Chicanas and black women.

*From *Twice a Minority*, edited by Margarita Melville (St. Louise: Mosby, 1980: pp. 217–234.

Chicanas were affected by the aftermath of the suffrage amendment, when women's movement activities slowed down, because white women achieved their desires, but Chicanas, like other minority women, had to continue to struggle for mere survival. They were affected when middle-class women were given preferential treatment in war industry, but blacks and Chicanas had to continue with unskilled, low-paid agricultural work and other service occupations. Chicanas were affected when white middle-class women went back home in the fifties, but minority women did not, and Chicanas, to boot, continued to suffer repression and deportation for their continued labor and civil rights advocacy. Chicanas have been affected when their community and their own gains in the 1960s have taken a back seat to the women's movement just as the black movement and black suffrage took a back seat to the suffrage movement in the latter part of the last century.

Minority women, whether black, Native American, Asian American, Chicanas, or even white ethnic women, are ambivalent about the promise of the present reemergence of the women's movement. One can even say they largely lean to the negative. Their ambivalence and apprehension are based on negative experiences suffered in contact with the movement over the past 10 years. Few minority women have read feminist archives nor the current classics; these historical analyses of the movement would definitely reinforce their apprehensions. But for those few minority and working-class women who have done extensive research, history does indeed seem to repeat itself. What is sad is that most minority, radical, and working-class women do need the movement.

The Women's Suffrage Movement and Minority Women, 1848 to 1900

This early period of the women's movement was both glorious and inglorious. The movement had started out to promote radical and lasting changes in the situation of all women in the home and in society. Even as the movement continued after 1848 and focused mainly on suffrage, the ideals remained solid. The basic premise among suffrageists in the 1850s, 1860s, and 1870s was that the vote is an intrinsic human right. When that ideal was abandoned for expediency's sake and restricitons were recommended to cut off the vote from the undesirables, minority women must have felt as did many in the early 1970s when the present movement decided that "women's liberation" was too drastic a term and we must focus on and call our movement a women's rights movement. Many wondered, "rights for *which* women?"

Mexican-American women, as part of ethnic groups of late arrivals to the national scene, had only limited participation in the women's movement in the 1848 to 1900 period. This potential for participation was further curtailed by the movement's ideological shift in the late nineteenth century against immigrants and the working class. In 1848, the very year of the historical Seneca Falls meeting when the "Declaration of Sentiments" was issued under the leadership of early feminists Elizabeth Cady Stanton and Lucrecia Mott, Mexican-American women were incorporated into the United States through conquest and the addition of Mexican territory.

During the first two decades of feminist activity in the United States, Mexican-American women were struggling along with the "social" bandits of the period like Joaquín Murieta and Nepomuceno Cortina to liberate Chicanos and Chicano territory. One of the first Chicanas to come into contact with the suffragist movements in the 1880s was Lucy Gonzalez Parsons, a Chicana socialist labor organizer. Lucy Gonzalez was born in Johnson County, Texas. As a young woman, she moved to Austin, Texas, where she worked in the state capitol and met Albert Parsons. She married

Parsons and in the 1880s they moved to Chicago where they became deeply involved in the struggling labor movement. They worked with the Workingman's Party and founded a labor newspaper, *The Alarm*. Lucy contributed to the paper as writer and editor. Her interest in labor organizing turned toward the organization of women workers. At the time of the famous Hay Market Riots in 1886, when her husband was accused as a conspirator, Lucy was involved in organizing women garment workers. During her husband's imprisonment and after his execution, Lucy continued her activities with the labor movement. In June 1905, she was listed as one of the leaders and founders of the Industrial Workers of the World (Cotera, 1976:73).

There is evidence that numerous attempts were made to bring labor organizers like Lucy Parsons and Emma Goldman into the fold of the women's movement, especially by leaders like Jane Addams and Florence Kelley, who were heavily involved with social work efforts to benefit working-class and immigrant women. Both Addams and Kelley spoke eloquently about the fact that these women needed the vote to effect changes in the home and on the job more desperately than did middle-class white, native-born women. Jane Addams and others spoke and acted on behalf of women labor leaders like Lucy Parsons, assisting them in rallies, providing bail when they were arrested, and using their tremendous power and influence on behalf of working women.

Unfortunately for poor and minority women, there were not enough "social" feminists to shift the suffragist movement away from a narrow human rights and universal voting rights platform. The ideals that were born within the abolitionist movement were cast aside to make way in the 1890s for a narrower goal of suffrage for white women at all costs. Two strategies were developed that adversely affected minority, immigrant, and working-class women and men. In the North, from the late 1880s to the early 1900s, suffragists advocated the vote for white middle-class women as an effective counter to the vote of workers and the foreign born. In the South, suffragists advocated enfranchising white women to dilute the effects of the Fourteenth Amendment and the votes of the newly enfranchised black men. It is true that in following these expedient strategies the suffragists attempted to diffuse attacks by the antisuffragists, that through suffrage black women and "ignorant immigrants" would be enfranchised. They attempted also to please politicians like President William Howard Taft who told the National American Woman Suffrage Association (NAWSA) that he was not supportive of woman suffrage because the intelligent and patriotic might not take advantage of it, but the undesirable classes might become political constituents (Cotera, 1976:72).

In 1889, at the NAWSA Convention, Elizabeth Cady Stanton called for literacy tests to abolish the ignorant vote. Carrie Catt's statement from the *Woman's Journal*, December 15, 1894, expresses alarm at the great danger faced by the United States:

> That danger lies in the votes possessed by the males in the slums of the cities, and the ignorant foreign vote which was sought to be bought by each part, to make political success. There is but one way to avert the danger—cut off the vote of the slums and give it to the women. (Quoted from *Woman's Journal*, December 15, 1894, by Kraditor, 1968:261)

Elizabeth Cady Stanton's own testimony to the House Committee on the Judiciary in 1896 presented the contrasting picture of drunken, illiterate, newly arrived immigrants trading votes for bribes, while women professors, writers, and teachers were deprived of the vote (Kraditor, 1971:109)

Stanton's plan also promoted the use of educational qualifications and literacy tests for voting. A resolution passed as early as 1893 at the NAWSA Convention read as follows:

> Resolved, That without expressing any opinion on the proper qualifications for voting, we call attention to the significant facts that in every State there are more women who can read and write then the whole number of illiterate male voters; more white women who can read than foreign voters; so that the enfranchisement of such women would settle the vexed question of rule by illiteracy, whether of home-grown or foreign-born production. (Kraditor, 1968:260)

An exception to the suffragist's mainstream was Mrs. Stanton's own daughter, Harriet Stanton Blatch, who wrote an open letter to her mother protesting the proposals for educational and literacy requirements. Her letter was published in the *Woman's Journal* (Kraditor, 1971:113).

At the 1899 convention, Mrs. Lottie Wilson Jackson would not support a resolution about black women having to ride in smoking cars. Susan B. Anthony spoke against the resolution in terms that have become very familiar to minority women today (Hymowitz and Weissman, 1978:276). After all, according to her, they were only powerless women and they could not very well get involved with any issues such as those. By 1903 the majority of the NAWSA members supported educational requirements for voting, and there was a final separation of the women's suffrage movement from the Black movement.

Although many social workers like Jane Addams, Florence Kelley, and Sophonisba P. Breckenridge, and socialists like Emma Goldman advocated the rights of immigrants and working women, in most instances during the 1890 to 1910 period their advocacy had little or no effect on the suffragist movement's attitude toward minority or working-class women (Kraditor, 1971:121).

Historian Aileen Kraditor analyzes this situation as a harsh indictment on white middle-class women. According to her analysis, women apparently did not feel humiliated when governed by white men, but if foreigners and blacks governed them, especially if they were of lower classes, it was unbearable. Kate M. Gordon, suffragist from Louisiana, proposed that only white women be granted suffrage. Others quoted extensive statistics to demonstrate that the votes of white women would offset the strength of black votes (Hymowitz and Weissman, 1978:276). White women objected to being governed by their former slaves (Kraditor, 1971:106).

Because of this classism and racism, the arguments of the need for universal suffrage and the negation of superiority of the male sex over the female sex were set aside (Kraditor, 1971:107). The abandonment of these two principles has lived to haunt all women to this day. Further, the promotion of barriers to universal suffrage such as literacy and educational requirements disenfranchised Black women, Chicanas, and poor and immigrant women until the passage of the Voting Rights Act of 1965.

With all the anti-immigrant, anti-slum, and anti-labor agitation, it is no wonder that the suffrage movement had almost no labor support by the end of the nineteenth century.

Labor, Socialism, and Suffrage, 1900–1920

Chicana feminist activity during the 1900 to 1920 period resembles the dynamics of the present Chicana feminists. Like Chicanas today, the early feminists were struggling for survival and for their development as individuals. Like Chicanas today, they had to work within their own movements and community. They had to attempt also to interact with a woman's movement that was directed toward fulfillment and not survival. And like Chicanas today, the women found, then, that while few battles were won in civil rights on behalf of their communities, fulfillment and the gains of the women's movement were never their gains. The suffragist movement had been manipulated since the 1870s to benefit those that eventually benefitted from it and no one else.

Chicana feminist activities in the 1904 to 1920 period were channeled through civil rights activities and labor organization work. Some outstanding women were Jovita Idar, a journalist and civil rights worker from Laredo, Texas; Soledad Peña, orator and educator; María Renteria; and María Villarreal. These women were speakers and participants in a historical civil rights conference, the Primer Congreso Mexicanista. On October 15, 1911 they also founded the Liga Femenil Mexicanista. The group's goals were to struggle on behalf of the Mexican-American and to educate and develop women (Cotera, 1976:82).

Mexican-American women from Texas to California worked through the Partido Liberal Mexicano (PLM), a political organization under Enrique and Ricardo Flores Magón, socialist organizers exiled from Mexico. Through PLM and many widely circulated publications such as *Regeneración* and *La Mujer Mexicana*, Chicanas raised the consciousness of other women in the Mexican-American community on matters relating to women's development and feminism. Some of the outstanding Chicanas of the period were involved as writers, advocates, and speakers for the organization. Modesta Abascal, Silvina Rembao de Trejo, Andrea and Teresa Villarreal, Francisca Mendoza, and Mariá Talavera were among the most active. One excellent example of the feminist content of *Regeneración* is the famous essay *A La Mujer*, which has been translated and reissued by California Chicana feminists. Contemporary Chicanas have seen in this essay evidence that within the worker and civil rights activities of the Chicano community there have been serious and progressive statements on women's rights. In this essay, Ricardo Flores Magón urges women to work for revolution and change.

In 1920, with the overwhelming support of labor and the big city vote, the suffrage amendment was passed, granting women the vote. While white women entered the flapper era uneducated about their mothers' struggle for enfranchisement and content to be conspicuous consumers, minority women, especially Chicanas, faced new and awesome tasks. Large corporations and the courts broke up generations of ties to the land and many Chicanos became the migrant peon class.

Chicanas had no time to bask in gains made in the name of womanhood in the United States. The most important gain of all, enfranchisement, was almost as universally denied to her as it was to Black women. Actually, the right to vote for Chicanas was not to become a reality until the passage of the 1974 amendments to the Voting Rights Act. Working-class women and Chicanas got a taste of some of the barriers recommended by the suffragists in the 1890s to keep undesirables from exercising the right to vote. Chicanas were barred through poll taxes, which were a burden to the poor, and by requiring proof of citizenship, which many second and third-generation citizens were afraid to put to a test because of the frequent deportations. They were submitted to literacy and educational tests and to intimidation by law-enforcement agencies who guarded the purity of the polling places by keeping Mexicans of both sexes out. Polling places in the southwestern states were almost always on the Anglo side of the tracks, where Mexicans were allowed for domestic work or other service jobs only.

Apparently, then, once suffrage was won for white middle-class women, there were few occasions for contact between white women and minority women.

The attitudes of even the strong feminists like Alice Paul did not encourage minority women about their future after 1920. June Sochen, in *Herstory*, indicates that after the suffrage amendment passed in 1920, reformers wondered about the fate of over 2 million Black women in the South who most assuredly would be disenfranchised like Black men were. Apparently, when this was brought to Alice Paul as a continuing concern for the Woman's Party, she replied that 1920 was not the time to discuss the issue. Consequently, Black women suffered through reading tests, intimidation, and violence at the polls (Sochen, 1974:279). And, of course, in Texas and many other states they were denied voting rights in the state primaries.

Repatriation and War, 1930 to 1950

The 1930s for Chicana and black women were really no easier than the 1920s had been. Chicanas continued as agricultural workers, domestics, and as workers in agribusiness, like the pecan shelling industry in San Antonio, Texas. Historians record that Black women suffered terrible discrimination from the New Deal and that their wages were in pennies, if they actually got to work. In the case of Chicanas, repatriation to Mexico was a constant spectre, whether or not they were on relief rolls. Despite the depression, there was no respite for the Chicano community in the areas of civil rights and labor organizing.

Chicana labor leaders and politicians, like Denver's Dolores McGran González, testified before congressional committees, ran for local office, and served as national delegates to the Progressive Party Convention in the late 1930s. Other women who have become models of female-inspired activities of the period are Dolores Hernández, who was killed on October 10, 1933 during a strike of 15,000 farm workers in Visalia, California. Another woman labor union leader made history in 1936 whe she led pecan sheller strikers in San Antonio in a successful strike effort. Emma Tenayuca Brooks, then a 17-year-old labor organizer and orator, became a beacon of hope to beleagured workers throughout the United States. For her efforts, she has had to live 40 years in obscurity and anonymity. In civil rights and educational reform, a strong women's advocate, Mariá L. Hernández of Lytle, Texas, worked tirelessly throughout the 1930s demonstrating, speaking, and protesting the educational status of Mexican-Americans in the United States.

The war effort in the 1940s affected Chicanas as they were recruited to occupy more service and domestic positions left vacant by the fortunate Black women who were recruited to work in the war industries. There is some evidence, however, that as much of the garment industry moved to the Southwest during this time, Chicanas took up these jobs. After the war, they were able to keep their place in this particular job market, while other women in heavier and better paid industries were sent home. War activities, repatriation in the 1930s, and the looming spectre of military conservatism did much in the late 1940s to discourage civil rights and labor advocacy, which had been the forums for female development in the Chicano community. However, the effort that women put forth, the extreme partiotism displayed by Chicano males, and the contact they established with the Anglo power bases yielded some seeds for the development of activism that was to come in the late 1940s and 1950s. The new activism among women was no longer the Socialist and Communist inspired advocacy of the early decades but a more subdued, club-woman reformist approach channeled through female auxiliary groups sponsored by the League of United Latin American Citizens (LULAC), founded in 1929, and the American G.I. Forum, founded in the 1940s. These new activities centered around educational reform, voter education, and employment opportunities. And, although the gains achieved were meager, an important factor is that they kept Chicanos and Chicanas involved in community development through the repressive, anticommunist McCarthy era.

The Chicano Movement and the Women's Movement, 1960 to 1970

Chicanas were actively involved from the very beginning of the Chicano civil rights movement in the 1960s. They are involved on behalf of the communities they represented and on their own behalf to speak about their community needs and their own needs as women. Some of the women who led the movement in its early days were Dolores Huerta of the United Farm Workers Organizing Committee, Alicia Escalante with the Welfare Rights Organization, and Gracia Molina de Pick and Anna Nieto-Gómez with feminist activities. Women politicians like Virginia Muzquiz of Crystal City, Texas, Mariana Hernández, and Grace Davies put Chicanas in the political forum. Like these women, there have been hundreds of others who, in the late 1960s and 1970s, have proved that Chicanas have come of age politically in this country.

In the mid-1960s, Chicanas were actively working for community and individual progress when the current women's movement loomed on the horizon. Chicanas felt as ambivalent about the new movement as the early twentieth century Chicana socialists felt about the suffragist movement. The new wave of the women's movement was firmly anchored in Alice Paul's Woman's Party platform of achieving an equal rights amendment. Again, white women were bringing forth a movement with a very attractive carrot. Who in their right political mind is going to challenge an equal rights amendment? Especially not minority activist women who were already heavily involved in a human rights movement.

In a blissful state of mutual ignorance about the history of the women's movement, the history of minority women, and our mutual relations, we went on to repeat the history of 1910 and 1920. Too much has occurred since 1968 to recount all the problems that have accompanied the clumsy attempts of the women's movement to incorporate minority and working-class women into the fold. As we have seen in the foregoing historical analysis, there are too many unresolved issues brought over from the 1920s. Working women's, housewives', and minority women's needs were not addressed then (Altbach, 1974:122). There is no evidence that they will be addressed by the present leadership. Unfortunately, the documentation of the legacy of the past is not easily available to instruct us and help us formulate a better future, but it is here to plague the present movment with the same attitudes of opportunism and power mongering.

Minorty women could fill volumes with examples of put-downs, put-ons, and out-and-out racism shown to them by the leadership of the [women's] movement. There are three major problem areas in the minority–majority relationship in this movement: 1) paternalism or maternalism, 2) extremely limited opportunities for minority women in the movement, and 3) outright discrimination against minority women in the movement. Paternalistic or maternalistic attitudes have kept white women from viewing minority women as anything but quaint, inarticulate ethnics, largely from the lower class. This has forced accomplished minority leaders out of the movement and has created a small group of Blacks, Chicanas, and other minority women who want to be accepted so badly by the movement that they will shuffle and "yes ma'am" to them to stay in favor. The power of these minority women is diminished accordingly, both in the movement and outside of it.

Opportunities for development for minority women within the [women's] movement have been very limited. Affirmative action resolutions for minority recruitment in the major organizations like the Women's Equity Action League, National Organization for Women, and the National Women's Political caucus have been scarce, and when they have been won after heated floor fights, they were either ovethrown in subsequent conventions or not implemented at all, especially at the local level. Opportunities for development are very limited, even once the women are in. Rhea Mojica Hammer, the chairwoman of the Chicana Caucus of the National Women's Political Caucus, is bypassed when critical information is forthcoming, excluded in meetings, insulted, ignored, and ridiculed by many of the women who have sat on the policy council with her during the past 8 years. Rose Marie Roybal, who worked with the National Office of the International Women's Year (IWY) Commission, was encouraged to seek a position elsewhere when it was discovered that she was giving information about IWY activities to Hispanic and other minority women.

The basic premise with this type of exclusion is that minority women are given observer status. Anytime they advocate for meaningful involvement to benefit their communities, they are tagged as divisive by women leaders. The same exclusion and discrimination exists in many women's studies courses, foundation-funded programs, minorities and women recruitment programs, "herstory" research, publishing, and women's service institutions. Activists and feminists who are trying to incorporate minority women into the ERA process for the sake of maintaining the gains made by the ERA movement and to assure its passage have fought a losing battle. So intent are the women in power on keeping the doors shut to minorities and the poor that they seem to prefer defeat than to give in—shades of the 1910s!

On a more positive note, Chicana feminists have continued undaunted, mostly outside the women's movement, now and then establishing ties and coalitions with it, to develop their own power base for the achievement of Chicana liberation and to provide increased opportunities for Chicanas. Current Chicana feminist organizations are actively pressing for their communities' development through advocacy in political activity at the local and national levels. Some of the major organizations are: Nacional Femenil (California), Chicana Service Action Center (California), Mujeres Unidas (Colorado), Mexican-American Women National Association (MANA, Washington, D.C.) Mexican-American Business and Professional Women (Texas), and Mexican-American Women Political Caucus (Texas).

Taking Stock

The Chicana is "together" but her progress is not commensurate with her potential or her goals as a woman.

The two great barriers to her achievement are: 1) the opportunism in the women's movement that has forced lower priorities to be set on public policy and governmental programming for minority populations and the poor, and 2) the conservatism of Chicano males.

Chicanas secretly hope that white women will quickly get the powerful positions that they want so that the movement can move on to more substantial changes in the overall status of women. In the meantime, Chicanas do intend to maintain a very alert posture to monitor and claim allocations and gains made on behalf of wom-ankind.

In regard to conservatism among Chicano males, Chicanas have had a decade of frustration. It is always easier to battle strangers than one's family. Chicanas have been remarkably restrained about accusing Chicanos publicly of discrimination and impos-ing barriers. And yet the Chicanas' growth is often stultified at home with fathers, brothers, and husbands who do not realize that this is wrong, that what they are doing is inhuman. Often their conservatism comes from belief in the macho myths spread by university sociologists in the 1930s. This conservatism often comes from ignorance about the roles that women have played in history and in the community.

Chicano males, like the white women, will demand commitment and support for their causes, and they will get it. Sometimes Chicanas break both their doors down to offer themselves solely for the sake of experience and participation. Yet, when Chicanas need political support, assistance in return, both claim repression, powerlessness, impotence. Both are potent enough and successful enough when they need to achieve it for themselves.

As feminists, Chicanas have more and more been left to their own devices—to rely on their own unity and strength. This is evident in the forceful poetry of Chi-cano journals and feminist literature. Perhaps it needs to be expressed next in ideolog-ical and academic terms, as well as on a one-to-one basis with the men in their fami-lies, without apologies. In order to complete their liberation, Chicanas will have to express their needs, not to strangers but to their own community. This courageous ac-tion, for those who survive it, will provide all Chicanas with the freedom to be equal with men who can appreciate human liberation, human value, and dignity.

References

Altbach, E.H. (1974) *Women in America*. Lexington, MA: D.C. Heath.

Cotera, Marta P. (1976) *Diosa y Hembra: History and Heritage of Chicanas in the U.S.* Austin: In-formation Systems Development.

Hymowitz, C. and M. Weissman. (1978) *A History of Women in America*. New York: Bantam.

Kraditor, A.S. (1968) *Up From the Pedestal: Selected Writings in the History of American Feminism*. New York: The New York Times Book Co.

Kraditor, A.S. (1971) *The Ideals of the Woman Suffrage Movement, 1890—1920*. Garden City, NY: Doubleday.

Sochen, J. (1974). *Herstory: A Woman's View of American History*. New York: Alfred Publishing Co.

CHICANA FEMINISM:
AN EVOLVING FUTURE

Introduction

By the end of the 1970's and the beginning of the 1980's, Chicana feminists could now look back at a decade of struggle and discourse, as seen in the following essays. What some of these writers concluded was that while Chicana feminists had made an impact it was relative to the many changes that were still needed. Moreover, the issues had become more complicated by the need to address a larger audience of other Latina women in the United States. As Chicanas came into increased contact with feminists from the Puerto Rican and other Latino communities in the country, the concept of Chicana was brought into question and a broader Hispana or Latina identity was introduced.

In their reflections, Chicana feminists observed that basic inequalities with Chicano men continued, although they remained hopeful of still eliminating these and of forging coalitions with Chicano men. In the labor market, Chicanas remained victims of employment discrimination. Stereotypes about Mexican-American women continued. Tensions with the Women's Movement had not abated and had increased due to questions about white women being the chief beneficiaries of affirmative action programs. In addition, as noted in the essays on the first National Hispanic Feminist Conference in 1980, new tensions and divisions became evident between more moderate Chicana feminists and more radical ones. Finally, academic Chicana feminists continued to press for a more thorough recognition and integration of Chicana issues in Chicano Studies programs.

Despite these lingering problems and obstacles, some Chicana feminists observed that in certain areas such as the emergence of new leadership among Chicanas and the success of some Chicanas in elective offices that real gains had been made. Still, the lack of fullfillment of the Chicana agenda would mean that into the 1980's and beyond, new and in some cases different efforts would be made to complete and expand the original agenda.

I Looked Up One Day (1973)

I looked up one day
and began
to see.

I looked up and began
to see
where I was
and
where I fit.

I began to suspect
that what I was doing
and what I wanted to do
to develop me
more completely
MIGHT
NOT
BE
THE
SAME.

And I began
to watch,
to listen,
and
to observe
all those activities that stifled
this growth.

And I became more particular
about
how I spent my time
and
who I spent it with.

Rose Marie Roybal

66

*La Década de la Mujer**

Marta Sotomayor

La Década de la Mujer—the specific meaning of this phrase is still uncertain to the majority of Hispanas. For involved women the meaning is as diverse as the various orientations and perspectives that characterize our communities. For some Hispanas, for example, the decade of women is best embodied in the Equal Rights Amendment, which clearly speaks of the legal framework for the exercise of some basic human rights. In the issue of abortion, that concept of human rights more often than not becomes diluted in the simplistic dichotomy of being either for or against abortion. For other Hispanas the feminist forum and agency (as varied as it is) provides one more arena to exercise their political skills regardless of the substance of the issues—the process, it is claimed, is what matters. For still another group of Hispanas the main issues revolve around a reevaluation of the roles, boundaries, and rules that have given a specific flavor to the transactional field between men and women.

The struggle becomes too easily translated into, and clouded by, the notion of *machos y hembras* [men and women] which is usually dealt with in the power arena.

One can go on to mention other perspectives of the feminist agenda but the truth of the matter is that Hispana leadership has yet to identify carefully and systematically the issues that could be meaningful and useful to engage the majority of Hispanas in the barrios and colonias in the process of self-change. While it is true that the majority of the issues being discussed by women in general are relevant to those Hispanas who have access to alternatives and choices, it is doubtful that those same issues, at this point, can be successfully utilized to organize the majority of average Hispanas and enable them to join that one other facet of the movement for liberation.

ERA, for example, as meaningful and important as it is, remains simply a legal strategy to guarantee certain rights to women; abortion, as crucial as it is in some instances, is merely a symptom of more severe and complex conditions that need to be understood, separated, and dealt with in a variety of approaches. While process is indeed important and political skills are indeed necessary to create change, process remains only the context and skills are only the tools to accomplish certain objectives. And while male and female relationships are quite basic and fundamental, and ascribed roles are often devastating for both sexes, a true reform movement must go beyond these sets of relationships.

It is true that certain principles are involved in the law, but the fact that a law exists does not necessarily mean that laws are enforced and that they will create basic

*From *Agenda*, Vol. 7, No. 6, Nov.–Dec., 1977: p. 2.

attitudinal change. All of us, I am certain, are painfully aware that civil rights legislation of the last 25 years has not created the basic changes that are so needed in this society to increase the life chances and open more doors of opportunity to the minorities of color.

Available data does not indicate that more Hispanas are graduating from professional schools, or entering managerial positions, or becoming entrepreneurs; some do, but not enough to make a dent. However, available data, as crude as they are, indicate that Hispanas continue to show a greater incidence of uterine cancer and tuberculosis; have large unplanned families, and not enough money to make it from day to day; and live in unsanitary and dilapidated housing that breeds all types of disease, which does not help in significantly lowering the infant death rate.

Available data also show that while some Hispanas are beginning to venture into the work world, the most they will be able to find is inadequately paid menial or domestic jobs, and that the majority of Hispanas do not finish high school and thus do not acquire sufficient skills to allow them to enter a competitive labor market. There are many barriers that Hispanas face from day to day that seem to have been there from generation to generation. All are symptoms of the way that society is organized and structured, of the rules of the game that exclude others and provide special privileges to the few.

But those forces that oppose change seem to be gaining momentum, as evidenced by the events that have taken place in a number of state conferences sponsored as part of the International Women's Year. Those Hispanas who as delegates engaged in a process of change faced in Houston [National Chicana Conference, 1971] a series of disruptive tactics, well-organized caravans, and well-disciplined organizational machinery that includes husbands, brothers, sons, and anyone who can be mustered to openly attack the values and changes that all of us have been working for.

Those Hispanas who were elected as delegates, and who identify themselves as Hispanas for our cause, will not have an easy task in the future, for they will have to deal with overt expressions of bigotry and racism. They must, however, formulate a meaningful Hispana agenda based on the nature of their positions as leaders. They will have to identify those issues with which la mujer en el barrio can identify, and develop strategies for change that are applicable and appropriate to the decades of the 70's and the 80's.

But equally important is the fact that these women can provide role models for many young Hispanas that will follow in the years to come. It will not be an easy task, but it is a most crucial and necessary one.

67

La Nueva Hispana e Hispanidad [*The New Hispanic Woman and Hispanicity*]*

Marta P. Cotera

Every time I start to write something really optimistic about Hispanas, especially for our own readers, my pen is paralyzed by reality: spectres of teenage girls pregnant, with their lives and leadership potential severed; flocks of masters degree and Ph.D. women in constant flight, without roots because they can't even get the mediocre jobs others discard; lonely, accomplished women who would be first-rate companions to our men, if only they believed that men could deal with the sublimity of the true history of the woman in Hispanic culture; *el clamor de la mujer hispana, "mejor sola que mal acompañada"* [the outcry of the Hispanic woman, "Better off alone than with bad company"]. Instead of optimisim, I am inspired by Erma Bombeck, universal humorist, whose words seem singularly directed to us: "If life is a bowl of cherries, what are we doing in the pits?"

Anglo women are "afraid of flying" [reference to Erica Jong's *Fear of Flying*, 1973] and we can't seem to master walking. And yet, the Eighties can be the threshold to the kind of future we deserve and have worked for as creators of the *Raza mestiza cosmica* in this continent. The past two decades have certainly picked up and built on our historical momentum of the 1900's and 1930's in this country. During the Civil Rights Movement of the Sixties, women who are now in mid-life relived with passionate consciousness the sentiments and activity that marked the lives of pre-Columbian and Independence-era heroines in the Americas. In the Seventies, many other Hispanas, too young for the Sixties activities, were spurred to action with the Women's Rights Movement. Both movements and both decades provided impetus, opportunities and vehicles for women's development, although, unfortunately, in both cases development was selected and often controlled by others—by our men in the Sixties and by Anglo women in power in the Seventies.

Nevertheless, as we face the Twenty-first Century, only two decades away in the Eighties, what exactly is our status as Hispanas in the United States? Where are we, the natives of this continent, originators of the mestizo race? A brief review of current literature epitomized by the timely *La Luz* article, "La Mujer En El Ochenta" by Alicia Valladalid-Cuarón, Arlene Vigil Sutton, and Dorothy M. Rentería outlines in

*From *La Luz*, Vol. 8, No. 4, Oct.–Nov., 1979: pp. 8–10.

great detail the discrepancy between Hispanic women's historic and economic contribution and the stark reality of our present socioeconomic condition.

We would never detract from the great women who have passed before us and from the present achievers who grace and have graced the pages of publications such as *La Luz*. If each one serves as a model for one other woman's growth, her life will have been worthwhile. But as Rosario Castellanos, a prominent Mexican writer warns in her excellent article, "Women's Contribution to Culture" (*Regeneración*, 1975) "one swallow does not a summer make." We cannot forget, for one moment, that there is much that we Hispanas and Hispanos must do yet to reclaim this continent.

In looking at qualitative versus quantitative development, we have fallen into our own analytical trap. We have let one successful woman, in high bureaucratic office, eclipse the litany of statistics that we have committed to memory: "80% of our women are in clerical, operative, and service positions, amen; median income of Hispanic women in 1977 was $3,700 per year, amen." The time has come to bring the high-positioned woman and the $3,700 a year Hispana down to the lowest common denominator, lest we retreat into a 1950's-type complacency in this next decade and bank our meager returns. We must face the gap represented by meager qualitative growth on one side, and the grossest statistic in the balance.

In the previously cited article, Rosario Castellanos describes the factors that blind women of Hispanic origin, regardless of class and educational status. She sees us as subject to the same rights and responsibilities under the law; as heirs to similar aggregation of tradition, norms of conduct, ideals, and taboos. We all have the liberty to reclaim our rights if they are curtailed, and to respond or not to respond to our responsibilities. We can choose to repeat ancestral practices or to break with them. We can also choose to expand or to reduce our expectations, and to reject prohibitions or respect them.

From these common factors, three major elements can be our common departure point for development in the Eighties. First of all, our people share the most unique historical experience in the world, involving a unique native American or Caribbean cultural heritage, from pre-Columbian historical roots to Hispanic acculturation and on to Anglo colonialism. This unique cultural history and genetic blend has made us heirs to an aggregation of cultural values with very specific moral, philosophical, and religious traditions. These traditions continue to be strong determinants in our lives, whether we are at the university or at the factory, and they serve to structure our basic relationships with family members and society. We also share equality with men under the law (Hispanos not excepted).

Whether we are Cuban, Puerto Rican, Bolivian, or Mexican-American we have uncannily similar historical backgrounds, including an American or Caribbean indigenous culture, conquest by Spain, a period of colonialism, *mestisaje* struggles for independence, nationalism—and for Hispanas in the United States, another colonial experience. Hispanas have already paid their dues in their native land, with their families and in this country. Ample archives of heroines in all ages and countries attest to the psychological and moral fiber of Hispanic women who have never backed off from their community's struggles. Again the moment in history is here to continue the tradition of involvement that has characterized our ancestors.

Hispanas are challenged to reclaim this as part of their cultural tradition in the Eighties. To do so will establish us firmly in a position of equality as individuals, *without departing one inch from our cultural tradition*. Further, we should act on Rosario Castellanos' challenge to document and trace the path toward the evolution of Hispana cultural tradition, our contribution and our status. It is important that the cultural evolution resulting from the Civil Rights Movement, our participation in the Woman's Movement, and the emergence of women as heads of families shall be incorporated into the ideological fabric of our intellectual expression. Thus, we are recording our own progress, our own innovations, our own institutional development consistent with our traditions. Hispanas should no longer leave unchallenged the irresponsible expressions of ideologies and rhetoric that both disregard the basic tenet of individual worth and ignore women's continued contribution to culture and to the political, artistic, and intellectual evolution of the Hispanidad. Until we do this, the detractors of womankind will continue to promote bastardized machismo as basic and inevitable in the Hispanic culture. Unless we do this, the majority society, and many of our own people, will continue their fantasized portrayals of Hispanas as objects; passive nonentities, social reactionaries, and nonproductive members of society. At a minimum, in the decade of the Eighties, concurrent with realizing our new emancipation, it is critical that Hispanas also aggressively continue to set straight the history of the Hispanic American. In this task, Hispanics, irrespective of gender, must close ranks to demand that dignity and self-respect that was criminally obliterated from the annals of the history of mankind. But within this overwhelming task of rescuing history, we must maintain the perspective that our overriding priority must be the redemption of the documented history of the Hispanic woman—a history rendered illegible by the cultural, sociological, economic, and political confrontations between colonizer and native of the New World.

Our group strategy for the Eighties must necessarily be group oriented, intellectual, education-based, and political. It will mean mobilizing our qualitative resources more effectively than we have in the past, so we may affect greater numbers of our women. Our strategies should be aimed at educational institutions—those depositories for young people where racism, extreme chauvinism, and anti-female feeling is the strongest. We need to address ourselves aggressively to educational textbooks in which Hispanas are the invisible minority. And if this task is too awesome to undertake, remember that local districts have been known to accept locally developed supplemental materials and that groups of women can organize lecturer's programs so that students can have regular cultural and feminist programs. Another alternative is for Hispanas with writing and media skills to write, write, write—and write some more. Media, communication, and group action are urgently needed if we're going to control our lives in the Eighties and beyond.

Besides the aggregates of Hispanic cultural traditions, Hispanas of this continent share with men (and other women) equal rights under the law. Only don't say it too loudly or print it too boldly, because 95 percent of the males aren't aware that most North American constitutions provide such protection for all their subjects. We actually do have this equal status. Saying it, yet believing and acting on this principle are different things. Hispanas need to decide now whether this is going to be an empty right, or whether they as individuals will claim it in marriage, in education, in the work force and in the political system.

In the Seventies, the alternative to claiming equality has seemingly been to stay out of marriage, out of education, and out of politics. This is certainly an easy way out, and some Hispanos have been relieved that so far they have not been challenged by Hispanas. This situation cannot last forever, and it should not be continued in the new decade. Hispanas and Hispanos together must confront the subject of equal rights. No one else is going to come in and resolve the situation for us. Hispanas are logically the ideal educators for Hispanos on equality of the sexes. After all, we don't want them to learn it in the streets or alleys or outside the family! Seriously speaking, as long as Hispanos are not prepared to deal with women's equality they will be handicapped in their relationship with Hispanas. A recent article in the *Harvard Educational Review* calls for the biculturalization of men, as a creative way to structure a healthier society. As other writers have done before them, the authors express the belief that men and women who understand both male and female cultures are better-adjusted individuals. In this respect they consider women far better adjusted than men, since women are bicultural and are able to perform in male and female cultures. It is time, they contend, that men become bicultural. They predict that men who cannot adjust to the new societal changes and more equilibrium between sexes will be woeful misfits in the coming world order.

In this respect, one of the challenges for Hispanas in the Eighties is to raise the consciousness of the community toward full and equal rights for all persons regardless of sex, to claim rights to personhood, which our Indian and Hispanic cultural heritage has never denied us. Further, we who have traveled the historic evolutionary path from the 1519 Spanish conquest to 1980 need to trace more innovative paths for our people.

We cannot hide the facts from men any longer. We will not use the proverbial shawl to protect them from reality. There is a new revolution to face together, a new independence to be fought for, together. Once again it's the cliche "all for one and one for all," so we may all be liberated.

Shake the *rebozo* [shawl] loose and let the men face the beautiful sun of the 1980's. They'll be dazzled.

68

Hispanas—Our Resources for the Eighties*

ANITA L. ESPINOSA

Never before in the history of this country has the social climate been so primed for the total emergence of our women. And given these opportunities to compete, our

*From *La Luz*, Vol. 8, No. 4, Oct.–Nov., 1979: pp. 10–13.

women are proving that we have the [wherewithal] to overcome the obstacles that impeded our integration on the national scene in the Sixties and the Seventies.

Civil Rights

In order to overcome the effects of systemic discrimination, Hispanas have tackled the more imposing institutions in their quest for justice, and won. These victories have only been possible at the expense of great personal sacrifice and a demonstrated tenacity that is enviable. *Tenemos tripas y tenemos chispa* [We have guts and we have spirit].

These successes reflect favorably *on all Hispanos*. The triumph of Aida Berio in her discrimination complaint against the Equal Rights Employment Opportunity Commission was sweet indeed for all Hispanos. (See *La Luz*, Vol. 8, No. 2 1979.) Cubanos, Chicanos, Mejicoamericanos, Sudamericanos, and Puertorriqueños alike, from one coast to the other felt a personal satisfaction and an ever-growing national unification in the pride Ms. Berio inspired. Receptions in her honor were held in Washington, D.C. after her victory was published in dailies all over the country. These functions were planned and attended by Hispanos of all persuasions. Aida Berio has given us an example that it is possible to fight "city hall" and win. Unquestionably, her name will become a household word as Hispanas and Hispanos as well as other minorities emulate her perseverance. Increasingly, we will note Hispanos from California to Miami to New York beginning to look to civil rights enforcement agencies with more hope and in the Eighties will demand more responsive action from those agencies. Individual and collective successes, as they come, will convince more and more of us that redress for wrongs can be wrenched, however laboriously, from the American justice system.

Education

In Colorado, Josie Luján (Luján et al. vs The Colorado Board of Education) and a handful of parents, with the assistance of the Chicano Education Project in Denver, Colorado, have shown us what a force of a few can accomplish in addressing the educational needs of our children. Mrs. Luján was the lead plaintiff in this landmark lawsuit.

In Denver, District Court Judge R. Quinn ruled on March 13, 1979 that the Colorado School Financing system was unconstitutional because of the extreme funding disparities among school districts in the State. A wide range of differences in personal income and property taxation in school disctricts across the State and subsequent corresponding funding levels per school district translated into lower per-pupil expenditures in the economically depressed areas of the state, most often where larger concentrations of Chicanos are found. The correction called for is to assure equal quality education to all children in the state, to be achieved by equity in funding levels to all school districts.

Unfortunately, the State Supreme Court stayed the order pending appeal by the defendants. Coupled with a tax relief package the Governor of Colorado signed into law on June 3, 1979, which eroded Colorado's 1979 $150 million tax surplus base by over $100 million, the legal maneuverings mean that our children may not benefit directly by Judge Quinn's decision, if upheld, for six to eight more years. Still, we are indebted to Josie Luján and people like her who have placed a foot in the door—a foot that is unlikely to be removed. It is evident by the increased participation of Chicanos in Colorado that the parents in Del Norte, where this struggle originated, have become "system wise" in a hurry.

The personal change in Mrs. Luján's daily life have been more direct. Mrs. Luján now has a seat on the local school board and finds herself writing articles about her experiences and addressing various groups of people about the developments of this drawn-out struggle. She has become a real education advocate for our people. Her biggest problem now is finding time to sandwich in all that she has committed her life's work to.

Politics

In California, Texas, Colorado, New Mexico, Miami, New York, and Chicago, as well as many other areas, Hispanas are being elected to offices where many of the so-called experts considered they didn't stand a chance.

Irma Rangel was the first Hispana elected to the Texas House of Representative.

A long-time politician and the first Hispana elected to a State Senate, Polly Baca-Barragan, Colorado, was the only Hispana invited to the Camp David brainstorming meeting in the aftermath of President Carter's massive overhaul of his cabinet.

Dr. Graciela Olivárez, head of the Community Services Administration, is the only Hispanic in President Carter's cabinet. During the Cabinet overhaul, she survived the axe.Carmela Lacayo serves as Vice Chair-person of the Democratic Central Committee.

Recently, Olga Moreno of Sacramento, California, was named Vice Chair to the National Women's Political Caucus.

Irene Hernández of Chicago, Illinois, ran a successful campaign and was elected Commissioner in Cook County, one of the most powerful, if not the most powerful, Democratic strongholds in the country.

Grace Montanez Davis is still serving a dynamic term as Los Angeles' Deputy Mayor.

And so it goes. Increasingly, Hispanics are running for local and state offices, as well as local boards of education. Although the reasons for their successes are still being dissected, and some, as Polly Baca-Barragan, muse on their token calling card, the overriding point to be made is that they are being nominated, elected, and named to office primarily because they are professional, knowledgeable, and politically astute.

Organizations

Denver's Chicana feminist organization, HEMBRA, Inc., founded in 1975 to improve the socioeconomic status of Chicanas (see *La Luz* Vol. 3/76), has decided to affiliate with M.A.N.A. The Chapter will be official in early 1980.

In Chicago, Mujeres Latinas en Acción (M.L.A.) concentrates on providing direct services and assistance to Hispanas at the grass roots level.

There are many local and state Hispana organizations developing in the Southwest and in the larger Hispanic "pockets" of the country. Some are ad hoc organizations, some are fledgling and loosely knit, others are becoming affiliated nationally, but all have in common a much-repreated purpose: to develop leadership.

69

La Mujer en el Ochenta
[*Women in the Eighties*]*

ALICIA V. CUARÓN, ARLENE VIGIL (KRAMER)
AND DOROTHY RENTERIA

Donde Estamos? [Where are we?]

Historically, the Hispanic family has been patriarchal and authoritarian. Economic, social, and political leadership in Hispanic communities traditionally have been based on the male. All that has been traditional is changing for La Hispana, just as it is changing for all women. How much is changing and how it is changing concerns many Hispana leaders.

Who is La Hispana? La Hispana has many characteristics. She may be of Mexican, Puerto Rican, Cuban, European Spanish, Central or South American descent, or a combination thereof. According to the Bureau of Census, March, 1978, in a population survey, over 12 million persons reported their origin or descent as Hispanic. Fifty one percent (6,196,000) were women. Specifically, the Hispanic-origin population in the United States includes about 7.2 million persons of Mexican origin, 1.8 million of Puerto Rican origin, 700,000 of Cuban origin, and about 2.4 million of Central of South American or other Hispanic origins. The largest concentration of Hispanics was in the five Southwestern states of Texas, Califonia, Arizona, Colorado, and New Mexico, as well as large numbers in the State of New York.

Hispanic women share with every other group in this country perplexing diversity and heterogeneity. An Hispana may have arrived from Mexico yesterday, or her ancestors may have been in this continent since 1520. She may be rural, urban, poor, middle class, a high school drop out, a Ph.D., a teacher, a saleswoman, or a migrant working the fields. She does share some basic roots in the development of Indian and Spanish culture, language and history. She also shares the history of participation in the development of this nation, which has been a way of life for the Hispanic community since 1848. Myths and stereotypes about Hispanas continue to abound because very few resources have ever been allocated to legitimate research on Hispanic women. Nonetheless, from every Hispanic community, from California to Texas, from Seattle to New York, Hispanas disagree with the positions and images foisted on them. Their feelings concerning their strengths as women, their status within their homes and communities, are currently under question by Hispanas themselves.

Current data suggests that 59 percent of Hispanic women 14 years and over are

*From *La Luz*, Vol. 8, No. 4, October–November, 1979: pp. 10–13.

married. Additionally, the research indicates that 85% of all Hispanic families are met-ropolitan dwellers. Families maintained by an Hispana were more likely to be below poverty level. Hispana-headed families generally experience special problems due to low income and a corresponding high incidence of poverty.

There is a direct correlation between educational attainment and employment opportunities for Hispanas. The median years of schooling completed by Hispanas 14 years and older was 10.4, as reported in a March, 1977 survey. Approximately six per-cent of all Hispanas completed four years of college or more. It is not surprising to find that employed Hispanic women are more likely than all other women to be con-centrated in low-paying occupations. Twenty nine percent of Hispanas are clerical workers; 25 percent are service workers; 25 percent are in semi-skilled professions; 10 percent are in professional and technical occupations; and four percent are in adminis-trative positions. Many jobs held by Hispanas are part-time, so while the figures seem to indicate that Hispanas are impacting the American labor market, the reality is that for Hispanas the world of work has done little to change the poverty situations that exist. One indication of this is the fact that the median income of Hispanic women in 1977 was $3,700 per year.

Historically, minority Hispanic women have been the victims of employment discrimination in their efforts to obtain status positions in business and professional areas. Only recently, very few have been able to overcome the barriers of discrimi-nation and have obtained positions of authority and policy levels in business, edu-cation, local, state, and federal agencies. A small number have achieved success in the private sector. The efforts of these few who have been successful have been exten-sive, laborious, and frustrating. Hispanic women have often experienced unique problems associated with transition to positions of supervision and managerial level, which have been dominated traditionally by Anglo males. Additionally, difficulties have also occured when Hispanas obtain positions that were held by other non-mi-nority women.

The working woman of today will, in most cases, find the absence of a relevant role model by which she can pattern her behavior and performance. Usually, the only model available is that of a male. The Hispanic woman has had to cope and adjust to the behavior pattern of the "culturally learned male role," which dominates the em-ployment field, and at the same time struggle to retain her individual identity as a woman and to maintain ethnic association. Due to the scarce availability of female models, and even greater scarcity of Hispanic female models in the work force, His-panas who have achieved success are to be highly commended. Hispanic women should be encouraged to make a commitment to personally and professionally pro-vide direction to other Hispanic women.

Hispanas have always been a part of the labor force that developed this country. Historians describe women who participated in the labor force as textile workers, artists, craft workers, salespersons, *curanderas* [women folk healers], midwives, seam-stresses, farmers, migrant workers, and teachers. Today the Hispana is confronted with grave difficulties in locating stable positions. Her generally low educational and train-ing level, coupled with inadequate and limited child care services, make employment difficult.

Currently, this nation is in the midst of a national energy-development upsurge. Specifically, these newest developments are in the area of oil, oil shale, uranium, gas, and coal and massive power plants. On July 15, 1979, President Carter, in his address to the nation, pinpointed some clear directions for energy development. This country will begin to see the most massive peace-time commitment for monies and resources to develop this nation's own alternative sources of fuel. At this very time, the entire Southwest is beginning to experience some intensive changes unprecedented hitherto in other economic development eras. Many new employment opportunities will begin to appear for those prepared to participate.

As of July, 1979, the mountain southwest has 355 communities designated as energy-impacted sites. These rural communities range in population from 12,000 to 70,000. Denver is becoming the national hub for resource development decisions. Currently, over 1,000 companies have opened offices in Denver to headquarter their resource development expansion efforts in the west. Already, energy companies have contributed to population increases in both the rural and urban areas. Historically, these companies have brought their own people with them to occupy both white- and blue-collar positions. Unless checked, energy companies will continue to bypass the native labor pool in the southwest. "New" people will be brought into communities historically settled and developed by Hispanics. Today, little concern has been shown by the private sector for the employment of minority women. Unless a process of intervention is initiated immediately it is doubtful that job opportunities for Hispanas will increase significantly in the future. Again Hispanas will find themselves delegated to traditional low-paying jobs.

Hispanas as a group need to begin to address the issue of energy development. Hispanas must plan to participate in the new labor market that will evolve.

Hispanic Women's Organizations will need to assure leadership roles to inform Hispanas about energy development as it relates to job opportunities and training programs. Discussion and negotiations should begin immediately with energy development companies to encourage them to seek federal funds to subsidize manpower programs for short- and long-term training in order to prepare Hispanic women for nontraditional energy related positions. Hispanic organizations should begin to develop job information systems with dissemination capability for Hispanics to have information and access to job opportunities as they relate to energy development. Additionally, community organizations should insist on adequate federal and state resources to meet the needs of children and elderly through day care services. Unless this is done, Hispanas will not find it possible to participate in the new labor market.

70

First Hispanic Feminist Conference Meets (1980)*

CHELA "CHE" SANDOVAL

Over 1,500 conference participants came from every state in the country, and from Uruguay, Argentina, Mexico, Bolivia, Spain, Cuba, Puerto Rico, and the Caribbean, to discuss the relationship of "Hispanics" to feminism. The following article is a preliminary critique of the Conference written by a few Chicanas who attended.

During the 60's, the political left among our peoples appropriated the term "Chicano" in order to redefine our own image within the dominant culture. Throughout the 70's, our increased awareness and the strong participation of Chicanos contributed to the organizing efforts of Spanish speaking peoples in general. So what is the meaning of naming these efforts "Hispanic"?

Also, the use of the term "feminism" has had an ambiguous quality in our organizational efforts. In the past, the term has been linked to the 60's women's liberation movement: its relationship to the Raza community has always been troublesome. A sampling of the workshops and presentations that were focused on this trouble included: "The Hispanic Woman as Separatist and Independent"; "Women's Studies and the Hispana"; "The Hispana in the Work Force"; "Lesbian Woman and the Bi-Cultural Experience in the United States"; "Luchas de la Mujer en Puerto Rico (1898–1929)"; and "Chicanas in the Movement: As Working Women, as Feminists, and as Socialists.".

This conference was an attempt at dialogue between researchers and scholars and community women. There has been confusion in some minds as to whether this was a conference for scholars or grass-roots women. It was the inclusion of both that made this meeting unique. However, in attempting to provide forums in which the first cadre of "Latina scholars" could communicate their work to one another, while at the same time having distinct forums for "grass-roots" women to discuss their work, the presentations were pitted against each other by scheduling them all at the same time. This structure added to the confusion of expectations on all sides. Community approaches were sometimes criticized as either being "too polemical" or "technical," while scholarly work was criticized as being "unconnected" to the "real world."

Thus, the organization of the Conference served two contradictory purposes. On the one hand, its structure "looked good" to outside observers. If someone examined the program booklet, they would see what seems to be a highly organized series of workshops and presentations. This may have been impressive to the federal govern-

*From *La Razón Mestiza/Union Wage*, June 20–22, 1980: pp. 3, 4, 6.

ment, which funded the conference, or to corporations interested in the "Hispanic" movement. But the same conference organizers who called for an "overturning of partiarchal power" also invited a female representative of *Playboy* magazine to address the Conference and describe all the ways in which Playboy Corporation supports the coming freedom and liberation of "Hispanas" (the audience booed her).

On a more profound level, the conference's structure, however, made it difficult for participants to achieve any real sense of unity or alliance. The divisions and unconnected events kept participants from seeing the overall effect of the conference and from easily engaging in practical criticisms of it. Ironically, when conference participants tried to challenge this oppressive structure, they were accused by the organizers of disrupting the "unity" of the conference.

Instead, the conference organizers continued to impose a highly rigid "following of the rules." For example, a workshop facilitator who wanted her 15-year-old sister to attend her only presentation had to pay an additional registration fee (no exceptions allowed). Another woman who was registered left for lunch and then returned without her identification card, and was initially refused admittance on the grounds that, "We don't have proof that you are really registered." This effort by the conference's organizers to (1) follow and enforce the "rules," and (2) emphasize a "good-looking" content at the expense of good communication among participants, suggested that the conference's organizers failed to achieve their aim of creating "liberating power structures."

Still, in spite of the differences in power between conference participants and organizers, as the four-day conference moved forward its structure was constantly challenged and ultimately forced to change.

The conference's organizers wanted to counter the dominant culture by presenting a coherent and unified voice with clarity, even if that meant silencing their own people, even if it meant accepting the very premises of the dominant culture. Their calls for "unity" in the midst of important ideological debate and division was a tactic that caused intense opposstition from the very people they sought to unify. They continued to treat so-called "radical" voices (especially Chicana, Native, Puerto Rican, and lesbian Feminist) as fringe elements that should be dismissed as irrelevant to the larger movement. However, as much as the conference organizers hoped to impose their so-called unity, the conference was not able to reconcile differences.

The struggles within the conference pointed out real differences among "Hispanic Feminists," but they do not suggest the divisiveness of defeat. Much of the excitement of "The First National Hispanic Feminist Conference" lay in a reworking of differences rather than their settlement. And after the many debates and dialogues, the conference participants were able to come together on Sunday night to forge thirty fundamental resolutions.

We Chicana feminists consider the conference another beginning.

71

Un Paso Adelante
[One Step Forward]*

DORINDA MORENO

Chicana and Third World women are aware that it can be beneficial to work within the Women's Movement. We are an integral part of that movement, but the often brutal clashing of ideas has made the building of that bridge a sometimes painful encounter, leaving each group frustrated and incapable of working together.

Conference after conference, issue after issue, "minority" women have stated: "We are a majority in the world." The dated and inaccurate reference to us as "less than" blocks further progress at drawing us into the fabric of feminist organization. These parallel movements are bound to spark controversises as the U.S. feminists, in their advocacy of women's rights, continue to base their cause almost solely on female/male role delineations and definitions.

In contrast, Third World women are emphatic in defining the issues based on the principal injustice of colonization inflicted on entire peoples. We have a history of imposed national boundaries, and of the suppression of human rights throughout developing nations. The two movements have not meshed or merged because of the unfortunate polarization.

White women, especially progressive feminists, know there is a chasm based not on personalities, but on issues and perspectives. Can *Union Wage* and other organizations devoting their enegergies to women's issues begin to evaluate these approaches? Can they accept criticism as constructive, acknowledge, respect, and work with these differences—for the necessary social changes?

Union Wage is a newspaper that has a proven track record in dealing with the issues of working women. While as a publications group they may not be perfect in their approach to solving this problem, they have nonetheless displayed a sensitive ear by working as a vehicle for the airing of the views of Third World women. They have agreed to grapple with the differences in order to find solutions and ways in which to work together to create a future, built on principles of unity.

We are living in a world that moves to extinction at a rapid pace, faster seemingly than we are able to organize against such self-destructive forces as the arms race. The threat of oncoming wars, possibly in Iran, the conflict in Afghanistan, and the U.S. financed intervention in Central America, etc., are a constant threat against which we need to mobilize our energies. Yet we are kept apart for crumbs. The paper

*From *La Razón Mestiza/Union Wage*, June 20–22, 1980: pp. 1–3.

tiger of competitiveness cancels out our effectiveness in finding areas of accord, as we grapple over basic civil rights issues.

The hesitancy revolves around such issues as affirmative action. Who is it serving? The white female must realize she is succeeding in new job areas oftentimes at the expense of non-white women and men, and similarly, sexual preference issues become secondary when compared to the typically explosive warfare syndrome, demonstrated so aptly by the U.S. in its international policies.

In general, Third World activists are no longer preoccupied with color, sex, or preference. Success for all means to live in a healthy environment, creating peaceful co-existence. Hunger, napalm, and discrimination know no sexual boundaries. Colonization and racism are sure vehicles for world destruction, promoting the atmosphere that will most assuredly bring a violent end to humankind.

At the recent Hispanic Women's Conference in San Jose [National Hispanic Feminist Conference, 1980], the Latina was symbolically "delivered" into the waiting arms of feminist national organizations such as the National Organization for Women (N.O.W.) and the National Women's Political Caucus (N.W.P.C.) A national coalition (or "Unity Celebration") was forced on us like cod liver oil. The Chicanas present who held opposing views from the conference leaders were further insulted by being barred from the "closed" press conference by security guards.

NOW, NWPC, and others, please take heed. Listen to the many Chicana voices at the conference who stated boldly, in unified strength, "We will not be used, abused, or misrepresented." For a respectful exchange of ideas and energies, a collective leadership based on principles of unity is the *only* bridge which will bring any coalition between white and Third World, grassroots and the professional, and between straight and gay women and men.

At the conference, almost 1,000 women chorused the profound sentiment, "we know who we are, and where we are going. We are the community, and cannot be sold out by a self-serving self-chosen few. We will not be moved."

When we first began to talk of doing an analysis of the "Hispanic" conference in San Jose, the ad-hoc editorial board for this *Union Wage* supplement issue discussed the importance of writing an inclusive overview of the events that took place and the issues that arose. The need to understand our own potential strength as *mujeres,* women, motivated us to analyze the source of the controversies so that we could become an organized force within our own movement. Now, after ten years, academic and political strength awaits us when our expertise is put to full strength.

There have been efforts over the years that inspired growth and development. Ethnic studies classes, La Raza Women's classes, Chicano/Latino studies, publications, and conferences, Cinco de Mayo fiestas, and the many *Diás de la Mujer* [Women's Day Celebrations] presented throughout Aztlán have all resulted in a support system of great value. Yet, though the conference was a timely event, the end result of the conference was bittersweet, both inspiring and at the same time hindering the solidarity of the mujeres attending.

To arrive at clarity out of the contradictions, we must examine the subject and our responsibilities towards its resolution. The conflicts that took place are indicative of the work to be done. This current newspaper issue is one of the many possible means of responding to the concerns and continuing the dialogue. Over the last ten years each of us has developed a base of support—a network within our isolated areas, geographical or professional. There is a need then for us to begin to hook up with each other to broaden our ideas and to strengthen our impact. We need to educate one another as to how crucial issues affect us in our own areas and then to unify. This

education, these dialogues, will inevitably bring conflict which can be the basis of later unified strength. But once the issues become clearer, the solutions become easier.

This conference was exploitive of the community and la mujer—in particular,
of Barrio women and Chicana professionals—for the purposes of an elitist few. The
politics of exploitation, which the conference direction attempted to implement, are
on the side of the oppressors, not ours. These oppressive politics rip off our *sentido*
[spirit] of Raza and our unity with Third World struggles around the world, thus
weakening our coalitions instead of strengthening them.

Several of the controversial issues that have come into focus are: 1) the politics of
Chicanas, 2) Latina lesbian women, 3) childcare, 4) the network of communication, 5)
Barrio women's participation, 6) the arts, 7) feminism, 8) solidarity with Third World
issues, 9) the Chicano movement, 10) relationships with white women, and 11) class
struggles/realities within Raza.

The innumerable efforts of diverse levels of community activism have produced
the sharing of resources, the launching of various vehicles of informational exchange,
the development of networks, and the promotion of issues pertaining to *la mujer, la familia,* and *la comunidad* [women, the family, and the community]. Even though most of
these activities emanated from the universities, many surged with the "*Movimiento
Chicano*" [The Chicano Movement], upholding Third World unity principles and
perspectives that encompass two levels of involvement, that of self-determination and
community control.

In assessing the last ten years, one must constructively criticize the lessons
learned and analyze the gains made. The women of la Raza, extremely active in efforts to achieve access, have consciously demanded entry into the decision-making
process. They have forged their way in preparation of and towards action. We have
our battle scars, and most importantly we have major victories—at the sides of our
families and men, in the labor force, in the universities, and in the community.

A quote from poet Nellie Wong, who was inspired to write regarding the conference, a poem which is the essence of this paper. With Nellie's words I wish to
[conclude]:

> It is easy, is it not,
> to move the anger out,
> from self expression to action,
> from individuality to community,
> from compromises to demands,
> for the right to live as women,
> as a people?

72

The Latina Feminist: Where We've Been, Where We're Going*

SYLVIA GONZALES

A decade has passed since those first days of the contemporary feminist movement. The 70's was the decade of feminism. Much as the 50's were to civil rights, the 60's to anti-war, the 70's signified the growth in women's consciousness. There can be no doubt that as all people are a product of their times and environment as much as their biology and culture, Latinas were impacted by the women's movement.

The feminist movement has been labeled a white, middle-class movement; and it is. As is typical of most historical movements, people must have the luxury to contemplate their status in order to rebel. The daily ritual of survival consumes too much energy from the poor and detracts from their ability to form a critical consciousness of their circumstance. The poor also become the victims of the mistaken notion that any improvement in their status is a remarkable accomplishment. In a sense, when one looks at the poverty of their conditions, a move from Mexican, Central American, Puerto Rican, or South American peasantry to United States poverty, for instance, does vastly improve their condition.

Historically, most peasant revolutions have originated with the intellectual elite. A close examination of the originators of this contemporary feminist movement will disclose a cadre of educated, sophisticated women with impressive credentials and intellectual experience. This was accomplished either by penetrating that bastion of male exclusivity, the academy, or by marriage to the intellectual elite.

The interesting thing about the women's movement is that although these women enjoyed exposure to the tools of the elite by virtue of birth or marriage, they still were not part of the elite. They were not accessories to power, only appendages to power. In essence, they were a part of the group they chose to liberate. That was their strength. Their weakness, however, was their inability to see further than their own liberation. In the spirit of the civil rights movement of a decade before, they professed to champion the cause of minority women. But in reality, they were too overwhelmed with their own cause to give more than token acknowledgement to the plight of these women.

Latina women's organizing occurred spontaneously and concurrently with the present phase of feminism. As early as 1968, Dr. Hector García, the founder of the American G.I. Forum, met with Polly Baca Barragan and this author in Washington, D.C. to discuss the formation of a national Chicana organization. Polly was charged

*From *Nuestro*, Vol. 5, No. 6, Aug. –Sept., 1981: pp. 45–47.

with meeting with Washington Chicanas to test the waters for such an organization. Leadership conflicts prohibited the idea from materalizing.

In 1971 the first attempt to form a national organization for Latinas was initiated by Lupe Anguiano, a Chicana employed with the Department of Health, Education, and Welfare. She joined ranks with a group of Puerto Rican women from New York. Among those from the Washington area involved in the effort were Lourdes Miranda King, Ana María Perera and this author. A conference was held in New York City but resulted in leadership conflicts. The attempt was a failure.

Also in 1971 Chicanas held a national conference in Houston, Texas. Resolutions generated by the conference called for legal abortions, birth control, and 24 hour childcare centers. And in 1972 Puerto Rican women on the East Coast founded the National Conference of Puerto Rican Women under the leadership of such women as Carmen Delgado Votaw and Paquito Vivo.

In communities all around the country, Latina women were organizing. In Los Angeles the Comisión Femenil Mejicana and the Chicana Service Action Center were founded to respond to the needs of California, and especially Los Angeles.

Finally in the mid-1970's, several national organizations strengthened and survived. Although the leadership squabbles continued, these organizations were able to build their bases and expand. Most notable among them are the National Conference of Puerto Rican Women and the Mexican-American Women's National Association.

In the Spring of 1980 Latinas entered a new phase of development. This decade opened with the National Hispanic Feminist Conference [held in San Jose, California]. The importance of the Conference is immeasurable in terms of organizational impact, public awareness, and most important, the leadership questions raised by the preceding decade.

The leadership struggles which produced failure for the early organizing attempts are questions that have always plagued the Latino movement as well as other grassroots movements. A direction for the future may be determined by reflecting on these questions and understanding their source.

Too often we Latinos have been too harsh on ourselves. We wonder why we can't "get it together." We look for role models and aspire for united action. The women's movement resembles our own in that respect, and we should recognize this as we dissect the causes for our disunity and negative political strategies that divide rather than unite.

The National Hispanic Feminist Conference was a classic example. The leadership struggles that surfaced were unmatched in recent years. The artificial boycott of the conference hotel by a disgruntled band of local Chicanas angry because they were not included as keynote speakers sufficiently disrupted events and disoriented participants to handicap the unifying efforts of the meeting. Yet, the conference proceeded successfully in spite of the destructive efforts of some.

There were several agendas occurring at the same time. Each latched onto the boycott of the conference hotel as leverage to push their specific cause. The Comisión Femenil Mejicana of Los Angeles was angered by what they perceived the predominant role of the Mexican-American Women's National Association and in fierce competition, proceeded to use the boycott as a rallying point for unhappy dissidents. These women, many long-time activists in the Chicano community and some intensely anti-feminist, sought to establish finally and resolutely their historical position in the Chicana leadership hierarchy at the expense of consensus and group priorities.

A contingent of young university activists of all backgrounds cuddled the boycott of the hotel as a springboard for their gay rights platform. Refugees from South American right-wing governments shied away from the boycott for the fear that their own cause would be unheard in the heat of an issue they felt insignificant compared to right-wing torture and repression.

What was amazing about the conference is that the agenda continued and people left with so many of these issues introduced, debated, and decided upon. Latinas decided to support gay rights, condemn right-wing governments, and showed sensitivity to the boycott by moving conference workshops from the hotel. Typical of the conference was the nature of the struggles, particularly the leadership struggles. Unique about the conference was its success in dealing with these struggles. And this perhaps can point to the direction for the future.

The leadership struggles that have caused us so much conflict in the past and continue to immobilize us in the present emanate from a lack of reflection on our goals. In the early and late sixties, the Chicano bible was Paulo Freire's *Pedagogy of the Oppressed*. Freire's book became the handbook for the Latino oppressed. Only recently the validity of Freire's methodology has been reinstated through his direction of the highly successful literacy campaign in Nicaragua. So, although we read Freire's words and instinctively identified with its message, we were still unable to internalize his methodology because of the strength of the social norms in which we live.

The kinds of leadership struggles which have plagued our movement and were so vividly highlighted at the National Hispanic Feminist Conference are those resulting from a group that has adopted the oppressors model and in reality seeks the power of the oppressor. And too often, the ambigious concepts of community and grassroots become the banner and rallying cry. The competition, the negative undermining and destructive disruptions (the forte of the Saul Alinsky radicals) are all tactics that have been taught to us by the system in which we live. We must recognize that every time we call for a "piece of the pie" we are asking to become the oppressors. Every time we struggle to be "the leader" we are struggling to become the "intermediary" oppressors of our communities.

What saved the National Hispanic Feminist Conferences was that the organizers were operating from the Freire model. Every time a leadership struggle emerged, they found no one to struggle with. Every time someone challenged "who's in charge here?" they were met with the response, "we all are." At first this was disorienting to a group unaccustomed to this approach. But in the end, the negative struggles dissipated into shallow motions.

The National Hispanic Women's Policy Studies Institute, the Latina Institute, is a result of the National Hispanic Feminist Conference. In organizing the conference, this author recognized the need for a national clearinghouse for Latina women, a research center for collecting data on Latinas, and the political education necessary for developing a critical consciousness. The Institute was incorporated in February, 1980, two months before the conference. Since that time, the Institute has developed its own model for social change which is an adaptation of Freire's model geared to contemporary United States society. The Institute proposes to engage in a wide campaign of political education of Latinas, but not in isolation of the research so important to critical planning and goal setting.

The Latina must move away from the model that has been given to us. We must stop struggling with each other for small insignificant symbols of power, which in reality are just that, symbols. In our recognition that it is the model that is wrong, we should form coalitions with other groups of like mind. It is my suspicion that the feminist movement and the Latino movement have not gotten it together because we are trapped by the model. In the women's movement, what started as grassroots consiousness-raising, turned into relabeling the model "the new girls network."

Latina women have not yet experienced the sweet taste of pseudo-success. We have not profited from the movements our Latino brothers initiated nor from the feminist movement. We are barely moving onto our own. And we are doing so within a climate of declining resources, self-righteous negativity, and anti-feminist and minority agendas. Perhaps we are entering the most critical period of our recent history. The forces of dogmatic judgements, selfish motivations, and narrow-minded governance are rampant. This is the model at its most extreme.

In a sense, this may be to the Latinas advantage. It can keep us honest and focused. Without that "piece of the pie" so readily available, we can direct our attention to the changes that need to be made in the pie. If we aspire to leadership, then let it be the leadership of cooperation and group consciousness to change our destinies and that of all people.

73

*Chicanas in the 80's: Unsettled Issues**

MUJERES EN MARCHA, UNIVERSITY OF
CALIFORNIA, BERKELEY

In keeping with a long tradition of struggle by women to assert their dignity, we, as members of Mujeres en Marcha at the University of California, Berkeley, organized a panel discussion for the 1982 National Association for Chicano Studies [NACS] conference in Tempe, Arizona. The purposes of the panel were 1) to generate discussion around significant issues of gender inequality that appeared to be unsettled, and 2) to generate suggestions of action to remedy the problems that women in NACS face in their attempts to be recognized as serious scholars.

Certainly, we were not exhaustive in the enumeration of issues, nor did we intend to be. Similarly, we were aware that the issues raised were particular to Chicana women in insitutions of higher education, and that a vast number of pressing issues

*From *Chicanas in the 80's: Unsettled Issues—1982*, (Berkeley: Chicano Studies Library Publication Unit: 1983).

remain to be addressed adequately for women in the Chicano community at large. The panel addressed an academic audience. This report continues in the same vein.

Three issues of concern were identified as topics for presentation:

1. For a number of years, Chicanas have heard claims that a concern with issues specifically affecting Chicanas is merely a distraction/diversion from the liberation of Chicano people as a whole. What are the issues that arise when women are asked to separate their exploitation as women from the other forms of oppression that we experience?
2. Chicanas are confronted daily by the limitations of being a woman in this patriarchal society; the attempt to assert these issues around "sexism" are often met with resistance and scorn. What are some of the major difficulties in relations amongst ourselves? How are the relationships between women and men affected? How are the relationships of women to women and men to men affected? How do we overcome the constraints of sexism?
3. It is not uncommon that our interests as feministas are challenged on the basis that we are simply falling prey to the interests of white middle-class women. We challenge the notion that there is no room for a Chicana movement within our own community. We, as women of color, have a unique set of concerns that are separate from white women and from men of color.

The issues raised in the panel evolved from a series of discussions that took place among members of Mujeres en Marcha during the 1981–82 academic year. The panel consisted of seven members from Mujeres en Marcha. As moderator, Teresa Córdova presented opening and closing remarks. The three sets of issues were introduced by Margarita Decierdo, Gloria Cuádraz, and Deena González, respectively. Other members of the panel included Sylvia Lizárraga, Linda Facio, and Lita de la Torre. Other members of Mujeres en Marcha included Maurilia Flores, Guadalupe Fríaz, and Beatríz Pesquera.

Topic I: Is The Concern with Issues Specifically Affecting Chicanas and Raised by Chicanas Merely a Distraction or Diversion from the Liberation of Chicano People as a Whole?

Speaker: Margarita Decierdo

What are the issues that arise when women are asked to separate their exploitation as women from the other forms of oppression that we experience? During the 1960's, while we struggled together against the structures that oppressed the Chicano/a community, the Chicana "had been cautioned to wait and fight for her cause at a later time for fear of dividing the Chicano Movement." Of course, this was unacceptable— and basically the issue evolved as to which of the two areas of discrimination the Chicana should adopt as priority—sexism or racism. Ana Nieto-Gómez elaborates on the situation:

> [M]any loyalists felt that these complaints from women were potentially destructive and could only divide the Chicano Movement. If sexual inequalities existed, they were an in-house problem which could be dealt with later. However, right then and there, there were more important priorities to attend to: Vietnam, La Huelga, and police brutality.

Well-known Chicana activist Yolanda Nava, for example, severely criticized this posture and states, "It is unacceptable to separate racial–sexual and economic struggle in a hierarchical list of priorities. It must be realized that it is illogical to ask a woman to ignore and postpone her struggle as a woman." Thus, our arguments were thought to be relevant only to Anglo women. Social and organizational ostracism were effectively used in the isolation of Chicana women. Anti-sexist criticism was interpreted as hatred of men.

Thus, women with or without their Chicano male counterparts, continued their struggle and began organizing to deal effectively with issues that concerned women. While the Chicano Movement activist strategized in dealing with the struggle against race and class domination, it neglected to embrace socio-economic, political issues critical to women—health, poverty, forced sterilization, racism, employment, child care, education, and abortion rights. We felt, therefore, that the fundamental criticism of the Chicano Movement was that it did not adequately incorporate the process of political strategies relevant to the Chicana. In other words, the movement could not survive merely on issues to liberate our people. The Movement, because it did not place nor identify the socio-political root of women's oppression, did not achieve as much as it would have if it had seriously dealt with the question of sexism. The political mobilization of women had to be linked with the liberation of a people and a class inasmuch as they were an integral part of these. By not understanding the dynamics of power, we failed to understand our own oppression.

Commentary: There was an indication that there was shared sentiment on three points: 1) that the Chicano Movement fell short of greater heights because of its exclusion of women; 2) that credit is due for the accomplishments that were attained, with the necessary help of women; 3) that the time has come for the Chicano Movement (and we assume there is still one operating) to incorporate fully the needs and voices of mujeres [women].

Topic I: Discussion

How is it true that we, together, as men and women, can begin to deal with feminism on a daily basis, especially in terms of organizational aspects?

A suggestion was made that decisions should be made in the plenary session to deal with issues of sexism. A panelist pointed out that we must keep in mind that women are not generally present at these meetings and that the men themselves should take the initiative to make progress rather than lean on a few token women who must not only bear the burden of responsibility for the issues of sexism, but bear the consequences as well.

A male member of the audience responded by saying that before a man could do this, he had to be educated. Several responded to this by saying that sexism has been seen as a woman's issue and not as a people's issue. "To say that women should educate men and make them repsonsible, not only for themselves, but for the men also, is ludicrous."

Panelist replied that it was a man himself who had to see to it that he was educated. It was clearly pointed out that "It was not the task of women to educate men. All we could do was to bring the awareness of what was going on. As women, we have discussed the issue among ourselves at length and essentially feel that it is a shared responsibility and that we want you to be responsible for educating yourselves."

It was suggested that we should ask the following series of questions:

1. Has there been any progressive change since the 1960s?
2. Where have the improvements been since the 1960s?
3. What are the areas we need to work on further?

NACS, to a certain degree, has done much to break down some of the sexual barriers, but still has some way to go. Women need to participate more on panels and committees, and as FOCO (group) representatives. Women are more apt to do this when they receive support not only from women, but also from men—without condescension.

Women's mobility in the world of academia (among other places) is limited, both structurally and systematically. We do not have, for example, tenured Chicanas with a solid institutional base and very few who have solid histories of publishing. We need a commitment in our universities to recruit women and to support them once they are there. The networkings of women are important in these endeavors.

Topic II: Chicanas are Confronted Daily by the Limitation of Being Women in this Patriarchal Society: The Attempt to Assert Issues Around "Sexism" is often met with Resistance and Scorn. What are Some of the Major Difficulties in the Arena of Relations Among Ourselves? How are The Relationships of Women to Women and Men to Men Affected? How do we Overcome the Constraints of Sexism?

Speaker: Gloria Holguín Cuádraz

Whether subtle or blatant, sexism is our reality. It is also yours. Whether intentional or non-intentional, the fact remains that Chicanas face sexism on a daily basis. Just as our Anglo counterparts hesitate to deal with their racism, so must Chicanos and Chicanas learn to deal with their sexism. The question we raise is: How do we deal with the sexism?

As we see it, Chicanas have two options: 1) We can remain silent; 2) We can confront it. Yet in remaining silent, we: 1) Remain frustrated and internalize our oppression; 2) Reinforce a false sense of manhood; 3) Reinforce the oppression of both men and women, because ultimately, our struggle for liberation suffers. Moreover, what are the consequences when we do confront the sexism? As we see it, the initial thing that occurs is that we become labeled. Be it as a "women's libber" or as a "radical feminist," by virtue of the labels imposed upon us and the reputation that accompanies it, often we are not only alienated but also ostracized from the "old boys network."

Topic II: Discussion

Many women, in response to the issues raised, expressed the frustrations they experience when attempting to achieve liberation from an oppression that is not only detrimental to women, but to the men as well. For example, women spoke of the defensiveness they encountered from men as a result of disagreeing with them. The hegemonic discourse requires them to be agreeably passive and they are considered out of place if they overstep this boundary. Many women asserted that if they were to achieve their dignity as scholars in a male-dominated world, then it would be necessary to refrain from being agreeably passive and instead assert their presence as thinking individuals. Because this is so challenging to assumptions long held about how the Chicana should behave, such assertion results in conflict.

Panelist: "Men are not aware of sexist acts and that's why they keep committing these sexist acts. If the woman brings this to the attention of men, then she has to pay the consequences, and she pays highly. The men have to want to educate themselves and become more aware. Men have to become aware of their own sexist acts, because men commit them."

Man: "What are those consequences you pay?"

Woman: " We are labeled, the word spreads and we are ostracized from the networks. If a job offer comes up [and] if you are too aggressive and too assertive, and possibly threaten the traditional role, you won't get considered. Rarely are qualified Chicanas pushed forward."

Woman: "Yes, there are consequences, but even without confronting men, you still get passed over. It is inexcusable, for example, that a faculty meeting is held to discuss funding possibilities, but the only woman faculty member is excluded."

Woman: "Even with the consequences it is important for us to examine the costs of sexism and the ways in which it hinders the growth of women and of us as a people."

Woman: "What about the kinds of things that women do to women? Women who have internalized their oppression experience the pains of jealousy, spurred by their insecurities. Women, too, have internalized and accepted the criteria of what a woman is as well as the ideological reinforcement."

Woman: "There are a lot of unresolved contradictions that we as women have to deal with."

There seems to be a fear that conflict—not confrontation—is unhealthy. Diversity in such settings as the National Hispanic Women's Conference [1980] are often ignored. A theme of the conference was to parade around our unity without any sort of substance. Yet questions of gay women and of class were ignored. "There are a number of questions on the agenda for us as women."

Topic III: It is not Uncommon that our Interests as Feministas are Challenged on the Basis that we are Simply Falling Prey to the Interest of White Middle-Class Women. We Challenge the Notion that There is no Room for a Chicana Movement within our Community. We, as Women of Color, Have a Unique Set of Concerns that are Separate Both From White Women and Men of Color.

Speaker: Deena González

White women and women of color come to feminism under profoundly different circumstances and with dissimilar issues in mind. What we define and interpret as our circumstances are primarily issues to white women. Therein lies what has come to signify the most crucial point of our divergence. Other distinctions demonstrate our differences, but this particular distinction between issues and circumstances holds great validity.

I discovered feminism largely under the auspices of the white women's movement. Through MS. Magazine, through group discussions at Women's Centers and Women's Buildings, I came to the conclusion that I was a feminist, in political and social orientation. But only when I came to the realization that I was a Chicana and a Latina feminist did I realize how fundamentally different and often how diametrically opposed my opinions and ideas were to white feminism, in fact, how contradictory they ran to that which white, middle-class feminism was attempting to achieve.

I remember participating in hundreds of hours of conversation with white women, in groups and in friendships, and not being stirred by the things that excited them. I mean, Emma Goldman was important, but she did not bring out in me what she seemed to move in white women, or Jewish women. But when I found other Latinas searching for similar people in our past, in other words, when many of us began to recapture a history and an identification that existed as it always has, in our communities, then I began to know what it was to admire a person from the past. When I read Julia de Burgos' poetry, when I read about Luisa Capetillo, when I heard about women's groups in Mexico City, when I learned about Black women and Native American women struggling and fighting, then I felt comfortable. Then, too, I began to develop an analysis whose great contradictions continue to move me toward the kind of intimate liberation that feminism induces. Our first step, however, is that of self-discovery, of recovery, of renewed identification.

Contrary to what has been said and written about us (in or out of academia) we have lost nothing. But we have begun the necessary steps toward reaffirming, in new contexts, what we have always known. For one thing, race and class oppression are our reality, but to white women these are merely issues; "they" do not consistently encounter themselves in situations like ours. I have come to believe that until white women (and also men) make our circumstances their own, subconsciously, what concerns us will remain topics for discussion, issues outside of their movements, and ultimately detrimental for their as well as our own liberation.

Neither our feminism nor our liberation depend on any white movement, but our hardest political struggles are pushed forward in alliances, no matter how tenuous or uneasy those might be. A similar parallel could be drawn over how feminism has infiltrated struggles around class. Our first step, however, must necessarily be that of self-discovery, of renewed commitment along with that reestablished identification.

Topic III: Discussion

The discussion generated by Topic III opened with a series of declarations by women differentiating their needs as women of color from those of white women. These testimonies included explicit descriptions of incidents where women could not relate to aspects of white feminism yet they could clearly identify needs that were specific to women who also encounter oppression due to hegemony based on race.

Some men pointed out that they do have the tendency to see issues of women's liberation as a middle-class set of issues and consequently block out any claims by third world women.

The women responded by pointing out that claims for women's liberation are not by any means necessarily bourgeois. Third world women have begun to speak out on issues such as health, poverty, forced sterilization, racism, unemployment, child care, education, and abortion rights.

A great amount of work needs to be done in promoting the elevation of women from a status of inferiority and submission to one of dignity and participation. In doing so, we encounter contradictions and dilemmas. This final comment by a woman reminds us of what we must do in spite of these dilemmas.

If we are going to take seriously the attempts toward social change, then we are going to be in a dilemma. People who don't want to accept the dilemma are basically supporters of the status quo. If we are going to challenge, then we have to accept the

dilemma. It doesn't mean we have to remain in a confused state, but we have to clarify what we want for ourselves, accept the dilemma and accept also that it is not easy.

Closing Remarks

Speaker: Teresa Córdova

We have only begun—all of us—to deal with the systematic hegemony—the systematic dominance of men over women. This dominance appears in many forms, at many
levels, throughout all realms of our lives. It is not an easy task; there are many issues,
many complications, many misunderstandings.

There is first the question of whether there is room for a feminist movement
within the Chicano community. Such a question is based, first of all, on the assumption that liberation is a zero-sum commodity; that there is only enough room for
some of us to be liberated. It is based on the assumption that hegemony based on race
is not related to hegemony based on sex. It is also based on the assumption that we
can separate ourselves as Chicano women. It is further based on the assuption that the
liberation of women precludes the liberation of our people. It is based on the assumption that women's active participation cannot contribute to the struggle. These assumptions, however, are not based on our reality.

The struggle of our people is better enhanced if we bring ourselves up together.
The struggle is better enhanced if we struggle together. United we stand. Divided we
fall

What is this thing we call sexism? It is like racism in many ways. It is both blatant and subtle. It is both psychological and institutionalized. There is "a systematic
body of knowledge that oppresses" Chicanas. We need to identify both a Chicanolo-
gy and a Chicanalogy—whether we call it that or not. We have here today begun to
enumerate together the assumptions, the actions, and the consequences of dominance
by men over women.

As we continue to do this, the process unfolds. It is important to emphasize that
it is a process. Like any other process, there are dynamics—the most striking to us is
what happens when we raise these issues to our men. Most typically we are reacted to
as though we are trying to cut off something. We are not. We are not castrating. We
are not bitches. We are not insignificant and we are not stupid. We are working together towards the liberation of all of us. What is in it for the women, is in it for the
men—cooperation, humanization, friendship, and liberation.

It is crucial, we agree, that situationally confronting the issues is ideal. When
"sexism" occurs, we need to deal with it. That is, the time to assert a right is when
that right is denied. To do this is something both men and women seem to agree is
important. This is the ideal, an ideal that we collectively have yet to achieve. Remember what happens when women do raise these issues. The men become defensive and
the women are defined as uppity or insolent. What is really being said is that women
have overstepped their boundaries. The point is, achieving this ideal is a process—a
process that collectively we can effectively develop.

There is also the question of whether we are a co-opted product of the white
feminist movement. There are charges that we are being used. Neither of these points
have been proven. What has been proven is that we, as Chicanas, experience oppression as women and as Chicanas. We cannot separate the two. There are, therefore, significant divergences between us and white women—differences of race and of class.
Similarly, to us and Chicano men, the issue of gender is significant.

There is a further issue that we have emphasized to many of you and wish to emphasize here again—the issue of intentionality. It is not necessary that one intends to act in a way that has hegemonic consequences. More often than not, the intention is not there. However, intention or not, the consequences remain. The point is, the pernicious assumptions and stereotypical understandings about Chicana women are deeply rooted. These assumptions and understandings have been perpetuated and sustained through history.

People act on the assumptions under which they were socialized. The point that we are making is that many of these underlying assumptions have served as the basis for a hierarchical structure that places men on top, women on the bottom. We challenge this on the basis that it is hierarchical and therefore requires that someone be on the bottom.

We know this is difficult for the men—it is even more difficult for us.

Our voices are becoming stronger and cannot be silenced. There are many men who are joining the struggle. Together we shall work for the eradication of a dehumanizing system of dominance.

III

CHICANA FEMINISTS SPEAK: VOICING A NEW CONSCIOUSNESS

Introduction

Indebted to the contributions and struggles of Chicana feminists during the intense period of the Chicano Movement, a new group of Chicana feminists evolved during the 1980s and into the 1990s. These later feminists can be considered post-Movement feminists in that their ideological constructions appear in a period when the Chicano Movement as a specific historical manifestation no longer exists or at least not in the same form or context that characterized its key political years.

This is not to say that the Movement does not continue to influence the second wave of Chicana feminists and activists, but it is to say that the Chicano Movement as a social movement possessed historical specificity. It took place in a particular time and in particular locations. *El Movimiento* lives on as an inspiration, but not as an on-going social movement.

Post-Movement Chicana feminists exhibit certain continuities but also disconti- nuities with movement feminists. The following essays reflect both these similarities as well as differences.

Some of the continuities include a recognition by some post-Movement fem- inists that the issue of sexism and of patriarchical oppression still need to be linked to race and class issues. That is, Chicanas continue to face particular forms of dis- crimination due not just to their gender or sexual identity, but also due to their race/ethnic and largely working-class positions within the United States. As Anna Castillo notes in her essay, Movement feminists understood sexism as a problem, but

261

they likewise understood race and class oppression as additional obstacles to the Chicana's liberation.

Some post-Movement feminists like their predecessors continue to link their struggles within the broader efforts of the Mexican-American and Latino communities. This linkage includes continued efforts to establish viable collective efforts with Chicano men. As Sandra Cisneros observes, the sexist attitudes and actions of Chicano men need to be critiqued and opposed, but Chicano men are not enemies or at least not the real enemies.

In their efforts to define themselves, post-Movement feminists agree with Movement feminists that they can draw inspiration from the history of strong Mexican women on both sides of the border including their own specific *antepasados*—their ancestors such as their *abuelitas* and *tías*—their grandmothers and aunts.

Like their predecessors, some post-Movement feminists continue to express reservations about the women's movement especially the continued concern that white, middle-class feminists are not sensitive to the particular race and class issues pertinent to Chicanas and other women of color. At the same time, post-Movement feminists like Movement feminists before them seem to agree with the general goal of the women's movement of ending the subordination of women. Finally, some post-Movement feminists also construct essentialist images of both Chicano men and white women rather than addressing the more complex and diverse relationships between and within these groups. While these continuities clearly reveal the linkages between Movement and post-Movement feminists, the discontinuities stress the fact that post-Movement feminists or at least some are not carbon copies of their predecessors, but instead are striking out in new directions.

These discontinuities with Movement feminists are expressed around the following issues: (1) there is a tendency to suggest, as Cynthia Orozco's essay does, that earlier feminists were not as clear about the nature of partiarchy; that is, Movement feminists focused too much on simply changing the sexist attitudes of Chicano men without understanding that patriarchy connotes not just attitudes but a deeply established system of social relationships requiring transformation; (2) there is a sharper focus on the victimization of Chicanas as opposed to a primary stress by Movement feminists on their agency to bring about change; (3) unlike Movement feminists, some post-Movement feminists privilege patriarchy and sexism as their major issues and in some cases their only issues; (4) the issue of gender identity has become more complex and multiple in order to accommodate differences among Chicanas, especially concerning sexual identity; (5) sexuality, specifically Chicana lesbianism, is now foregrounded whereas such issues were largely untouched during the Movement years due to a more constrictive and oppressed climate on such matters; (6) some post-Movement feminists, as suggested in Carla Trujillo's essay, besides giving priorty to issues of sexuality, in addition advance the hypothesis of Chicana lesbians as representing the most progressive sector within the Chicano community; (7) despite the efforts by some post-Movement feminists to argue for a more multiple interpretation concerning gender, essentialist notions concerning Chicana heterosexuals and about the Chicano community's attitudes regarding issues of sexuality have often accompanied these new assertions.

Together these continuities and discontinuities give voice to an evolving Chicana feminism, but one whose contemporary roots lie in the struggles of the first wave of Chicana feminists during the period of the Chicano Movement.

DESERT WOMEN (1986)

Desert women know
about survival.
Fierce heat and cold
have burned and thickened
our skin. Like cactus
we've learned to hoard,
to sprout deep roots,
to seem asleep, yet wake
at the scent of softness
in the air, to hide
pain and loss by silence,
no branches wail
or whisper our sad songs
safe behind our thorns

Don't be deceived.
When we bloom, we stun.

Pat Mora

Chicana at student strike, University of California at Los Angeles, 1993. Courtesy
Raul Ruiz, *La Verdad* magazine, Los Angeles, California.

STRONG WOMEN (1991)

Some women hold me when I need to dream,
rock, rocked my first red anger through the night.
Strong women teach me courage to esteem,

to stand alone, like cactus, persevere
when cold frowns bite my bones and doubts incite.
Some women hold me when I need to dream.

They walk beside me on dark paths I fear,
guide with gold lanterns: stories they recite.
Strong women teach me courage to esteem.

In their safe arms, my visions reappear:
skyfire voices soar, blaze, night ignite.
Strong, women teach me courage to esteem.

They sing brave women, sisters, we revere
whose words seed bursts of light that us unite.
Some women hold me when I need to dream.
Strong women, teach me courage to esteem.

Pat Mora

74

Sexism in Chicano Studies and the Community*

CYNTHIA OROZCO

I would like to address the significance of gender and its relationship to sexism in the Chicano community and Chicano studies. Three questions are discussed: (1) How did the Chicano movement deal with women and how did Chicano studies treat the category of gender? (2) What is the significance of gender for understanding and ending the oppression Chicanas experience as women? and (3) What is the relationship between gender and feminism, and what does this mean for social change?

The Chicano movement was a nationalist struggle for the liberation of the Mexican people in the United States, though class struggle was a conscious component among various sectors. It must be clear that this movement did *not* attempt to end patriarchy, the system by which men dominate women.

Though we can speak of a Chicana movement in which women argued that women's life experiences and oppression were different and worse than men's and acted against this particular oppression, lack of ideological clarity on what gender meant hindered the Chicana movement.[1] At the time, Chicana activists did not recognize patriarchy as a system separate in origins and in everyday life and quite distinct from racism and capitalism. Chicanas struggled against the interconnectedness of this triple burden, but largely battled racism and capitalism on the ideological front. For instance, Anna Nieto Gómez, California's best-known and most controversial feminist, argued in 1977 that sexism "is part of the capitalist ideology which advocates male supremacist values."[2]

When Chicanas raised the issue of male domination, both the community and its intellectual arm, Chicano studies, put down the ideology of feminism and put feminists in their place. Utilizing ideology and its corresponding actions, Chicanos continued to manifest the sexism feminists sought to eradicate.

Various sexist ideologies about feminism (and feminists) emerged from the Chicano movement. Four common ones can be discerned: (1) "El problema es el gabacho no el macho." ["The problem is the Anglo not the Macho"]. (2) Feminism was Anglo, middle-class, and bourgeois. (3) Feminism was a diversion from the "real" and "basic" issues, that is, racism and class exploitation. (4) Feminism sought to destroy "la familia" supposedly the base of Mexican culture and the basis for resistance to domination.[3]

These ideologies raised some legitimate concerns, but blurred the feminist vi-

*From *Chicana Voices: Intersections of Class, Race, and Gender,* edited by Teresa Córdova et al. (Austin: Center for Mexican American Studies, 1986: pp. 11–18).

sion. Machismo was disregarded. Activists defined racism and capitalism as fundamental problems, but such issues as equal pay for equal work, sex segregation in employment, and rape were hardly considered "basic." Many feminists were Anglo and middle class, but there were also black and other Third World working-class feminists. Chicanos stereotyped feminism to mean liberal feminism; radical feminism was ignored. Moreover, Chicana radicals had begun to redefine feminism to fit their particular triple oppression when the case against feminism was made. Similarly, while the family has embodied essential emotional and human relationships, the idea that it did not sustain oppressive or hierarchical relationships, especially for women and girls, was asserted.

While the attack on feminism in community action was overt and conscious, Chicana feminism was also undermined in Chicano studies. Chicano intellectuals argued that race and class were the determining factors in understanding the subordinate position of Mexicans in the United States.[4] They interpreted the condition of Mexican men and women to be synonymous; gender was irrelevant in determining life experience and power. Most intellectuals were unconscious of their exclusion of the category of gender, since male thought permeates our thinking and does not allow for the female perspective and opinion. In community life, Chicano activists like César Chávez advanced male thought: he proudly asserted, "We are not beasts of burden, we are not agricultural implements or rented slaves, we are men."[5]

Rodolfo Acuña's *Occupied America*, perhaps the most widely read book about Chicanos—a work which should be considered the "Chicano Bible"—epitomizes the lack of a conceptualization of gender.[6] Acuña cogently describes racial and class oppression, but he does not mention gender oppression.[7] In not doing so, he suggests a male ideology: sexism is not a problem, and therefore feminism is irrelevant to Chicanas. We must not underestimate the power of Acuña's book: teachers have organized courses around it, and it has taught thousands how to think about the oppression Mexicans experienced.

In the Chicano studies document "El Plan de Santa Barbara," the theoretical rationale for Chicano studies, a lack of consciousness about sexism and gender can be inferred.[8] Sociologist Mary Pardo's analysis of "El Plan" shows that not once did it make reference to women, female liberation, or Chicana studies. Indeed, "El Plan" was a "man"-ifesto.[9]

College course offerings by Chicano studies centers exemplify a lack of awareness about the problem of sexism and the importance of gender. Most small centers offered the token "La Chicana" (usually as a result of Chicana feminists' annual struggle to ensure it) which usually covered all topics briefly and none thoroughly.[10] At some schools, even this class has not been institutionalized. The women teaching these courses have overwhelmingly been part-time workers.[11] The omission of courses on women and the lack of Chicana faculty help to explain the weak feminist consciousness among students and the lack of support systems for young women.[12]

In short, feminism has been suppressed and feminists have been repressed. What is the significance of this? Many lack an understanding of male domination in society; therefore, the oppression that Mexican women suffer which is specific to their gender has hardly been challenged. Moreover, Chicana studies today are underdeveloped. It is time to study problems specific to Chicanas and to rectify them.[13]

To do so, we must understand the significance of gender. It determines life experience, power, and privilege, and the division of labor is created on the basis of it.[14] Our identities are formed by work. Thereby, men learn to be men and women learn to be women; gender is largely a social construction.[15] This varies according to historical period and culture and is subject to change.

Society gives social significance to gender, and a system of power is organized around it. This system is patriarchy or male domination or machismo, if we extend its usual connotation. Its origins are different from those of racism and capitalism, and it is the most universal and historical system.

Patriarchy is sophisticated: it has both structural and ideological features.[16] The key structural feature is the division of labor by sex. Arising from this is the ideological feature of femininity and masculinity, our gender identities. Femininity must not be seen solely as a female-creation; it complements masculinity, which also serves as a foundation for male dominance.[17]

In contrast to patriarchy is feminism. Feminism is a recognition of the domination of men over women and attempts by women to end male privilege. It also seeks to redefine female-to-female relations. Feminism is all-encompassing since it is a theory, a method, and a practice which seeks to transform human relations.[18] Feminism is necessary for liberation.

How can feminism affect social change? How does it relate to women and higher education? To begin, "higher education" demands redefinition, since only 6 percent of our Latina population attend institutions of higher learning.[19] We must broaden our strategies to include the majority of our community.

Schools alienate and exclude women and men, girls and boys. Alternative institutions and mediums must be created, and we must take higher education to common people. Here, higher education is defined not as institutions, but as the realm of thought. We must disseminate our knowledge and progressive perspectives to the community by presenting strategies for change. At the same time, we must listen to the community, for it speaks to us. We must move beyond the barriers that the university seeks to maintain between a privileged sector and the mass of exploited and oppressed Mexicans. Sexism has no geographical barriers—it thrives at the university—nor should feminism stay in the college setting. Feminism belongs in the community.

Higher education promotes the liberation of the oppressed and rejects hierarchy. Feminism as theory and daily practice should be an integral feature of this higher education so we can end the exploitation of women in the home, sexual harassment on the job, sex segregation in employment, wife abuse, and rape.

These strategies imply a vision of the future, a vision of hope. In the spirit of change, visions are revisions. Today, we revise "El Plan de Santa Barbara" to encompass the feminist voice it lacked in 1969.[20] We have appropriately called it "El Plan de Santa y Barbara" since it is a proposal written to Chicano studies across the nation in hope that feminism will reemerge in strength. It follows:

> We will move forward toward our destiny as women. We will move against those forces which have denied us freedom of expression and human dignity. Due to the sexist structure of this society, to our essentially different life style, and to the socioeconomic functions assigned to our community by male society-as suppliers of free labor and a dumping ground for male aggression, the female community remains exploited, impoverished, and abused.

As a result, the self-determination of the female community is now the only acceptable mandate for social and political action; it is the essence of Chicana commitment.

Culturally, the word "feminism," in the past a pejorative and class-bound word, has now become the root idea of a new cultural identity for women. Feminism draws its faith and strength from two main sources: from the just struggle of women and from an objective analysis of our community's strategic needs.

It is in this spirit, that we meet in Austin, Texas, in mid-March, over 400 Chicano students, faculty, administrators, and community delegates representing Aztlán.

Let us part with the words of a Chicana feminist named Sra. Josefa Vasconcelos. She said, "At this moment we do not come to work for Chicano studies and the community, but to demand that Chicano studies and the community work for our liberation too."

Acknowledgments

I would like to thank members of Raza Women's Organization, UCLA for their moral support and help. Particular thanks to Luz Calvo.

NOTES

1. Carlos Vásquez has pointed to the problem of ideological clarity among Chicana feminists yet subsumes the feminist cause under the Marxist-Leninist struggle and fails to acknowledge patriarchy. "Women in the Chicano Movement," in *Mexican Women in the United States: Struggles Past and Present*, ed. Magdalena Mora and Adelaida R. Del Castillo (Los Angeles: Chicano Studies Research Center Publications, 1980), pp. 27–28. For a critique of the socalled "woman question," see Heidi Hartman, "The Unhappy Marriage between Marxism and Feminism," *Capital and Class* 8 (Summer, 1979): pp. 1–33.

2. Nieto-Gómez was the Chicana movement's eminent intellectual/activist; she waged war on the triple oppression Chicanas suffer. Her writing reflects lack of clarity on the origins and nature of this burden, but to some extent this can be attributed to the interconnectedness of capitalism, racism, and sexism. Adelaida R. Del Castillo notes that "Chicana feminism itself was delineated not so much through cohesive political statements as through the focus of issues and activities" (Anna Nieto-Gómez, "Sexism in the Movimiento, " *La Gente* (February, 1975): 10; Adelaida R. Del Castillo, "Mexican Women in Organization," in *Mexican Women in the United Slates*, p. 11). *This Bridge Called My Back* should be credited with adding new vigor to women's studies and Third World women's studies in particular. [*This Bridge Called My Back: Writings by Radical Women of Color*, ed. Cherríe Moraga and Gloria Anzaldúa (Watertown, Mass.: Persephone Press, 1981).]

3. Both antifeminist and feminist writings of the Chicano movement and other Third World movements have been collected by Dorinda Moreno, *La Mujer en Pie de Lucha* (San Francisco: Espina del Norte, 1973). A critique of the notion of feminism as an Anglo, bourgeois diversion is Cynthia Orozco, "Feminism: How Chicanos 'Skirt' the Issue," *La Gente* (June, 1983): p. 17, and a critique of the "cult of la familia" has been launched by Beatriz Pesquera. See also Cherríe Moraga, "A Long Line of Vendidas," *Loving in the War Years, Lo Que Nunca Paso Por Sus Labios* (Boston: South End Press, 1983).

4. Students have transformed intellectual analysis and theory into action, and therefore MECHA's agenda has also reflected the lack of understanding of patriarchy. Mechistas have challenged sexist behavior and attitudes but fail to perceive the systematic nature of women's oppression. See Irene Rodarte, "Machismo vs. Revolution" in Moreno, *La Mujer*, pp. 36–40, and Marta Arguello, "Phallic Politics," *La Gente* (March/April, 1984): p. 5.

5. Quoted in Paul Fusco and George D. Horwitz, *La Causa: The California Grape Strike* (New York: Collier Books, 1970), n.p.

6. Rodolfo Acuña, *Occupied America: The Chicano's Struggle Toward Liberation* (San Francisco: Canfield Press, 1972).

7. Acuña made various changes in his second edition but no fundamental change in his conceptualization of women in history. His changes reflect what historians have called "compensatory history." The Mexican-American Studies Program at the University of Houston sponsored a Symposium on the classic, but no women were invited, nor was gender analyzed. See Rodolfo Acuña, *Occupied America: the Chicano's Struggle toward Liberation*, 2nd ed. (New York: Harper and Row, 1981); Mary Pardo, "Mexicanas/Chicanas: Forgotten Chapter of History," *El Popo* 14/4 (February/March, 1980):8; *Occupied America: A Chicano History Symposium* (Houston: Mexican-American Studies Program, 1982); and Cynthia Orozco, "Chicana Labor History: A Critique of Male Consciousness in Historical Writing," *La Red* 77 (February, 1984); and Acuña's sexist and paternalistic response, Rudy Acuña, "Letter to the Editor," *La Red* 79 (April, 1984).

8. Chicano Coordinating Council on Higher Education, *El Plan de Santa Barbara: A Chicano Plan for Higher Education* (Oakland: La Causa Publications, 1969).

9. Mary Pardo, "A Selective Evaluation of El Plan de Santa Barbara," *La Gente* (March/April, 1984): pp. 14–15. While it could be argued that the feminist movement in the United States was still at an incipient stage in 1969, recent Chicano studies documents and activities continue to reflect limited consciousness.

10. The fundamental base, Chicana history, has only recently been promoted by some Chicano studies centers. The product of the first symposium on Chicana history is forthcoming; see *Women's History in Transition: Content, Theory, and Method in Chicana/Mexicana History*, ed. Adelaida R. Del Castillo (Los Angeles: Chicano Studies Research Center Publications, 1985).

11. Chicano studies must be recognized not only as centers for the production of Chicano ideology, but as workplaces. Female teachers and clerical workers have confronted sex segregation, sexual harassment, and the lack of recognition for their work.

12. See California State University at Los Angeles, Mecha, "Chicano Studies Accused of Fostering Male Chauvinism," in Moreno, *La Mujer*, p. 22; and Mujeres en Marcha, *Chicanas in the 80's: Unsettled Issues* (Berkeley: Chicano Studies Library Publications Unit, 1983) for a recent critique. Of more than 500 individuals listed, Julio Martínez's reference work on Chicano scholars listed only 97 women. The National Chicano Council on Higher Education listed 38 women out of 144 members in 1982 (Julio Martínez, *Chicano Scholars and Writers: A Bio-Bibliographical Directory* (Metuchen, NJ: Scarecrow, 1979); Richard Chabran, "Chicana Reference Sources," *La Gente* (February/March, 1984): pp. 18–19; National Chicano Council on Higher Education List of Members, 1982.

13. Chicana feminists made early attempts to delineate Chicana studies but lacked the positions of center directors and professorships to disseminate and distribute curriculum. A rationale, course proposals, outlines, and a bibliography on Chicana history, sociology, literature, and higher education can be found in *New Directions in Education, Estudios Femeniles de la Chicana*, ed. Anna Nieto-Gómez (Los Angeles: UCLA Extension and Montal Educational Associates, 1974); and Odalmira L. García, *Chicana Studies Curriculum Guide, Grades 9–12* (Austin: National Educational Laboratory Publishers, 1978). For a summary of recent literature, see Cordelia Candelaria, "Six Reference Works on Mexican-American Women: A Review Essay," *Frontiers*, 5/2 (1980): pp. 75–80.

14. *Women, Culture, and Society*, ed. Michelle Zimbalist Rosaldo and Louise Lamphere (Stanford: Stanford University Press, 1974); *Towards an Anthropology of Women*, ed. Rayna Reiter (New York: Monthly Review Press, 1975); Heidi Hartman, "Capitalism, Patriarchy, and Job Segregation by Sex," *Signs: Journal of Women in Culture and Society*, 1/3 (Spring, 1976), part 2: pp. 137–169.

15. Joan Kelly-Gadol, "The Social Relations of the Sexes: Methodological Implications of Women's History," *Signs*, 1/4 (Summer, 1976): pp. 809–824; Nancy Chodorow, *The Reproduction of Mothering: Psychoanalysis and the Sociology of Gender* (Berkeley: University of California Press, 1978).

16. *Capitalist Patriarchy and the Case of Socialist Feminism*, ed. Zillah R. Eisenstein (New York: Monthly Review Press, 1979).

17. Susan Brownmiller, *Femininity* (New York: Linden Press/Simon and Schuster, 1984).

18. Catharine A. MacKinnon, "Feminism, Marxism, Method, and the State: An Agenda for Theory," *Signs*, 7/3 (Spring, 1982): pp. 515–544. See also Cynthia Orozco, "Cronica Feminista," *La Gente* (February/March, 1983): p. 8.

19. Current issues on Chicanas and higher education can be found in the Stanford newsletter *Intercambios Femeniles*. Pioneer Chicana feminists raised the issues facing Chicanas and their access to education. See Corinne Sánchez, "Higher Education y la Chicana?" and Anna Nieto-Gómez, "The Chicana-Perspectives for Education," *Encuentro Femenil*, 1/1(September, 1973): pp. 27–33, 35–61.

20. Chicano Coordinating Council on Higher Education, "Manifesto," *El Plan de Santa Bárbara*, pp. 9–11.

75

La Conciencia de la Mestiza: Towards a New Consciousness*

Gloria Anzaldúa

Por la mujer de mi raza
hablará el espíritu.[1]

José Vasconcelos, Mexican philosopher, envisaged *una raza mestiza, una mezcla de razas afines, una raza de color—la primera raza síntesis del globo*. He called it a cosmic race, *la raza cósmica*, a fifth race embracing the four major races of the world.[2] Opposite to the theory of the pure Aryan, and to the policy of racial purity that white America practices, his theory is one of inclusivity. At the confluence of two or more genetic

*From *Making Face, Making Soul: Haciendo Caras: Creative and Critical Perspectives by Women of Color*, edited by Gloria Anzaldúa (San Francisco: Aunt Lute Foundation Book, 1990: pp. 377–389).

streams, with chromosomes constantly "crossing over," this mixture of races, rather than resulting in an inferior being, provides hybrid progeny, a mutable, more malleable species with a rich gene pool. From this racial, ideological, cultural and biological cross-pollinization, an "alien" consciousness is presently in the making—a new *mestiza* consciousness, *una conciencia de mujer.* It is a consciousness of the Borderlands.

Una Lucha de Fronteras/A Struggle of Borders

> Because I, a *mestiza,*
> continually walk out of one culture
> and into another,
> because I am in all cultures at the same time,
> alma *entre dos mundos, tres, cuatro,*
> me zumba la cabeza con *lo contradictorio.*
> *Estoy norteada por todas las voces* que me hablan
> simultáneamente.

The ambivalence from the clash of voices results in mental and emotional states of perplexity. Internal strife results in insecurity and indecisiveness. The *mestiza*'s dual or multiple personality is plagued by psychic restlessness.

In a constant state of mental nepantilism, an Aztec word meaning torn between ways, *la mestiza* is a product of the transfer of the cultural and spiritual values of one group to another. Being tricultural, monolingual, bilingual or multilingual, speaking a patois, and in a state of perpetual transition, the *mestiza* faces the dilemma of the mixed breed: which collectivity does the daughter of a darkskinned mother listen to?

El choque de un alma atrapado entre el mundo del espiritu y el mundo de la técnica a veces la deja entullada. Cradled in one culture, sandwiched between two cultures, straddling all three cultures and their value systems, *la mestiza* undergoes a struggle of flesh, a struggle of borders, an inner war. Like all people, we perceive the version of reality that our culture communicates. Like others having or living in more than one culture we get multiple, often opposing messages. The coming together of two self-consistent but habitually incompatible frames of reference[3] causes *un choque,* a cultural collision.

Within us and within *la cultura chicana,* commonly held beliefs of the white culture attack commonly held beliefs of the Mexican culture, and both attack commonly held beliefs of the indigenous culture. Subconsciously, we see an attack on ourselves and our beliefs as a threat and we attempt to block with a counterstance.

But it is not enough to stand on the opposite river bank, shouting questions, challenging patriarchal, white conventions. A counterstance locks one into a duel of oppressor and oppressed; locked in mortal combat, like the cop and the criminal, both are reduced to a common denominator of violence. The counterstance refutes the dominant culture's views and beliefs, and, for this, it is proudly defiant. A reaction is limited by, and dependent on, what it is reacting against. Because the counterstance stems from a problem with authority—outer as well as inner—it's a step towards liberation from cultural domination. But it is not a way of life. At some point, on our way to a new consciousness, we will have to leave the opposite bank, the split between the two mortal combatants somehow healed so that we are on both shores at once and, at once, see through serpent and eagle eyes. Or perhaps we will decide to disengage from the dominant culture, write it off altogether as a lost cause, and cross the border into a wholly new and separate territory. Or we might go another route. The possibilities are numerous once we decide to act and not react.

A Tolerance For Ambiguity

These numerous possibilities leave *la mestiza* floundering in uncharted seas. In perceiving conflicting information and points of view, she is subjected to a swamping of her psychological borders. She has discovered that she can't hold concepts or ideas in rigid boundaries. The borders and walls that are supposed to keep the undesirable ideas out are entrenched habits and patterns of behavior; these habits and patterns are the enemy within. Rigidity means death. Only by remaining flexible is she able to stretch the psyche horizontally and vertically. *La Mestiza* constantly has to shift out of habitual formations; from convergent thinking, analytical reasoning that tends to use rationality to move toward a single goal (a Western mode), to divergent thinking,[4] characterized by movement away from set patterns and goals and toward a more whole perspective, one that includes rather than excludes.

The new *mestiza* copes by developing a tolerance for contradictions, a tolerance for ambiguity. She learns to be an Indian in Mexican culture, to be Mexican from an Anglo point of view. She learns to juggle cultures. She has a plural personality, she operates in a pluralistic mode—nothing is thrust out, the good, the bad and the ugly, nothing rejected, nothing abandoned. Not only does she sustain contradictions, she turns the ambivalence into something else.

She can be jarred out of ambivalence by an intense, and often painful, emotional event which inverts or resolves the ambivalence. I'm not sure exactly how. The work takes place underground, subconsciously. It is work that the soul performs. That focal point or fulcrum, that juncture where the *mestiza* stands, is where phenomena tend to collide. It is where the possibility of uniting all that is separate occurs. This assembly is not, one where severed or separated pieces merely come together. Nor is it a balancing, of opposing powers. In attempting to work out a synthesis, the self has added a third element which is greater than the sum of its severed parts. That third element is a new consciousness—a *mestiza* consciousness—and though it is a source of intense pain, its energy comes from a continual creative motion that keeps breaking down the unitary aspect of each new paradigm.

En unas pocas centuries, the future will belong to the *mestiza*. Because the future depends on the breaking, down of paradigms, it depends on the straddling of two or more cultures. By creating a new mythos—that is, a change in the way we perceive reality, the way we see ourselves and the ways we behave—*la mestiza* creates a new consciousness.

The work of *mestiza* consciousness is to break down the subject—object duality that keeps her a prisoner and to show in the flesh and through the images in her work how duality is transcended. The answer to the problem between the white race and the colored, between males and females, lies in healing the split that originates in the very foundation of our lives, our culture, our languages, our thoughts. A massive uprooting of dualistic thinking in the individual and collective consciousness is the beginning, of a long struggle, but one that could, in our best hopes, bring us to the end of rape, of violence, of war.

La encrucijada/the Crossroads

A chicken is being sacrificed
    at a crossroads, a simple mound of earth
a mud shrine for *Eshu*,
    Yoruba god of indeterminacy,

who blesses her choice of path.
She begins her journey.

Su cuerpo es una bocacalle. La mestiza has gone from being the sacrificial goat to becoming the officiating priestess at the crossroads.

As a *mestiza* I have no country, my homeland cast me out; yet all countries are mine because I am every woman's sister or potential lover. (As a lesbian I have no race, my own people disclaim me; but I am all races because there is the queer of me in all races.) I am cultureless because, as a feminist, I challenge the collective cultural/religious male derived beliefs of Indo-Hispanics and Anglos; yet I am cultured because I am participating in the creation of yet another culture, a new story to explain the world and our participation in it, a new value system with images and symbols that connect us to each other and to the planet. *Soy un amasamiento*, I am an act of kneading, of uniting and joining that not only has produced both a creature of darkness and a creature of light, but also a creature that questions the definitions of light and dark and gives them new meanings.

We are the people who leap in the dark, we are the people on the knees of the gods. In our flesh, Revolution works out the clash of cultures. It makes us crazy constantly, but if the center holds, we've made some kind of evolutionary step forward. *Nuestra alma el trabajo*, the opus, the great alchemical work; spiritual *mestizaje*, a "morphogenesis,"★ an inevitable unfolding. We have become the quickening serpent movement.

Indigenous like corn, like corn, the *mestiza* is a product of crossbreeding, designed for preservation under a variety of conditions. Like an ear of corn—a female seed-bearing organ—the *mestiza* is tenacious, tightly wrapped in the husks of her culture. Like kernels she clings to the cob; with thick stalks and strong brace roots, she holds tight to the earth—she will survive the crossroads.

Lavando y remojando el maíze en agua *de cal, despojando el pellejo. Moliendo, mixteando, amasando, hacienda tortillas de masa.*★★ She steeps the corn in lime, it swells, softens. With stone roller on *metate*, she grinds the corn, then grinds again. She kneads and moulds the dough, pats the round balls into *tortillas*.

> We are the porous rock in the stone metate
> squatting on the ground.
> We are the rolling pin, *el maíze y agua,*
> *la masa harina. Somos el amasijo.*
> *Somos lo* molido en el metate.
> We are the comal sizzling hot,
> the hot *tortilla*, the hungry mouth.
> We are the coarse rock.
> the mixed potion, *somos el molcajete.*
> We are the pestle, the comino, ajo, pimienta.
> We are the *chile colorado,*
> the green shoot that cracks the rock.
> We will abide.

NOTES

★To borrow chemist Ilya Prigogine's theory of "dissipative structures." Prigogine discovered that substances interact not in predictable ways as it was taught in science, but in different and fluctuating ways to produce new and more complex structures, a kind of birth he called "morphogenesis," which created unpredictable innovations.[5]

★★*Tortillas de* masa harina: corn tortillas are of two types, the smooth uniform ones made in a tortilla press and usually bought at a tortilla factory or supermarket, and *gorditas*, made by mixing masa with lard or shortening or butter (my mother sometimes puts in bits of bacon or *chicharrones*).

1. This is my own "take-off" on José Vasconcelos' idea. José Vasconcelos, *La Raza Cósmica: Missión de La Raza Ibero-Americana* (México: Aguilar S.A. de Ediciones, 1961)

2. Vasconcelos.

3. Arthur Koestler termed this "bisociation." Albert Rothenberg, *The Creative Process in Art, Science, and Other Fields* (Chicago, IL: University of Chicago Press, 1979), p. 12.

4. In part, I derive my definitions for "convergent" and "divergent" thinking from Rothenberg, pp. 12–13.

5. Harold Gilliam, "Searching for a New World View," *This World* (January, 1981), p. 23.

76

Canto, locura y poesía★

OLIVIA CASTELLANO

In Comstock, the Tex–Mex border town about 15 miles from the Rio Grande where I spent the first 12 years of my life, I saw the despair that poverty and hopelessness had etched in the faces of young Chicano men who, like my father, walked back and forth on the dusty path between Comstock and the Southern Pacific Railroad station. They would set out every day on rail carts to repair the railroad. The women of Comstock fared no better. Most married early, I had seen them in their kitchens toiling at the stove, with one baby propped on one hip and two toddlers tugging at their skirts. Or, they followed their working mothers' route, cleaning house and doing laundry for rich Texan ranchers who paid them a pittance. I decided very early that this was not the future I wanted.

In 1958 my father, tired of seeing days fade into each other without promise, moved us to California, where we became farmworkers in the San José area (then a major agricultural center). I saw the same futile look in the faces of young Chicanos

★From *Women's Review of Books*, Vol. VII, No. 5, Feb., 1990: pp. 18–20.

and Chicanas working beside my family. Those faces already lined so young with sadness made me deadly serious about my books and my education.

At a young age—between 11 and 14—I began my intellectual and spiritual rebellion against my parents and society. I fell in love with books and created space of my own where I could dare to dream. Yet, in school I remained shy and introverted, terrified of my white, male professors. In my adolescence, I rebelled against my mother's insistence that a Mexican girls should marry young, as she did at 18. But, I didn't care if my cousins Alicia and Anita were getting married and having babies early "I was put on this earth to make books, not babies!" I announced and ran into my room.

Books became my obsession. I wanted to read everything that I was not supposed to. By 14 I was already getting to know the Marquis de Sade, Rimbaud, Lautréamont, Whitman, Dostoyevsky, Marx. I came by these writers serendipitously. To get from home to Sacramento High School, I had to walk through one of the toughest neighborhoods in the city, Oak Park. There were men hanging out with liquor in brown paper bags, playing dice, shooting craps and calling from cars: "Hey, baby, get in here with me!" I'd run into the small Oak Park Library which turned out to have a little bit of everything. I would walk around staring at the shelves, killing time till the shifty-eyed men would go away.

The librarians knew and tolerated me with skepticism: "Are you sure you're going to read the Marquis de Sade? Do your parents know you're checking out this material? What are you doing with the Communist Manifesto?" One librarian even forbade me to check the books out, so I'd sit in the library reading for hours on end. Later, at 16 or 17, I was allowed to check out anything I wanted.

The librarians gave me *carte blanche* circulation, so it was that I came to grapple with tough language and ideas. These books were hot! Yet I also was obsessed with wanting to be pretty, mysterious, silent and sexy. I wanted to have long curly hair, red lips and long red nails; to wear black tight dresses and high heels. I wanted desperately to look like the sensuous femmes fatales of the Mexican cinema—María Félix, one of the most beautiful and famous of Mexico's screen goddesses, and Libertad Lamarque, the smoky-voiced, green-eyed Argentinian singer. These were the women I admired when my mother and I went to the movies. But these were my "outward" models. My "inward" models, the voices of the intellect that spoke to me when I shut the door to my room, were, as you have gathered, a writer of erotica, two mad surrealists, a crazy Romantic, an epileptic literary genius, and a radical socialist.

I needed to sabotage society in a major, intellectually radical way. I needed to be a warrior who would catch everyone off guard. But to be a warrior, you must never let your opponent figure you out. When the bullets of racism and sexism are flying at you, you must be very clever in deciding how you want to live. I knew that everything around me—school, teachers, television, friends, men, even my own parents, who in their own internalized racism and self-hatred didn't really believe I'd amount to much though they hoped like hell life would prove them wrong—everything was against me and this I understood fully.

To protect myself, I fell in love with Language—all of it, poems, stories, novels, plays, songs, biographies, "cuentos" or little vignettes, movies—all manifestations of spoken and written language. I fell in love with ideas, with essays by writers like Bacon and Montaigne. I began my serious reading crusade around age 11, when I was already convinced that books alone would save my life. Only through them and through songs, I felt, would I be free to shape some kind of future for myself.

I wanted to prove to anyone who cared to ask (though by now I was convinced no one gave a damn) that I, the daughter of a laborer-farmworker, could dare to be somebody. Try to imagine what it is like to be full of rage—rage at everything: at white teachers who could never pronounce my name (I was called anything from "Odilia" to "Otilia" to "Estela"); rage at those teachers who asked me point blank, "But how did you get to be so smart? You are Mexican, aren't you?"; rage at my 11th-grade English teacher who said to me in front of the whole class, "You stick to essay writing; never try to write a poem again because a poet you are not!" (This after I had worked for two diligent weeks on an imitation of "La Belle Dame Sans Merci"! Now I can laugh. Then it was pitiful).

From age 13, I was also angry at boys who hounded me for dates. When I'd reject them they'd yell, "So what do you plan to do for the rest of your life, fuck a book?" Angry at my Chicana classmates in high school who, perhaps jealous of my high grades, would acuse, "What are you trying to do, be like the whites?" And regrettably, I was angry at my parents, exasperated by their docility, their limited expectations of life. I knew they were proud; but sometimes, in their own misdirected rage (maybe afraid of my little successes), they would make painful comments. "Te vas a volver loca con esos jodidos libros" ("You'll go nuts with those damned books") was my mother's frequent warning. Or the even more sickening, "Esta nunca se va a casar." ("Give up on this one; she'll never get married.") This was the tenor of my adolescent years. When nothing on either side of the two cultures, Mexican or Anglo-American, affirms your existence, that is how rage is shaped.

While I managed to escape at least from the obvious entrapments—a teen pregnancy, a destructive early marriage—I did not escape years of being told I wasn't quite right, that because of my ethnicity and gender I was somehow defective, incomplete. Those years left wounds on my self-esteem, wounds so deep that even armed with my books and stolen knowledge I could not entirely escape deep feelings of unworthiness.

By the time I graduated from high school and managed to get a little scholarship to California State University, Sacramento, where I now teach (in 1962 it was called Sacramento State College), I had become very unassertive, immensely shy. I was afraid to look unfeminine if I raised my hand in class, afraid to seem ridiculous if I asked a "bad" question and all eyes turned on me. A deeper part of me was afraid that my rage might rear its ugly head and I would be considered "one more angry Mexican accusing everybody of racism." I was painfully concerned with my physical appearance: wasn't I supposed to look beautiful like Felix and Lamarque? Yet while I wanted to look pretty for the boys, the thought of having sex terrified me. What if I got pregnant, had to quit college and couldn't read my books any more? The more I feared boys, the more I made myself attractive for them, the more they made advances, the more I rejected them.

This constant tension sapped my energy and distracted me from my creative journeys into language. Oh, I would write little things (poems, sketches for stories, journal entries), but I was afraid to show them to anyone. Besides, no one knew I was writing them. I was so frightened by my white, male professors, especially in the English department—they looked so arrogant and were so ungiving of their knowledge—that I didn't have the nerve to major in English, though it was the subject I loved.

Instead, I chose to major in French. The "Parisiens" and "Québecois" in the French department faculty admired my French accent: "Mademoiselle, êtes-vous certaine que vous n'êtes pas Parisienne?" they would ask. In short, they cared. They engaged me in dialogue, asked why I preferred to study French instead of Spanish ("I already know Spanish," I'd say.) So French became my adopted language. I could play with it, sing songs in it and sound exotic. It complemented my Spanish; besides, I did-n't have to worry about speaking English with my heavy Spanish accent and risk be-ing ridiculed. At one point, my spoken French was better than my oral Spanish and my written French has remained better than my written Spanish.

Thus, at 23, armed with a secondary school teaching credential and a B.A. in French with an English minor, I became a high school teacher of French and English. Soon after that, I began to work for a school district where the majority of the students were Chicanos and Blacks from families on welfare and/or from households run by women.

After two years of high school teaching, I returned to Cal State at Sacramento for the Master's degree. Professionally and artistically, it was the best decision I have ever made. The Master's program in which I was accepted was a pilot program in its second year at CSU Sacramento. Called the "Mexican American Experienced Teach-ers Fellowship," it was run by a team of anthropology professors, central among whom was Professor Steven Arvizu. The program was designed to turn us graduates into "agents of social change." It was 1969 and this was one of the first federally funded (Title V) programs to address Mexican-American students' needs by re-educating their teachers.

My interests were literary, but all 20 of us "fellows" had to get an M.A. in social anthropology, since this experiment took the "anthropolgizing education" approach. We studied social dynamics, psycholinguistics, history of Mexico, history of the American Southwest, community activism, confrontational strategies and the nature of the Chicano Movement. The courses were eye-openers. I had never heard the terms Chicano, biculturalism, marginality, assimilation, Chicanismo, protest art. I had never heard of César Chávez and the farmworkers nor of Luis Valdéz and his Teatro Campesino. I had never studied the nature of racism and identity. The philosophy of the program was that culture is a powerful tool for learning, self-expression, solidarity and positive change. Exploring it can help Chicano students understand their bicul-tural circumstances.

The program brought me face to face with nineteen other Chicano men and women, all experienced public school teachers like myself, with backgrounds like mine. The program challenged every aspect of my life. Through group counseling, group encounter, classroom interaction, course content and community involvement I was allowed to express my rage and to examine it in the company of peers who had a similar anger. Most of our instructors, moreover, were Chicano or white professors sensitive to Chicanos. For the first time, at 25, I had found my role models. I vowed to do for other students what these people had done for me.

Eighteen years of teaching, primarily white women students, Chicanos, and Blacks at California State University, Sacramento have led me to see myself less as a teacher and more as a cultural worker, struggling against society to undo the damage of years of abuse. I continue to see myself as a warrior empowered by my rage. Racism and sexism leave two clear-cut scars on my students: internalized self-hatred and fear of their own creative passion, in my view the two most serious obstacles in the classroom. Confronting this two-headed monster made me razor-sharp. Given their tragic personal stories, the hope in my students' eyes reconfirms daily the incred-ible beauty, the tenacity of the human spirit.

Teaching white women students (ages 30–45) is no different from working with Chicano and Black students (both men and women): you have to bring about changes in the way they view themselves, their abilities, their right to get educated, and their relation to a world that has systematically oppressed them simply for being who they are. You have to help them channel and understand the seething rage they carry deep inside, a rage which, left unexpressed, can turn them against each other and, more sadly, against themselves.

I teach four courses per semester: English 109G, Writing for Proficiency for Bilingual Bidialectal Students (a course taken mainly by Chicano and Black students, ages 19–24); English 115A, Pedagogy/Language Arts for Prospective Elementary School Teachers (course taken mainly by women aged 25–45, 50 percent white, 50 percent Chicano); English 180G, Chicano Literature, an advanced studies General Education course for non-English majors (taken by excellent students, aged 24–45, about 40 percent white, 40 percent Chicano, 20 percent Black/Vietnamese/Filipino/South American). The fourth course is English 1, Basic Language Skills, a pre-freshman composition course taken primarily by Black and Chicano freshmen, male and female, aged 18–22, who score too low on the English Placement Test to be placed in "regular" Freshman Composition.

Mine is a teaching load that, in my early teaching years, used to drive me close to insanity from physical, mental and spiritual exhaustion—spiritual from having internalized my students' pain. Perhaps not fully empowered myself, not fully emplumed in the feather of my own creativity (to borrow the "emplumada" metaphor coined by Lorna Dee Cervantes, the brilliant Chicana poet), I allowed their rage to become part of mine. This kind of rage can kill you. And so through years of working with these kinds of students I have learned to make my spirit strong with "canto, locura y poesia" (song, madness and poetry).

Truly, it takes a conjurer, a magus with all the teaching cards up her sleeve, to deal with the fragmented souls that show up in my classes. Among the Chicanos and Blacks, I get ex-offenders (mostly men but occasionally a woman who has done time), orphans, single women heads of household, high school dropouts who took years to complete their Graduation Equivalency Diploma.

I get women who have been raped or have been sexually abused either by a father figure or by male relatives—Sylvia Tracey, for example, a 30–year-old Chicana feminist, mother of two, whose parents pressured her to marry her rapist and who is going through divorce after ten years of marriage. I get battered women who are still in a violent marriage or finally got the courage to say enough. And, of course, I get the young Chicano and Black young yuppies who don't believe the world existed before 1970, who know nothing about the sixties' history of struggle and student protest, who—in the case of the Chicanos—feel ashamed that their parents speak English with an accent or were once farmworkers. Most of my students are ashamed of their writing skills and have never once been told that they could succeed in school.

Annetta Jones is typical. A 45–year-old Black woman who single-handedly raised three children, all college-educated and successful, she is still married to a man who served ten years in prison for being a "hit man." She visited him faithfully in prison and underwent all kinds of humiliation at the hands of correctional officers—even granting them sexual favors for conjugal visits with her husband. When her husband completed his time, he fell in love with a young woman from Chicago, where he now lives.

Among my white women students (ranging in age from 25 to 40, though occasionally I get a 45- or 50-year-old "re-entry" woman who wants to be an elementary or high school teacher and "help out young kids so they won't have to go through what I went through"—their exact words) I get women who are either divorced or divorcing; rarely do I get a "happily" married woman. This is especially true of the white women who take my Chicano literature and my credential-pedagogy classes. Take Lynne Trebeck, for instance, a white woman about 40 years old who runs a farm. When she entered the university, her husband objected, so she divorced him! They continue to live in the same house (he refused to leave), "but now he has no control over me," as she told me triumphantly midway through the semester. She has two sons, 15 and 18-years-old; as a young woman, she did jail time as the accomplice of a convicted drug dealer.

Every semester I get two or three white lesbian feminists. This semester there was Vivianne Rose, about 40, in my Chicano literature class. On the first day of class she wore Levi pants, a baggy sweat shirt, white tennis shoes and a beige baseball cap. But, apparently sensing too much conservatism in the students, and knowing that she wanted to be an elementary school teacher, she chose to conceal her sexual orientation. By the end of the first week she had switched to ultrafeminine dresses and flowery skirts, brightly colored blouses, nylons and medium-heeled black shoes, along with lipstick and eye makeup. When she spoke in class she occasionally made references to "my husband who is Native-American." She and Sylvia Tracey became very close friends. Halfway through the course, they informed me that "Shit, it's about time we tell her." (This from Sylvia.) "Oh, hell, why not," Vivianne said; "my husband is a woman." Vivianne Rose lived on a reservation for years and taught Native-American children to read and write. She speaks "Res" (reservation speech) and has adopted her "husband's" last name.

Among my white women students there are also divorced women who are raising two to four children, usually between the ages of eight and seventeen. The most confident are the older, widowed white women who are taking classes for their own enjoyment, not for a degree. They also tell stories of torment: rapes, beatings, verbal and emotional harassment from their men. On occasion, as I said, I get women who have done jail time, usually for taking the rap for drug-connected boyfriends. Among the older married women, the litany echoes again and again: "My husband doesn't really want me in school." "My husband doesn't really care what I do in college as long as I take care of his needs and the kids' needs." "My husband doesn't really know what I'm studying—he has never asked and I've never told him."

Most of the white women as well as the minority students come to the university through special programs. There is the "Educational Opportunity Program" for students who do not meet all university entrance requirements or whose high school grade point average is simply too low for regular admission. The "Student Affirmative Action Program" is for students who need special counseling and tutoring to bring their academic skills up to par or deal with emotional trauma. And the "College Assistance Migrant Program" assists students whose parents are migrant farmworkers in the agricultural areas surrounding the city of Sacramento. There is a wonderful program called PASAR for older women students entering the university for the first time or returning after a multiple-year absence. The Women's Resource Center also provides small grants and scholarships for these re-entry women. A large number of my students (both white and minority women) come severely handicapped in their basic language, math and science skills; a large number have never used a computer. It is not uncommon (especially among Chicanos and Blacks) to get an incoming student who scores at the fifth- and sixth-grade reading levels. Imagine the damage I must help repair!

The task is Herculean, the rewards spiritually fulfilling. I would not have it any other way. Every day is a lesson in humility and audacity. That my students have endured nothing but obstacles and put-downs yet have the courage and strength to seek a college education, humbles me. They are, like me, walking paradoxes. They have won against all the odds, (their very presence on campus attests to that). Yet, they haven't won: their deeply ingrained sense of inferiority convinces them that they are not worthy of success.

This is my challenge, I embrace it wholeheartedly. There is no other place I'd rather be, no profession more noble. Sure, I sometimes have doubts; every day something new, sad, even tragic comes up. Just as I was typing this article, for instance, Vicky, one of the white students in my Chicano literature class, called in tears, barely able to talk. "Professor, I can't possibly turn in my paper to your mailbox by four o'-clock," she cried. "Everything in my house is falling apart! My husband just fought with my oldest daughter [from a previous marriage], has thrown her out of the house. He's running up and down the street, yelling and threatening to leave us. And I'm sitting here trying to write your paper! I'm going crazy. I feel like walking away from it all!" I took an hour from writing this article to help her contain herself. By the end of our conversation, I had her laughing. I also put her in touch with a counselor friend of mine and gave her a two-day extension for her final paper. And naturally I was one more hour late with my own writing!

I teach in a totally non-traditional way. I use every trick in the book: much positive reinforcement, both oral and written; mny one-on-one conferences. I help women develop a network women with each other, refer them to professor friends who can help them; connect them with graduate students and/or former students who are already pursuing careers. In the classroom, I force students to stand in front of their classmates, to explain concepts or read and evaluate their essays aloud. I create panels representing opposing viewpoints and hold debates—much oral participation, role-playing, reading their own texts. Their own writing and opinions become part of the course. On exams I ask them questions about their classmates' presentations. I meet with individual students in local coffee houses or taverns; it's much easier to talk about personal pain over coffee or a beer or a glass of wine than in my office. My students, for the most part, do not have a network of support outside of the university. There are no supportive husbands, lovers (except on rare occasions, as with my lesbian students), no relatives saying, "Yes, you can do it."

Is it any wonder that when these students enter the university they have a deep sense of personal shame about everything—poor skills, being older students. They are angry at the schools for having prepared them poorly; at their parents for not having had high enough expectations of them or (in the case of the women) for having allowed them to marry so young. Sylvia, my Chicana feminist student, put it best when I was pointing out incomplete sentences in her essay: "Where the hell was I when all this was being taught in high school? And why didn't anybody give a damn that I wasn't learning it?"

I never teach content for the first two weeks of the semester. I talk about anger, sexism, racism and the sixties—a time when people believed in something larger than themselves. I allow them space to talk—about prisons and why so many Chicano and Black young men are behind bars in California; why people fear differences; why our society is gripped by homophobia. I give my students a chance to talk about their anger ("coraje" in Spanish). I often read them a poem by my friend and colleague José Montoya, called "Eslipping and Esliding," in which he talks about "locura" (craziness) and says that with a little locura, a little eslipping and esliding, we can survive the madness that surrounds us. We laugh at ourselves, sharing our tragic, tattered pasts, undoing everything and letting the anger out. "I know why so many of you are afraid of doing well," I say. "You've been told you can't do it, and you're so angry about it, you can't concentrate." Courage takes pure concentration. By the end of these initial two or three weeks we have become friends and defined our mutual respect. Only then do we enter the course content.

I am not good at endings; I prefer to celebrate beginnings. The struggle continues, and the success stories abound. Students come back, year after year, to say " Thank you." Usually, I pull these visitors into the classroom: "Tell my class that they can do it. Tell them how you did it!" The visitors start talking and can't stop. "Look, Olivia, when I first came into your class," said Sylvia, "I couldn't even put a fucking sentence together. And now look at me, three years later I'm even writing poetry!"

77

Chicana Lesbians: Fear and Loathing in the Chicano Community*

CARLA TRUJILLO

The vast majority of Chicano heterosexuals perceive Chicana lesbians as a threat to the community. Homophobia, that is, irrational fear of gay or lesbian people and/or behaviors, accounts for part of the heterosexist response to the lesbian community. However, I argue that Chicana lesbians are perceived as a greater threat to the Chicano community because their existence disrupts the established order of male dominance, and raises the consciousness of many Chicana women regarding their own independence and control. Some writers have addressed these topics (Moraga 1983, pp. 103, 105, 111, 112, 117), however an analysis of the complexities of lesbian existence alongside this perceived threat has not been undertaken. While this essay is by no means complete, it attempts to elucidate the underlying basis of these fears which, in

*Chicana Lesbians: The Girls Our Mothers Warned Us About edited by Carla Trujillo (Berkeley: Third Woman Press 1991: pp. 86–194).

the very act of the lesbian existence, disrupt the established norm of patriarchal oppression.

Sexuality

As lesbians, our sexuality becomes the focal issue of dissent. The majority of Chicanas, both lesbian and heterosexual, are taught that our sexuality must conform to certain modes of behavior. Our culture voices shame upon us if we go beyond the criteria of passivity and repression, or doubts in our virtue if we refuse (Castillo 1991; Alarcón, Castillo, and Moraga 1989). We, as women, are taught to suppress our sexual desires and needs by conceding all pleasure to the male. As Chicanas, we are commonly led to believe that even talking about our participation and satisfaction in sex is taboo. Moreover, we (as well as most women in the United States) learn to hate our bodies, and usually possess little knowledge of them. Lourdes Arguelles (1990) did a survey on the sexuality of 373 immigrant Latina women and found that over half of the women possessed little knowledge of their reproductive systems or their own physiology. Most remarked they "just didn't look down there."

Not loving our bodies affects how we perceive ourselves as sexual beings. As lesbians, however, we have no choice but to confront our sexuality before we can confront our lesbianism. Thus the commonly held viewpoint among heterosexuals that we are "defined by our sexuality" is, in a way, partially true. If we did not bring our sexuality into consciousness, we would not be able to confront ourselves and come out.

After confronting and then acknowledging our attraction, we must, in turn, learn to reclaim that what we're told is bad, wrong, dirty, and taboo-namely our bodies, and our freedom to express ourselves in them. Too often we internalize the homophobia and sexism of the larger society, as well as that of our own culture, which attempts to keep us from loving ourselves. As Norma Alarcón states, "[Chicana lesbians] must act to negate the negation."[1] A Chicana lesbian must learn to love herself, both as a woman and a sexual being, before she can love another. Loving another women not only validates one's own sexuality, but also that of the other woman, by the very act of loving. Understanding this, a student in a workshop Cherríe Moraga and I conducted on lesbian sexuality stated, "Now I get it. Not only do you have to learn to love your own vagina, but someone else's too."[2] It is only then that the subsequent experiences of love and commitment, passion and remorse can also become our dilemmas, much like those of everyone else. The effort to consciously reclaim our sexual selves forces Chicanas to either confront their own sexuality or, in refusing, castigate lesbians as *vendidas* to the race, blasphemers to the Church, atrocities against nature, or some combination.

Identification

For many Chicanas, our identification as women, that is, as complete women, comes from the belief that we need to be connected to a man (Flores-Ortíz 1990). Ridding ourselves of this parasitic identification is not always easy, for we grow up, as my Chicana students have pointed out, defined in a male context: daddy's girl, some guy's girlfriend, wife, or mother. Vying for a man's attention compromises our own personal and intellectual development. We exist in a patriarchal society that undervalues women.[3] We are socialized to undervalue ourselves, as well as anything associated with the concept of self. Our voice is considered less significant, our needs and desires secondary. As the Chicanas in the MALCS workshop indicated (Flores-Ortíz 1990), our toleration of unjust behavior from men, the church, the established order, is considered an attribute. How much pain can we bear in the here-and-now so that we may be better served in the afterlife? Martyrdom, the cloth of denial, transposes itself into a gown of cultural beauty.

Yet, an alliance with a man grants a woman heterosexual privileges, many of which are reified by the law, the church, our families and, of course, "La Causa." Women who partake in the privileges of male sexual alliance may often do so at the cost of their own sense of self, since they must often subvert their needs, voice, intellect, and personal development in these alliances. These are the conditional contradictions commonly prescribed for women by the patriarchy in our culture and in the larger society. Historically, women have been viewed as property (Sanday 1974). Though some laws may have changed, ideologically little else has. Upon marriage, a father feels he can relinquish "ownership" and "responsibility" of his daughter to her husband. The Chicana feminist who confronts this subversion, and critiques the sexism of the Chicano community, will be called *vendida* if she finds the "male defined and often anti-feminist" values of the community difficult to accept (Moraga 1983, p. 113).

The behaviors necessary in the "act of pursuing a man" often generate competition among women, leading to betrayal of one another (Castillo 1991; Moraga 1983, p. 136). When a woman's sense of identity is tied to that of a man, she is dependent on this relationship for her own self-worth. Thus, she must compete with other women for his attention. When the attention is then acknowledged and returned, she must work to ensure that it is maintained. Ensuring the protection of this precious commodity generates suspicion among women, particularly single, unattached women. Since we're all taught to vie for a man's attention, we become, in a sense, sexual suspects to one another. The responsibility is placed entirely upon the woman with little thought given to the suspected infidelity of the man.

We should ask what role the man places himself in regarding his support of these behaviors. After all, the woman is commonly viewed as his possession. Hence, in the typical heterosexual relationship both parties are abetting the other, each in a quest that does not improve the status of the woman (nor, in my view, that of the man), nor the consciousness of either of them.

How does the Chicana lesbian fit into this picture? Realistically, she doesn't. As a lesbian she does many things simultaneously: she rejects "compulsory heterosexuality" (Rich 1980); she refuses to partake in the "game" of competition for men; she confronts her own sexuality; and she challenges the norms placed upon her by culture and society, whose desire is to subvert her into proper roles and places. This is done, whether consciously or unconsciously, by the very aspect of her existence. In the course of conducting many workshops on lesbian sexuality, Chicana heterosexuals have often indicated to me that they do not associate with lesbians, since it could be assumed that either (1) they too, must be lesbians, or (2) if they're not, they must be selling out to Anglo culture, since it is implied that Chicana lesbians do and thus any association with lesbians implicates them as well. This equivocation of sexual practice and cultural alliance is a retrograde ideology, quite possibly originating from the point of view that the only way to uplift the species is to propagate it. Thus, homosexuality is seen as "counter-revolutionary."

Heterosexual Chicanas need not be passive victims of the cultural onslaught of social control. If anything, Chicanas are usually the backbone of every *familia* [family] for it is their strength and self-sacrifice which often keeps the family going. While heterosexual Chicanas have a choice about how they want to live their lives (read: how they choose to form their identities),[4] Chicana lesbians have very little choice, because their quest for self-identification comes with the territory. This is why "coming out" can be a major source of pain for Chicana lesbians, since the basic fear of rejection by family and community is paramount.[5] For our own survival, Chicana lesbians must continually embark on the creation or modification of our own familia, since this institution, as traditionally constructed, may be non-supportive of the Chicana lesbian existence (Moraga 1986, p. 58).

Motherhood

The point of view that we are not complete human beings unless we are attached to a male is further promoted by the attitude that we are incomplete as women unless we become mothers. Many Chicanas are socialized to believe that our chief purpose in life is raising children (Moraga 1983, p. 113). Not denying the fact that motherhood can be a beautiful experience, it becomes rather, one of the few experiences not only supported, but expected in a traditional Chicano community. Historically, in dual-headed households, Chicanas (as well as other women) were relegated to the tasks of home care and child rearing, while the men took on the task of earning the family's income (Sacks 1974). Economic need, rather than feminist consciousness, has been the primary reason for the change to two-income households. Nevertheless, for many Chicanas, motherhood is still seen by our culture as the final act in establishing our "womanhood."

Motherhood among Chicana lesbians does exist. Many lesbians are mothers as by-products of divorce or earlier liaisons with men. Anecdotal evidence I have obtained from many Chicana lesbians in the community indicates that lesbians who choose to become mothers in our culture are seen as aberrations of the traditional concept of motherhood, which stresses male-female partnership. Choosing to become a mother via alternative methods of insemination, or even adopting children, radically departs from society's view that lesbians and gay men cannot "successfully" raise children. Therefore, this poses another threat to the Chicano community, since Chicana lesbians are perceived as failing to partake in one of their chief obligations in life.

Religion

Religion, based on the tradition of patriarchal control and sexual, emotional, and psychological repression, has historically been a dual means of hope for a better afterlife and social control in the present one. Personified by the *Virgen de Guadalupe*, the concept of motherhood and martyrdom go hand in hand in the Catholic religion. Nevertheless, as we are all aware, religion powerfully affects our belief systems concerning life and living. Since the Pope does not advocate a homosexual lifestyle, lesbians and gay men are not given sanction by the largely Catholic Chicano community—hence, fulfilling our final threat to the established order. Chicana lesbians who confront their homosexuality must, in turn, confront (for those raised in religious households) religion, bringing to resolution some compromise of religious doctrine and personal lifestyle.[6] Many choose to alter, modify, or abandon religion, since it is difficult to advocate something which condemns our existence. This exacerbates a sense of alienation for Chicana lesbians who feel they cannot wholly participate in a traditional religion.

In sum, Chicana lesbians pose a threat to the Chicano community for a variety of reasons, primarily because they threaten the established social hierarchy of patriarchal control. In order to "come-out," Chicana lesbians must confront their sexuality, therefore bringing a taboo subject to consciousness. By necessity, they must learn to love their bodies, for it is also another woman's body which becomes the object of love. Their identities as people alter and become independent of men, hence there is no need to submit to, or perform the necessary behaviors that cater to wooing the male ego. Lesbians (and other feminist women) would expect to treat and be treated by men as equals. Men who have traditionally interacted with women on the basis of their gender (read femininity) first, and their brains second, are commonly left confused when the lesbian (or feminist) fails to respond to the established pecking order.

Motherhood, seen as exemplifying the final act of our existence as women, is practiced by lesbians, but usually without societal or cultural permission. Not only is it believed that lesbians cannot become mothers (hence, not fulfilling our established purpose as women), but if we do, we morally threaten the concept of motherhood as a sanctified entity, since lesbianism doesn't fit into its religious or cultural confines. Lastly, religion, which does not support the homosexual lifestyle, seeks to repudiate us as sinners if we are "practicing": and only tolerable if not. For her personal and psychological survival, the Chicana lesbian must confront and bring to resolution these established cultural and societal conflicts. These "confrontations" go against many of the values of the Chicano community, since they pose a threat to the established order of male control. Our very existence challenges this order, and in some cases challenges the oftentimes ideologically oppressive attitudes toward women.

It is widely assumed that lesbians and heterosexual women are in two completely different enclaves in regard to the type and manner of the oppression they must contend with. As illustrated earlier in this essay, this indeed, may be true. There do exist, however, different levels of patriarchal oppression which affect all of us as women, and when combined inhibit our collective liberation. If we, as lesbian and heterosexual Chicana women, can open our eyes and look at all that we share as women, we might find commonalities even among our differences. First and foremost among them is the status of *women*. Uttered under any breath, it implies subservience; cast to a lower position not only in society, but in our own culture as well.

Second, the universal of the body. We are all female and subject to the same violations as any woman in society. We must contend with the daily threat of rape, molestation, and harassment—violations which affect all of us as women, lesbian or not.

As indicated earlier, our sexuality is suppressed by our culture—relegated to secrecy or embarrassment, implicating us as wrongful women if we profess to fulfill ourselves sexually. Most of us still grow up inculcated with the dichotomy of the "good girl–bad girl" syndrome. With virtue considered as the most admirable quality, it's easy to understand which we choose to partake. This generates a cloud of secrecy around any sexual activity, and leads, I am convinced, to our extremely high teenage pregnancy rate, simply because our families refuse to acknowledge the possibility that young women may be sexually active before marriage.

We are taught to undervalue our needs and voices. Our opinions, viewpoints, and expertise are considered secondary to those of males—even if we are more highly trained. Time and again, I have seen otherwise sensible men insult the character of a woman when they are unable to belittle her intellectual capacities.[7] Character assassinations are commonly disguised in the familiar "*vendida* to the race" format. Common it seems, because it functions as the ultimate insult to any conscientious *política*. Because many of us are taught that our opinions matter little, we have difficulty at times, raising them. We don't trust what we think, or believe in our merits. Unless we are encouraged to do so, we have difficulty thinking independently of male opinion. Chicanas must be constantly encouraged to speak up, to voice their opinions, particularly in areas where no encouragement has ever been provided.

As Chicanas (and Chicanos), most of us are subject to the effects of growing up in a culture besieged by poverty and all the consequences of it: lack of education, insufficient political power, and health care, disease, and drugs. We are all subject to the effects of a society that is racist, classist, and homophobic, as well as sexist, and patriarchally dominant. Colonization has imposed itself and affected the disbursement of status and the collective rights of us as individuals. Chicana women are placed in this order at a lower position, ensconced within a tight boundary which limits our voices, our bodies, and our brains. In classic dissonant fashion, many of us become complicit in this (since our survival often depends on it) and end up rationalizing our very own limitations.

The collective liberation of people begins with the collective liberation of half its constituency—namely women. The view that our hierarchical society places Chicanos at a lower point, and they in turn must place Chicanas lower still, is outmoded and politically destructive. Women can no longer be relegated to supporting roles. Assuaging delicate male egos as a means of establishing our identities is retrograde and subversive to our own identities as women. Chicanas, both lesbian and heterosexual, have a dual purpose ahead of us. We must fight for our own voices as women, since this will ultimately serve to uplift us as a people.

NOTES

1. Personal communication with the author at MALCS (Mujeres Activas en Letras y Cambio Social) Summer Research Institute, 3–6 August 1990, University of California, Los Angeles.

2. Chicana Leadership Conference, Workshop on Chicana Lesbians, 8–10 February 1990, University of California, Berkeley.

3. There are multitudes of feminist books and periodicals which attest to the subordinate position of women in society. Listing them is beyond the scope of this essay.

4. As Moraga (1983, p. 103) states, "only the woman intent on the approval can be affected by the disapproval."

5. Rejection by family and community is also an issue for gay men, however their situation is muddied by the concomitant loss of power.

6. Joseph Cardinal Ratzinger, Prefect, and Alberto Bouone, Titula Archbishop of Caesarea in Numedia, Secretary, "Letter to the Bishops of the Catholic Church in the Pastoral Care of Homosexual Persons:" 1 October 1986. Approved by Pope John Paul II, adopted in an ordinary session of the Congregation for the Doctrine of Faith and ordered published (Grammick and Furey 1988, pp. 1–10).

7. This occurred often to the women MEChA, (Movimiento Estudiantil Chicano de Aztlán) leaders who were on the Berkeley campus between 1985–1989. It also occurred to a Chicana panel member during a 1990 National Association for Chicano Studies presentation, when a Chicano discussant disagreed with the recommendations based on her research.

REFERENCES

Alarcón, Norma, Ana Castillo, and Cherríe Moraga, eds. 1989. "The Sexuality of Latinas," *Third Woman*, 4.

Arguelles, Lourdes. 1990. "A Survey of Latina Immigrant Sexuality." Paper read at National Association for Chicano Studies Conference, 29 March–1 April, Albuquerque, New Mexico.

Castillo, Ana. 1991. "La Macha: Toward a Beautiful Whole Self." In *Chicana Lesbians: The Girls Our Mothers Warned Us About*, ed. Carla Trujillo. Berkeley: Third Woman Press.

Flores-Ortíz, Yvette. 1990. Workshop on Chicana Lesbians at MALCS (Mujeres Activas en Letras y Cambio Social) Summer Research Institute, 3–6 August, at University of California, Los Angeles.

Gramick, Jeannine, and Pat Furey, eds. 1988. *The Vatican and Homosexuality*. New York: Crossroad Publishing Co.

Moraga, Cherríe. 1983. *Loving in the War Years: Lo que nunca pasó por sus labios*. Boston: South End Press.

Moraga, Cherríe. 1986. *Giving Up the Ghost*. Los Angeles: West End Press.

Rich, Adrienne. 1980. "Cumpulsory Heterosexuality and Lesbian Existence." In *Women: Sex and Sexuality,* eds. Catherine R. Stimpson and Ethel Spector Person, pp. 62–91. Chicago: University of Chicago Press.

Sacks, Karen. 1974. "Engles Revisited: Women, the Organization of Production and Privately Property." In *Women, Culture and Society*, eds. Michelle Rosaldo and Louise Lamphere, pp. 207–222. Stanford: Stanford University Press.

Sanday, Peggy. 1974. "Female Status in the Public Domain." In *Women, Culture and Society*, eds. Michelle Rosaldo and Louise Lamphere, pp. 189–206. Stanford: Stanford University Press.

78

---

*Interview with Sandra Cisneros** *

FEROZA JUSSAWALLA AND REED WAY DASENBACK

F. J.: It strikes me as you are describing your new novel that one of the things it is about is class politics. What would you say your politics are now?

Cisneros: I have lived in socialist countries, so I can't call myself a socialist, because I know that doesn't work. When I traveled in Europe for a year, I went from country to country and I met women and men, and women helped me and men helped me, but it turned out to be too expensive when you got anything free from a man (*laughter*), so I realized I'd only depend on women. Women helped me and they asked for nothing in return, and they gave me great compassion and love when I was

*From *Interviews with Writers of the Post-Colonial World,* edited by Feroza Jussawall and Reedway Dasenbrack (Jackson, Mississippi and London: University Press of Mississippi, 1992: pp. 298–301).

feeling lost and alone. I, in turn, listened to their stories, and I think I made so many friendships that crossed borders. It was like we all came from the same country, the women, we all had the same problems. I don't know what my politics are, except my stories tell it to you. I can't give it to you as an -ism or an -ist.

F. J.: How about as feminist?

Cisneros: Well, yes—it's a feminism, but it's a feminism that is very different from the feminism of upper-class women. It's a feminism that's very much tied into my class.

F. J.: What would be the difference?

Cisneros: I guess my feminism and my race are the same thing to me. They're tied in one to another, and I don't feel an alliance or an allegiance with upper-class white women. I don't. I can listen to them and on some level as a human being I can feel great compassion and friendships; but they have to move from their territory to mine, because I know their world. But they don't know mine. Then I moved to Texas, and that made me so angry. I don't know why Texas did that to me. Texas made me angry. In some way that I never had before, I started getting racist towards white people. I was wandering around like this colonized fool before, trying to be like my women friends in school. I didn't have any white women friends when I was in Texas. Once, Norma Alarcón [associate Professor of Chicano/Ethnic Studies at U.C. Berkeley] came to visit me when I was working in San Antonio and she said, "Don't you have any white friends?" It suddenly occurred to me that she hadn't met one and I thought, "I don't!" You know, that's because I was working in the barrio, I was doing community arts, I didn't have time. White people never came to the neighborhood where I worked. I wasn't about to go into their neighborhood and start telling them about Chicano art. I was creating Chicano art, and I was bringing Chicano writers to the neighborhood. I was up to my elbows in work. I didn't have time to be going off to UTSA [University of Texas, San Antonio] telling them where Chicano writers are.

I was committed to the neighborhood; I was committed to creating a small press book fair—the first one that was there. And if people were scared of my neighborhood, well, they better start thinking what our cultural center was all about to begin with and who we were supposed to serve first. Something ugly happened during that time that I didn't realize. I have to say now that I'm in a more balanced place than I was at that period. And so my politics have been changing, and some of my white women friends who have come into my life—I think it was divine providence that put them there—have taught me a lot. Those white women friends who have bothered to learn about my culture have entered into my life now and have taught me something. Maybe a little sliver of glass of the Snow Queen in my heart has dissolved a bit. But I'm still angry about some things, and those issues are going to come up in my next book.

F. J.: What are those?

Cisneros: I'm really mad at Mexican men, because Mexican men are the men I love the most and they disappoint me the most. I think they disappoint me the most because I love them the most. I don't care about the other men so much. They don't affect my personal politics because they're not in my sphere whereas Latino men, and specifically Mexican men, are the ones that I want to be with the most. And they keep disappointing me. I see so many intelligent Mexican women in Texas and they can't find a Mexican man because our Mexican men are with white women. What does that say about Mexican men? How do they feel about themselves if they won't go out with Mexican women, especially professional Mexican women? What does that say about themselves? They must not love themselves or, like someone said, "You must not love your mama." You know? You must not. That's an issue we talk about only among ourselves—the Latina women. That's really hard for me to tell my white women friends and make them understand without offending them. And these issues have to come up, and they will come up. Now these are some of the things on my agenda that I didn't get to in this book, but I'll get to in the next one.

F. J.: Could it be that you are an exception among Latina women?

Cisneros: No! I'm not the exception! I came to Texas, I met so many major mountain movers here, especially in Texas. The Chicanas I met in Texas, my God they're something! They're like *nopalitos* [cactus]. And I think it's because they're like the landscape. But it's hard to be a woman in Texas.

F. J.: They are not women who want to assume the traditional Mexican female role?

Cisneros: I have to say that the traditional role is kind of a myth. I think the traditional Mexican woman is a fierce woman. There's a lot of victimization but we are also fierce. We are very fierce. Our mothers had been fierce. Our women may be victimized but they are still very, very fierce and very strong. I really do believe that.

F. J.: Is the same kind of gender politics involved in writing?

Cisneros: How specifically?

F. J.: Certainly, male Chicano writers were recognized and published before the women. Do you think that's a function of some of the same kinds of things you've been talking about?

Cisneros: The men who were published first, Tomás Rivera, Rudolfo Anaya, Rolando Hinojosa, they were all in universities, no? Whereas with the women, it's taken us this long to get educated. Or some of them have educated their husbands first. It's taken us a while to get to this level where we are educated enough so that we can feel confident enough to even compete. It's taken us this long to take care of our sense of self. There's a lot of stuff going on with women, as far as getting your education, and as far as figuring out you don't have to go the route that society puts on you. Men are already in a privileged position. They don't have to fight against patriarchy; it put them in a great place. But the women did; it took us a little while to figure out, "I don't have to get married just yet," or "Wait a second, I don't have to have a baby now." And some of us figured it out a few babies later.

I think it took a little while for the women who wanted to get their education, and to fight for that education, because our fathers didn't want us to go to school or they wanted us to go to school to get married. As for me, I went through great trauma in my twenties trying to figure out that my life had no role model, so I had to invent that. I don't know if Rolando Hinojosa went through the trauma of wondering if he should have children in his twenties and should he get married. I don't think he did. He had other pressures, supporting his family, sure, but I had pressures too. You know, we all did. I wasn't even applying for a job in a university with an MFA. Imagine that. With an MFA from one of the famous writing schools, and even with an NEA I didn't dare apply for a job at a university. I was making $12,000 a year working at an alternative high school in inner-city Chicago when I came out of Iowa. Why? Because as women, we think we're not good enough. Because as people of color, we have been led to believe, we're colonized to think, we're not smart enough, we're not good enough, we have nothing to share at the university. And where would I have gone at the university had I gone into the schools that I left? Would I be teaching Moby Dick? You know I don't want to teach Moby Dick! (Laughter)

79

The Last Generation*

CHERRÍE MORAGA

I call myself a Chicana writer. Not a Mexican-American writer, not a Hispanic writer, not a half-breed writer. To be a Chicana is not merely to name one's racial/cultural identity, but also to name a politic, a politic that refuses assimilation into the U.S. mainstream. It acknowledges our mestizaje-Indian, Spanish, and Africano. After a decade of "hispanicization" (a term superimposed upon us by Reagan-era bureaucrats), the term Chicano assumes even greater radicalism. With the misnomer "Hispanic," Anglo America proffers to the Spanish surnamed the illusion of blending into the "melting pot" like any other white immigrant group. But the Latino is neither wholly immigrant nor wholly white; and here in this country, "Indian" and "dark" don't melt. (Puerto Ricans on the East Coast have been called "Spanish" for decades and it's done little to alter their status on the streets of New York City.)

The generation of Chicano literature being read today sprang forth from a grassroots social and political movement of the sixties and seventies that was definitively anti-assimilationist. It responded to a stated mandate: art is political. The proliferation of poesía, cuentos, and teatro that grew out of El Movimiento was supported by Chicano cultural centers and publishing projects throughout the Southwest and in every major urban area where a substantial Chicano population resided. The Flor y Canto poetry festivals of the seventies and a teatro that spilled off flatbed trucks into lettuce fields in the sixties are hallmarks in the history of the Chicano cultural movement. Chicano literature was a literature in dialogue with its community. And as some of us became involved in feminist, gay, and lesbian concerns in the late seventies and early eighties, our literature was forced to expand to reflect the multifaceted nature of the Chicano experience.

The majority of published Chicano writers today are products of that era of activism, but as the Movement grew older and more established, it became neutralized by middle-aged and middle-class concerns, as well as by a growing conservative trend in government. Most often gains made for farm workers in California were dismantled by a succession of reactionary governors and Reagan/Bush economics. Cultural centers lost funding. Most small press Chicano publishers disappeared as suddenly as they had appeared. What was once a radical and working-class Latino student base on university campuses has become increasingly conservative. A generation of tokenistic affirmative-action policies and bourgeois flight from Central America and the Caribbean has spawned a tiny Latino elite who often turn to their racial/cultural

*From *The Lost Generation*. Boston: South End Press, 1993: pp. 56–59.

identities not as a source of political empowerment, but of personal employment as tokens in an Anglo-dominated business world.

And the writers . . . ? Today more and more of us insist we are "American" writers (in the North American sense of the word). The body of our literary criticism grows (seemingly at a faster rate than the literature itself), we assume tenured positions in the University, secure New York publishers, and our work moves further and further away from a community-based and national political movement. A writer will write. With or without a movement.

Fundamentally, I started writing to save my life. Yes, my own life first. I see the same impulse in my students—the dark, the queer, the mixed-blood, the violated—turning to the written page with a relentless passion, a drive to avenge their own silence, invisibility, and erasure as living, innately expressive human beings.

A writer will write with or without a movement; but at the same time, for Chicano, lesbian, gay, and feminist writers—anybody writing against the grain of Anglo misogynist culture—political movements are what have allowed our writing to surface from the secret places in our notebooks into the public sphere. In 1990, Chicanos, gay men, and women are no better off than we were in 1970. We have an ever-expanding list of physical and social diseases affecting us: AIDS, breast cancer, police brutality. Censorship is becoming increasingly institutionalized, not only through government programs, but through transnational corporate ownership of publishing houses, record companies, etc. Without a movement to foster and sustain our writing, we risk being swallowed up into the "Decade of the Hispanic" that never happened. The fact that a few of us have "made it" and are doing better than we imagined has not altered the nature of the beast. He remains blue-eyed and male and prefers profit over people.

Like most artists, we Chicano artists would like our work to be seen as "universal" in scope and meaning and reach as large an audience as possible. Ironically, the most "universal" work—writing capable of reaching the hearts of the greatest number of people—is the most culturally specific. The European-American writer understands this because it is his version of cultural specificity that is deemed "universal" by the literary establishment. In the same manner, universality in the *Chicana* writer requires the most Mexican and the most female images we are capable of producing. Our task is to write what no one is prepared to hear, for what has been said so far in barely a decade of consistent production is a mere *bocadito*. Chicana writers are still learning the art of transcription, but what we will be capable of producing in the decades to come, if we have the cultural/political movements to support us, could make a profound contribution to the social transformation of these Américas. The retort, however, is to remain as culturally specific and culturally complex as possible, even in the face of mainstream seduction to do otherwise.

80

Nepantla: Essays from the Land in the Middle*

PAT MORA

The Desert

How normal the starkness is when we live in it and know no other landscape. Geographical terrains are seldom awesome to their inhabitants. Many Mexican-American women from the Southwest are desert women. We "know about survival / . . . Like cactus / we've learned to hoard."[1] We hoard what our mothers, our *tías*, our *abuelitas* hoarded: our values, our culture. Much as I want us, my daughters, my niece, Chicanas of all ages, to carry the positive aspects of our culture with them for sustenance, I also want us to question and ponder what values and customs we wish to incorporate into our lives, to continue our individual and our collective evolution. Such emergence, the wriggling from our past selves and experience as both women and women of Color, brings with it mixed blessings. We can learn from the desert, from the butterflies and snakes around us, how vulnerable a creature is in transition. We can offer one another strength and solace, protection from harsh elements, from the painful cold of sexism, racism, ageism, elitism; faith, the space for exploration.

Our cities are changing, though far too gradually. We have lived to see bicultural and bilingual librarians, principals, superintendents. We have lived to see Latinas as alderwomen, lawyers, doctors, judges, directors. Much as we want young people to view this as appropriate and normal, we want them to be keenly aware that Mexicans were part of this open, uncluttered Southwest landscape long before the arrival of Anglos. But women and men of Mexican descent have, like American-Indians, been both excluded from shaping many aspects of their societies and unrecognized for the contributions they did make. Late in the last century, Anglos became the dominant culture. English, which had been foreign to our region, the language of the second colonizer, became the correct and valued language. Work viewed as menial too often became the province of the dark-skinned, of Mexicans. Ours.

Mexican women contributed to the intellectual history of this land of promise, the West, before the region was part of the United States. Thanks to the work of Chicana and Chicano literary historians such as Tey Diana Rebolledo, Rosaura Sánchez, and Clara Lomas, we are beginning to learn the names of some of the early women writers. How much all of us will profit from this research and from endeavors such as

---

*From *Nepantla: Essays from the Land in the Middle*. Albuquerque: University of New Mexico Press, 1993: pp. 53–56.

the ten-year Arte Público Press project funded by the Rockefeller Foundation, titled "Restoring the Hispanic Literary Heritage of the United States," which will publish work written from the colonial period to 1960.

"The struggles, lives and dreams of Hispanic women in the West from 1580 to 1940 is just beginning to be pieced together," Rebolledo tells us.[2] Women such as Nina Otero Warren, Cleofas Jaramillo, Fabiola Cabeza de Baca, Jovita González, and Josephina Niggli are finally receiving a degree of attention—women who sat in their long dresses, hearing the mix of indigenous languages, Spanish, and English that is part of our heritage, looking out at our mountains and moon, writing diaries, drama, fiction, poetry. For most of us, those women remain in the shadows. I think of them, pen poised above a sheet of blank paper, frowning, struggling as I do to find the right words.

But they were the exception. Most of our foremothers lived unsung lives, seldom if ever realizing their intellectual potential, renouncing personal ambition to give steadily and unstintingly to their families, to their children, to us. How they have worked—in their own homes and in the homes of others, in department stores, in churches, in fields, in canneries, in factories, in restaurants, in hospitals. Some supported their families financially, endured and endure; some supported husbands, endured and endure. We have drawn strength since we were in grade school from the pride of our female relatives. We were encouraged by the nods of approval from *Abuelita* when we recited the Pledge of Allegiance, even when she didn't understand a word we said, and perhaps even stubbornly refused to learn English, carving linguistic space for herself, denying those foreign sounds a place inside of her.

The prices have been high, then, for succeeding generations of Latinas to complete college and university educations. Often, "We are the first / of our people to walk this path."[3] The climate in our schools remains cold. Studies continue to reveal that educational institutions are not appropriately encouraging women of all ages and colors to explore their potential. Do we create a supportive climate for ourselves and for others? We know our students, female and male, need to study the history and literature of women. In a particular way, women of color deserve role models to give them faith that they too can advance and contribute to society. As the educator James Banks reminds us, simply observing, for example, Hispanic Heritage Month and the quincentenary will not suffice. The educational system must be transformed. Our students should study Latina contributions, perspectives, and values, as an integral part of their curriculum, a curriculum in which they see themselves. Textbooks that don't include diverse perspectives should be rejected by responsible educational institutions-for their bias *mis*-educates.

We, and all women, need and deserve our past. We can value the resourcefulness of our mothers and the homes they created, the space they shaped for us. There is much to be learned from the strengths of *tías* and *abuelitas*, and from our experiences in cooking, gardening, mothering. The seventeenth-century Mexican poet Sor Juana Inés de la Cruz quipped, "*Si Aristótoles hubiera guisado, mucho mas hubiera escrito.*" "Had Aristotle cooked, he would have written more."[4] Obviously, Sor Juana lived a privileged life and knew that housework can be true drudgery when a woman has no options. But rather than focusing on the drudgery of work, her words present such work as a source of creativity.

Our womanness, heritage, culture, language all deserve preservation. To transform our traditions wisely, we need to know them, learn from them, be inspired and saddened by them, choose for ourselves what to retain. But we can prize the past together, valuing the positive female and Mexican traditions. We can prize elements of the past as we persist in demanding, and creating, change. I remember looking up at a huge abandoned church outside of Ciudad Oaxaca and seeing a cactus somehow thriving and growing high up near the bell tower. I pointed to it in delight, and the Mexican with me said, "*Aun en los lugares mas dificiles el nopal da frutas.*" "Even in inhospitable places, cactus bears fruit."

NOTES

1. Pat Mora, "Desert Women," in *Borders* (Houston: Arte Público Press, 1986), p. 80.
2. Tey Diana Rebolledo, "Introduction," in *Infinite Divisions: An Anthology of chicano Literature,* edited by Tey Diana Rebolledo and Eliana Riviero (Tucson: University of Arizona Press, 1993).
3. Pat Mora, "University Avenue," in *Borders,* p. 19.
4. Margaret Sayers Peden, *A Woman of Genius: The Intellectual Autobiography of Sor Juana Inés de la Cruz* (Salisbury, Conn.: Lime Rock Press, 1987).

81

*There is no Going Back: Chicanas and Feminism**

BEATRIZ M. PESQUERA AND DENISE A. SEGURA

American feminism has inspired a tremendous amount of research, little of which attends to feminist expressions among Chicanas, or women of Mexican descent, who form the second largest racial-ethnic group in the United States. This inattention is disturbing inasmuch as feminism purports to explain the nature of women's oppression and develop strategies for social change. Without sustained analysis of the diverse feminism among women and the conditions that motivate them, theoretical formulations and strategies for change will continue to veer away from historically subordinate groups.

The paucity of knowledge about Chicana feminism, as well as the range of their political activities, results in researchers relegating Chicanas to the margins of social

*From *Chicana Critical Issues,* edited by Norma Alarcón, et al. (Berkeley: Third woman Press, 1993: pp. 95–115).

inquiry (Moraga & Anzaldúa 1981; Chabram & Fregoso 1990). Intellectual marginal-ization of Chicanas leads to an uncritical acceptance of the discourse of the late 1960s that situated Chicanas three paces behind Chicano men in the movement to overturn race-ethnic and class systems of oppression but silent on the question of patriarchy (Longeaux y Vásquez 1970; López 1977; García 1989). Positioned thusly, Chicanas were largely excluded from the feminist debates of the time—a dilemma yet to be systematically reversed (Lizárraga 1977; Sandoval 1982; Alarcón 1990).

This article[1] explores feminism among two groups of Chicanas; 101 members of a group of Chicanas in higher education (MALCS) and 152 Chicana white collar workers. We analyze how Chicanas' social locations—their race-ethnicity, gender, and class—shape their political consciousness and orientation toward feminist politics. This analysis inquires into the contradictions posed by these simultaneous social memberships. We begin our investigation by presenting three scenarios based in the late 1960s to capture symbolically the dialectical tension between women's lives and the ideological configurations of the Chicano Movement, which privileged a Chi-cano subject, and the American women's movement which posited a universal woman.[2] We follow this with a brief critique of American feminism and the Chicano Movement advanced by leading Chicana activists of the late 1960s and early 1970s.[3] Then, using a 1988–1989 survey of 101 Chicanas in higher education we discuss their appraisals of American feminism and the contours of Chicana feminism. Finally, we examine attitudes toward feminism expressed by 152 Chicana white collar workers from a study conducted in 1989–1990. Our research is grounded in a feminist histor-ical-social constructionism that analyzes structural conditions, Chicanas' interpreta-tions of their social locations and life options, and how these interpretations shape their consciousness.

On Feminist Consciousness

What is feminist consciousness? Tolleson Rinehart (1988) argues that feminist con-sciousness is a specific type of gender consciousness anchored in a commitment to egalitarian relations between the sexes. Klein (1984) and Cook (1989), on the other hand, assert that feminist consciousness includes not only advocacy of gender equality but a sense of subjective unity with women and a desire to change existing institu-tional arrangements that maintain the status quo as well. Klein (1984) proposes three prerequisites to feminist consciousness. First, members must recognize their member-ship in the group and that they share interests with the group (or group identifica-tion). Second, members must reject the rationale for the situation of the group. Third, they must recognize the need for group solutions. "Only women who reached this third stage, where they believed that they deserved equal treatment but were denied opportunities because of sex discrimination, had a feminist consciousness" (Klein 1984, p. 3). According to Cook (1989, pp. 84–85), people with "politicized feminist consciousness are significantly more likely to assign blame to societal factors than are those who are not feminists." Moreover, one must embrace a political stance that moves away from individualistic goals and action to a collectivist orientation to achieve group goals. These formulations imply a unidimensional source of group identification based on gender when in fact, women experience gender, racial-ethnic, and class statuses concurrently. We argue that analyses of feminist consciousness should attend to the dynamics of each social location in framing women's experi-ences. It is theoretically possible and likely that Chicanas' multiple sources of group identification conflict at times with one another, rendering the development of a group consciousness based on the privileging of one social location over the others ahistorical and untenable. The interplay of the multiple axes of class, race-ethnicity, and gender informs a unique Chicana perspective or world view that guides their assessment of the relevancy of feminism. This cross-positioning motivates a distinct Chicana feminism grounded in the experience of being female and Mexican from largely working-class backgrounds. This experience is not monolithic, however, but one that highly educated Chicanas interpret somewhat differently than white collar Chicana workers. These differences reflect Chicanas' varied social locations, networks, and experiences.

Three Scenarios

Scenario 1: ". . . the Chicana woman does not want to be liberated"

On 19 February 1990, we interviewed Martha Cotera, a prominent Chicana feminist and activist from Texas. In her interview, she recounted her involvement with alternative Chicano politics (specifically the rise of the "third" party in Texas, La Raza Unida), feminism, and civil rights. When we asked her to elaborate on the social context of Chicana feminism in the late 1960s, she related several accounts of the tension between male-defined Chicano political discourse and gender. One narrative centered on Enriqueta Longeaux y Vásquez, a Chicana activist and one of the editors of *El Grito del Norte*, a Chicano Movement newspaper published in New Mexico. Cotera related that twenty years ago, Longeaux y Vásquez had telephoned her to discuss the March 1969 First National Chicano Youth Conference held in Denver, attended by several thousand people from across the United States.[4] Cotera recalled that Longeaux y Vásquez was extremely upset—to the point of tears—that the Chicana Caucus at this conference had adopted the position that ". . . the Chicana woman does not want to be liberated." Longeaux y Vásquez (1970) chronicled the Chicana Caucus position in an article in the best-selling book *Sisterhood is Powerful*, edited by Robin Morgan. Albeit unintentionally, this article reinforces stereotypes of Chicanas as submissive and passive and uninterested in feminism.

Scenario 2: "El Plan Espiritual de Aztlán," March 1969

One of the major conferences of the Chicano movement was the First National Chicano Youth Conference hosted by the Crusade for Justice, a Denver-based, militant grassroots Chicano movement organization. This Conference gave birth to "El Plan Espiritual de Aztlán," also known as "The Chicano Movement Manifesto." The "Plan" provided an ideological framework and concrete political program for the Chicano Movement emphasizing nationalism and self-determination. The "Plan" stated: "Cultural values of our people strengthen our identity and are the moral backbone of the movement. Our culture unites and educates the family of La Raza towards liberation with one heart and one mind. . . . Our cultural values of life, family, and home will serve as the powerful weapon to defeat the gringo dollar value system and encourage the process of love and brotherhood" (Anaya & Lomeli 1989).

    The symbolic representation of familism (or family solidarity) and political cultural nationalism occurred with the marriage of Rodolfo "Corky" Gonzales's daughter and a militant member of the Crusade for Justice. Corky Gonzales, an ex-boxer and writer, headed the Crusade for Justice.

Scenario 3: "The Redstockings Manifesto"

A few months after the March 1969 Denver Conference, in New York, the "Redstockings Manifesto" appeared in *Notes from the Second Year: Women's Liberation, Major Writings of the Radical Feminists* (Firestone & Koedt 1970). Section III reads: "We identify the agents of our oppression as men. Male supremacy is the oldest, most basic form of domination. All other forms of exploitation and oppression (racism, capitalism, imperialism, etc.) are extensions of male supremacy: men dominate women, a few men dominate the rest. . . . *All men* have oppressed women" (Firestone & Koedt 1970, p. 113). In August, 1969, *The Feminists*, another radical women's liberation group, implemented a membership quota: "That no more than one-third of our membership can be participants in either a formal (with legal contract) or informal (e.g., living with a man) instance of the institution of marriage. (Firestone & Koedt 1970, p. 117). This membership quota grew out of their critique of marriage as a primary locus of female subordination and oppression.

On 22 November 1969, the Congress to Unite Women held workshops in New York on "What Women Want." One of the workshops was titled: "How Women are Divided: Class, Racial, Sexual, and Religious Differences." Evelyn Leo, who participated in this workshop reported, "The first exchange that took place is worth noting. A Black woman said she had been at a workshop that morning and went on to complain about what a waste it had been because everyone was talking around the subject and not at it, etc. A white woman responded and said, 'It was not as black as you are painting it.' Need I say more?" (Leo in Tanner 1970, pp. 127–128)

These scenarios highlight the polarized nature of insurgent politics during this period. Each position articulated an analysis of oppression based on race-ethnicity or gender. The Chicano Movement exalted marriage and reproduction as integral to the politics of cultural reaffirmation. A fundamental feminist position, on the other hand, indicted marriage and reproduction within the traditional patriarchal family as a primary source of all women's subordination. Although Chicanas recognized the need to struggle against male privilege in the Chicano community, they were reluctant to embrace a feminist position that appeared anti-family (Orozco 1986; García 1989). Caught between two incompatible ideological positions, Chicanas developed their own discourse reflecting their multidimensional sources of oppression and validation (Alarcón 1990; Apodaca 1986; Moraga and Anzaldúa 1983).

Chicanas and the American Women's Movement

The writings of Chicana feminists of the late 1960s and early 1970s demonstrate considerable ambivalence toward American feminism. Chicanas, both those who called themselves feminists and those who eschewed this label, characterized the movement as predominantly white and middle-class with interests distinct from their own (Cotera 1977, 1980; Del Castillo 1974; Hernández 1971; Nieto-Gómez 1973, 1974; Vidal 1971). With few exceptions, Chicanas did not distinguish between the "women's rights" branch and the "women's liberation" or "left" branch.[5] The women's rights branch concentrated on programs to integrate women into the mainstream of American society (Freeman 1984; Jagger 1983). The women's liberation branch called for a radical restructuring of society to eliminate patriarchy, or the system of male control and domination of women (Andersen 1988. Jaggar 1983). Although both branches of the women's movement advocated for women, the issues of women of Color[6] were often overlooked (Davis 1981; Garcia 1989; hooks 1981, 1984; Hull, Bell Scott, & Smith 1982; Moraga & Anzaldúa, 1983). Chicanas questioned the feminist call to "sisterhood" because it assumed unity based on one set of shared interests (gender-oppression) and overlooked the historical class, race-ethnic, and cultural antagonisms between women. Chicana activists contended that the American women's movement and feminism could not be relevant to Chicanas until race-ethnic and class concerns became integrated into their political and theoretical formulations (Flores 1973; Moraga & Anzaldúa 1983; Nieto-Gómez 1973, & 1974; Sosa-Riddell 1974). Chicanas doubted, however, that such an integrative approach would emerge in light of the racism and what Anna Nieto-Gómez (1973) referred to as "maternal chauvinism" in the women's movement. With this term, Nieto-Gómez directed attention to Chicanas virtual exclusion from feminist agendas and writings as well as the condescending attitudes among some Movement activists toward Chicanas.[7] In the rare instances Chicanas were included, their experiences tended to be cast in ways that reinforced cultural stereotypes of them as women who did not "want to be liberated" (Longeaux y Vásquez 1970). Most often, however, Chicanas have been silent objects within feminist discourse because they are neither included or excluded by name. Thus, Chicanas in this period concluded they were not "equal" sisters in the struggle against sexual oppression (Cotera 1980; Moraga & Anzaldúa 1983).

Chicana feminists also criticized what they interpreted as an individualistic upward mobility ethos within the American women's movement (Sutherland 1970). They posited an alternative view; one rooted in the collective struggle for liberation of the entire Chicano community.

Chicanas and Cultural Nationalism

Chicanas' critique of American feminism and the women's movement resonate with a strong collective orientation formed during the heyday of Chicano cultural nationalism. Ideologically, this perspective identified the primary source of Chicano oppression in the colonial domination of Mexican-Americans following the annexation of Northern Mexico by the United States after the U.S.-Mexico War of 1846–48 (Acuña 1981; Almaguer 1971; Barrera, Muñoz, & Ornelas 1972; Blauner 1972). As part of the process of colonial domination, Chicanos were limited in their access to education, employment, and political participation. Thus, race-ethnicity defined the life chances of Mexican-Americans rather than individual merit. Cultural differences between Anglos and Mexicans became the ideological basis that legitimized the unequal treatment and status of Mexicans in the United States (Blauner 1972; Montejano 1987; Takaki 1979). Ideologically, Mexicans were viewed as intellectually and culturally inferior.

Cultural nationalist ideology countered this pejorative perspective by celebrating the cultural heritage of Mexico in particular, indigenous roots, la familia, and political insurgency (Macías 1974; Mirandé 1985). The term, "Chicano," arose as the symbolic representation of self-determination (Chicano Coordinating Committee on Higher Education 1969; Álvarez 1971; Acuña 1981). It conveys a commitment to politically struggle for the betterment of the Chicano community. Cultural nationalism idealized certain patterns associated with Mexican culture. For example, Chicano movement groups often organized around the ideal of la familia.[8] Any critique of unequal gender relations within the structure of the family was discouraged. Cynthia Orozco's historical research on Chicanas in the Chicano movement and the Chicana movement speaks to the dilemma of raising a critique of gender inequality: "When Chicanas raised the issue of male domination, both the community and its intellectual arm, Chicano Studies, put down the ideology of feminism and put feminists in their place" (1986, p. 12).

Chicanas who deviated from a nationalist political stance were subjected to negative sanctions including being labeled *vendidas* (sell-outs), or *agabachadas* (white identified) (López 1977; Nieto Gómez 1973, 1974). Once labeled thus, they became subject to marginalizaition within Chicano movement organizations. Martha Cotera points out how even the label "feminist" was a social control mechanism: "We didn't say we were feminist. It was the men who said that. They said, 'Aha! Feminista!' and that was a good enough reason for not listening to some of the most active women in the community" (1977, p. 31). Such social and political sanctions discouraged women from articulating feminist issues.

The ideological hegemony of cultural nationalism was exemplified in the first official position taken by the Chicana Caucus at the 1969 National Chicano Youth Conference. While the motives behind caucus participants' decision to take the position that Chicanas are not interested in women's liberation have not been documented, the hostile climate to feminism within the Chicano movement undoubtedly played a role in their decision.

Chicana writings and organizational activities of this period resounded with frustration over patriarchy in the Chicano Movement and a "maternal chauvinism" in the women's movement. Time and time again Chicanas argued that ending race-class oppression would not automatically eliminate sexual oppression (Del Castillo 1974; Flores 1973; Martínez 1972). Similarly, freedom from sexual oppression would not end oppression on the basis of race-ethnicity and class. They sought various ways to reconcile the tension between cultural nationalism and feminism. Chicana feminism reverberates with the dialectical tension between their lives and the ideological configurations that dichotomize their experiences and exploit their political loyalties. We now consider the extent to which this tension exists today among two groups of Chicana women.

The Women of MALCS

To explore the context of Chicana attitudes toward feminism and their feminist consciousness, we analyze the relationship between the Chicano Movement, the American women's movement, and Chicana feminism based on a questionnaire administered to women on the mailing list of MALCS (Mujeres Activas en Letras y Cambio Social). This organization of Chicana/Latina women in higher education was founded in 1983 at the University of California, Berkeley. MALCS's charter and activities demonstrate familiarity with Chicana concerns, a feminist orientation, and sensitivity to cultural concerns. Each year MALCS organizes a four-day summer institute which includes panels on Chicana research and workshops on Chicana empowerment. In our questionnaire, we asked women to answer a series of largely open-ended questions (with some closed-ended questions) on the Chicano movement, the American women's movement, the Chicana movement and feminism. In 1988, we mailed the questionnaire to all 178 women on the MALCS mailing list; 101 were completed and returned for a response rate of 57 percent.

Nearly all of the women who answered our questionnaire are associated with colleges and universities: 38.6 percent of them are faculty; 25.7 percent are graduate students; 8.9 percent are undergraduates; and 8.9 percent are professional staff at a college or university campus. Eleven women said they were employed outside of a university setting, and seven did not provide us with information on their employment or education.

The women were between 22 to 65 years old with a median age of 35 years, and a mean age of 38.1 years. This age distribution means that a majority of the women were college-age (17–22) during the heyday of the women's movement (1967–1977). Moreover most of the women have activist backgrounds. Over three-fourth (78.2 percent) of the women either belong to, or have previously been involved in women's organizations. Women overwhelmingly (84.2 percent) self-identified as a "Chicana feminist."

The women of MALCS shared certain perceptions about their current and past experiences. They have varied work, family, community, political backgrounds, and attitudes. Thus, it is impossible to characterize one single type of Chicana feminism. Hence, we offer a typology of Chicana feminism to try and capture the broad range of their critical interpretations of their feminism. We hope this not only counters stereotypical views of Chicanas as non-feminists, or even anti-feminists, but presents them as women whose self-reflections demonstrate resistance, accommodation, and change—sometimes in contradictory ways rooted in simultaneously privileged and marginalized social locations. This analysis contributes to research on feminist consciousness by giving life and a historical base to the multidimensional social contexts that frame Chicana feminism. We emphasize that this group of Chicanas is not a representative sample of U.S. women of Mexican descent. But, as academicians or highly educated women, the women of MALCS inform the public discourse on feminism and Chicana issues. While their perceptions offer considerable insight on possible formulation Chicana feminism, they may not be generalizable to other Chicana women-an issue we explore later in this chapter among a group of Chicana white collar workers.

The Women's Movement and Chicana Concerns

Nearly all MALCS survey informants criticize the America women's movement for failing to "adequately" address Chicana concerns. MALCS Chicanas argue that the American women's movement largely articulates issues best relevant to relatively privileged, well-educated middle- and upper-class white women. They object to what they perceive as a marked tendency with the American women's movement to present itself in global terms (e.g., *The* women's movement). Women feel this obscure important racial-ethnic and class differences among women. As one twenty-four-year-old graduate student writes:

> The "movement" has failed to adequately address classism and racism and how it impacts on women as a class and in dealing with of areas of common concern (i.e. women and the family). I think we have been used to present a collective voice on behalf of women but have not been extended the same degree of importance to areas that concern us differently, i.e., class and race issues. In other words white women also have to overcome their own prejudices as they try to overcome prejudice altogether.

Most of the women also object to any analysis of oppression that puts gender first. They argue that overreliance on a gender critique inhibits the development of a more inclusive perspective sensitive to the ways race—ethnicity, class, *as well* as gender, shape the Chicana experience. Although informants rarely distinguished between the different segments of the American women's movement, those that did (make this distinction) tended to have similar criticisms. This suggests that informants feel Chicana concerns are neglected across all the political or ideological groupings within the American women's movement.

Despite their criticisms of the American women's movement, nearly all of the informants endorse its key maxim—that ending female subordination is essential. Many women credit the movement for developing a critique of patriarchy—something that influenced their own development of Chicana feminism. Yet, while they acknowledge that Chicanas can benefit from the struggle to overthrow male privilege, most feel that any gains netted from this particular struggle will be inadequate and largely incidental. Moreover, since white, middle-class women tend to define the direction of the struggle against patriarchy, they are likely to benefit the most.

A few informants credit feminists for beginning to move the concerns of working-class and racial-ethnic women from, what bell hooks (1984) terms, "margin to center." Many women feel, however, this action has come from the *critiques* and *demands* of women of color. Not all women share this view however, as the following twenty-seven-year-old graduate student indicates: "Women of Color, particularly Chicanas themselves, have struggled as a group since the late 1960s, early 1970s to raise their/our own issues as women from an oppressed nationality group in the U.S. Our fight within the predominantly white, middle-class women's movement has been to address the issues of class and race, as *inextricable* [her emphasis] to our gender issues." This woman's words speak to the need for white feminists to acknowledge Chicanas active resistance to patriarchy *as well* as race-ethnic and class oppression.

Chicana Feminism

Nearly all of the informants (85 percent) self-identify as Chicana feminists–only 16 do not. 62 women discussed the meaning of Chicana feminism.[9] From their descriptions of Chicana feminism, we developed the following typology: *Chicana Liberal Feminism* (*n* = 28), *Chicana Insurgent Feminism* (*n* = 21), and *Chicana Cultural Nationalist Feminism* (*n* = 13). Each category is grounded in the material condition of the Chicano people and highlights different aspects of Chicana feminism. Each encompasses diverse ways of interpreting oppression and advocating strategies for social change.

Chicana Liberal Feminism centers on women's desires to enhance the well-being of the Chicano community, with a special emphasis on improving the status of women. This perspective advocates change within a liberal tradition emphasizing access to social institutions, employment and equal treatment in all areas of life. Women in this category endorse political strategies to improve the status of the Chicano community through education, employment, health care services, and political involvement. As one twenty-six-year-old graduate student said: "[The] term 'Chicana' in itself represents a certain degree of feminism. She strives to understand the political, social, and economic state her people are in and actively seeks to make change that will advance her *raza* [people]." This perspective affirms Chicanas' desires to develop a personal awareness of women's needs and espouses an active commitment to improve the social and economic condition of the Chicano community-at-large.

Chicana Insurgent Feminism, on the other hand, emanates from a political tradition that contests the social relations of production and reproduction. Women who articulate these sentiments call for Chicana self-determination which encompasses a struggle against both personal and institutional manifestations of racial discrimination, patriarchy, and class exploitation. For example, the following fifty-year-old Chicana faculty member advocates revolutionary change to end oppression:

> I believe that the impact of sexism, racism and elitism, when combined, results in a more intensely exploitative, oppressive and controlling situation than when these conditions exist independently of one another. The status and quality of life of the Chicano community as a whole can only improve/change when that of women within that community changes/improves. Any revolutionary change must include a change in relationships between men and women.

This woman argues that the cumulative effects of oppression are particularly pronounced for Chicanas. Similar to the previous informant, she links the liberation of Chicanas to the overall struggle of the Chicano community. Her words, however, contain a more strident and uncompromising tenor. For her, Chicana feminism ties liberation of the Chicano community to the struggle against patriarchy. Politically, she espouses a radical praxis advocating revolutionary change.

Other informants discussed the need for feminism to incorporate oppression based on sexual orientation and international solidarity with other oppressed peoples. One forty-year-old Chicana faculty member said, "I am active and critical with respect to political, social, and cultural manifestations of sexism, racism, hispanophobia, heterosexism, and class oppression, and committed to working with others to create a more just society. It also means that I am moved by a sense of ethnic solidarity with Chicano, Mexican and other Latino people." This informant and a small, but vocal group of women advocate recognizing oppression on the basis of sexual orientation as central to Chicana feminism. Resonating the sentiments of the majority, this woman views political activism as a critical component of Chicana feminism. In general, *Insurgent Feminism* engages in a critique that calls for the radical restructuring of society.

Finally, *Chicana Cultural Nationalist Feminism* includes a small group of women that identify as feminists but are committed to a cultural nationalist ideology. They believe that change in gender relations should be accomplished without annihilating traditional cultural values. For example, one forty-one-year-old Chicana graduate student wrote: "I want for myself and for other women the opportunities to grow, and develop in any area I choose. I want to do this while upholding the values (cultural, moral) that come from my being a part of the great family of Chicanos."

Reminiscent of the slogan popularized within the Chicano Movement (that all Chicanos are members of the same family—*la gran familia de la raza*), *Chicana Cultural Nationalism* articulates a feminist vision anchored in the ideology of la familia. While advocating feminism this perspective retains allegiance to cultural nationalism which glorifies Chicano culture. *Chicana Cultural Nationalism* overlooks the possibility that these cultural traditions often uphold patriarchy. This speaks to the difficulty of reconciling a critique of gender relations within the Chicano community while calling for the preservation of Chicano culture.

Despite their different interpretations of oppression and strategies for social change, MALCS Chicanas articulate a feminist consciousness. They demonstrate a subjective identification with multiple groups each reflecting an affinity with women's unequal access to power vis-a-vis men, their membership in a socially subordinate racial-ethnic group, and a symbolic attachment to their working-class origins. Moreover, they reject the ideological and structural configurations that maintain

Chicanas in a socially subordinate position. By and large they consider themselves Chicana feminists with interests that both intersect and diverge from those of Chicano men and white women. Both their sense of belonging to socially subordinate groups and their awareness of their social locations in society contribute to the high level of feminist consciousness within this group of women. MALCS Chicanas advocate social change-reformist in nature for some, revolutionary in nature for others. Chicana feminism then, exhibits what Cook refers to as a politicized feminist consciousness.

The attitudes of MALCS Chicanas towards feminism led us to consider whether their views are shared by other Chicana workers. In the following section we discuss white collar women's attitudes toward the women's movement and feminism. We also offer a preliminary view related to feminist consciousness. We explore the extent to which the strong sense of group consciousness we found among MALCS members resonates among the Chicana/Latina white collar workers.

Chicana White Collar Workers

The Chicana white collar workers selected for this study work at a major public university in Northern California.[10] We chose this site because it allowed us to access Chicana workers who work in an academic setting (like MALCS women) but are outside the relatively privileged research and teaching sector. We feel that exploring attitudes toward feminism among a group closer in income, working conditions, and status to the MALCS Chicanas is the next logical step in an inquiry on feminism that begins with academic Chicanas. Moreover, it provides us with a sense of the extent to which Chicana academics actually represent views beyond their relatively privliged realm.

For this study, we designed a mail survey containing a series of closed-ended questions on work, issues of race and ethnicity, the women's movement, and feminism. The actual questions were based on the views of the MALCS respondents as well as selected questions from other studies on American feminism.

In 1989, we mailed the questionnaire to all 312 self-identified "Hispanic" women workers at the research site; 152 women (48.7 percent) returned the questionnaire. The women's ages ranged from twenty to sixty-one years, with an average age of 36.5 years. They are well-educated: all but three women have high school diplomas; 65 percent have post-high school educations short of a bachelor's degree; and 15 percent have B.A.'s or above. About one-third of the informants belong to an Hispanic workers advocacy group on the campus. Nearly half have been involved in organizations aimed at promoting the needs of their racial-ethnic group and community. Relatively few women (20 percent) indicated they had been members of a group to promote women's needs or interests.

Chicana White Collar Workers and Feminism

Women in the study are familiar with the women's movement. Most of the informants (72.2 percent) feel the women's movement tries to empower all women.[11] About half of the Chicana/ Latina workers believe that all women have benefited from the women's movement. When asked whether or not the women's movement advocates specifically for Chicana/Latina women, however, few respondents agree (20.3 percent). It is important to note that a relatively high number of women (37 percent) did not express an opinion on this particular question. Moreover, about one-quarter of the respondents feel the women's movement is not comprised of women from diverse racial backgrounds. This suggests that the Chicana/Latina workers are either unsure about the relevancy of the women's movement to their group, or are ambivalent about it. They do, however, appreciate its beneficial aspects.

Most of the women express opinions compatible with feminist positions on key issues including a high level of concern with women's rights (94.7 percent) and agreement that women's roles should continue to change (93.2 percent). With respect to the controversial issue of women's right to a legal abortion, the respondents lean toward a pro-choice position with 43.4 percent favoring women's right to a legal abortion under "any" circumstances and another 48.7, percent favoring this right under "certain" circumstances. Only 5.9 percent denounce abortion under all circumstances. Concurrently many of the respondents would feel comfortable calling themselves, "feminists" (52 percent), but most would not join a feminist organization (66.9 percent).

Some of the sentiments expressed by Chicana/Latina white collar workers complement those of the MALCS study. That is, both groups of women recognize the contributions of the women's movement to improve the status of women in our society. They are ambivalent, however, with respect to the lack of a specific focus on Chicana/Latina issues. In general, the Chicana/Latina workers are more positive about the women's movement and American feminism. Unlike the MALCS respondents, the white collar workers do *not* believe that the women's movement is primarily a white, middle-class movement. When presented with a "feeling thermometer" designed to gauge their feelings toward feminists, most Chicana/Latina workers indicated they felt warm or hot toward feminists.[12] Perhaps most surprising is the high number of women (52 percent) who feel they would feel comfortable calling themselves "feminists." There is a high degree of support for issues commonly associated with feminists, including the opinion that women's roles need to continue changing, and support for abortion rights. These findings are significant in that they counter commonly-held assumptions that Chicana/Latina women sustain more traditional gender values and are less likely to embrace feminist attitudes.

Chicana/Latina white collar workers demonstrate considerable attachment to key features of Mexican/Chicano cultural identity including Spanish/English bilingualism (60 percent) and Catholicism (67.8 percent). They also reveal a high degree of race-ethnic consciousness. Specifically, they are aware of the unequal location of their group in U.S. society—85 percent believe that "Mexicans do not share equally in the good life." By and large, women reject individualistic explanations for the persistent, low social status of Mexicans in society. Rather, over half cite institutional discrimination in education and employment. Further, they recognize the need for group solutions (e.g., 70 percent advocate bilingual education; and 70 percent support teaching Mexican history and culture to all students).

Women also demonstrate high awareness of the ways gender construction intersects with Chicano/Mexican culture to constrain Chicana/Latina workers. When we asked women why Chicanas/Latinas are not employed in high-paying jobs, a majority cited both institutional and familial circumstances. That is, Chicanas are limited both by inadequate access to good jobs as well as " traditional" familial roles and gender expectations of women embedded in the ethnic community.

Women in this study affirm the need to formulate group solutions to eradicate gender inequality, often in support of key feminist positions (e.g., equal pay for comparable work). Their awareness of the unique social location of their group suggests elements of a combined race-ethnic and feminist consciousness.[13] In sum, Chicana/Latina white collar workers recognize and affirm their membership in a subordinate group and endorse group solutions to redress inequality.

Conclusion

The Chicanas in this study express feminist consciousness. For Klein, constituent features of feminist consciousness include the recognition of shared membership and shared sets of interests with the group, rejection of the rationale for the situation of the group, and affirmation of the need for collective solutions.

Using this criteria, MALCS survey informants express a feminist consciousness along all three dimensions. They identify themselves as Chicana feminists with a set of interests separate from both Chicano men and white feminists. Moreover, MALCS informants articulate an understanding of the ways that social, economic, and political forces maintain their subordinate status. Finally, this group of women calls for social change-reformist in nature for some; revolutionary in nature for others. Irrespective of the specific form their feminism takes, MALCS Chicanas affirm their struggle as integrally bound to the social and political struggles of the Chicano/Latino community-at-large.

Chicana white collar workers also demonstrate a feminist consciousness. A majority would feel comfortable calling themselves "feminists." They believe women's roles need to continue change and uphold a pro-choice stance. They also articulate awareness of the unique social vulnerability of Mexicans in the U.S., and advocate structural changes. Although the majority do not belong to organizations that focus specifically on women's issues, most of the women are or have been involved in organizations that address community and/or ethnic concerns.

MALCS and Chicana white-collar workers share a strong group consciousness and espouse collective solutions to inequality. They differ however, with regard to their evaluation of the women's movement-a movement aimed at redressing gender inequality. MALCS informants express more negative criticisms of the Movement's efficacy to address Chicana concerns. This critique is influenced by their perception that the women's movement primarily constitutes middle- to upper-class white women whose concerns reflect their class status. They assert that the benefits netted by Chicanas result from a "trickle-down effect" as opposed to advocacy of working class, racial-ethnic women grounded in a direct understanding of their distinct material conditions.

The majority of the Chicana white-collar workers in this study do not perceive the women's movement as primarily comprised of white middle-class women. They express more positive evaluations of the gains to Chicana women resulting from the movement's struggle to eradicate gender inequality. Similar to MALCS informants, however, Chicana white collar workers do not believe the women's movement addresses the *specific* concerns of Chicana women.

How can we account for the differences in attitudes toward feminism between Chicana academics and Chicana white collar workers? Convergence in the mean ages of both groups of women places them in a similar political generation. That is, they represent a cohort that has experienced the emergence of the "second wave" of American feminism and has been exposed to potent benefits from this movement's activities.

Although both groups of women constitute a political generation, they differ in their social locations, networks, and experiences. MALCS members have direct experience in both the Chicano movement and the American women's movement; therefore they form a "politicized generation." With few exceptions, the white collar informants have not been involved in either social movement. The MALCS women work in close proximity to white feminist academics; most are also involved in women's studies programs. Moreover, their place within the university situates them to engage in the debate over the production of ideologies and agendas that comprise modern-day feminism. One result of this contestation across race-ethnic and class lines is a more critical or negative evaluation of American feminism and white feminists. This negative evaluation is compounded by the relatively greater access to opportunity in the academia of white women visa-vis Chicana faculty and graduate students (Baca Zinn, Cannon, Higginbotham, & Dill 1986).

The warmer attitudes toward feminism among Chican/Latina workers may reflect their employment in situations where reforms advocated by the women's movement can benefit them (e.g. training opportunities, equal pay, affirmative action). Lewis (1983) observes that women do, in fact, articulate greater support for feminism when they perceived immediate benefits. Although Chicana/Latina white-collar workers are critical of race or class barriers, they do not always see feminist issues in class or racial-ethnic terms. Because the overwhelming majority of Chicana white-collar workers have not participated in the Chicano movement or the women's movement, they do not have the same sense of the contradictions and contestations within these movements experienced first-hand by the MALCS women. These differences in social location, networks, and experiences between MALCS women and white-collar workers shape each woman's evaluation of feminism. Irrespective of these differences, both the MALCS women and the Chicana white collar workers affirm the significance of the struggle to eradicate all forms of social inequality. Their feminist consciousness flows from their group status as Mexican women in the United States.

NOTES

1. The authors would like to acknowledge that the first part of our article title is the final line from Ana Castillo's poem, "We Would Like You To Know," in *My Father Was a Toltec* (1988). Our research was supported, in part, by research grants from the Academic Senates of U.C. Davis and U.C. Santa Barbara as well as the University of California Consortium on U.S.–Mexico Relations (U.C. Mexus). Authors' names are randomly ordered.

2. We recognize that there are various branches of the American women's movement and numerous types of feminism that are currently the subject of intense analysis. We use these larger terms because we are not interested in entering the debate of what American feminisms are, but rather discuss the shape and forms of Chicana feminism.

3. In the late 1960s and early 1970s there were numerous Chicana activists that identified themselves as feminists. The constraints of space do not allow us to include all of them in our analysis. The Chicanas highlighted in this chapter are among the most prolific writers of the time period under review.

4. One of the coauthors of this chapter, Beatriz M. Pesquera, also attended this conference while an undergraduate student at Merritt College, Oakland, California. Her recollections inform Scenarios I and 2.

5. One notable exception is Anna Nieto-Gómez (1974, pp. 4–5) who stated: "What is the Anglo women's movement? First, you have to understand that it is not a unified movement. There are at least three positions. There are the liberal feminists who say, 'I want access to power. I want access to whatever men have. . . .' Then there are radical feminists, who say that men have the power, and that men are responsible for the oppression of women. A third position is that of women's liberationists which says that women's oppression is one of the many oppressions in the economic system of this country. . . ."

6. We capitalize the word, "Color" as in women of Color since it refers to specific racial-ethnic groups. See Hurtado (1989).

7. Anna Nieto-Gómez (1973, p. 43) stated: "The women's movement seems to perpetrate a sense of maternalism by treating the Chicana in a childlike manner. During the 1972 National Women's Political Caucus Convention, the lack of Chicana representation, negative attitudes towards the Chicana caucus structure and the actions taken in respect to the Women's Education Act of 1972 seem to demonstrate this kind of *maternal chauvinism* [our emphasis] as an extension of racism."

8. For example, the Denver-based Chicano Movement organization, the Crusade for Justice stressed the concept of family unity as one of the central principles for self-and community-development (López 1977). The national student organization, MEChA (Movimento Estudiantil Chicano de Aztlán) called upon students to recreate a feeling of *familia*, and "promote brotherhood" among Chicano students (Chicano Coordinating Committee on Higher Education 1969).

9. Thirteen women provided non-specific answers that did not fall into any discernable pattern; seven women did not elaborate on the meaning of Chicana feminism.

10. One shortcoming of this study is that we do not distinguish native-born Chicanas from foreign-born Mexican women. There is little published work on women of Mexican descent that makes this distinction. Also, relatively few of the informants in both studies indicated they were foreign-born Mexicans or Latinas. For readers interested in the differences between native-born and foreign-born Mexican women, see Tienda and Guhleman (1985).

11. We should note that we are in the process of interviewing one-third of this group of informants ($n = 50$). Thus far we have spoken with 40 women. All of these women assert they are "fairly familiar" with the American women's movement. They indicate that their main source of information is the media. Few have taken women's studies courses; few have good friends they consider "strong" feminists.

12. Feeling thermometers were introduced in the 1964 American National Election Study. Wilcox, Sigelman and Cook (1989, p. 246) observe they are "standard tools in survey-based political research. Respondents use feeling thermometers to locate attitude objects on an imaginary scale ranging from 0 (very cold) to 100 (very warm)."

13. Inasmuch as our questionnaire did not have open-ended questions, the white collar respondents could not elaborate on this issue. Follow-up interviews (in progress) should shed additional insight on this important question.

REFERENCES

Acuña, Rodolfo. 1981. *Occupied America: A History of Chicanos.* 2nd ed. New York: Harper and Row.

Alarcón, Norma. 1983. "Chicana Feminist Literature: A Re-Vision Through Malintzinl or Malintzin: Putting Flesh Back on the Object." In *This Bridge Called My Back: Writings By Radical Women of Color,* eds. Cherríe Moraga and Gloria Anzaldúa. 2nd ed. New York: Kitchen Table Press.

Alarcón, Norma. 1990. "The Theoretical Subject(s) of *This Bridge Called My Back* and *Anglo-American Feminism.*" In *Making Face, Making Soul: Haciendo Caras,* ed. Gloria Anzaldúa, pp. 356–369. San Francisco: Aunt Lute Foundation.

Almaguer, Tomás. 1971. "Toward the Study of Chicano Colonialism." *Aztlán, Chicano Journal of the Social Sciences and Arts* 2: 7–22.

Alvarez, R. 1971. "The Unique Psycho-historical Experience of the Mexican-American." *Social Sciences Quarterly* 52: 15–29.

Anaya, R. A., and F. Lomeli. 1989. *Aztlán: Essays on the Chicano Homeland.* Albuquerque: University of New Mexico Press.

Anderson, M. L. 1988. *Thinking About Women, Sociological Perspectives on Sex and Gender.* 2nd ed. New York: Macmillan.

Apodaca, María Lida. 1986 "A Double-Edged Sword: Hispanas and Liberal Feminism." *Crítica: A Journal of Critical Essays* 1 (Fall): 96–114.

Baca Zinn, M., L. Weber Cannon, E. Hinninbotham, and B. Thorton Dill. 1986. "The Costs of Exclusionary Practices in Women's Studies." *Signs: Journal of Women in Culture and Society* 11 (Winter): 290–303.

Barrera, Mario, Carlos Muñoz, and C. Ornelas. 1972. "The Barrio as an Internal Colony." In *People and Politics in Urban Society, Urban Affairs Annual Review*, Vol. 6, ed. H.H. Hahn, pp. 465–99. Beverly Hills: Sage Publications.

Blauner, R. 1972. *Racial Oppression in America*. New York: Harper and Row.

Castillo, Ana. 1988. *My Father Was A Toltec*. Novato, Calif: West End Press.

Chabram, Angie, and Rosalinda Fregoso, eds. 1990. *Cultural Studies* 4 (October): 3.

Chicano Coordinating Committee on Higher Education. 1969. *El Plan de Santa Barbara: A Chicano Plan for Higher Education*. Santa Barbara: La Causa Publications.

Cook, E. A. 1989. "Measuring Feminist Consciousness." *Women and Politics* 9: 71–88.

Cotera, M. P. 1977. *The Chicana Feminist*. Austin: Information Systems Development.

Cotera, M. P. 1980. "Feminism: The Chicana and Anglo Versions, A Historical Analysis." In *Twice a Minority: Mexican-American Women,* ed. Margarita Melville, pp. 217–234. St Louis: C.V. Mosby.

de la Torre, Adela. 1990. "Latino Health in the 1980's: Critical Health Policy Issues." In *Income and Status Differences Between White and Minority Americans*, ed. Sucheng Chan. Lewiston, Maine: Edwin Mellon Press.

Del Castillo, Adelaida. 1974. "La Visión Chicana." *Encuentro Femenil* 12: 46–48.

Firestone, S., and A. Koedt, eds. 1970. *Notes from the Second Year: Women's Liberation Major Writings of the Radical Feminist*. New York: Radical Feminist.

Flores, F. 1971. "Conference of Mexican Women: Un Remolino." *Regeneración* 1:1–4.

Flores, F. 1973. "Equality." *Regeneración* 2:4–5.

Freeman, J. 1984. "The Women's Liberation Movement: Its Origins, Structure, Activities, and Ideas." In *Women, A Feminist Perspective*, ed. J. Freeman, 3rd ed., pp. 543–556. Palo Alto: Mayfield Publishing.

García, Alma M. 1989. "The Development of Chicana Feminist Discourse, 1970–1980." *Gender and Society* 3(June): 217–38.

Hernández, Carmen. 1971. "Carmen Speaks Out." *Paper Chicano* 1(June):8–9.

hooks, bell. 1981. *Ain't I a Woman: Black Women and Feminism*. Boston: South End Press.

hooks, bell. 1984. *Feminist Theory: From Margin to Center*. Boston: South End Press.

Hull, G., P. Bell Scott, and B. Smith. 1982. *All Men are Black, All Women are White, But Some of Us Are Brave*. Old Westbury, N.Y.: Feminist Press.

Jaggar, A. M. 1983. *Feminist Politics and Human Nature*. Totowa, NJ: Rowman and Allanheld.

Klein, E. 1984. *Gender Politics*. Cambridge: Harvard University.

Lewis, D. K. 1983. "A Response to Inequality: Black Women, Racism and Sexism." In *The Signs Reader: Women, Gender and Scholarship*, eds. E. Abel and E.k. Abel, pp. 169–91. Chicago: University of Chicago Press.

Lizárraga, Sylvia S. 1977. "From a Woman to a Woman." In *Essays on La Mujer*, eds. Rosaura Sánchez and Rosa Martínez Cruz, pp. 91–96. Los Angeles: University of California Chicano Studies Research Center.

Longeaux y Vásquez, Enriqueta. 1970. "The Mexican-American Woman." In *Sisterhood is Powerful: An Anthology of Writings from the Women's Liberation Movement*, ed. Robin Morgan, pp. 379–384. New York: Vintage.

López, S. A. 1977. "The Role of the Chicana Within the Student Movement." In *Essays on La Mujer*, ed. Rosaura Sánchez and Rosa Martínez Cruz, pp. 16–29. Los Angeles: University of California Chicano Studies Research Center.

Macías, Anna. 1982. *Against All Odds*. Westport, CT: Greenwood Press.

Martínez, E. 1972. "La Chicana." In *Third World Women*, pp. 130–132. San Francisco: Third World Communications.

Mirandé, Alfredo. 1985. *The Chicano Experience: An Alternative Perspective*. Notre Dame: University of Notre Dame Press.

Montejano, David. 1987. *Anglos and Mexicans in the Making of Texas, 1836–1986*. Austin: University of Texas Press.

Moraga, Cherríe, and Gloria Anzaldúa, eds 1983. *This Bridge Called My Back: Writings By Radical Women of Color*. 2nd ed. New York: Kitchen Table Press.

Nieto-Gómez, Anna. 1973. "La Feminista." *Encuentro Femenil* 1:34–47.

Nieto-Gómez, Anna. 1974. "Chicana Feminism." *Encuentro Femenil* 1:3–5.

Orozco, Cynthia. 1986. "Sexism in Chicano Studies and the Community." In *Chicana Voices: Intersections of Class, Race, and Gender*, ed. Teresa Córdova, et al., pp. 11–18. Austin: University of Texas Center for Mexican-American Studies.

Sosa-Riddell, Ada. 1974. "Chicanas and El Movimiento." *Aztlán: Chicano Journal of the Social Sciences and the Arts* 5 (Spring/Fall): 155–65.

Sutherland, E., 1970. "Colonized Women: The Chicana, An Introduction." *Sisterhood is Powerful, An Anthology of Writings from the Women's Liberation Movement*, ed. Robin Morgan, 376–79. New York: Vintage.

Takaki, R. T. 1979. *Iron Cages: Race and Culture in Nineteenth Century America*. New York: Alfred Knopf.

Tienda, Marta, and Patricia Guhleman. 1985. "The Occupational Position of Employed Hispanic Women." In *Hispanics in the U.S. Economy*, ed. George J. Borjas and Marta Tienda, 243–73. New York: Academic Press.

Tolleson Rinehart, S. 1988. The Consequences of Gender Consciousness for Public Policy and Participation. Paper presented at the annual meeting of the Midwest Political Science Association, Chicago.

Vidal, M. 1971. "New Voices of La Raza: Chicanas Speak Out." *International Socialist Review* 32(October):7–9, 31–33.

Wilcox, C., L. Sigelman, and E. Cook. 1989. "Some Like It Hot: Individual Differences in Responses to Group Feeling Thermometers." *Public Opinion Quarterly* 53: 246–57.

Chicanas at a Los Angeles rally during the early 1990s; sign uses inclusive language: "Chicana/o Power." During the 1960s and 1970s, the the term "Chicano" was used for men and women.

82

Massacre of Dreams: Essays on Xicanisma*

ANA CASTILLO

The early feminista, as the Chicana feminist referred to herself then, had been actively fighting against her socioeconomic subjugation as a Chicana and as a woman since 1968, the same year the Chicano movement was announced. I am aware that there have been Chicana activists throughout U.S. history, but I am using as a date of departure an era in which women consciously referred to themselves as feministas.

An analysis of the social status of la Chicana was already underway by early feministas, who maintained that racism, sexism, and sexist racism were the mechanisms that socially and economically oppressed them. But, for reasons explained here, they were virtually censored. The early history of la feministas was documented in a paper entitled, "La Feminista," by Anna Nieto- Gómez and published in *Encuentro Femenil: The First Chicana Feminist Journal*, which may now be considered, both article and journal, archival material.[1]

The early feminists who actively participated in the woman's movement had to educate white feminist groups on their political, cultural, and philosophical differences. Issues that specifically concerned the feminists of that period were directly related to her status as a non-Anglo, culturally different, often Spanish-speaking woman of lower income. Early white feminism compared sexism (as experienced by white middle class women) to the racism that African-Americans are subjected to. But African-American feminists, such as those of the Rio Combahee Collective,[2] pointed out that this was not only an inaccurate comparison but revealed an inherent racist attitude on the part of white feminists who did not understand what it was to be a woman and black in America.

By the same token, brown women were forced into a position in which we had to point out similar differences as well as continuously struggle against a prevalent condescension on the part of white middle-class women toward women of color, poor women, and women who's first language is Spanish and whose culture is not mainstream American. *This Bridge Called My Back*, first published in 1981, as well as other texts by feminists of color that followed serve as excellent testimonies regarding these issues and the experiences of feminists of color in the 1970s.

At the same time, according to Nieto-Gómez, feministas were labeled as *vendidas* (sell-outs) by activists within *La Causa*. Such criticism came not solely from men but

*From *Massacre of the Dreamers: Essays on Xicanisma* (Albuquerque: University of New Mexico Press, 1994: pp. 33–36).

also from women, whom Nieto-Gómez calls Loyalists. These Chicanas believed that racism not sexism was the greater battle. Moreover, the Loyalists distrusted any movement led by any sector of white society. The early white women's movement saw its battle based on sex and gender, and did not take into account the race and class differences of women of color. The Loyalists had some reason to feel reluctant and cynical toward an ideology and organizing effort that at best was condescending toward them. Loyalists told the feministas that they should be fighting such hard-hitting community problems as police brutality, Viet Nam, and La Huelga, the United Farm Workers labor strike. But white female intellectuals were largely unaware of these issues. While the Chicana resided in a first world nation, indeed the most powerful nation at that time, she was part of a historically colonized people.

I am referring to the approximate period between 1968 through the 1970s. However, more than twenty years later, the Chicana—that is a brown woman of Mexican descent, residing in the United States with political consciousness—is still participating in the struggle for recognition and respect from white dominant society. Residing throughout her life in a society that systematically intentionally or out of ignorance marginalizes her existence, often stereotypes her when she does "appear," suddenly represented (for example by mass-media or government sources), and perhaps more importantly, relegates her economic status to among the lowest paid according to the U.S. Census Bureau, the Chicana continues to be a countryless woman. She is—I am, we are—not considered to be, except marginally and stereotypically, United States citizens.

Nevertheless, according to las feministas, feminism was "a very dynamic aspect of the Chicana's heritage and not at all foreign to her nature."[8] Contrary to ethnographic data that portrays Chicanas as submissive followers who are solely designated to preserve the culture, the feminists did not see herself or other women of her culture as such. While the feminist dialogue remained among the activists in el Movimiento, one sees in *Encuentro Femenil* that there indeed existed a solid initiative toward Chicana feminist thought, that is, recognition of sexism as a primary issue, as early on as the late 1960s. Clarifying the differences between the needs of the Anglo feminist and the feministas was part of the early feminista's tasks.

And if the focus of the Chicano male-dominated movement with regard to women had to do with family issues, the feminista zeroed in on the very core of what those issues meant. For instance, the feministas believed that women would make use of birth control and abortion clinics if in fact they felt safe going for these services; that is, if they were community controlled. Birth control and abortion are pertinent issues for all women, but they were particularly significant to the Chicana who had always been at the mercy of Anglo controlled institutions and policies.

Nonconsenting sterilizations of women—poor white, Spanish speaking, welfare recipients, poor women of color—women in prison among them—during the 1970s were being conducted and sponsored by the U.S. government. One third of the female population of Puerto Rico was sterilized during that period.[4] The case of ten Chicanas (*Madrigal v. Quilligan*) against the Los Angeles County Hospital who were sterilized without their consent led to activism demanding release of the Health, Education and Welfare (HEW) guidelines for sterilizations. During that period, HEW was financing up to 100,000 sterilizations a year.[5]

The feminista also wanted a bicultural and bilingual child care that would validate their children's culture and perhaps ward off an inferiority complex before they had a chance to start public school; traditionally, monolingual and anglocentric schools had alienated children, causing them great psychological damage.[6]

The early feminista understood the erroneous conceptions of the white woman's movement that equated sexism to racism because she was experiencing its compounding effects in her daily life. The feministas were fighting against being a "minority" in the labor market. According to Nieto-Gómez, more Anglo women had jobs than did women of color. We must keep in mind that most women of color in this country have always needed employment to maintain even a level of subsistence for their families.

The mestiza still ranks in the labor force among the least valued in this country. In Susan Faludi's best-selling *Backlash*, which focuses on the media's backlash against the white feminist movement, the only noteworthy observation of women of color refers to our economic status in the 1980s. Faludi states that over all income did not increase for the African-American woman and for the Hispanic woman, it actually got worse.

NOTES

1. *Encuentro Femenil: The First Chicana Feminist Journal* 1 (1974); no. 2. (CA: Hijas de Cuauhtémoc). I can't recall how, but it seems fortuitously for me this document came into my hands in Chicago around this time.

2. Please read their essay in *This Bridge Called My Back: Writings by Radical Women of Color*, edited by Cherríe Moraga and Gloria Anzaldúa (Watertown, MA: Persephone Press, 1981).

3. Anna Nieto-Gómez, "La Feninista," *Encuentro Femenil: The First Feminist Journal* 1 (1974); no. 2, 38

4. See Angela Davis, *Women, Culture and Politics* (New York: Random House, 1989).

5. Thomas Shapiro, *Population Control Politics: Women, Sterilization and Reproductive Choice* (Philadelphia: Temple University Press, 1985), pp. 91–93.

6. I am reminded of two stories I have heard from U.S.-born Spanish speaking women who went to public schools in the United States. One was sent with her sister, upon starting, to the class for the hearing impaired. Another, attending a school with a majority Chicano population was sent to "girls' math" class. For further reading on the education of Chicanos please refer to Fernando Peñalosa's *Chicano Linguistics*.

Index

R

Racism
  in Anglo feminism, 203
  as barrier to Chicana employment, 128–129
  in capitalist ideology, 97–100
  Chicana feminism and, 56, 86–92
  Chicano movement and, 55
  in education, 238
  versus sexism, 214, 219–220
  in suffrage movement, 224–226
  in workplace, 126–127
Racism-sexism, and Chicano/Chicana, 98
Radical Woman's Position Paper on Race and Sex, 213
Rangel, Irma, 189, 241
Raza
  Chicana activism and, 80–81
  children of, in reform schools, 111
  discrimination against women in, 21–22
  new voice of, 21–24
  women of, 110–112
Raza cósmica, 270
Raza Unida, 57
Raza Unida Party, 2, 3, 11, 22
  Chicana in, 176
  Chicana's role in, 79
  feminist agenda in, 139
  founding of, 202
  presentation by Chicanas of, 180–181
Raza Unida Party of Northern California, party platform on Chicanas of (1971), 165–167
Raza Unida Party of Texas, platform of (1972), 167–169
Razón Mestiza, La, 8
Rebolledo, Tey Diana, 292–293
"Redstockings Manifesto, The," 297
Reform schools, Chicano children in, 111
Regeneración, La, 5, 8, 113
Religion. *See also* Catholic Church
  Chicana lesbian and, 284–286
  Chicanas and, 130
Religious life, Chicana women in. *See* Chicana religious
Rentería, Dorothy M., 236
Rentería, María, 227
Republican Party, Chicana and, 176
Respuesta, 54
Revolutionary movements, women in, 4
Rights, political, Mexican-American woman and, 133–134
Rincón, Bernice, 5, 148
Rinehart, Tolleson, 295
Rio Combahee Collective, 310

Rivera, Tomás, 289
Rose, Vivianne, 279
Roybal, Rose Marie, 230, 233
Ruiz, Julia, 156, 163

S

Sabio, Mercedes, 190
Saenz Rayo, Artenmisa, 42
Sager, Manuela, 43, 215
Salt of the Earth, 43
Sampaio, Anna, xiii
Schnier, Miriam, 11–12
Scott, Joan W., 9–10
Seifer, Nancy, 215
Seminars, Chicana, from 1970-1975, 142–144
Serrano, Sandy, 189
Sex
  Chicana and, 38, 134–135, 158, 205
  Chicanos' attitudes toward, 82–83
Sexism
  as barrier to Chicana employment, 128–129
  in Catholic Church, 103
  Chicana and, 126–127, 254
  in Chicano movement, 5, 97, 254–257, 265–266
  in Chicano studies, 265–270
  defined, 97
  in educational institutions, 103, 238
  in legal institutions, 103
  versus racism, 214, 219–220
Sexuality, cultural attitudes toward, 282, 285
Sisterhood is Powerful, 296
Sisters, religious. *See* Chicana religious
Smith, Barbara, 10
Sánchez, David, 118
Sánchez, Elisa, 188, 189–190
Sánchez, Rosaura, 292
Sochen, June, 228
Socialism, 287
  Chicana and, 226–228
  and Mexican women's rights, 41
  scope of, 222–223
Socialists, Chicana/Chicano, 215
Spanish women, model of, 48–50, 57
Stanton, Elizabeth Cady, 224
  and call for literacy tests, 225–226
Stereotyping, by dominant culture, 92–94
Sterilization
  nonconsensual, 107, 140, 311
Strong Women, 264
Struggle of Borders, A, 271
Student movement, Chicano. *See* Chicano student movement